The Economics of Lawmaking

The Economics of Lawmaking

FRANCESCO PARISI  VINCY FON

OXFORD
UNIVERSITY PRESS

OXFORD
UNIVERSITY PRESS

Oxford University Press, Inc., publishes works that further Oxford University's objective of excellence in research, scholarship, and education.

Oxford New York
Auckland   Cape Town   Dar es Salaam   Hong Kong   Karachi   Kuala Lumpur   Madrid
Melbourne   Mexico City   Nairobi   New Delhi   Shanghai   Taipei   Toronto

With offices in
Argentina   Austria   Brazil   Chile   Czech   Republic   France   Greece   Guatemala
Hungary   Italy   Japan   Poland   Portugal   Singapore   South Korea   Switzerland   Thailand
Turkey   Ukraine   Vietnam

Copyright © 2009 by Oxford University Press, Inc.

Published by Oxford University Press, Inc.
198 Madison Avenue, New York, New York 10016

Oxford is a registered trademark of Oxford University Press
Oxford University Press is a registered trademark of Oxford University Press, Inc.

Library of Congress Cataloging-in-Publication Data

Parisi, Francesco.
   The economics of lawmaking / Francesco Parisi and Vincy Fon.
      p. cm.
   Includes bibliographical references and index.
   ISBN 978-0-19-537415-5 ((hardback) : alk. paper)
1. Legislation–Economic aspects. 2. Law–International unification.
      I. Fon, Vincy. II. Title.
   K3316.P37 2009
   340'.11–dc22   2008030832

1 2 3 4 5 6 7 8 9

Printed in the United States of America on acid-free paper

Note to Readers
This publication is designed to provide accurate and authoritative information in regard to the subject matter covered. It is based upon sources believed to be accurate and reliable and is intended to be current as of the time it was written. It is sold with the understanding that the publisher is not engaged in rendering legal, accounting, or other professional services. If legal advice or other expert assistance is required, the services of a competent professional person should be sought. Also, to confirm that the information has not been affected or changed by recent developments, traditional legal research techniques should be used, including checking primary sources where appropriate.

(Based on the Declaration of Principles jointly adopted by a Committee of the American Bar Association and a Committee of Publishers and Associations.)

You may order this or any other Oxford University Press publication by visiting the Oxford University Press website at www.oup.com

To my parents, Raffaele Parisi and Clara Sdino Starace,
who showed me the beauty of analytical rigor and the power
of simple thinking. 🐝 F.P.

To my late father, Mincio Fon, who inspired and encouraged
me to become an academic, and my mother, K. C. Au, who enticed
me to work hard by drawing my attention to my
brother's accomplishments. 🐝 V.F.

Contents

Acknowledgments

SCHOLARS WITHIN THE SO-CALLED LAW and economics tradition have traditionally taken a normative or positive approach to the study of law. Both approaches focus on the role of law as an instrument of behavioral control and treat lawmaking processes and institutions as exogenous. A more recent trend in the literature, developed at the intersection of law, economics, and public choice theory, has extended the economic analysis to the institutional design of lawmaking. This literature revisits the traditional conceptions of lawmaking, treating lawmaking process and institutions as endogenous. Alternative sources of law are evaluated considering their respective advantages in the production of legal order. With this book we wish to contribute to this literature, providing a comprehensive study of alternative lawmaking processes, which emphasizes the respective advantages and proper scope of application of legislation, judge-made law, customary law, and international law in the creation of a legal order.

This book is the result of several years of collaborative efforts of its authors. We wish to thank our mutual friend and former teacher David Levy for giving us the idea of collaboration during a holiday party in 1999. At different points in time, David Levy was our economics professor and knew our complementary skills (and weaknesses). His suggestion led to the fruitful collaboration and friendship of the present authors. The decision to write a book on the economics of lawmaking was far from the plans at the beginning of our collaboration. Our prior research and teaching interests were quite different from one another. One of us was teaching in a law school in the field of comparative and international law, while the other was teaching mathematical economics and economic theory courses in an economics department. Our backgrounds brought different insights and layers of understanding to the problems that we chose to study in the course of our collaboration. One topic after another, we began to realize that the problems that we chose to analyze followed a clear logical structure—a structure that we ultimately chose to carry forward in a more systematic fashion for the writing of this book.

Several of the chapters in this book were published before in some form and, unless otherwise noted, were jointly authored by the present authors. The adaptations of the original articles for the present book were made by Francesco Parisi to improve the unity of the analysis and cohesion of the presentation, while preserving the structure and mathematical formulations of the original papers. We thank the copyright holders for their permission to reprint our articles in this book. The first three sections of Chapter 2 are based on our article "On the Optimal Specificity of Legal Rules," originally published in the *Journal of Institutional Economics* (2007), © 2007 by Cambridge University Press; the fourth section of Chapter 2 is based on an article by Francesco Parisi originally published under the title "Harmonization of European Private Law: An Economic Analysis" in M. Bussani and F. Werro (eds.), *European Private Law: A Handbook* (Staempfli Publications Ltd., 2008), © 2008 by Staempfli Publications Ltd. Chapter 3 is based on material originally published as "The Value of Waiting in Lawmaking" in the *European Journal of Law and Economics* (2004), © 2004 by Springer Publishing Company. Nita Ghei was a coauthor of that article, and we are grateful to her for allowing us to include it in this book. Chapter 4 was written by Francesco Parisi in collaboration with Emanuela Carbonara and Barbara Luppi and is based on a working paper originally circulated under the title "Self-Defeating Subsidiarity" in Minnesota Legal Studies Research Paper 08-15. We are grateful to Emanuela Carbonara and Barbara Luppi for allowing us to include this chapter in the book. Chapter 6 is based on our article "Litigation and the Evolution of Legal Remedies" published in *Public Choice* (2003), © 2003 by Springer Publishing Company. Chapter 7 was originally published as "Litigation, Judicial Path Dependence, and Legal Change" in the *European Journal of Law and Economics* (2005), © 2005 by Springer Publishing Company. Ben Depoorter was a coauthor of that article, and we are grateful to him for allowing us to include it in this book. Chapter 8 is based on our article "Judicial Precedents in Civil Law Systems: A Dynamic Analysis," published in the *International Review of Law and Economics* (2006), © 2006 by Elsevier. Chapter 10 is based on an article published as "Role Reversibility, Stochastic Ignorance, and Social Cooperation" in the *Journal of Socio-Economics* (2008), © 2008 by Elsevier. Chapter 11 is based on our article "International Customary Law and Articulation Theories: An Economic Analysis," published in the *International Law and Management Review* (2007), © 2008 by BYU International Law and Management. Chapter 12 is based on our article "Stability and Change in International Customary Law," to be published in the *Supreme Court Economic Review* (forthcoming, 2009), © 2009 by University of Chicago Press. An earlier draft of that article was awarded the 2004 Garvin Prize in Law & Economics for Best Workshop Paper by the University of California at Berkeley. Chapter 14 was previously published as "Formation of International Treaties" in *Review of Law and Economics* (2007), © 2007 by BEPress. Chapter 15 is based on our article "The Economics of Treaty Ratification," originally published in the *Journal of Law, Economics and Policy* (2008), © 2008 by Journal of Law, Economics and Policy. Chapter 16 is based on a working paper originally circulated under the title "The Hidden Bias of the Vienna Convention on the International Law of Treaties," to be published in the *Review of Law and Economics* (forthcoming, 2009), © 2009 by BEPress. The remaining chapters—1, 5, 9, and 13—as well as the introductory and concluding chapters were written for the present book by Francesco Parisi, who wishes to express his personal gratitude to Professors Robert Cooter and Pietro Trimarchi for their friendship and guidance in academia.

This book could not have been completed without the support of our families and friends during these years of research. We are especially grateful to our spouses for their inspiration, their unwavering support, and their willingness to accept our long absences while we worked together. More colleagues than we could have hoped to enlist have provided comments and suggestions on prepublication drafts of the articles included in this book. We particularly want to thank Alessandra Arcuri, Daniel Benoliel, Omri Ben-Shahar, Lisa Bernstein, Margaret Brinig, Frank Buckley, Guido Calabresi, Emanuela Carbonara, Loyd Cohen, Robert Cooter, Tyler Cowen, Anthony D'Amato, Giuseppe Dari-Mattiacci, Gerrit DeGeest, Ben Depoorter, Gianluca Fiorentini, Luigi Franzoni, Nuno Garoupa, Claire Hill, Bruce Kobayashi, Eugene Kontorovich, Ejan Mackaay, Richard McAdams, Brett McDonnell, Jacob Nussim, Jide Nzelibe, Daniel Polsby, Eric Posner, Richard Posner, Felix Reinshagen, Charles Rowley, Alan Sykes, Paul Rubin, Thomas Ulen, Georg Von Wangenheim, Richard Wagner, David Weissbrodt, and Todd Zywicki for their valuable comments and constructive criticisms. We are also extremely grateful to Dan Milkove and Julie Hunt for their help and careful suggestions throughout the production of this book, to Catherine Sevcenko for her willingness to share her extensive knowledge of the literature, and to Ben Week, Joshua Rusenko, Ian Beed, and Matt Hurm for their research and editorial assistance.

As is customary in our profession, previous incarnations of this book went through an extensive refereeing process. The current version reflects changes (in both substance and organization) that were suggested by the anonymous reviewers. The current version of the book has greatly benefited from their input. Finally, we are grateful to the participants in the 2004, 2005, and 2006 American Law and Economics Association Annual Meetings; the 14th John M. Olin Conference in Law and Economics at the University of Toronto, Canada; the Workshop in Economic Dynamics at the Max Planck Institute in Jena, Germany; the CASLE Workshop in Law and Economics at the University of Ghent, Belgium; the Levy Workshop in Law and Economics at George Mason University; the 2005 European Association of Law and Economics Annual Meeting; the Economic Analysis Workshop at the U.S. Department of Justice; and the participants in the Faculty Workshops at the New York University Economics Department, the University of California at Berkeley School of Law, the University of Amsterdam Economics Department, the University of Hamburg Graduate College, the University of Aix-Marseille, the Northwestern University School of Law, the University of Minnesota Law School, and the University of Chicago Law School Workshop in International Law and Economics for their valuable comments, criticisms, and suggestions on individual portions of this book presented at those events.

Introduction

ALL LEGAL SCHOLARS, at some time in their legal careers, ponder the fundamental questions concerning the sources of law. How should laws be made? Who should make them? Despite their theoretical and practical importance, sources of law have not enjoyed a systematic treatment in the existing law and economics literature. This book attempts to remedy this shortcoming, providing some novel insights for the institutional theory of lawmaking. We consider four different methods of lawmaking, which we describe respectively as (1) lawmaking through legislation; (2) lawmaking through adjudication; (3) lawmaking through practice; and (4) lawmaking through agreement.

The sources of law considered in this book have different degrees of importance depending on the legal system in question. It is well known, for example, that there is a substantial historical difference between the role played by legislation and judicial precedents in the civil law and common law and traditions. In early legal systems, written legislation was utilized with great parsimony and great weight was given to customary sources of law. Occasionally, sources of customary law were unable to provide solutions to emerging legal issues and to satisfy the changing needs of society. In these cases, precedents were recognized and followed as a matter of outright necessity. With the gradual expansion of statutory law, the recognition of precedents as sources of law was no longer a practical necessity. In this historical context, legal systems have developed a variety of doctrines to determine the effective role of customary rules and judicial decisions in the presence of legislation. In past decades we have also witnessed a great expansion in the role of international treaties in affecting substantive areas of domestic law. The resulting transformations in the legal landscape and the persistent variations in the role played by these sources of law in contemporary legal systems have, in many ways, inspired us to examine this increasingly important type of lawmaking.

The aim of this book is to provide insight on the relative advantages and the respective limits of alternative sources of law. We consider some characterizing features of our sources of law and examine them with the aid of the formal methods of economic analysis and public choice theory. We have proceeded in the analysis despite the absence of established conventions in the literature regarding the identification of relevant topics. The selection of issues and organization of the book was far from easy and greatly benefited from the early feedback of various anonymous readers and referees. The final selection of topics strikes a balance between the need for systematic exposition of the chosen topics and attentiveness to their practical relevance. We are hopeful that our chosen approach and findings will shed some light on the important issues that concern the institutional design of lawmaking.

The book is divided into four parts, each focusing on one of the above four methods of lawmaking. For each part we provide a brief introduction to the main issues and a brief review of the relevant literature. In Part 1 we consider sources of law that depend on political collective decision making, such as legislation, codifications, and regulations. We organize the analysis in three substantive chapters considering (1) optimal specificity of legal rules (Chapter 2); (2) optimal timing of legal intervention when lawmaking is carried out under uncertainty (Chapter 3); and (3) optimal territorial scope of law, addressing issues of subsidiarity and legal harmonization (Chapter 4). In Part 2 we consider sources of law derived from adjudication, such as legal precedents and judge-made law. We again organize the analysis in three substantive chapters considering (1) biases in the evolution of legal remedies through litigation (Chapter 6); (2) the role of litigation and judicial path-dependence on judge-made law (Chapter 7); and (3) the effect of alternative doctrines of legal precedent, such as *stare decisis* and *jurisprudence constante*, on the dynamics of legal change (Chapter 8). In Part 3 we consider sources of law derived from practice, such as customary law and other spontaneous sources of law. The three substantive chapters consider (1) which conditions are best capable of fostering the emergence of customary law (Chapter 10); (2) the role of articulation theories in the formation of customary law (Chapter 11); and (3) the dynamics of change of customary law (Chapter 12). In Part 4 we consider sources of law derived from explicit agreements, such as international treaties and conventions. The three substantive chapters cover (1) the process of formation and accession to international treaties (Chapter 14); (2) the ratification and reservations to international treaties (Chapter 15); and (3) the effect of the 1969 Vienna Convention governing the law of treaties, and the possible bias created by this treaty when heterogeneous states are involved (Chapter 16).

Throughout the book, our findings are examined with the discussion of some of their normative corollaries. We revisit the traditional presentation of sources of law by considering the important issue of the institutional design of lawmaking through the lens of economic analysis and public choice theory. Our analysis addresses several key issues from public choice theory. They are (1) issues of minimization of lawmaking costs, (2) agency problems in representation, and (3) issues of stability of collective decision-making outcomes. These concerns influencing the institutional design of lawmaking should be kept in mind as the reader progresses through the book, and they will prove helpful in identifying commonalities and differences in the various sources of law considered. Our functionalist approach to legal analysis will hopefully shed new light on the process of law formation, emphasizing the respective advantages and proper scope of application of legislation, judge-made law, customary law, and international law in the creation of a legal order.

PART I

Lawmaking through Legislation
Codified Law

ONE

Lawmaking through Legislation
An Introduction

THE DIFFERENCES IN LEGAL SYSTEMS often reflect different ideologies and conceptions of the political economy of lawmaking. In recent decades, modern countries have been giving increasing importance to written statutes among their sources of law. The supremacy of written law over other sources of legal order is not, however, universal. The conventional distinction between common law and civil law systems is based on conceiving legal traditions as a dichotomy. Systems of the civil law tradition, the conventional thinking goes, tend to give greater weight to written and statutory sources of law. Generally speaking, these systems derive historically from a legal tradition that recognized the authority of a comprehensive body of written law (e.g., the Roman Corpus Juris). The common law tradition, by contrast, evolved from the tradition of casuistic reasoning pioneered by Aristotle; this tradition consisted of comparing the case to be decided against a paradigmatic case (i.e., a precedent). Unlike a legal code written ex ante that can remain more or less static over time, the law would evolve as judges subsequently relied on some decided cases but not others for their precedential value.

In most legal traditions, legal pragmatism has informed much of the debate and traditional dogmatic principles are no longer seen as providing bright-line guidelines in the balance between legislative and judicial sources of law. During the last several decades this pragmatism has allowed substantial methodological convergence between legal systems of the world. In the common law tradition, the proliferation of legislative intervention has gradually corroded the traditional dominance of judge-made law; in the civil law tradition, increasing weight is given to judicial decision making, and statutes and case law coexist, more or less happily, with one another.

In the following three chapters, we will examine three related dimensions of legislative lawmaking. Lawmakers can choose among different variables: the level of specificity of a law, the timing of legal intervention and revision of the law, and the territorial scope of application of the law. These interrelated choices represent critical ingredients in any legislator's attempt to maximize the net present value of legislation.

1. Optimal Specificity of Legislation

With respect to the issue of optimal level of specificity, we should consider that lawmakers can craft laws with different levels of detail to guide judges in their decision-making process, incorporating detailed rules or more general standards into the laws they write. In the existing literature, the problem of optimal degree of specificity of laws was first discussed by Ehrlich and Posner (1974) and Schwartz and Scott (1995), who structured their seminal papers around the rules versus standards dichotomy. Ehrlich and Posner (1974) offer a formal optimization model that is static. Schwartz and Scott (1995) model rule making in the context of private legislatures as a single-shot, multistage game. They outline a theory of the legal process which holds that the degree of precision in the formulation of laws is largely based on the desire to minimize social costs. With the knowledge that specific legal rules and general legal standards lie at opposite ends of the spectrum, Ehrlich and Posner articulate the criteria for determining the optimal degree of specificity, given cost minimization as a dominant consideration. They discuss the benefits that precision brings to the legal system, including increased predictability and the consequential reduction in litigation expenditures, increased speed of dispute resolution, and reduced information costs associated with adjudication. Yet precision also involves costs: the costs of rule formulation, which are often substantial, given the high transaction costs of statutory decisions; allocative inefficiency arising from both the over- and under-inclusive effects of rules; and information barriers for the layman, who is more likely to understand general standards than specific rules, which employ technical language.

In Chapter 2 we address this issue with the aid of the analytical tools of modern investment theory (a theory analogizing a law to an investment), studying the optimal degree of specificity and the functionality of rules or standards under different environmental conditions. In the presence of uncertainty, we can view legal systems as making investment decisions that create present lawmaking costs and which generate uncertain future benefits. Lawmaking costs are at least partially sunk (i.e., lawmaking costs cannot be recovered if the enacted rule proves to be ineffective or undesirable at a later time) and exogenous changes in the regulated environment affect the benefits of legislation over time (e.g., social or economic changes may render enacted rules obsolete). We present a basic model of optimal specificity of laws, clarifying the relevance of legal obsolescence and volume of litigation in the optimal specificity of a law. We then consider the important influence of codification style, judges' specialization, and complexity of reality on the optimal choice of legislative instrument. In the conclusion of this chapter, we reexamine the implications of our results in light of the more complex institutional reality that characterizes contemporary legislative processes in various areas of the law.

2. The Optimal Timing of Legislation

In Chapter 3 we apply the instruments of modern investment theory to consider the issue of optimal timing of legal intervention. Extending the analysis of the previous chapter, we observe that political actors and legislative bodies often invoke net present value calculations to support proposed legislative change. Building on the idea of law as an investment in a productive asset, we identify some misleading applications of net present value calculations. Legal systems can be regarded as making investment decisions when incurring present lawmaking costs will generate benefits over time. Like any investment decision, timing is an issue for lawmakers to determine: lawmaking innovation or revision of current rules can be postponed. Often delays in such investment decisions come at a cost, given the forgone benefits of the investment in the immediate future. Our analysis focuses on the value of waiting in lawmaking, illustrating the interaction among the above factors in identifying the conditions that determine the optimal timing of legal intervention. Building on the insights of option pricing theory, we observe that the choice of optimal timing in lawmaking should consider the option-like characteristics of lawmaking decisions. This suggests that the net present value methodology is inappropriate for dealing with lawmaking decisions under uncertainty. We illustrate the different results obtained considering the option value of deferring legal intervention, showing how the resulting lawmaking choices depend on various parameters of the regulated environment. The basic model is followed by two extensions. In the first extension, we allow for some learning and informational benefit from the immediate implementation of the new law. In a second extension, we allow for political time preference to affect the lawmaking choice.

The two issues of optimal timing and optimal specificity of legal rules are clearly interrelated. The lawmaker has two control variables: first, the option to innovate (or delay intervention); second, the choice of either fully specifying the rule ex ante (i.e., choosing a "rule") or stating the law in general terms, which requires an ex post interpretation of the law (i.e., choose a "standard"). Well-specified rules may require larger up-front investments, inasmuch as they require a large outlay in the initial acquisition of information, but the choice of well-specified rules may reduce operating costs later. A standard requires smaller initial investments but may require larger outlays in its interpretation and enforcement. The option value of delaying legal intervention varies in the two cases. In the presence of uncertainty and sunk investment costs, the lawmaker is faced with a wedge between the economies of scale obtainable with the implementation of a specified rule and the increased value of the forgone option to postpone the lawmaking decision. The dual optimization problem facing the lawmaker, then, is that of determining the optimal level of specificity and timing of intervention in consideration of the above factors. The understanding of the optimal specificity problem discussed in Chapter 2 and the optimal timing problem presented in Chapter 3 serves as a building block for understanding the dual lawmaking problem, where timing and specificity are allowed to vary simultaneously. Indeed, at any point in time, lawmakers decide their legislative action controlling both the timing and the degree of detail of laws, likely with an awareness of the interrelationship between the two variables. The solution to these interrelated lawmaking problems generates several implications concerning the pattern of lawmaking under different legal, social, and economic conditions. The hypothesis is that legal systems respond to exogenous changes by adopting varying patterns of lawmaking, thus maximizing the value of a legal intervention. This hypothesis provides the basis for further study analyzing the likely departures from such optimal lawmaking pattern due to specific public choice failures.

3. The Optimal Territorial Scope of Legislation

We conclude the analysis of lawmaking through legislation by considering the factors that influence the optimal territorial scope of legal rules. The question regarding the optimal territorial scope of law is, in many ways, related to two trends in the literature, respectively addressing issues of federalism and legal uniformity. Two opposing tendencies are observable in the current process of transformation of the global political geography: a movement toward devolution, subsidiarity, and local autonomy and a movement toward legal unification and harmonization. These tendencies represent symmetric departures from the traditional principles of territoriality of national law.

In the evolving structure of European law, notions of subsidiarity, devolution, and regionalism are used to legitimize the existence and autonomy of local units within a larger confederation. At the same time, European lawmakers are undertaking important steps toward the harmonization, unification, and possible codification of some areas of European law. Instruments of legal harmonization and unification have emerged to promote the convergence of legal systems across politically distinct geographical entities. Both phenomena show how the territorial scope of law is becoming detached from the political boundaries of the nation-state. Harmonization of substantive law and choice of law regimes are the complementary instruments achieving this result. From a welfare perspective, legal uniformity may be desirable for reducing externality problems that individual systems may impose on other legal regimes. The elimination of external effects through uniform legislation is in turn likely to lead to the choice of laws that maximize global rather than domestic welfare. The law-as-a-product metaphor provides the inspiration for a general theory of competitive supply of laws (Romano 1985). In an ideal world of frictionless legal competition, individuals could choose among alternative legal regimes, just as consumers choose among competing products and services in the marketplace. The competitive supply of legal rules coupled with institutional meta-rules of mutual recognition and freedom of choice would thus lead to a competitive legal equilibrium that could ideally maximize the aggregate welfare of the legal subjects. From a public choice perspective, promoting legal diversity creates an effective constraint on the arbitrariness of lawmakers. Just as demand-driven competitive markets impose a limit on the suppliers' unwarranted production choices, freedom of choice of law narrows the lawmakers' unwarranted discretion. Rules that do not conform to the consumers' preferences will not be chosen in equilibrium. Liberal rules for the enforcement of choice of law provisions may be seen as instrumental to reducing the transaction costs of the parties' bargain. On this basis, law and economics scholars formulated a testable hypothesis: choice of law gives states an incentive to compete by providing efficient legal rules (Ribstein 1993). The efficiency hypothesis postulates a correlation between the degree of freedom of choice and the efficiency of legal rules. This correlation was successfully tested by Kobayashi and Ribstein (1997). Against this position, externality-based arguments have been put forth to determine the benefits of legal uniformity. Negative externalities can arise from parties engaging in choice of law decisions. The literature has identified three cases of externalities created through contractual choice of law: (1) externalities that the choice of law may impose on third parties not in privity with the contract, (2) externalities that the choice of law may impose on the forum state, and (3) externalities that the choice of law may impose on the judicial system (Parisi and O'Hara 1997; Parisi and Ribstein 1997).

In Chapter 4 we develop a model of subsidiarity which encompasses some of the issues discussed in the previous literature. According to the subsidiarity principle, introduced in the Maastricht Treaty to limit the interference of the central government of the European Union in the policy of member states, central lawmaking should have a subsidiary function, performing only those tasks that cannot be performed effectively at a local level (Swaine 2001). Empirical evidence has shown that, in the European Union, substantial harmonization and centralization have occurred in areas where heterogeneity of preferences is predominant (like social protection or agricultural policy) whereas other areas characterized by strong economies of scale have remained in the local domain (like defense and environmental protection). In these areas, all normative prescriptions on the optimal level of centralization have been mixed-up.

We argue that the discrepancy between the normative prescription of the theory and the present allocation of policy responsibilities can be explained by the presence, in the Treaty on European Union, of the subsidiarity principle. The presence of both economies of scale and scope in the provision of policies and regulatory functions can lead to some paradoxical results. First of all, the subsidiarity principle may favor centralization rather than putting a limit to it. Our model allows us to formulate a conjecture according to which a piecemeal application of the subsidiarity principle can trigger path-dependent centralization and ultimately turn subsidiarity into a self-defeating principle. Second, the application of a subsidiarity principle leaves ample room for strategic manipulation of centralization. As the principle of subsidiarity comes of age, future scholars will have an opportunity to investigate this question empirically. Our results further provide a basis for a normative theory of lawmaking in changing transnational legal environments and provide some policy recommendations for the ongoing process of legal reform in both the European context and other legal systems in transition.

TWO

Optimal Specificity of Laws
Rules versus Standards*

A PROBLEM THAT LAWMAKERS need to address when crafting legislation concerns the degree of specificity of their laws. When enacting new laws, lawmakers cannot effectively foresee all of the particular circumstances for which they could apply. This renders legislation general in nature and incomplete as a matter of practical necessity. In ancient Greece, Aristotle (350 B.C.: bk. V, § 10) realized the unavoidability of incomplete laws. But at times, incompleteness of legislation is not only a matter of unavoidable necessity. Incomplete legal precepts can be purposefully enacted as a way to optimize the legislating and adjudication functions, transferring to the judiciary some of the tasks that would otherwise have to be carried out ex ante by the legislature. In this setting, Jeremy Bentham (1776) addressed the question of optimal specificity of laws, providing fertile ground for the modern debate on rules versus standards. Bentham's idea of a two-tiered system, where the public learns of the general standards while the judges implement those standards by creating rules for the individual cases, provides a good example of the possible role of purposeful incompleteness of laws.

Since Bentham, contemporary legal theorists have attempted to formulate principles that should be used to determine the optimal degree of specificity of legislation. In considering these criteria, legal and economic scholars have utilized instruments from optimal decision theory, public choice theory, and constitutional political economy. This strand of literature, far from being purely theoretical, is acquiring increasing practical significance in the

---

* The first three sections of this chapter are based on material originally published as Fon, Vincy, and Francesco Parisi, "On the Optimal Specificity of Legal Rules," *Journal of Institutional Economics* 3: 147–64 (2007); the fourth section is based on material originally published as Parisi, Francesco, "Harmonization of European Private Law: An Economic Analysis" in M. Bussani and F. Werro (eds.), *European Private Law. A Handbook* (Staempfli Publications Ltd. 2008).

European and Israeli contexts. In Europe, the ongoing process of unification of some areas of law poses the question of choice among alternative legislative instruments. The preparatory work of new codifications, such as the Draft European Civil Code and the new Israeli Civil Code, poses the important question of how detailed these codes should be.

The current chapter contributes to this literature in general, and in particular offers a framework for identifying the optimal degree of specificity of legal rules in various legal and institutional contexts. Section 1 introduces the problem with brief references to the existing literature. Section 2 formulates a model of optimal specificity of laws to analyze how legal obsolescence, the volume of litigation, legal traditions and codification styles, judges' specialization, and the complexity of reality affect the choice of optimal legal instruments. Section 3 revisits the results of the theoretical section, considering implications of the model in more complex institutional scenarios. These include the absence of benevolent planning, the dangers of instrumental use of legal specificity by legislators, and the way political time preference may affect the degree of legal specificity. Section 4 provides some historical and comparative illustrations and identifies areas where our propositions could be validated by future empirical research.

1. Rules, Standards, and the Optimal Degree of Specificity of Laws

In the law and economics literature, scholars have paid much attention to the difference between "standards" and "rules." Standards and rules can be visualized as two extremes on a continuum representing the degree of precision of laws.[1] A standard is the legal or social criterion that adjudicators use to judge actions under particular circumstances. In that sense, standards are circumstantial; they are open-ended, allowing the adjudicator to make a fact-specific determination such as whether a driver used "reasonable care" in a given situation. Standards, such as reasonableness, are largely intuitive, which makes them easy for the general public to understand. A rule, conversely, withdraws from the adjudicator's consideration the circumstances that would be relevant to decision making according to a standard. Rules are more specific than standards; they create bright-line tests such as whether a driver exceeded the speed limit of 55 miles per hour. Greater specificity decreases the flexibility of a rule. This often results in an imperfect fit between the specific wording of a rule and the varying fact patterns of the regulated conduct.

When legislators choose between rules and standards, they must consider when, and at what cost, the rules and standards should be applied to specific situations. For instance, rules require advance determination of the law's content because of the high degree of specificity involved in their formulation. Lawmakers must perform research in advance to determine the appropriate rule to create. Therefore, rules are more costly for legislators to promulgate than standards, which require less specificity. Laws that are less specific, however, impose greater implementation and decision-making costs by judicial and administrative bodies. Standards are more costly for legal advisors to predict or adjudicators to apply because they require determinations of the law's content with less guidance than rules.[2] Hence, in the event of a car accident where the driver was traveling more than 55 miles per hour, liability would be automatic under a 55 miles per hour rule. However, under a standard such as "reasonableness," the judge or jury would have to determine the facts and circumstances at the time of the accident and decide whether to impose liability. The application of a standard is more fact specific but naturally less consistent in the long run. Thus, from an ex ante perspective, rules provide better guidance to the subjects of the law, and from an ex post perspective, standards may be more easily adapted to the varying circumstances of a case.

Generally, scholars have postulated that laws articulated as standards leave a greater margin of discretion to judges and administrative agencies in their implementation. On the other hand, rules are laws that are specified up front with a greater level of detail and thus leave a lesser margin of discretion in implementation. The imperfect fit between the ex ante legal rule and the circumstances of individual cases may create social losses. From an efficiency perspective, standards allow ad hoc custom-tailoring of the law to the circumstances of the case at bar, reducing problems of over-inclusion and under-inclusion. These problems are more serious when there is greater heterogeneity in regulated conduct and a faster rate of change in the regulated environment.[3]

In our analysis, we take the value of the law as a function of legal precision. Rules advance certainty, consistency, and predictability to private parties and promote judicial economies by minimizing the need for a detailed consideration of facts and circumstances each time a law is applied (Sullivan 1992). Individuals and businesses often need to obtain professional legal advice to determine whether certain conduct violates the law.[4] Attorneys can more easily provide legal advice when the consequences of an actor's conduct are clearly specified up front in detailed rules. Given the greater accessibility and predictability of detailed rules, more individuals are likely to become informed in a regime dominated by rules than in a regime dominated by standards. This is a value of law's specificity. Under rules, individuals are more likely to adjust their conduct to the precepts of the law. Under a standard such as reasonableness, what is reasonable under the circumstances can vary widely. Applying standards may require some guesswork by less experienced legal actors. As a result, standards tend to be more costly for individuals to interpret when deciding how to act, because standards are given content and substance only after individuals act. The forward-looking and deterrent functions of law are thus more effective when laws are formulated as precise rules. This is another benefit of law's specificity.

In the literature, scholars often point out that when the regulated environment is subject to exogenous changes over time, laws may require more frequent revisions (e.g., Ehrlich and Posner 1974; Landes and Posner 1976). In other words, changes in the regulated environment lead to legal obsolescence. The fact that more specific rules become obsolete at a faster rate should imply that the optimal level of specificity of legal rules should depend on the expected rate of change of the regulated environment. The existing models, however, do not explicitly formulate the optimal level of specificity of law as a function of the expected rate of change of the regulated environment. In the following, we extend the results of the existing literature to consider how obsolescence and frequency interact in choosing the optimal detail of laws. We also consider the relevance of other factors in the choice of appropriate legislative instruments.

2. Lawmaking with Obsolescence and Economies in Adjudication

We view the lawmaking process as a production function with both fixed and variable costs. The creation of law can be thought of as investing a fixed cost in the production of legal order. Lawmakers choose the level of specificity of laws by allocating fixed capital in the production process.[5] After a law is promulgated, there is a variable adjudication cost whenever it is applied. A greater level of specificity of the law generally increases the cost of promulgation but requires lower implementation costs by courts and administrative agencies. That is, the more specific the law is, the greater the fixed investment and the lower the variable implementation costs will be. Clearly, the more frequently the law is applied, the higher the total variable cost.

The optimal degree of specificity of laws should be chosen to maximize the value of the law considering the fixed cost of lawmaking and the variable cost of adjudication. In addition to the costs and benefits discussed in the previous literature, we concentrate on some factors that have not been previously highlighted.

2.1. The Model

Our model of optimal specificity of laws includes the frequency of the law's application, the rate of obsolescence of law, the cost of coordination and harmonization of new laws within existing legal systems, the degree of specialization of courts, and the complexity of the regulated environment. We will investigate the impact of these variables in the choice of optimal specificity of laws.

Assume that the average value of a law V, appropriately discounted by the social discount rate, depends on the degree of specificity chosen in the formulation of the law (s) and the expected rate of obsolescence (ω). Following the existing literature, we assume that as the legal issue is specified in more detail, the value obtained from the law increases. For example, when a law is more specific, it becomes less costly for parties to interpret, increasing the value of the law at a decreasing rate ($V_S > 0$ and $V_{SS} < 0$).[6] As the rate of obsolescence increases, the value of the law clearly decreases ($V_\omega < 0$). We postulate that the marginal value of the level of specificity decreases as the obsolescence rate increases ($V_{S\omega} < 0$). If the frequency of application of the legal rule is N, then the total value of the legal rule becomes $N \cdot V(s, \omega)$.

There are two cost components to lawmaking: a fixed promulgation cost and a variable adjudication cost. We will discuss them in turn.

The fixed promulgation cost F depends positively on the degree of specificity of the law: more specific laws require more up front research; hence, the greater the specificity of a law, the higher the fixed cost ($F_S > 0$). Further, the marginal cost of promulgation increases as the level of specificity increases ($F_{SS} > 0$). A second factor that influences the fixed promulgation cost is the need to coordinate the new law with existing legislation or to comply with other institutional constraints. We refer to this as coordination cost or degree of difficulty in legislation λ and assume that $F_\lambda > 0$. In a civil law system characterized by a comprehensive and coordinated codification, the cost of enacting a law that amends a provision of an existing codification is high, given the need to coordinate the new law with other rules and principles already contained in the code. The degree of difficulty in legislation λ may include the need for bargaining between different political parties to reach consensus, the existence of institutional constraints, or constitutional procedures to follow for the legal enactment. The promulgation cost due to a higher level of specificity becomes larger as legislative coordination difficulties increase ($F_{S\lambda} > 0$). A third determinant of the fixed promulgation costs is the complexity of the regulated environment κ. We assume that the fixed promulgation costs increase with the complexity of the regulated environment ($F_\kappa > 0$). Further, $F_{S\kappa} > 0$ is assumed. Our assumptions rest on either of two reasons. First, when reality becomes more complex, the additional fixed cost of specificity becomes larger due to the obvious difficulty of specifying the contingencies of a complex environment. Lawmakers need to account for the complex interaction of a large number of contingent events, specifying the factual scenario under which a legal rule applies. Second, when the legal system becomes more complex, the fixed promulgation cost of specific legal intervention increases due to the need to coordinate the new legal rule with a more complex system of preexisting legal rules. Lawmakers will need to avoid conflicts of law, specifying how new laws relate to preexisting laws (e.g., abrogating a prior law or carving an exception to a preexisting law), specifying the timing of application of new laws vis-à-vis prior laws (e.g., retroactive versus nonretroactive application), and specifying the territorial scope of application of new laws.

The second cost component of lawmaking is related to the adjudication of the law. If N is the frequency of application of the law, the total adjudication cost is $N \cdot C$, where C is the unit adjudication cost, appropriately discounted by the social discount rate. The adjudication cost C depends on the degree of specificity s, the degree of specialization of the court σ, and the complexity of reality κ.

First, greater specificity implies lower unit adjudication cost ($C_S < 0$). In absolute value, this change in adjudication cost can be thought of as the lowering of adjudication cost caused by a greater specificity of the rule, or more simply as an additional benefit of greater detail in the law.[7] With higher levels of specificity, the additional benefit of greater specificity $|C_S|$ decreases, implying a higher C_S. Thus, we assume $C_{SS} > 0$.

Next, we assume that the unit adjudication cost decreases as the courts become more specialized ($C_\sigma < 0$). The additional benefit of greater specificity of laws is greater when those laws are interpreted and applied by a specialized court. In other words, as σ increases, $|C_S|$ increases, resulting in $C_{S\sigma} < 0$. This assumption captures the simple intuition that specialized judges are better able to interpret and apply complex law, given the greater familiarity acquired over time with the legal system that is relevant to their subject-matter jurisdiction. So, for example, it seems reasonable to assume that a specialized tax judge is better able to handle a complex tax rule than a judge sitting in a court with general jurisdiction.

Lastly, when reality becomes more complex, the unit adjudication cost increases ($C_\kappa > 0$). The additional benefit of greater specificity is higher when reality is more complex. That is, as κ increases, $|C_S|$ increases, resulting in $C_{S\kappa} < 0$.

The level of specificity is chosen to maximize the net total value:

$$\max_s \; N \cdot V(s, \omega) - F(s, \lambda, \kappa) - N \cdot C(s, \sigma, \kappa)$$

With the assumptions made above, the second-order sufficient condition for the optimization problem is fulfilled. Specifically, the assumptions that greater specificity increases the value of the legal rule at a decreasing rate ($V_{SS} < 0$), that marginal cost of promulgation increases with greater specificity ($F_{SS} > 0$), and that the lowering of unit adjudication cost induced by a greater specificity of the rule decreases ($C_{SS} > 0$) imply that $N \cdot V_{SS} - F_{SS} - N \cdot C_{SS} < 0$. Then the optimal level of specificity must fulfill the following condition:

$$N \cdot V_S(s^*, \omega) - F_S(s^*, \lambda, \kappa) - N \cdot C_S(s^*, \sigma, \kappa) = 0 \qquad 2.1$$

For now, assume that λ, σ, and κ are fixed and concentrate on the impact of changes in frequency of application N and in the rate of obsolescence ω on the optimal specificity level s^*. To that end, the optimality condition to be fulfilled can be obtained by totally differentiating equation (2.1):

$$dN \cdot V_S + N \cdot V_{SS} \cdot ds^* + N \cdot V_{S\omega} \cdot d\omega - F_{SS} \cdot ds^*$$
$$- dN \cdot C_S - N \cdot C_{SS} \cdot ds^* = 0$$

Equation (2.2) details how the different impacts generated by exogenous changes in the frequency of application dN, exogenous changes in the rate of obsolescence $d\omega$, and the required optimal changes in the level of specificity ds^* must be balanced. Rearranging the terms, we have

$$dN \cdot (V_S - C_S) + d\omega \cdot (N \cdot V_{S\omega}) = ds^* \cdot \left|(N \cdot V_{SS} - F_{SS} - N \cdot C_{SS})\right|$$
$$+ \qquad\qquad\qquad\qquad -$$

Equation (2.3) must be satisfied for the optimal specificity to be chosen in the face of changes in the frequency of application of the law and the rate of obsolescence. The first term in equation (2.3) indicates the total impact induced by changes in the volume of application of the legal rule. Since $V_S - C_S > 0$, this impact is positive if, for example, there is an increase in the frequency of application of the legal rule. The second term in (2.3) represents the total impact induced by changes in the rate of obsolescence. This impact is negative if, for example, there is an increase in the rate of obsolescence, as $V_{S\omega} < 0$. Thus, equation (2.3) specifies that the total impact, positive and/or negative, from changes in N and in ω must be balanced by an adjustment in the chosen level of specificity s^*.

2.2. The Relevance of Economies of Scale in Adjudication

Consistent with Kaplow (1992), our result suggests that the frequency of a law's application is important in determining optimal specificity. First, consider the simple cases where there is only one exogenous change. If there is no change in the rate of obsolescence ($d\omega = 0$), then the optimal change in specificity must go in the same direction as the change in frequency of application of the legal rule ($ds^*/dN > 0$).[8]

For legal issues that arise frequently in settings with common characteristics, a rule with a higher degree of specificity is desirable. If a law is frequently applied, variable adjudication costs will tend to be higher than promulgation costs. Because a rule is more specific than a standard, it is easier, and hence less costly, to learn up front. This necessarily means that rules will be more efficient than standards when the law is frequently applied.

Conversely, where legal issues rarely arise and the circumstances are varied, designing a rule that accounts for every relevant contingency would require a high fixed cost and would be wasteful, as most of such hypothetical circumstances would never arise in actual cases. Thus, when frequency is low, a standard is preferable.

OPTIMAL SPECIFICITY OF LAWS   17

2.3. The Obsolescence Problem

Circumstances change over time causing some laws to become obsolete. An important cost of legal regulation by means of rules is the cost of altering obsolete laws to keep pace with social, economic or technological change. Obsolescence is not as serious a problem with standards as it is with rules. Standards are relatively unaffected by changes over time since standards are much broader than rules and hence much more adaptable to varying circumstances. The reasonableness concept is still useful despite immense changes of the optimal course of conduct over time. Thus, we expect specific rules when there is a stable environment and general standards when there is a fast rate of change.

The existing literature points out that specific rules are more sensitive to exogenous, unforeseen changes in the regulated environment and thus are more prone to obsolescence (Ehrlich and Posner 1974). Our model shows that if we expect volatility in the environment and consequent obsolescence in the legal order, legislators should choose lower levels of specificity. Our model further clarifies that if there is no change in the frequency of application of the legal rule ($dN = 0$), the optimal change in specificity must go in opposite direction as the change in the rate of obsolescence ($ds^*/d\omega < 0$).[9]

2.4. Economies of Scale in Adjudication and Obsolescence

Next, consider the cases in which there are changes in both the rate of obsolescence and the frequency of application of the legal issue. In these cases, the total impacts on changes in the optimal specificity are generally unknown. Various possibilities are conceivable. In the case where there is an increase in the frequency of application of the legal rule and a decrease in the rate of obsolescence, the two positive impacts induced by these exogenous changes reinforce each other to create a positive change, increasing the optimal level of specificity. This may be the case when certain new areas of the law become more established, with an increase in both the frequency of application of the law and the stability of the regulated environment. As a new area of the law consolidates and grows in relevance, greater detail in the formulation of laws becomes desirable. Likewise, when there is a decrease in the frequency of application of the law and an increase in the rate of obsolescence, the two impacts reinforce each other and lead to a reduction in the optimal level of specificity.

In cases in which changes in the rate of obsolescence and the frequency of application of the legal issue are in the same direction, the impacts counterbalance each other. Depending on the relative magnitudes and the scaling effects of these changes, the optimal level of specificity may increase or decrease. For example, consider the case in which both the frequency in the application of a law and the rate of obsolescence increase. This may be the case of a booming area of the law where the increase in frequency of a legal issue is also accompanied by instability and change of the regulated environment. The impacts of these two factors go in different directions. When the positive impact, induced by the increase in the frequency of application of the law, outweighs the negative impact, induced by the increase in the rate of obsolescence, abbreviated here by $N \uparrow$ and $\omega \uparrow$, the optimal level of specificity increases ($s^* \uparrow$). The relatively large and positive impact induced by changes in N may be due either to the large increase in magnitude dN, or to the large, positive scaling factor of marginal net value of adjudication $V_S - C_S$, or to both. The relatively weak and negative impact induced by changes in the obsolescence rate may be due either to the small increase in the rate of obsolescence $d\omega$, or to the small decrease in marginal value due to obsolescence $N \cdot V_{S\omega}$, or to both.

It is straightforward to consider the total impact on the optimal level of specificity s^* for the other cases in which both frequency of application and the rate of obsolescence change in the same direction. In Figure 2.1 we summarize the resulting changes in the optimal specificity under different scenarios when there are simultaneous changes in ω and in N.

2.5. Optimal Detail of Legal Rules in Civil Law Systems with Specialized Courts and Complex Regulated Environments

After concentrating on the effects induced by changes in frequency of application and rate of obsolescence on the optimal specificity of legal rules, we now shift our attention is now shifted to the impact caused by other exogenous variables. We consider how the methodological approach used by legal systems, the existence of specialized courts, and the complexity of the regulated environment affect the optimal level of detail in the formulation of law.

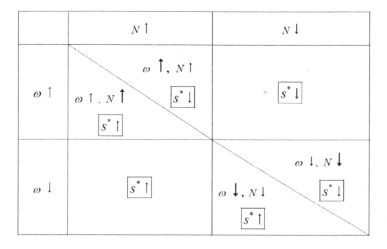

FIGURE 2.1 Changes in the Optimal Specificity of Legal Rules
Source: This table splits the main body into 4 quadrants. The second (northwest) and the fourth (southeast) quadrants are further split into two triangles. Each of these triangles specifies the movements of the variables N and ω and gives the resulting movement of S^* (in a box). In the first (northeast) and third (southwest) quadrants, no movements of variables N and ω are given, only the definitive movement of S^* (in a box) is provided.

With respect to the impact of the methodological approach, it is important to consider the peculiar conception of "codification" in civil law systems. In a civil law system, codifications are aimed at providing a comprehensive and coherent set of principles and rules, capable of application through deductive techniques of interpretation (Merryman 1969). Like a set of mathematical theorems and corollaries, law is organized in a rigorous scheme of principles and rules, arranged in a pyramid-like fashion, from broad to specific, from general rules to particular exceptions. This conception of civil law codification results from efforts of the seventeenth- and eighteenth-century French scholars and the later rational jurisprudence that inspired modern European codifications. The change of any specific provision in a civil law codification is fairly problematic. The amendment of a provision often requires coordination and harmonization with other rules and principles of the code, with complex chain effects on yet other code provisions. In fact, codes in a civil law system are infrequently revised, compared with the relative frequency with which ordinary legislation is introduced in the same civil law system. Further, when revisions do occur, they are carried out by committees of experts that attempt to revise entire sections of the code in a systematic fashion, avoiding piecemeal intervention.

Given these system-specific methodological constraints, the cost of legislative revisions is higher for civil law codifications than for other forms of legislation or codification. Using our first order condition for the net value optimization problem, equation (2.1), we can study how the codification method influences the optimal level of specificity. The relevant comparative static results can be obtained directly: $ds^*/d\lambda < 0$.[10] This reveals that when it is more difficult to codify and amend a legal rule (λ increases), a lower level of specificity is desirable. We should thus observe less detail and greater use of standards.

Another component that affects the optimal level of detail of legal rules is the degree of specialization of courts. Most civil law jurisdictions have specialized sections of the bench to deal with given set of issues of the law. For example, in ordinary civil law courts (tribunals, courts of appeal, and supreme courts), specialized panels (generally referred to as "sections" or "divisions" of the court) are formed to deal with particular recurring legal issues. Thus, most courts will have a division specializing in labor disputes, a division specializing in bankruptcy proceedings, another with contract disputes, another with succession disputes, and so on. In yet other cases, specialized jurisdictions, for example tax courts, are created to deal with particular sets of legal issues.

Furthermore, some laws affect only specific areas of the law that fall under the jurisdiction of a specialized panel of judges. A tax law will most frequently be applied by a tax judge and will have only limited occasion to become relevant in a dispute pending before a different type of court. The optimal level of specificity of these laws of narrow application can thus be evaluated with respect to the specialized court. On the other hand, other laws affect matters that can fall under the jurisdiction of a large number of different courts. For example, laws concerning legal capacity or duress are potentially relevant to almost every area of the law. The optimal level of specificity of these laws of widespread application has to be considered with respect to the entire judicial system.

We thus want to see how the existence of specialized courts affects the optimal level of specificity of a law. For the interpretation of this result, we refer to the specificity of laws that primarily fall under the jurisdiction of the specialized court. The relevant comparative static results can be obtained directly: $ds^*/d\sigma > 0$.[11] The optimal level of specificity increases for laws that are applied and interpreted by more specialized courts (σ increases). In these cases we should expect to see greater use of detailed legal provisions and to observe more rules.

Lastly, we discuss the effect of the complexity of the regulated environment on the choice of optimal specificity. Recall that a more complex reality raises the legislative fixed cost and also increases the adjudication cost. An increase in the legislative fixed cost favors a lower degree of specificity (laws should be formulated more like a standard) while an increase in the adjudication cost favors a higher degree of specificity (laws should be formulated more like a rule).

The relevant comparative static result shows that the sign of $ds^*/d\kappa$ is indeterminate.[12] In spite of the indeterminacy of the overall sign due to the two effects, if the force induced by an increase in legislative fixed cost of specificity dominates the force induced by an increase in adjudication cost, the optimal degree of specificity is lowered when reality becomes more complex.[13] Intuitively, with an increase in the complexity of the regulated environment, greater use of rules will be warranted when legislative costs are lower than judicial costs. An increase in judicial human capital, on the other hand, would lower judicial costs and thus justify the use of less specific laws in response to an increase in complexity of the regulated environment.

🎟 3. Contextualizing the Analysis

Lawmakers can choose to craft laws with different levels of specificity. We considered factors that may affect the optimal degree of specificity of laws, including the relevance of legal obsolescence, volume of litigation, judges' specialization, and complexity of the regulated environment. In order to keep things tractable, our model necessarily abstracts from reality to isolate effects that would otherwise be obfuscated by the many different forces in practice. In recognizing these limits, we consider our results further under the more complex institutional reality that characterizes contemporary legislative processes in various areas of the law.

3.1. Legislative Information and Legal Experimentation

Lawmakers often undertake legal intervention with incomplete information about the current or future circumstances of the regulated issue. When lawmakers lack current information about the regulated issue, they adopt standards because they expect information to be revealed through implementation and enforcement of legislation. In light of information acquired during the initial phase, legal amendments to increase the level of specificity can be implemented later. Standards are also useful to cope with legislative uncertainty about future events. Standards are more adaptable to surprises, since judges can more easily cope with unexpected shocks in the regulated environment through adaptive adjudication.

Standards imply ex post regulation by courts. Our model ignores the intrinsic benefit of judicial lawmaking in terms of experimentation and gradual accretion of legal certainty. As is well-known in the law and economics literature—the Chicago School efficiency of the common law hypothesis is an example—courts may have an institutional advantage in designing and experimenting with alternative rules in light of case experience. This is an advantage if the adversarial process and the repeat filing of cases reveal otherwise unavailable private information to third parties, allowing courts to better specify the proper domain of a law. However, the institutional advantage of courts over legislators may disappear when selections of cases going to courts are biased (Fon, Parisi, and Depoorter 2005) or when ideological decision making is taken into account (Fon and Parisi 2003a). Furthermore, hindsight bias often leads courts to depart from the optimal balancing of type I and type II errors (Rachlinski 2000).[14]

Our model assumes that greater levels of specificity lead to greater certainty and predictability of the system. Obviously, there are diminishing returns—excessive specificity and complexity may ultimately lead to less predictability than general standards. Unlike specific rules (a speed limit rule is applicable to specific categories of vehicles), standards generally have broader scope of application (a safe speed standard is applicable to all means of transportation). The advantage of rules in terms of predictability may quickly disappear due to the uncertain boundaries of rules (should horseback riding be covered under speed limit rules?) or because it is not clear ex ante which set of rules is applicable (are electric bicycles subject to the speed limit of bicycles or can they take advantage of higher limits allowed for motorcycles?).

The assumed relationship between specificity and adjudication costs (specific rules are easier and cheaper to adjudicate than general standards) ignores another relevant social cost: information costs faced by subjects of the law. Unlike courts and professional lawyers, subjects of the law may find it easier to gain a sense of what a legal standard requires of their behavior, rather than navigating through a complex web of detailed rules. Furthermore, as a stylized fact, the drafting styles of standards and rules may differ substantially. Standards are often formulated in plain language easily comprehensible to a lay person, while rules frequently incorporate statutory jargon that requires doctrinal interpretive techniques.

3.2. Beyond the Benevolent Lawmaker

Our stylized model of legal intervention assumes that lawmakers act benevolently, without considering the impact of political failures and selfish behavior by legislators, courts, and subjects of the law. There may be advantages and disadvantages of legal specificity when agency problems are taken into account, from the public choice or social choice viewpoints. For example, Mahoney and Sanchirico (2005) suggest standards as a tool for legislators to make lobbying less effective. However, this poses an inconsistency problem, inasmuch as lobbying generates potential benefits for the legislators. Hence it might be in the interest of lawmakers to precommit to enacting rules, rather than standards, as a way to maximize their rents from lobbying. Thus, only higher-order rules, such as constitutions or other institutional constraints, may be capable of creating an effective long-term constraint to reduce the risk of special-interest lobbying.

When legal intervention is used to deliver selective benefits over time, rules, especially when contained in a code, may be a more effective tool for legislators to enhance the durability of their political decisions in the face of potential political turnover and unstable majority coalitions (Majone 2001). Specificity in legislation thus increases the present value of legislative rents. Choosing specificity of legislation is also relevant in the face of strategic actions by subjects of the law. Individuals and businesses expend effort to find ways around specific commands of the law. Standards are more robust to attempts by subjects of the law to bypass legal constraints (Wegner 1997). Thus, lawmakers may choose standards to protect the effectiveness of their legal enactments in the face of detrimental creativity by subjects of the law. Lawmakers must weigh the costs and benefits of specificity, because greater specificity enhances the durability of legislation in the face of later political changes but renders it more vulnerable to strategic actions by individuals and businesses to bypass the effectiveness of legal provisions.

Specificity of law is also relevant in the presence of misaligned objectives of different branches of government. Standards transfer lawmaking authority to courts. When courts and legislatures have different political makeups, legal specificity may be a relevant political instrument. General standards allow courts to resist legislation; specific rules may reduce the ability of courts to corrode legislative enactments.

In mixed jurisdictions where legislative and judge-made sources compete to create legal order, the effect of legal specificity should be considered in conjunction with strategic judicial intervention. The interpretation and future application of a newly enacted standard is greatly affected by the first applicable cases. This creates an opportunity for strategic adjudication, where interventionist courts may race to adjudicate new standards, affecting the future interpretation of similar cases. On the other hand, rules are generally less vulnerable to strategic adjudication.

Lastly, lawmakers often operate under binding legal and institutional constraints. Legislation and regulation may be subject to higher-order rules (for example, constitutional rules, presidential vetoes, and international law). In the presence of binding constraints, lawmakers may use vague standards to avoid an open conflict with the higher source that could lead to an invalidation of their legislative efforts.[15] Likewise, the use of standards may be driven by political expediency when lawmakers serve conflicting demands of different constituencies.[16]

3.3. Social versus Political Time-Preference

Legislation imposes current lawmaking costs, producing benefits while incurring additional costs over time. Discount rates become a critical factor in computing the net present value of alternative legislative interventions. Our model assumes the presence of a benevolent lawmaker who weighs current costs against the future benefits of lawmaking and uses the appropriate social discount rate. The discounted present value of legislation is implicitly captured and approximated by our benefit variable. Although this analysis is appropriate to understand the factors that affect the optimal level of specificity of laws, a more realistic extension should allow the political discount rate to differ substantially from that of society as a whole, as lawmakers are political actors with a time horizon. This may affect the cost-benefit calculation in a number of ways. Interestingly, our analysis generates indeterminate results regarding the impact of political time-preference on specificity of legislation.

Whether a lawmaker's limited time-horizon leads to a greater use of standards over rules depends largely on context. When lawmakers use legal intervention to deliver future benefits that depend on the degree of specificity of laws, a higher political time preference will lead to inefficiently low levels of specificity. Although both the benefits of legislation and the adjudication costs occur in the future, the political discount factors have more impact on benefits than on costs. This is because, assuming that legal intervention is cost-justified, the expected benefits are larger than the costs. Thus, higher political discount rates would lead to less specificity and an increased use of standards. Put differently, if the benefits of legal intervention are only captured over time, a short-sighted lawmaker may give greater weight to the immediate costs of lawmaking, tilting towards the use of general standards. From an institutional perspective, the myopic behavior of lawmakers can be aggravated by institutional factors such as term-limits, shorter legislative periods, and unstable majority coalitions.

Political discount rates also affect the rate of legal change and the specificity of legal rules. When a new law is enacted, a learning period may create costs for both courts and subjects of the law. Once this period is over, these costs fade out and the net benefits of legal innovation begin to accrue. Depending on the duration of the learning period relative to the time horizon of the lawmakers, legal innovation may be discouraged and standards may be preferred to rules to reduce short-term costs. An extension of our analysis could consider optimal lawmaking patterns in light of alternative social and normative discount rates.

4. The Evolving Structure of Codifications

Results of this analysis may shed light on the historical trends in legislation of special areas of private law, concentrating on the degree of detail utilized by European codifications. The peculiar structure of the modern codifications of Europe reveals heterogeneity in the degree of detail used in codifying different areas of the law, a variance that could be explained with the institutional and environmental variables identified in our analysis. A similar analysis can be carried out with respect to the recent draft codifications of Europe, which also reveal changes in codification style across different areas of the law.

European national codes have been fairly resilient over the course of centuries. The French *Code Civil* enacted in 1804 by emperor Napoleon Bonaparte still stands as the central body of private law in France. The same is true for many other national codifications of the nineteenth and early-twentieth century, such as the Italian *Codice Civile* and the German

Bürgerliches Gesetzbuch. The Italian *Codice Civile* came into force in 1865 and remained in force until 1942. The German *Bürgerliches Gesetzbuch* that came into force in the year 1900 has maintained much of its structure and content to the present time.

The model of optimal level of specificity of legal rules sheds some light on the structures of these codifications and the different levels of detail used in regulating different areas of law. Table 2.1 illustrates the point with reference to three representative codifications of modern Europe, each of which played an important role in influencing subsequent codifications throughout the world, and two draft codifications, the European and Israeli Civil Codes. Table 2.1 lists the number of provisions utilized by different codes to regulate specific areas of law. A larger number of provisions to regulate the same area of the law suggest a greater level of specificity.

The French codification was enacted after the fall of the feudal era. The fall of feudalism brought about a substantial change in the structure of property, with a resulting need for innovation in the law of property. This is a period of reaction to the fragmentation of property rights that was characteristic of the feudal era (with the problems of infeudation and subinfeudation) and proclamation of absolute conceptions of property. Fundamental principles of property law are under reconsideration and property law is in flux. Given the rapid economic and institutional changes brought about by the end of the feudal era, detailed property rules risked becoming obsolete. This explains the relative simplicity of French property law compared to earlier (and later) regimes. Property law gradually settled and was regulated in greater detail in the later Italian and German codes. This is illustrated by

TABLE 2.1 The Evolving Structure of Civil Codes

	Property	Contracts and Sales	Torts	Agency	Gifts and Successions
French Civil Code of 1804	194[17]	387[18]	5[19]	26[20]	389[21]
Italian Civil Code of 1865	278[22]	275[23]	5[24]	26[25]	376[26]
German Civil Code of 1900	442[27]	273[28]	30[29]	17[30]	481[31]
Netherlands Civil Code of 1990	335[32]	277[33]	21[34]	37[35]	247[36]
Israeli Civil Code (Draft 2004)	232[37]	385[38]	54[39]	14[40]	N.A.[41]
European Civil Code (Draft 2004)	N.A.[42]	267[43]	62[44]	48[45]	N.A.[46]

the fact that the number of provisions dealing with the law of property increases substantially from the 1804 French code to the 1865 Italian code and more than doubles by the time of the German code of 1900. The same probably holds for the regulation of property by the Israeli Civil Code, given the developing principles of property law and the unsettled resolution of historic claims.

An opposite trend is observed in contract and sales law. French and Israeli codes have a substantially higher number of provisions, compared to their Italian, German, and other European counterparts. This is explainable considering that in France and Israel at the time of their respective codifications there was already a unitary and established commercial tradition. On the other hand, nineteenth-century Germany and Italy, and twenty-first-century Europe utilize codifications as an instrument to achieve unification of otherwise diverse regimes. In the European context, reduced specificity is further due to the increase in the linguistic and legal diversity and the need to simplify contract and sales laws.

An interesting discrepancy is observed in Table 2.1 between the level of specificity in the law of contracts and torts. In the French code, there are 77 times as many contract law provisions than tort law provisions. The entire area of tort law is governed by five simple principles with very little degree of specificity. By the time of the German code the number of tort provision increases but the discrepancy with the number of contract law provisions remains noticeable nevertheless. The extreme minimalism used in the drafting of tort rules is even more striking when compared to the much greater detail used in older systems to regulate tort liability (e.g., Emperor Justinian's *Corpus Juris Civilis* enacted in the year 533 C.E.), where specific causes of actions were created to remedy specific tort situations, with a large number of detailed provisions regulating liability in each particular situation. This peculiar feature of nineteenth and early-twentieth-century codifications can be explained by the fact that the shock brought about by the industrial revolution rendered older fact-specific tort rules obsolete. Reference to specific fact patterns in the description of a tort action would have given opportunity for iterated obsolescence in such a dynamic economic reality. Although in the present reality some volatility continues to characterize the world of accidents, the rate of change in the accident environment (and the resulting rate of obsolescence of tort law) is probably lower than it was during the industrial revolution. This explains why the Drafts Codes of European law and Israeli law show greater levels of detail used in the area of tort law.

The same holds for the law of agency. In the early twentieth century, in a world of rapid changing from local rural economies to more complex industrial relations, agency law became at the same time highly relevant and in a state of rapid flux. Any detailed form of regulation of this dynamic reality would have risked rapid obsolescence. This explains the parsimony used by nineteenth- and early-twentieth-century lawmakers in regulating this area of the law. As this reality approached stability in more recent times, rules gradually increased in number and became more detailed in their formulation.

These findings suggest that lawmakers appear to realize that the increased opportunity for obsolescence of laws renders standards preferable to specific rules, preventing the legislature from incurring the cost of legislative amendment to adapt existing rules to new development in the external environment. European codes are thus characterized by different levels of specificity in different areas of the law, with greater specificity in areas characterized by stability and lesser specificity in areas characterized by rapid change.

The data in Table 2.1 further supports the conclusion that specificity of laws is also affected by the number of cases that are likely to be adjudicated in each area of the law. More frequent usage of rules justifies greater fixed expenditures in rule drafting, inasmuch as these expenditures help reduce average adjudication costs. In the historical context of nineteenth-century codifications, this can be seen by the fact that greater specificity was given to laws of successions, in spite of the fairly narrow scope of this area of the law. The law of successions was in fact given a disparately greater prominence in the codes than other areas of the law, such as the laws on quasi contracts or privacy.

The solution to our lawmaking problem generates several implications concerning the patterns of lawmaking under different legal, social, and economic conditions. These implications are relevant for both positive and normative analyses. From a positive standpoint, these results can be used to formulate a testable hypothesis: legal systems respond to exogenous changes in the external environment by adopting varying patterns of lawmaking, thus maximizing the value of legal intervention. The anecdotal, historical evidence discussed in this chapter is consistent with this hypothesis. Modern codifications provide useful points of comparison because they were written and enacted in a unitary fashion. European national lawmakers probably realized that volatility in the external environment creates an increased opportunity for rule obsolescence. This led them to prefer standards over rules in order to avoid the need for costly legislative amendments when developments in the external environment rendered previously enacted rules obsolete. The historical and comparative illustrations presented above should be corroborated by further empirical analysis to assess the consistency of these evolving patterns of codification with predictions by the economic model.

In a normative context, our results should be used with caution. Models necessarily assume away many institutional factors that form an important part of reality. This is necessary to isolate effects and formulate results with predictive or explanatory power. In real life, optimal patterns of codification should be determined on the basis of a richer contextual analysis, in light of current circumstances. We can, nevertheless, offer some general criteria to lawmakers on the basis of our stylized analysis, calling for an increased attentiveness to environmental changes in the optimal choice of legal intervention.

THREE

Optimal Timing of Legal Intervention
Lawmaking under Uncertainty*

A SECOND PROBLEM THAT LAWMAKERS need to address when considering the enactment of new laws concerns the timing of legal intervention. The choice of timing of legal intervention is interrelated to the problem discussed in Chapter 2, concerning the optimal degree of specificity of laws. Despite their fundamental relevance for policy purposes, the economic principles that guide the optimal timing of legal intervention remain poorly understood. Modern investment theory offers valuable insights into the problem of timing of laws, based on the similarity that adopting a law bears to the decision to invest in a productive asset. Lawmaking shares three critical characteristics with investment in physical assets: (1) irreversibility of investment (sunk costs); (2) uncertainty about future returns; and (3) discretion with respect to the timing of the investment. Lawmaking investment costs are largely sunk and cannot be recovered if an enacted law proves to be ineffective or undesirable at a later time. Most legislative choices are often carried out under uncertainty over the future benefits of the new law. Chosen law may prove ineffective or changes in the social or economic circumstances may render them obsolete over time. In many situations, the lawmaker has some discretion as to the timing of the lawmaking intervention; deciding to invest today often means giving up the option to invest tomorrow using the same resources.

The traditional applications of the net present value rule typically ignore the option to delay an investment and therefore fail to correctly estimate the true opportunity cost of immediate investment and the potential benefits of waiting. A rational investor should take into account the benefits from waiting whenever investments are irreversible and can be postponed. Similarly, in the context of lawmaking, taking the value of

---

* This chapter is based on an article previously published as Parisi, Francesco, Vincy Fon, and Nita Ghei, "The Value of Waiting in Lawmaking," *European Journal of Law and Economics* 18: 131–48 (2004).

waiting into account alters the traditional rule of thumb of the optimal time to legislate, by which a rational lawmaker should enact a new rule when the present expected value from the legal innovation is equal to or greater than its investment cost. Correctly valuing the option of waiting is important whenever the costs of legal intervention are irreversible and innovation can be postponed. In this chapter we build on this premise to study the main determinants of the optimal timing of legal intervention under uncertainty.

Section 1 frames the lawmaking problem as an investment problem. We contemplate the choice of a benevolent planner whose preferences and incentives are perfectly aligned with those of society. We discuss the important factors that affect the optimal timing of lawmaking, given the possibility of waiting until a later time to enact the law. Section 2 presents a basic model to illustrate the value of waiting in lawmaking. A simple dynamic lawmaking problem under uncertainty is used to characterize the optimal timing issue. The model also considers lawmaking by a benevolent planner to illustrate the effect of the option to delay legal intervention on the optimal timing of lawmaking, under different parameters of the regulated environment. We explore the significance of those results for legislative and judicial policy. We consider two extensions of the basic model in Section 3. In the first extension, we allow for some learning and informational benefit from the immediate implementation of the new law. In a second extension, we introduce a political agency problem by allowing the subjective discount rate of the regulator to differ from the social discount rate. We then suggest some areas for future research.

Although our model contemplates legal intervention by a benevolent lawmaker in the absence of timing constraints and agency problems, it provides a valuable benchmark against which to measure the action of real-life lawmakers. There may be important exceptions to the existence of an option to delay intervention. For example, in the case of judge-made law, courts do not have the privilege of postponing decision making, even when they have full control on the decision of whether to overturn a precedent. Whenever presented with a novel legal issue, courts have an obligation to provide a decision in the case at bar. This eliminates their freedom in the choice of timing for the creation of a new legal precedent.

In spite of such institutional or strategic constraints, in most cases, delay in legal intervention remains to a large extent feasible. As public choice theory tells us, however, there are several strategic and political variables that influence the timing of legal intervention. For example, there can be several situations in which strategic concerns render it important for a legislative coalition to act promptly in order to preempt possible intervention by alternative coalitions. Likewise, under certain institutional settings, optimal waiting may violate time-consistency. Given a binding budget on the legislature, there is an opportunity cost of adopting a new rule, represented by the forgone possibility to enact a new rule in the subsequent time period. However, if the cost of subsequent legal change is borne by a different legislature, the decision to legislate now would create an externality that is not captured by the current decision maker. This problem has been recognized in the recent literature (Parisi and Ghei 2005; Gersen and Posner 2007), suggesting that this may yield a rate of legal change that exceeds or otherwise departs from the socially optimal rate.[1] Constitutionally mandated waiting periods for the enactment of new law and budgeting rules aimed at forcing lawmakers to internalize the cost of future revisions of their laws can facilitate the optimal rate of legal change in situations of political instability. More generally, our results provide a relevant key in the design of constitutional and institutional constraints, from a constitutional political economy perspective.

1. Lawmaking as Investment: Methodological Premises

We begin by considering the legal problem of optimal lawmaking as analogous to an investment problem. The legal and economic analysis of the issue can greatly benefit from the methodological premises and substantive findings of modern investment theory. An investment is the choice of an economic agent to incur a present cost in the expectation of future benefits (Dixit and Pindyck 1994). A legal system can be regarded as making investment decisions when incurring present lawmaking costs that will generate benefits over time.

Traditionally, investment theory has suggested that an investment should be undertaken whenever it generates a positive net present value of benefits; that is, the present value of benefits exceeds the present value of costs. But this rule does not yield the optimal result when the investment is irreversible (Dixit and Pindyck 1994). As the emerging investment literature has shown, the ability of an investor to delay an irreversible investment may affect a decision on whether and when to invest. McDonald and Siegel (1986), and Pindyck (1991), among others, have highlighted the value of the option to delay investment. This implies that the rule to invest whenever the net present value is positive should be revised to include the value of the waiting option.

The results of the investment literature have important implications for the choice of optimal timing in lawmaking. Drawing from this literature, we suggest that the value of waiting ought to be included as part of the cost of an immediate lawmaking investment.[2] Although delays in investment decisions come at a cost, given the forgone benefits of the investment in the immediate future, lawmakers can control the timing for legal intervention in order to exploit the benefits from waiting.

As mentioned above, lawmaking investments share, to varying degrees, three important attributes with other investment decisions. First, the initial lawmaking costs are largely sunk and the investment is correspondingly irreversible. That is, lawmaking costs cannot be fully recovered if the enacted rule proves to be ineffective or undesirable at a later time.[3] In this sense, lawmaking investments are partially or completely irreversible. Second, there is often uncertainty over the future benefits of the legislation. Chosen rules may prove ineffective in achieving the desired goal. Changes in the social or economic circumstances may also reduce the value of legal intervention, even in the very short term. Third, as in many investment decisions, there is the choice of the timing of the investment. Legislative innovation or revision of current rules can be postponed.

We suggest that these three characteristics are crucial in determining the optimal decisions of legal planners. Building on investment theory under uncertainty, this chapter focuses on the optimal timing of legal intervention, illustrating the interaction among the above factors in identifying the optimal patterns of lawmaking.

1.1. The Value of the Law and the Benefit of Legal Intervention

Much like investing in a productive asset, adoption of a new law requires a direct investment cost (I). Like other investments, the value of the law (V) is given by the present discounted value of the law's future benefits. In this context we distinguish between long-run and short-run benefits of the law.

1.1.1. Long-Run Benefit

We assume that the value of the law (the asset) changes, and generally grows, over time, although with some uncertainty. The assumption is justified by the fact that the value of the law is a function of the scale of application of the law, which is itself generally related to the growth of the economy or society. We denote the growth rate and the variance parameter of the value of the law V as α and σ, respectively. We may want to think of α as the long-run growth rate and σ as the volatility measure of the value of the law. In our model, we assume that the value of the law V is a stochastic process that follows a Brownian motion. Thus, even though information arrives over time, the future is always uncertain.

1.1.2. Short-Run Benefits

Just like real assets, a law has a return in current period, which we denote as δ. This short-run benefit is derived from the adoption of a legal rule in the present time period. The adoption of a legal rule may produce short-run benefits in two alternative ways. First, in the event of an area of the law which was previously unregulated, the new rule provides the immediate advantage of a certain legal standard for the previously unregulated human behavior. Second, if the new legislation falls in an area of the law that is already regulated, the new law may provide legislators with an opportunity to improve over the current rule, which may have become less effective over time with changes in the environment. These short-run benefits are forgone when legal intervention is delayed. It is thus appropriate to think of this short-run return rate as a benefit of immediate legal intervention (i.e., a cost of waiting in lawmaking).[4]

In sum, adopting a law has a short-run benefit, δ, which is the immediate payoff rate. This is analogous to the dividend rate earned in an investment problem. Likewise, adopting a law has a long-run benefit, α, which is the expected rate of growth in the value of the law, much like the expected rate of appreciation of the investment in a traditional investment problem.

1.2. Sunk Costs in Lawmaking

In the context of lawmaking, a variety of legislative (or judicial) costs required to implement legal innovation are sunk and cannot be recovered if the enacted rule proves to be undesirable over time.[5] First, there are the obvious costs of legal intervention, which include the direct legislative and political costs, publication and notice costs. Second, there are the learning costs for courts, enforcement agencies, lawyers, and the general public.[6] The costs associated with making a new law indeed include the costs of disseminating information (Kaplow 1992) and acquiring information about the new law (Ehrlich and Posner 1974). In addition, the process of lawmaking through the private legislature, explored by Schwartz and Scott (1995), should be taken into account. These costs may be substantial and for the most part are irreversible, given the limited value of having learned a law, if the law is repealed. Once the law is formulated and promulgated, these costs cannot be recovered. Third, there may be adjustment costs from legal innovation whenever it results in a change in the existing set of legal entitlements. Finally, there may be institutional costs involved in the change in a law. For example, there may be sunk costs associated with the discontinued operation of an existing rule, given the lost value in the specialization of attorneys and other agents, and other sunken investments by law enforcement agencies.

As we will show in Section 2, the irreversibility of lawmaking costs has important implications for our understanding of optimal lawmaking behavior. It requires lawmakers to be sensitive to uncertainty over future costs and benefits derived from the enforcement of the new rule and changes in the regulated environment that may render the law obsolete. Any model of optimal lawmaking that fails to consider the option value of delaying innovation is necessarily assuming, explicitly or implicitly, that the legal system can avoid all the above sunk costs and can abrogate and enact laws without sunken expenditures. For most real-life applications, however, the substantial sunk costs involved in regulatory or legal innovation necessitate a revision of the simple net present value rule in the context of lawmaking.

1.3. The Cost of Waiting in Lawmaking

In addition to the direct investment cost I, there is also an implicit cost to adopting a law that results from giving up the opportunity to delay intervention. If the law is not passed now, there is the option to pass it in the future. In the presence of sunken investment costs, the option to invest in the future thus creates an opportunity cost, given the forgone opportunity to use the same investment to pass the law in subsequent time periods. It should be noted that this additional element brings the model closer to real-life politics, where frequent amendments to the same rule are either unfeasible or impose severe reputational costs, given the unavoidable public distaste for unstable legislation.[7] This opportunity cost should be considered in addition to the direct investment cost I. In this chapter we refer to this opportunity cost as the "value of waiting" and discuss how this cost affects the choice of optimal timing of legal intervention.

1.4. Social Discount Rates

The model presented in Section 2 considers the optimal timing of lawmaking for a benevolent risk-neutral lawmaker. Such a lawmaker faces a discount rate equal to the risk-free market discount rate. Optimal allocation of governmental investments in lawmaking requires that $\alpha + \delta$ be at least equal to such market return. The intuition is that a benevolent legal planner should limit lawmaking investments to the point in which the rate of return on those investments, $\alpha + \delta$, equals the market return rate. Any lawmaking investment that yields less than such rate of return would, in fact, constitute a misallocation of valuable governmental resources, given the opportunity cost of investing in the market with a higher return.[8] We assume that the optimal allocation of governmental resources and lawmaking investments by a benevolent planner is determined by the same profit maximization exercise that determines other investment decisions in the marketplace. Put differently, limited legislative resources would be used toward the best lawmaking opportunities, much like in a traditional investment problem. In Section 3 we will relax this assumption, introducing another variable to reflect political agency problems and the resulting differences in political time preference. The introduction of a political agency problem implies that lawmakers' "political" discount rate may differ from the social discount rate.

2. Optimal Timing in Lawmaking

In this section we present a basic model of lawmaking that uses the characteristic of irreversibility, and the corresponding value of waiting, to examine the choice of timing of the adoption of a legal rule in a world of uncertainty.[9] We consider a world with a single supreme adjudicator, with sole lawmaking authority. The external environment changes at a stochastic rate. Lawmakers can choose the optimal legislative instrument and control the time of legal intervention.[10] The lawmaker has the option of changing the law at any time. The new law is always a better fit with the new environment and is thus more efficient. The lawmaker also always has the option of waiting until another period to change the law. The legal planner's problem is that of determining the optimal timing of legal intervention.

2.1. A Basic Model

To make the analysis tractable, we assume that the value of the law V is a stochastic process that follows the geometric Brownian motion:

$$dV = \alpha V \, dt + \sigma V \, dz \qquad\qquad 3.1$$

where dz is the increment of a standard Wiener process with mean zero and variance dt. At each period, V can increase or decrease by a fixed percentage.[11] The steps of change are of equal proportions. When the time period for each step is very short, the distribution of logarithm of V_t for future t is approximately normal. Thus the current value V is known, but future values are always uncertain with a variance σ^2 that grows linearly with the time horizon.

We formulate this problem as a binary dynamic programming problem. At each time t, let $P_t(V_t)$ be the net present value of the optimal payoff of the law-adopting opportunity. The legislature can decide to adopt the new law, terminating the wait, or opt to postpone legal intervention, continuing the status quo. If the legislature chooses to terminate the wait and adopt the new law, the termination payoff will be $V_t - I$. On the other hand, if the legislature chooses to wait, then there is no immediate payoff flow for the current period. There is, however, a value to waiting, given by the expected future (optimal) adoption payoff in the next period, discounted to the present period: $\frac{1}{1+\alpha+\delta}E[P_{t+1}(V_{t+1})]$. Given the recurring choice between immediate legal intervention and waiting at any point in time, the optimal payoff value for the period $P_t(V_t)$ is always equal to the larger value of the two choices. Hence, the optimal stopping problem is given by the Bellman equation:

$$P_t(V_t) = \max\left\{ V_t - I, \; \frac{1}{1+\alpha+\delta}E\big[P_{t+1}(V_{t+1})\big]\right\} \qquad\qquad 3.2$$

Because of the stochastic nature of the problem, the precise timing of adoption cannot be found. We can, however, formulate the problem in terms of finding a threshold value for V, which we call V^*, such that whenever $V \geq V^*$, it is optimal to adopt the law. When the value falls below such critical level, an optimizing lawmaker should maintain the status quo; that is, delay the legal innovation. In order to facilitate the understanding of the problem, we have cast our initial Bellman equation in a discrete form. We proceed, however, to solve the problem in continuous form. In particular, in the continuation region where it is optimal to wait, the optimal payoff to the legal adoption problem, the left-hand side of equation (3.2), should be equal to the expected future payoff, the second term in the right-hand side of (3.2). That is,

$$(\alpha + \delta)P\,dt = E(dP) \qquad\qquad 3.3$$

Note that this optimal payoff value, when it is equal to the value in the continuation/waiting region, represents the opportunity cost of waiting to adopt the law. Applying Ito's lemma to expand dP, and recalling that V follows the geometric Brownian motion, we have[12]

$$E(dP) = \tfrac{1}{2}\sigma^2 V^2 P''(V)\,dt + \alpha V\, P'(V)\,dt \qquad\qquad 3.4$$

Substituting (3.4) into (3.3) gives the following second-order differential equation:

$$\tfrac{1}{2}\sigma^2 V^2 P''(V) + \alpha V\, P'(V) - (\alpha + \delta)P(V) = 0 \qquad\qquad 3.5$$

In addition to this differential equation, the optimal value P must satisfy the following boundary conditions:

$$P(0) = 0, \; P(V^*) = V^* - I, \; P'(V^*) = 1 \qquad\qquad 3.6$$

The first boundary condition specifies that, as $V = 0$, the option to adopt the law has no value. The second boundary condition is the "value-matching" condition: at the threshold value V^*, the optimal value of passing the law is $V^* - I$. The third boundary condition is the "smooth-pasting" condition: at the threshold V^* where the opportunity cost to adopt the law and the net benefit in the event of immediate investment meet, the two functions should meet continuously and smoothly.

It can easily be checked that, $P(V) = AV^\beta$, where $\beta > 1$, is the solution of (3.5).[13] Note that $P(V) = AV^\beta$ is the value of waiting (i.e., the opportunity cost of immediate legal intervention). Further note that β satisfies the following equation:

$$\tfrac{1}{2}\sigma^2 \beta(\beta - 1) + \alpha\beta - (\alpha + \delta) = 0 \qquad\qquad 3.7$$

Using the value-matching and the smooth-pasting conditions in (3.6), A and β can be specified in the solution $P(V) = AV^\beta$. In particular, the optimal threshold V^* is given by

$$V^* = \frac{\beta}{\beta - 1} I$$ 3.8

In Figure 3.1, curve VW represents AV^β, the value of waiting. The straight line NB represents $V - I$, the net benefit from immediate lawmaking.

At any point to the left of V^*, the value of waiting exceeds the net benefit of legal intervention. Hence $P(V) = AV^\beta$ the solid portion of VW curve is relevant because delaying intervention is preferable. At all points after V^*, the net benefit of legal intervention exceeds the cost of waiting, rendering immediate intervention desirable. Hence $P(V) = V - I$, or the solid portion of the line NB is now relevant, because legal intervention becomes desirable in this region.[14] At the critical value V^*, the opportunity cost of immediate legal intervention equals the net benefit of immediate investment. Put differently, this means that the value of adopting the law is equal to the full cost of adopting the law $V^* = I + AV^{*\beta}$, where $AV^{*\beta}$ is the value of waiting. At this critical point, the lawmaker would be indifferent between adopting a new law now and waiting to adopt a more efficient rule later. The smooth-pasting conditions at point V^* are represented by the fact that the smooth curve

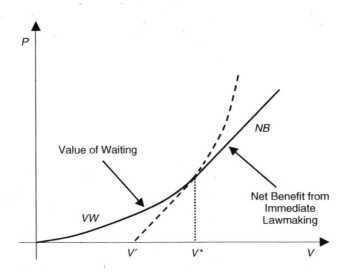

FIGURE 3.1 The Optimal Waiting in Lawmaking

(the opportunity cost of waiting curve) is tangent to the straight line (the net benefit of immediate lawmaking) at V^*.

At this point, it is easy to contrast the optimal value V^* with the critical value V' generated by the simple net present value rule. Points to the left of V' correspond to negative net present values and would thus imply that no lawmaking is desirable under both the simple net present value rule and the different value of waiting rule presented in this chapter. Points between V' and V^* correspond to situations where lawmaking would be desirable according to the traditional simple net present value rule, but would call for no lawmaking at the present time, if legal intervention can be delayed. Finally, points to the right of V^* correspond to situations where lawmaking would be desirable according to both the traditional simple net present value rule and our value of waiting rule.

2.2. The Determinants of Optimal Waiting

There are four relevant variables that can affect the optimal timing of legal innovation. First, the extent to which the investment costs are irreversible. Intuitively, one would expect the value of waiting would increase with the extent of irreversibility. The second variable that matters is the extent of uncertainty in the system. The greater the uncertainty, the greater the cost of giving up the option of waiting. The third factor that matters is the value of the law over time. The greater the expected value of the law over time, the greater should be the value of waiting. For example, legislating in a field dominated by rapidly changing technology, such as the Internet, carries a high value of waiting. The field is growing in importance, and legislating today may leave the system with inefficient laws in the future. On the other hand, the greater the short term benefits of legal intervention, the lower is the net value of waiting. Thus, for example, environmental legislation may have substantial immediate benefits, and irreversible losses that might result from delay. This reduces the value of waiting. Thus, the greater the immediate value of legal innovation, the more likely is immediate adoption of the new rule.

The comparative statics from the model bear out these intuitions. Simple comparative statics shows that[15]

$$\frac{\partial V^*}{\partial I} > 0, \quad \frac{\partial V^*}{\partial \sigma} > 0, \quad \frac{\partial V^*}{\partial \alpha} > 0, \quad \frac{\partial V^*}{\partial \delta} < 0. \qquad 3.9$$

The sensitivity results in (3.9) show that the optimal waiting in lawmaking increases in (1) the extent to which the lawmaking expenditures are sunk; (2) the level of uncertainty in the regulated environment or the variance of the expected benefits from legal intervention; and (3) the expected rate of growth in the value of the law, such as when the law becomes more important overtime. Lastly, less waiting is commanded by an increase in the short-term benefits of legal intervention.

2.3. Timing of Legal Intervention and the Option Pricing Analogue

As discussed above, the general problem facing the lawmaker is that of choosing the right moment to switch to the new law. One extreme possibility is for lawmakers to change the law every time there is a change in the external environment; the other extreme is never to change the law. The former option would mean incurring the sunk costs for each switch, which could be prohibitive. The latter could result in laws that are in effect obsolete and inefficient, because they do not address the needs of the society they are designed to serve. In between the two extremes, there should be a range of points where the benefits of the switch exceed the sunk cost of making the switch.

The importance of the option in the context of law depends on the fact that, by waiting, the legislator preserves the opportunity of making a better informed legislative change in the future, rather than simply the choice to abstain from acting at all in the future.[16] The opportunity to delay an irreversible investment can be analogized to a financial call option.[17] In our lawmaking investment application, we should note that unlike most financial options, the lawmaking opportunity is always available, and thus is comparable to a perpetual option with no expiration date.[18] As with financial options, the opportunity to delay legal intervention is intrinsically valuable whenever the future benefit from the lawmaking investment is uncertain.[19]

When a lawmaker decides to legislate, she exercises (or "kills") her lawmaking option, giving up the possibility of waiting for new events and information that might influence the desirability of the legislative innovation. By deciding to intervene, the lawmaker exhausts the full option value. Therefore, legal innovation should be undertaken only when the expected value of lawmaking exceeds the lawmaking costs by an amount equal to the value of keeping the lawmaking option alive. In the presence of uncertainty, this result modifies considerably the criterion that suggests proceeding with legal innovation any time the present value of the expected benefits of lawmaking exceed the expected costs of lawmaking. Indeed, in the presence of sunk costs and uncertainty, such incomplete application of the net present value rule would likely lead to nonoptimal decisions.

Thus, lawmaking guidelines that ignore the value of waiting principle can be grossly in error. Most importantly, as was shown in this section, the value of waiting in lawmaking increases when higher sunk investment costs are involved and when there is more uncertainty in the regulated environment or when the law becomes more important over time. On the other hand, less waiting is preferable when there are higher short-term benefits from legal intervention.

Some of these results generate conclusions that are complementary to the results reached by Heiner (1986) in the context of judicially driven legal innovation[20] and the general wisdom in the political economy of regulation stressing the importance of stability and certainty in the legal system (Barro 1991).[21] The results of this analysis, however, suggest that there is an option value of waiting in lawmaking that is independent of the imperfect decision making of judges and legislators or the social preference for stable laws. Even lawmakers with perfect decision-making abilities, when acting under uncertainty, may rationally choose to postpone legal intervention, if they have an option to delay their decision. This optimal delay strategy would obviously be reinforced if any of the traditional arguments for delayed intervention are also present, such as when lawmakers have less than perfect cognitive abilities (such as in Heiner 1986), or when society intrinsically values stability and certainty in law.

3. The Value of Waiting in Lawmaking: Some Extensions

The model presented in Section 2 illustrates how a proposed legal change can be viewed as an option and valued accordingly. This insight can be extended to a variety of situations involving lawmaking under uncertainty. In the following, we explore some extensions and then offer some ideas for future research on the subject. These extensions address real world problems, allowing us to discuss some additional implications for regulatory policy.

3.1. Trial and Error, and the Benefits of Legal Experimentation

In our general model of lawmaking presented above, we assume that no learning takes place. That is, future benefits from legal intervention are always uncertain, and the degree of uncertainty does not depend on whether legal intervention has actually taken place. Our model thus assumes away the possible informational benefits generated by legal experimentation. In real life, even an unsuccessful legal innovation can occasionally generate informational benefits, because it discloses the intrinsic value of attempted legal solutions and reduces the risk of similar legislative errors in the future. Legislative experimentation may indeed provide valuable information about the net benefits (or lack thereof) of alternative legal rules.[22] Put differently, by "investing" (i.e., adopting a law), it may at times be possible to learn at a faster rate than one would without such investment.

The possibility of positive informational value of past legislative action affects the results reached in Section 2 of this chapter, because present legal innovation yields information that reduces the uncertainty over the value of future legal alternatives.[23] The consideration of the value of learning may lead to counterintuitive results. For example, paradoxically, even legal proposals that have a negative expected present value may be worth carrying out, if the external informational benefits generated by such form of legal experimentation are sufficiently large.

These results may partially offset the tendency suggested by our basic model. As we have seen above, in the absence of learning, option value of immediate legal action yields a test for the optimal timing of legal innovation that is stricter than the net present value rule. This is our "value of waiting" in lawmaking. If we take into account the value of learning from past errors, the above result may be considerably changed in the opposite direction. With learning, we may have a more permissive test concerning the optimal timing of legal innovation, given the external informational benefits from past experience. We may think of these benefits as the "value of experimentation" in lawmaking.[24]

In order to appreciate the scope (and limits) of the value of experimentation argument, we need to identify two relevant types of learning. First, if the underlying reality evolves stochastically, the value of learning is given by the opportunity to observe the unknown reality. To the extent that this "learning" is only obtainable in conjunction with actual legal innovation and experimentation (e.g., the only way to estimate the effect of a given law on human behavior is to experiment with such law), delayed legal intervention would preclude the acquisition of such informational benefits. Second, learning can be independent of any stochastic uncertainty. Indeed, this is often the case in investment models with learning. The implied and most crucial assumption of models with learning is that the underlying reality does not evolve stochastically. The identity of the best legal rule may not be known (at least until all possible rules have been tried), but the identity of such rule, whichever it may be, does not evolve stochastically over time. Also in this case, if the only source of information comes from actual trial and error, there is no gain from waiting. To the contrary, there is an opportunity cost to delaying experimentation, given the informational value of innovation.[25]

These two forms of learning benefits could be included in the short-term benefits from lawmaking (δ) in our basic model.[26] As our comparative statics show, when δ increases, the threshold determining immediate action V^* decreases, thus justifying faster legal intervention.

3.2. Political Agency Problems and the Rush to Legislation

Our basic model contemplates a benevolent planner whose preferences and incentives are perfectly aligned with those of society. In real world politics, however, the private and social costs of delaying legal intervention are likely to differ. A more complex formulation of the problem should allow the subjective discount rate of the lawmaker to differ from the social discount rate. The normative results of the basic model could thus be contrasted with those where the preferences and subjective time horizon of the legal planner differ from the preferences of society as a whole, explaining why, in certain areas of lawmaking, we are more likely to observe a departure from the socially optimal waiting rule.

In the previous analysis, all the waiting costs are socially relevant costs, such as the lost opportunity to govern a specific area of the law in the short term, and the long-run increase in the value of the law. In the process of lawmaking, however, political choices are likely to be driven also by other considerations that do not reflect social preferences. Politicians often have limited terms in office and/or face reelection constraints. As public choice theory teaches us, there are several strategic reasons for political actors to manipulate the timing of policy intervention as a way to maximize the chances of reelection (Mueller 1989; Olson 1965; Grossman and Helpman 1996). These institutional constraints often affect the timing of legal intervention, adding a political cost of delayed intervention for the individual lawmaker. This additional cost is a private or political cost for the lawmaker. The lost opportunity for individual legislators to enact laws that may prejudice their reputation or their leverage with specific interest groups is an example. Likewise, in the case of judge-made law, individual judges face the private cost of a lost opportunity to generate a law-changing legal precedent, without fully internalizing the social benefits of waiting.

The divergence between private and social incentives in the choice of timing of legal intervention is the unavoidable consequence of political agency problems. The introduction of such political agency problems implies that lawmakers' discount rate may differ from the social rate. Here, we introduce another variable π to reflect such political time preference. In the choice of timing for legal intervention, there would thus be three relevant discount factors instead of two. This implies that the total discount rate used in the lawmaking process is $\alpha + \delta + \pi$, instead of $\alpha + \delta$. This means that $\alpha + \delta$ can fall below the social return rate and yet it could be subjectively rational for lawmakers to invest in new laws. In turn, this may lead to too little waiting and excessive lawmaking, compared to the social optimum.

3.3. Future Research

The model presented in Section 2 viewed a proposed legal change as an option and valued the option accordingly. This insight should be extended to a variety of situations involving lawmaking under uncertainty. In the following, we explore some of them.

3.3.1. The Timing versus Specificity Trade-Off

There are two interrelated issues concerning the adoption of legal rules: the timing of adoption of legal rules, and the degree of specificity of the rule (discussed in Chapter 2). Law and economics scholars have treated these issues as independent, often concentrating on the question of optimal degree of specificity (e.g., rules versus standards) and assuming no degree of freedom in the choice of timing in the implementation of legal rules. Such a simplifying assumption is useful for rendering the problem more tractable; nonetheless it should be relaxed to examine the important interrelations between timing and specificity of legal rules. In this chapter we focused on the related problem of optimal timing in the adoption of legal rules. In doing so, we have undertaken a different simplification, treating the level of specificity of legal rules as a constant. Future research should more explicitly consider the tradeoff between timing and specificity of legislative intervention, where the lawmaker has the option to innovate (or delay intervention) and the choice of different degrees of specificity. In this context, less specificity in a legal rule can be viewed as a form of delayed lawmaking, because the fuller specification of the law will take place at a later time, through practice and judicial interpretation.[27]

Given that the different sunk investment costs of a well -specified rule are greater than those of a general standard, in the presence of uncertainty, the option value of delaying legal intervention may be greater in the case of rules with a greater degree of specificity. The lawmaker faces a wedge between the economies of scale obtainable with the implementation of a specified rule and the increased value of the forgone option to postpone the lawmaking decision. The dual optimization problem facing the lawmaker, then, is that of determining the optimal level of specificity and timing of intervention, taking into account irreversibility, uncertainty, and the other factors discussed above.[28] It is likely that in times of high uncertainty, the expected value of investment in well-specified rules declines relative to general standards, and one would expected to see more standards and fewer rules with an increase in the volatility of the regulated environment. These are testable hypotheses that are grounds for further work.

3.3.2. Incremental Legal Intervention and Sequential Lawmaking Decisions

Many regulatory objectives involve multistage legal intervention that needs to be carried out in sequence (e.g., several programmatic laws require implementing legislation and/or subsequent governmental intervention; international treaties require ratification and subsequent implementation and harmonization at the national level).[29] Sequential lawmaking processes like those mentioned above can take substantial time to complete. Furthermore, they can be temporarily or permanently abandoned midstream if the expected net benefit of the final legal innovation declines. How does the existence of multistage regulatory objectives (when the benefits of undertaking each step are uncertain) change the results of the one-time legal intervention discussed above? It is likely that the effects of uncertainty and irreversibility become more important in the sequential lawmaking problem. The longer it takes for a legal enactment to come into force (whether the delay is due to a time lag in legal implementation or to a complex multistage regulatory process) the greater is the uncertainty regarding the value of the innovation at the time it is finally enforced. Because the value of the law upon completion is more uncertain, an even higher expected discounted benefit from regulation will be necessary to justify legal intervention.[30]

But this may also work to explain why valuable, but difficult to achieve, targets are often pursued with multistage, sequential lawmaking. Disarmament treaties (Nicholson 1989) and trade treaties, such as the GATT Agreement that finally created the World Trade Organization, are examples on point. Generally, the gains from both types of treaties are enormous. At the same time, there are strong incentives to defect, rendering the final objective uncertain in its achievement. Such treaties, then, are often set up in a way that implementation takes place in several steps.[31]

This point also relates to the other issue concerning the optimal degree of specificity of legal rules. One of the key insights of the modern investment literature is that investing in stages can increase the value of an investment. This would suggest that setting standards, and then later (after some learning has taken place) implementing rules, may be an optimal approach to lawmaking.

4. Conclusions

In this chapter we have discussed the optimal timing decision of lawmaking by applying some key results in the modern investment literature. There is a "hidden" opportunity cost associated with exercising the option to adopt a new law. This cost and the corresponding value of waiting are particularly large if (1) there is significant uncertainty about future benefits of the law, (2) there are large costs of implementation that are difficult to recover if the law were later abandoned, or (3) the value and importance of the law is likely to grow over time.

The basic model of optimal timing is then extended to two situations that may lead to less waiting. First, if implementing one law can inform the decision of whether to adopt future laws, then the value of this learning should be incorporated in the evaluation of the "present value" of the law under consideration today. In this first case, less waiting is socially optimal, because the informational value of legal intervention is a social benefit.

Second, if lawmakers have a political discount factor in addition to the social discount factor, there could also be a higher rate of legal innovation. In this second case, the higher rate of innovation is socially inefficient, because the faster production of laws creates a private benefit for lawmakers while imposing an external cost on society. These scenarios provide alternative hypotheses for why there may be less than optimal waiting in lawmaking. Additional extensions were suggested for future research, including the availability of continuous or incremental lawmaking, and the simultaneous choice of timing and specificity of legal rules.

The analysis contained within this chapter suggests that uncertainty may be a more crucial determinant of optimal timing in lawmaking than usually believed under the simple net present value criterion. This has both positive and normative implications, for the explanation of regulatory and judicial behavior and for the institutional design of lawmaking and legislative policy. This chapter focused largely on the criteria that *should* guide lawmaking and legal innovation. Our analysis, we hope, provides insight into the importance of the latent opportunity costs of lawmaking in different lawmaking environments. The sensitivity results and the various extensions provide testable hypotheses that could be evaluated against historical trends in the rate of legal innovation within given areas of legislation. The results of this chapter provide a valuable benchmark against which to test evidence concerning legislative action. For example, stable political regimes with lower turnover should be more likely to follow optimal patterns of legal change. Institutions and political bodies whose actors do not face term limits should more frequently account for the opportunity cost of legal intervention under uncertainty and the option value of waiting in lawmaking. On the contrary, the presence of instability in political coalitions, term limits, special interest pressure, and corruption should negatively affect the willingness of political actors to account for the option value of waiting lawmaking. In these cases, delay in legal intervention is likely to generate private costs for the political actors that dominate the benefits of waiting. These systems should experience a higher frequency of legal change. Finally, subsequent research should more explicitly contemplate the hypothesis that legal systems, through evolved institutional constraints, developed instruments to induce courts and lawmakers to account for the option value of a lawmaking investment.

FOUR

Optimal Territorial Scope of Laws
Subsidiarity and Legal Harmonization*

A THIRD PROBLEM FACED BY lawmakers when planning their legislative intervention concerns the territorial scope of application of their laws. Because political units are frequently subdivided into smaller units, rules can be enacted and enforced at different levels, whether by the central government or by local governments. What factors should be considered when allocating a given policy function at a particular level, and how do these factors affect the growth and evolution of multilevel governments? In this chapter we consider this question, with reference to the existing economic literature and with the aid of a model of subsidiarity and rule competition. After discussing the interplay of economies of scale, economies of scope, and heterogeneity of preferences in determining the optimal level of legal intervention, we show that the subsidiarity principle can have mixed effects as a firewall against progressive centralization.

Our economic model of subsidiarity reveals that once some functions become centralized, further centralization becomes easier and often unavoidable. Contrary to its intended function, a piecemeal application of the subsidiarity principle can trigger a path-dependent avalanche of centralization, turning subsidiarity into a self-defeating statement of principle.

※ 1. Centralization, Devolution, and Subsidiarity

One of the fundamental issues facing federal governments and unions of states is the allocation of policy responsibilities (i.e., the creation and enforcement of policy) between the federal (central) government and the

---

* This chapter has been written in collaboration with Emanuela Carbonara and Barbara Luppi and is based on the paper by Carbonara, Emanuela, Barbara Luppi, and Francesco Parisi, originally circulated under the title "Self-Defeating Subsidiarity" in Minnesota Legal Studies Research Paper 08–15.

local governments. There is a flourishing literature trying to establish the optimal level of centralization of policy responsibilities. This literature focuses on the trade-offs between the costs and benefits of centralization.

A helpful contribution in this field is Alesina, Angeloni, and Etro (2005a). Their paper characterizes the benefit of centralization as the possibility of exploiting economies of scale in the central allocation of policy responsibilities. It characterizes the costs of harmonization, principally, as those related to dealing with heterogeneity of preferences across the regions. Balancing the benefits from economies of scale with the varying preferences of the citizenry, the optimal degree of centralization should ensue: all functions where economies of scale are predominant should be held at the central level, whereas all functions with high heterogeneity of preferences should be kept at the local level.

In a related paper, Alesina, Angeloni, and Schuknecht (2005) provide empirical evidence on the expansion of the policy-making role of the European Union (EU) in the years between 1971 and 2000. They find that the range of functions attributed to the central level (for instance to the European Commission, to the Parliament, or to the Court of Justice) has expanded markedly, "far away from the EEC's original mandate," which only established a free market zone and harmonized trade policy.[1] Moreover, they find that in the European Union something seems to have drawn the process of allocation of policy responsibilities away from the optimal balance of economies of scale and the heterogeneity of preferences set down by the literature above. Substantial harmonization and centralization have occurred in areas where heterogeneity of preferences is predominant (like social protection or agricultural policy) whereas other areas characterized by strong economies of scale have remained in the local domain (like defense and environmental protection).

In this work, we argue that the discrepancy between the optimal balance and the present allocation of policy responsibilities can be explained by the presence, in the Treaty on European Union, of the subsidiarity principle.

According to the subsidiarity principle, regulation should be made at the lowest possible level of government. In the short term the subsidiarity principle may actually accomplish its stated goal, but we conclude that in long run, clinging to the subsidiarity principle may actually trigger a mechanism that could lead to an avalanche of centralization.

We begin our analysis by assuming the presence of both economies of scale and scope in the creation and enforcement of policies. Economies of scale are present when the cost of producing a given output Y is lower if only one entity produces it rather than if two or more entities produce outputs that add up to Y. In our setting, the presence of economies of scale implies that the allocation of policy responsibilities to the central level for all member states yields lower costs than allocation policy responsibilities at the local level. For instance, there is evidence that economies of scale are present in areas like common market policies, monetary policy, and environmental protection (Alesina, Angeloni, and Schuknecht 2005).

Economies of scope are present when creating and enforcing two or more policies together costs less than doing so separately. In our framework, economies of scope signify that shifting one or more policy responsibilities to the central level, while keeping other functions at the local level, means the costs of those policy responsibilities left at the local level will be greater.[2] Typically, economies of scope are present when one policy responsibility requires some fixed resource that can also be used for another policy responsibility at no additional cost. We suggest that economies of scope are present in many policy areas. For instance, the regulation of the banking and insurance sectors may share many common costs. If the same centralized police corps can enforce the policies applying to these two sectors at a lower cost than enforcement by multiple, local entities then efficiency will be served. It seems a plausible assumption, therefore, that, in a given policy area, centralized policy responsibilities will yield some economies of scope.

The assumption of economies of scope, coupled with the more traditional assumption of economies of scale, leads to several interesting and paradoxical results.

First of all we show that, contrary to its stated goal, the subsidiarity principle may trigger a mechanism favoring centralization. This mechanism is strongly path dependent and, once started, may lead to strong centralization even in policy areas where local preferences are quite heterogeneous. Conversely, whenever the mechanism leading to centralization is not triggered, the subsidiarity principle exerts its function of limiting centralization and protecting local policy responsibilities. However, given that the mechanism facilitating centralization is path dependent, different degrees of centralization may occur based on the particular process adopted for allocating policy responsibilities. The application of a subsidiarity principle thus leaves room for strategic manipulation of the process of allocation of policy responsibilities and may explain some anomalies characterizing the European Union such as the low level of centralization of environmental protection, where special interest groups try to avoid a centralized policy.

Although the subsidiarity principle is still too young to allow for a significant empirical verification of our hypothesis, our conjecture that once some functions become centralized further centralization becomes easier and often unavoidable is supported by the preliminary evidence presented by Alesina, Angeloni, and Schuknecht (2005), who date the period of most intense centralization to the 1990s. The subsidiarity principle was, in fact, formally introduced to the EU in 1991 by the Maastricht Treaty.

In this chapter we also look at the interplay between rule competition and centralization. Competition favors the unification of regulatory settings among states.[3] Carbonara and Parisi (2007b), although proving that evolution does not necessarily favor the diffusion of the best rules, shows that rule competition leads to the universal adoption of a single rule when switching costs are sufficiently low. Starting from the mid-1980s, in the European Community, the "Principle of Mutual Recognition" has been increasingly advocated for and applied.[4] According to the principle of mutual recognition, rules implemented in one member state must be lawful also in all other member states. This principle had been introduced with the primary intent of preventing strategic and discriminatory regulations in order to promote trade among member states. The principle's functional outcome, however, is that of promoting rule competition and reducing switching costs. We show that when rule competition promotes efficient rules, the combination of rule competition and subsidiarity may have the effect of slowing down the centralization of policy responsibilities. Subsidiarity alone does not promote allocation of policy responsibilities to local units, but may reach such result when the subsidiarity principle is applied in conjunction with rule competition. This is to say that without an efficient mechanism providing national regulators with wide responsibilities, the benefits of economies of scope at the local level and heterogeneity of preferences are not enough to outweigh the benefits of economies of scale and scope at the central level. In fact, when rule competition triggers an inefficient "race to the bottom," a path-dependent evolution under the subsidiarity principle would favor centralization rather than limiting it.

Unlike previous literature on the optimal level of centralization, we adopt a dynamic framework. Previous literature used static models with the structure of costs not changing over time. In our model, the structure of costs evolves according to previous centralization decisions.

This chapter is structured as follows. Section 2 provides a description of the subsidiarity principle and of its main characteristics. In Section 3 we introduce a simple model for subsidiarity. Section 4 looks at how the subsidiarity test is performed in a union of states. From there we move to Section 5, showing, in a dynamic setting, how the outcomes generated by the subsidiarity principle are path-dependent. We further illustrate how the results of the subsidiarity test can be manipulated strategically, either to limit or to boost centralization. Section 6 concludes modeling the interplay of the principle of mutual recognition and the subsidiarity principle, and proving that the combined application of these principles may limit the problems of progressive centralization observed under subsidiarity.

2. The Philosophy of Subsidiarity: From Human Rights to Political Compromise

As introduced above, since the Treaty on European Union (or Maastricht Treaty) of 1991, the European Commission has explicitly adopted the subsidiarity principle, according to which policy responsibility should be allocated at the lowest possible level of government. The purpose of this principle is to reduce the number of centralized policy. In other words, the subsidiarity principle was created in order to slow down the centralization of policy responsibilities.

The concept of "subsidiarity" has ancient roots. Some historians trace it back to classical Greece. Subsidiarity made a new appearance in the middle ages, taken up by Thomas Aquinas and medieval scholasticism. Later, it was revived by many politicians and political scientists such as Althusius, Montesquieu, Locke, Tocqueville, and Abraham Lincoln (Carozza 2003). The Articles of Confederation, created by the United States in 1781, relied heavily on the subsidiarity principle, with a resulting deference to states over a federal government.

Catholic social theorists started to apply the concept of subsidiarity to social life at the end of the nineteenth century. In 1891 Pope Leo XIII included the subsidiarity principle in his encyclical *"Rerum Novarum."* At that point in time the concept of subsidiarity was put forth as an alternative to the opposing claims of decentralized capitalism and centralized Marxian socialism.

The perspective on subsidiarity changed markedly a few decades later. In a famous passage of his *"Quadragesimo Anno"* Pius XI wrote "the more faithfully this subsidiarity principle function is followed and a graded hierarchical order exists among the various associations, the greater also will be both social authority and social efficiency, and the happier and more prosperous too will be the condition of commonwealth" (Bermann 1994). Those words were written in 1931 when the major concern was to protect society against the rise of totalitarianism rather than protecting various social groups from failures of the state. The subsidiarity principle thus evolved from advocating a cooperative balance between the state and the civil society toward setting limits on centralized authority (Carozza 2003).

It seems that originally subsidiarity was not seen as a way to achieve social efficiency or as an instrument for political compromise, reasons for which it was later included in the Treaty on the European Union. Rather, subsidiarity was and is primarily a declaration about the inherent and inalienable dignity of individual human beings. It reflects the belief that the individual should be "ontologically and morally prior to the state or other social groupings" (Carozza 2003: 42).

In the Treaty on European Union the concept of subsidiarity is more an empty shell than an operative concept. The definition provided by the Treaty can be found in Article 5: "In areas which do not fall within its exclusive competence, the Community shall take action, in accordance with the subsidiarity principle, only if and insofar as the objectives of the proposed action cannot be sufficiently achieved by the member states and can therefore, by reason of the scale or effects of the proposed action, be better achieved by the Community. Any action by the Community shall not go beyond what is necessary to achieve the objectives of this Treaty."

How should this principle be applied in practice? How should an effective subsidiarity test be constructed, which effectively defends the sovereignty of individual states, but which encourages cooperation and the intervention of superior hierarchical layers when efficient?

How this test is constructed (i.e., the manner in which the subsidiarity principle is applied) is crucial in assuring the subsidiarity principle functions properly. As effectively put by Carozza (2003), subsidiarity is, in itself, a paradoxical principle because it is instituted to limit the intervention of higher layers of hierarchy yet it also justifies those very interventions. Political scientists and philosophers frequently disagree on the proper way to apply the principle, and, when applied in different ways, the subsidiarity principle can have very different outcomes. Our simple model of subsidiarity seeks to balance the competing aims of the subsidiarity principle and to bring reason to this paradoxical chaos.

✎ 3. A Simple Model of Subsidiarity

In this section we introduce a simple model to explain how the subsidiarity test works in an economic framework. We model the decision to allocate policy responsibilities either at a local or central level according to the subsidiarity principle. As argued above, the optimal territorial scope of rules can be thought of in terms of economies of scale and economies of scope.

We consider a single federal government (or a union of states like the European Union), divided into a finite number of regions (for example, states in case of the EU). Initially, we analyze the simplest possible case: the federal government divided into only two regions, indexed with the subscript $i = 1, 2$. Moreover, we consider only one policy area (say, financial or common market policies). The federal government and its regions have to decide whether policy responsibilities should be allocated to the federal government (centralization) or to the local level. To simplify analysis, we also assume that there is a set consisting of only two policy functions (say, financial regulation and banking supervision). Both functions, indexed by f_j ($j = 1, 2$), are initially allocated to the local level. Each region (or state in case of a union of states) is asked to decide whether it is more convenient to keep the function at local level or to allocate it to the central level.

In order to allocate policy responsibilities to the local level, each region has to bear costs. The cost function C_i^R for region i ($i = 1, 2$) is

$$C_i^R(f_1, f_2) = C_i^{1R}(f_1, f_2) + C_i^{2R}(f_1, f_2) \qquad 4.1$$

Equation (4.1) is the total cost that region i sustains when it provides regulation on both functions f_1 and f_2 and is given by the sum of the costs of provision of regulation on each single function. The variable f_j is an indicator function that takes value 1 if the function is allocated at the same level (be it local or central) and zero otherwise.[5]

When policy responsibility is allocated to the central level, the federal government has to provide regulation for both regions and encounters a regulation cost. Suppose, for example, that the central government provides function 1, whereas function 2 is left to the regions. Then the cost for the federal government to provide function 1 for both regions is

$$C^{1C}(2f_1, 0) \qquad 4.2$$

It is important to note that the decision to allocate a specific function to the central level or to the local level can be motivated by the interplay of two countervailing incentives: economies of scale versus economies of scope.

One argument that is often brought in favor of centralization and harmonization is that allocating policy responsibilities to the central level results in economies of scale, thus reducing the overall cost of providing that specific function.[6] The concept of economies of scale is often used loosely in this context to include benefits from coordination that are more readily obtained through centralized policy responsibilities.[7]

In applying the subsidiarity test, it should be kept in mind that some of the policy functions for which economies of scale are present, are best done together with other functions at the same level of government, either local or central. These functional synergies between two governmental functions create valuable economies of scope. The economies of scope that are created by performing two or more functions at the same level of government are generally due to the opportunity to pool information, share organizational infrastructures, or internalize other administrative externalities between two or more governmental functions (e.g., regulation and enforcement of the same subject matter, regulation of different but interrelated subject matters).

We can thus represent economies of scale and scope in the central and local cost functions. To have economies of scale at the central level, the cost of allocating a policy function (say function 1) to that level should be less than the sum of the costs for allocating policy responsibility to each region. Analytically this can be written as

$$C^{1C}(2f_1,0) < C_1^{1R}(f_1,0) + C_2^{1R}(f_1,0)$$
$$C^{2C}(0,2f_2) < C_1^{2R}(0,f_2) + C_2^{2R}(0,f_2)$$

4.3

and also

$$\sum_{j=1}^{2} C^{jC}(2f_1,2f_2) < \sum_{j=1}^{2} [C_1^{jR}(f_1,f_2) + C_2^{jR}(f_1,f_2)]$$

4.4

In order for economies of scope to be present, on the other hand, the cost functions at the central and local levels respectively must satisfy the following conditions:

$$C^{1C}(2f_1,2f_2) < C^{1C}(2f_1,0)$$
$$C^{2C}(2f_1,2f_2) < C^{2C}(0,2f_2)$$

4.5

$$C_i^{1R}(f_1, f_2) < C_i^{1R}(f_1, 0)$$
$$C_i^{2R}(f_1, f_2) < C_i^{2R}(0, f_2)$$

4.6

for $i = 1, 2$. Both equations (4.5) and (4.6) mean that performing both functions at the same level of government, be at the central or regional level, costs less.

Let us assume now that the federal government is willing to centralize a given policy function (say, function 1). The decision to shift a function from local to central government imposes financial, social, and political costs associated with the necessary changes in the organizational management of the function (e.g., human capital costs associated with the changed role of public officials, physical capital investments for new bureaucratic infrastructures, organizational shocks, and political and social costs on local communities).[8]

We shall refer to these switching costs, faced when reallocating government functions between levels, as k^R. Specifically, we define $k_i^R(j)$ as the switching cost experienced by region i following the decision to allocate function j at central level. The switching cost $k_i^R(j)$ is assumed to be (weakly) decreasing in the number of functions allocated at the central level. In other words, the cost experienced by each region is lower when other functions were previously allocated to the central level.[9] Analytically, (weakly) decreasing centralization costs can be expressed as follows:[10]

$$k_i^R(f_1 | f_2) \leq k_i^R(f_1 | 0)$$

4.7

This indicates that the switching costs due to the transfer of function 1 are lower when function 2 is already centralized.

4. The Subsidiarity Principle and Harmonization

Having introduced all elements of our simple model we are able to provide a formalization of the subsidiarity principle. In order to centralize a given function, a "subsidiarity test" has to be passed. The test is generally viewed as consisting of three steps:[11] (1) identify whether a function falls within the area of shared competences (if exclusive to the federal government—or to the EU—the test does not apply); (2) apply a cost-benefit analysis (taking into account both economies of scale and scope) to assess the optimal level of allocation of a given function; and (3), if step 1 is confirmed and step 2 indicates the efficiency of centralizing the function, then centralization occurs. Otherwise, the function is left at the local level.

For the purpose of our model, we assume that the step 1 above is resolved exogenously by the legal and institutional rules that govern the union or federation. The analysis that follows develops an economic framework for carrying out the remaining steps 2 and 3 of the subsidiarity test, evaluating the benefits and the costs of centralization for a given policy function and allocating that function to the optimal level of government. In order to describe how the subsidiarity test should be applied in our model, suppose that initially all functions f_1 and f_2 are allocated at local levels and that the central government wishes to exercise one of the functions at a central level. Suppose for example that the central government aims to centralize function 1, currently allocated at the local level in both regions.

The subsidiarity test requires that a cost-benefit analysis of the proposed centralization be performed. In case of centralization, the federal government bears the entire cost of providing the function to all regions but enjoys economies of scale. Single regions bear switching costs and some of the preexisting economies of scope may be forgone. If the benefits from economies of scale outweigh the sum of switching costs plus the cost of the forgone economies of scope, the subsidiarity test is satisfied and the function is centralized.

Assuming that the central government is planning to centralize function 1, step 2 of the subsidiarity test can be written analytically as follows:

$$C^{1C}(2f_1, 0) + C_1^{2R}(0, f_2) + C_2^{2R}(0, f_2) + [k_1^R(f_1|0) + k_2^R(f_1|0)] \leq$$

$$\sum_{j=1}^{2} \left[C_1^{jR}(f_1, f_2) + C_2^{jR}(f_1, f_2) \right] \qquad \text{4.8}$$

Equation (4.8) presents the subsidiarity test from the point of view of a benevolent central planner maximizing aggregate (Kaldor-Hicks) welfare. This formulation is equivalent to the idea of "centralized federalism" as defined by Inman and Rubinfeld (1998). The subsidiarity test could however lead to different results if administered by taking into account the individual payoffs of the relevant regions. Consider the case where all policy functions are initially allocated at the local level and the decisions of whether to centralize are made at the local level. This is the case of "decentralized federalism," where regions decide whether to transfer some (or even all) of their functions to a central government.[12] When the decision to centralize is made at the local level, the centralization result would necessarily depend on the decision rule used to aggregate the preferences of the various regions into a collective outcome. If single regions had to vote in order to approve the shift in power from the local to the central level, the outcome of the proposed centralization would hinge upon the adopted voting rule. The results of the test may be different if the voting rule required unanimity rather than majority voting, as it will be seen in the next sections.[13]

If the subsidiarity test is performed at the local level and the unanimous consent of each region is required for centralization to occur, the subsidiarity test should be carried out for each region i. Similar to a Pareto test, the unanimity rule implies that centralization can take place only if the switch from local to central does not reduce the payoff for any of the affected regions. To formulate the subsidiarity test from the point of view of region i, consider that when the function f_1 is provided at the local level, region i bears the cost $C_i^{1R}(f_1, f_2)$. Conversely, if f_1 is reallocated to the central level, region i bears the switching cost $k_i^R(f_1|0)$. Additionally, region i will bear a share S_i of the total cost of providing function 1 at the central level. In the simplest case, with two regions, in the absence of asymmetries across regions, each region bears a share of the cost equal to $\frac{1}{2}C^{1C}(2f_1, 0)$. In the general case, each region bears a share of the overall cost $S_i[C^{1C}(2f_1, 0)]$ $(i = 1, 2)$, established according to factors such as territorial size, population, gross domestic product, and other social or political factors. Clearly, the shares are determined so that $S_1[C^{1C}(2f_1, 0)] + S_2[C^{1C}(2f_1, 0)] = C^{1C}(2f_1, 0)$.

From the point of view of an individual region, centralization is desirable when the shared cost of centralized policy responsibility for f_1 plus the switching cost associated with the shift of responsibility and the cost of providing function 2 locally are lower than the total cost of providing both functions locally. Analytically, region i will choose to allocate function 1 at the central level if and only if the following conditions are satisfied:

$$S_i[C^{1C}(2f_1, 0)] + k_i^R(f_1|0) + C_i^{2R}(0, f_2) \leq \sum_{j=1}^{2} C_i^{jR}(f_1, f_2), i = 1, 2 \qquad 4.9$$

Under a unanimity rule, function 1 will be allocated to the central level if, and only if, both regions agree. Analytically, this is equivalent to carrying out a Pareto test, verifying if equation (4.9) is verified for all affected regions. Notice that the test in equation (4.9) is especially difficult to pass, because the cost $C_i^{jR}(f_1, f_2)$ is particularly low due to the presence of economies of scope. In general, when few functions are performed at the central level, centralization based on the subsidiarity test will be more difficult than at later stages, when more functions will have been reallocated to the central level and forgone economies of scope at the local level will be relatively small. This characteristic of the cost function will play a crucial role in later sections, where we will analyze the possibility of making strategic use of the subsidiarity principle. It is worth mentioning that, for the case of a majority rule, given the distribution of the switching costs and the costs of providing the function among regions, equation (4.9) would have to be satisfied for the median region.[14]

We are now able to use our model to analyze how the subsidiarity test is performed and to understand the process used for reallocating functions to central level under the subsidiarity principle. The test can be centralized or carried out at the local level, and outcomes are likely to vary under different decision rules. Generally, a test performed at the local level is more restrictive.

First of all, it is possible to show that if the test in equation (4.9) is satisfied for both regions, then the centralized subsidiarity test in equation (4.8) is also satisfied. This result is rather intuitive: if all regions benefit from centralization, then the aggregate benefits must outweigh the aggregate costs.

To see why this is the case, take the two inequalities in expression (4.9)

$$S_1 \left[C^{1C}(2f_1, 0) \right] + k_1^R (f_1 \mid 0) + C_1^{2R}(0, f_2) \leq \sum_{j=1}^{2} C_1^{jR}(f_1, f_2)$$

$$\text{4.10}$$

$$S_2 \left[C^{1C}(2f_1, 0) \right] + k_2^R (f_1 \mid 0) + C_2^{2R}(0, f_2) \leq \sum_{j=1}^{2} C_2^{jR}(f_1, f_2)$$

Summing over the left-hand sides and the right-hand sides of the two expressions, obtains

$$S_1 \left[C^{1C}(2f_1, 0) \right] + S_2 \left[C^{1C}(2f_1, 0) \right] + \left[k_1^R (f_1 \mid 0) + k_2^R (f_1 \mid 0) \right]$$

$$+ C_1^{2R}(0, f_2) + C_2^{2R}(0, f_2) \leq \sum_{j=1}^{2} [C_1^{jR}(f_1, f_2) + C_2^{jR}(f_1, f_2)]$$

which is exactly expression (4.8).

It is interesting to notice that the opposite is not necessarily true. Satisfaction of the centralized subsidiarity test in equation (4.8) does not imply simultaneous satisfaction of the two inequalities in expression (4.9).

To prove this, we can easily find sharing rules $S_i \left[C^{1C}(2f_1, 0) \right]$ $(i = 1, 2)$ such that the centralized test is passed but one of the regions votes against centralization if the test is administered locally.[15]

Consider the following example, where $C^{1C}(2f_1, 0) = 8$, $k_1^R(f_1|0) = 1$, $k_2^R(f_1|0) = 3$, $C_1^{1R}(f_1, f_2) = 7$, $C_2^{1R}(f_1, f_2) = 9$, $C_1^{2R}(f_1, f_2) = 6$, $C_2^{2R}(f_1, f_2) = 8$, $C_1^{2R}(0, f_2) = 7$, $C_2^{2R}(0, f_2) = 9$. According to these figures, the centralized subsidiarity test in expression (4.8) is passed, because $8 + 7 + 9 + (1 + 3) < 7 + 9 + 6 + 8$. Assume that the test is performed locally and that the central government is going to set the shares of the costs as follows: $S_1 \left[C^{1C}(2f_1, 0) \right] = 2$, $S_2 \left[C^{1C}(2f_1, 0) \right] = 6$. Now the first region will vote in favor of centralization of function 1, whereas the second will vote against it. In fact, the test is passed in the first region, because $2 + 1 + 7 < 7 + 6$, whereas it is not passed in the second, as $6 + 3 + 9 > 9 + 8$.[16]

Hence, a test at the local level is more restrictive. This result should not be surprising if we think of this problem in welfare terms. Satisfaction of the Pareto subsidiarity test in expression (4.9), guarantees satisfaction of the Kaldor-Hicks test in equation (4.8), but the Kaldor-Hicks subsidiarity test in equation (4.8) does not imply simultaneous satisfaction of the Pareto test for the two regions in expression (4.9).

This problem becomes even more crucial where regions vote on the centralization of a function according to a majority rule. In that case there is a wider array of instances where satisfaction of the centralized subsidiarity test does not imply satisfaction of the local tests. However, in those cases, in order to have centralization, it suffices that satisfaction of the centralized test implies satisfaction of the test for the median region. It is therefore possible to devise many instances where rule sharing is manipulated strategically in order to guarantee centralization (or lack thereof) of a given function. For instance, consider a central government with three regions, two of them with stronger bargaining power than the third. One can see the vast potential for manipulation and abuse under majority rule voting that could take place. The likely outcome in such cases is that weaker regions end up with less favorable distributions of costs.

5. Dynamic Subsidiarity and Path Dependence

In this section we consider two effects of subsidiarity. Both effects suggest that the principle of subsidiarity can lead to a path-dependent reallocation of policy responsibilities and have mixed effects as a firewall against progressive centralization.

In the first application discussed in Section 5.1, our economic model of subsidiarity revealed that once some functions become centralized, further centralization becomes easier and often unavoidable. Our model showed that piecemeal applications of the subsidiarity principle can trigger a path-dependent avalanche of centralization. The dynamics of piecemeal decision making may turn subsidiarity into a self-defeating statement of principle.

In the second application discussed in Section 5.2 we showed that the application of a subsidiarity principle as a constitutional constraint to the reallocation of power may determine a status quo bias, with a consolidation of the current allocation of power. The model showed that a status quo bias is possible when the subsidiarity test bars the transfer of a function to central level, preventing the exploitation of economies of scale and the creation of economies of scope at that level.

Both cases suggest that the initial applications of the subsidiarity test may have path-dependent effects on later decisions. As the now young principle of subsidiarity comes of age, future scholars will have an opportunity to investigate the extent to which either of these forms of path-dependence can be observed empirically.

5.1. Dynamic Subsidiarity: The Paradox of Progressive Centralization

In the following we will show that, when considered in a dynamic setting, the subsidiarity principle can trigger a gradual trend toward harmonization and full centralization of all policy functions. Subsidiarity, introduced as a safeguard against complete centralization, becomes a self-defeating principle leading to path-dependent centralization: once some functions are centralized, further centralization is often unavoidable.[17]

To see how this can happen, assume that the subsidiarity test is performed at the local level.[18] Using our simplest hypothetical model with two regions, both regions would have to decide whether to transfer function 1, currently performed at the local level, to the central government. Suppose that the subsidiarity test for the transfer of function 1 is passed in both regions, so that, analytically, the inequalities in expression (4.9) are satisfied for all regions $i = 1, 2$. As a consequence, function 1 will be reallocated to the central level of government. The subsidiarity test, applied to function 1, has no direct impact on function 2, which is therefore kept at the local level.

If in a subsequent period the central government wants to also allocate function 2 to the central level, the proposed centralization would have to be evaluated according to a new subsidiarity test. Each region would thus have to evaluate the proposed reallocation of f_2 to the central level. A region will choose to retain the function at the local level if and only if the sum of the shared cost of providing the function at the central level and switching costs is higher than the cost of keeping it at the local level.

Region i will favor the proposed centralization of f_2 if the following condition is satisfied:

$$S_i[C^{1C}(2f_1, 2f_2)] + S_i[C^{2C}(2f_1, 2f_2)] + k_i^R(f_2 \mid f_1) \leq$$
$$S_i[C^{1C}(2f_1, 0)] + C_i^{2R}(0, f_2)$$

4.11

As before, function 2 will be allocated to central level if and only if both regions agree to do so. Analytically, equation (4.11) is the analogue of condition (4.9) and would have to be verified for both regions.

Economies of scale and economies of scope play a crucial role in determining the subsequent decisions at the regional level. It is possible to prove that, under the assumption of economies of scope at central and local levels, inequality (4.11) is always satisfied whenever inequality (4.9) is satisfied. According to the assumptions in (4.5) and (4.7), $C^{1C}(2f_1, 2f_2) < C^{1C}(2f_1, 0)$ and switching costs are decreasing in the number of functions allocated at central level: $k_i^R(f_2 \mid f_1) < k_i^R(f_1 \mid 0)$.

Additionally, for the case where $S_i[C^{2C}(2f_1, 2f_2)] \leq C_i^{2R}(f_1, f_2)$, when inequality (4.9) is satisfied, inequality (4.11) would also be satisfied. This follows from the fact that countries are unwilling to bear a share of the total costs of performing function 2 at the central level when such shared cost is actually higher than the cost they would face by performing the function on their own at the local level.[19]

Therefore, once function 1 has passed the subsidiarity test, it is easier to allocate functions to the central level. Contrary to the aim for which it was introduced, we show that the subsidiarity test does not play a significant role in slowing down the process of centralization. Rather, it is likely that the subsidiarity test leads to excessive centralization, because over time it becomes an increasingly weaker instrument for keeping policy responsibilities at the local level.

The paradox of full centralization is established under the assumption of economies of scale at a central level and economies of scope at central and local levels. The results could change if we assumed that at least some functions present diseconomies of scale at the central level. This concept captures the idea that there are some things that are best done locally, despite the presence of economies of scope, according to which some functions are best done in conjunction with other functions. For instance, if the two functions are financial regulation and its enforcement, we may think that enforcement is best done locally (diseconomies of scale), whereas regulation is best done centrally (economies of scale). In this case, the presence of diseconomies of scale could put a limit to the centralization of functions, depending on the relative strength of economies of scope and diseconomies of scale in the process of the allocation of functions to the central level. However, a general bias toward a process of avalanche centralization remains.

A second relevant assumption is that the switching costs borne by individual regions when transferring functions from the local to the central level decrease with the number of functions that have been already transferred. This is an assumption on the dynamics of the switching costs and seems consistent with the empirical evidence provided by Alesina, Angeloni, and Schuknecht (2005): when most functions are already allocated to the central level, the degree of resistance to further centralization is likely to be weaker, given that the political power of the single region vis-à-vis the central government is gradually decreasing.

This assumption per se may reinforce the likelihood of the "status quo" bias. This is a typical behavior of unions, who usually try to resist change, be that change an effort to harmonize or even an enlargement of the union (Alesina, Angeloni, and Etro 2005). Interestingly, it may also foster a completely opposite result.

Assume that switching costs increase when more functions have already been centralized. This would be the case if the main source of switching costs is political and social: for local governments it becomes more and more difficult to have voters accepting further depletion of their sovereign powers. As a result, the likelihood that one of the subsidiarity tests fails at some point, after some centralization already occurred, would increase. We would not observe full centralization in this case. However, the mechanism that drives centralization following the application of a subsidiarity principle would still work and not necessarily at a weaker pace. Consider the possible dynamic tradeoffs between switching costs and economies of scope. Imagine that switching costs increase with the number of functions previously centralized; initially such switching costs will be relatively low, and this facilitates early centralizations, boosting economies of scope at the central level. If the effect of economies of scope at the central level outweighs the increase in switching costs, we could also observe progressive centralization in this type of situation.

5.2. Dynamic Subsidiarity: The Case of Status Quo Bias

In this section we examine whether the application of a subsidiarity principle as a constitutional constraint to the reallocation of power may determine a status quo bias, with a consolidation—rather than optimal reallocation—of the current assignment of policy responsibilities across different levels of government. As mentioned above, the subsidiarity principle was introduced as a constitutional principle of the European Union to limit the expansion of central levels of government and to leave power and responsibilities for the formation and the implementation of policies at the lowest possible level of government consistent with efficiency (Carozza 2003).

The model presented above shows that a status quo bias may occur when the initial process of centralization is prevented by the subsidiarity test. When the subsidiarity test bars the transfer of a function to central level, it may in fact prevent the creation of economies of scope at the central level—economies that may have in turn facilitated the absorption of other functions by the central government. Initial applications of the subsidiarity test may thus have an important effect on subsequent decisions, leading to a path-dependent evolution of governance. Unlike the case of progressive centralization considered in the previous sections, in the present case we can observe a "conservative trend" limiting harmonization and centralization.[20]

To see how this can happen within the framework of our model, consider the case where the first function proposed for centralization is f_2. Parameters are as above: function 1 would pass the test if proposed first.

If for one or both regions the following condition is observed

$$C_i^{1R}(f_1, 0) + S_i \left[C^{2C}(0, 2f_2) \right] + k_i^R (f_2 \mid 0) > \sum_{j=1}^{2} C_i^{jR}(f_1, f_2) \qquad 4.12$$

the proposed centralization of function 2 would be barred by the sub-sidiarity test.[21] The result would be completely different if the process of centralization began with function 1 and such function successfully passed the subsidiarity test. An initial transfer of f_1 could in fact provide the prospect for economies of scope, facilitating the subsequent absorption of f_2 by the central government.

These results should be considered in conjunction with those examined in the previous sections, noting that the application of the subsidiarity principle is likely to lead to a path-dependent reallocation of policy responsibilities. The temporal sequence of subsidiarity tests becomes crucial to determine the final level of centralization. Whether path-dependence leads to progressive centralization or to a conservative status quo bias may heavily depend on the sequence of decisions, and outcomes that are determined by the application of subsidiarity may thus represent local, rather than global maxima. This path-dependence opens the doors to strategic manipulations by agenda setters. The central government may put forth a proposed centralization of f_1 to create the prospect of economies of scope and enhance the opportunities of absorption of f_2 at a later stage. Similarly, groups that oppose centralization may attempt to preempt the progressive centralization of these functions initially barring the centralization of f_2 through subsidiarity. This strategic manipulation can lead to a less than optimal allocation of governmental functions.

As a preliminary conclusion we can therefore state that the outcome of the application of the subsidiarity principle on the final level of harmonization may be controversial. Such ambiguity in its final effects leaves substantial room for strategic behavior on behalf of either the central or local governments.

6. Mutual Recognition and Rule Competition: Rethinking the Optimal Territorial Scope of Rules

As discussed in Section 5, whenever both economies of scale and economies of scope are present, a dynamic application of the subsidiarity principle may lead to the perverse effect of facilitating progressive centralization, rather than limiting it. In this section we shall illustrate another effect of the subsidiarity principle. The subsidiarity principle is meant to favor decentralization whenever that enhances efficiency. Rule competition is also meant to favor efficiency, guaranteeing the selection of the best rules.[22] The inclusion of rule competition in a constitutional setting characterized by the subsidiarity principle may limit the tendency toward progressive centralization observed under simple subsidiarity.

When considering rule competition as a barrier to centralization, it is helpful to view function allocation in two parts: rule sharing and the physical performance of the function. Centralization produces both these results while rule competition instead provides the rule sharing, but keeps the performance of the function at the local levels. By instituting this half-measure, proponents of local control have created what appears to be a significant barrier to complete centralization. This issue is particularly relevant in the European Union, where the combination of the subsidiarity principle with mutual recognition has created room for competition among national lawmakers. Mutual recognition *de facto* implies that regulations in place in one member state must be recognized and, whenever applicable, given enforcement in all member states. The principle of mutual recognition, in combination with choice of law principles, creates the opportunity for a controlled market for legal rules. Under certain conditions, this market may generate a valuable mechanism where more efficient national regulations could be utilized by other countries according to the principle of mutual recognition (Neven 1992).

The general claim is that subsidiarity favors rule competition, slowing down the centralization process (Neven 1992). We aim to examine this claim within the analytical model of subsidiarity developed in the previous sections. We model the decision to centralize a given function considering the interplay of the subsidiarity principle and of mutual recognition within the model developed in the previous sections.

As a consequence of rule competition, the most efficient rules enacted in a particular state have a higher chance of being adopted by other states by means of legal transplantation or by application of choice-of-law rules.[23] A similar effect is played in the European Union by the principle of mutual recognition: the best regulation on a given function performed at the national level will become available to all other states in the union. This makes it likely that the most efficient regulation is generally adopted, which implies a reduction in the cost of regulating that specific function at the local level.[24]

To understand why that happens, the principle of mutual recognition can be interpreted in economic terms as a reduction in the cost of regulation across states. According to that principle, the best regulation existing at local level about a given function will be implemented in each state of the union. This produces an overall reduction in the cost of regulation, because each state will deliver the function at local levels at the minimum available cost. In this context, it is possible to identify an additional cost of full centralization given by the disappearance of virtuous rule-competition, which could provide ways to minimize the costs of regulation at the local level but also, by extension, at the central level.

In the simple model of subsidiarity with two regions and two functions, region i will be in favor of allocating function f_1 to the central level if the cost of regulation at central level plus switching costs is lower than the minimum cost of delivering function 1.

$$S_i \left[C^{1C}(2f_1, 0) \right] + k_i^R (f_1 \mid 0) + C_i^{2R}(0, f_2) \leq \min \left\{ \sum_{j=1}^{2} C_i^{jR}(f_1, f_2) \right\} \qquad 4.13$$

where $\min\{\sum_{j=1}^{2} C_i^{jR}(f_1, f_2)\}$ indicates the minimum cost of regulation (between the regions) of function 1, given that function 2 is still allocated at local levels. Rule competition therefore lowers the right-hand side of the analytical expression for the subsidiarity test, thus making it more difficult that a proposed centralization of a given function (in this case f_1) will pass the subsidiarity test.[25] It should be noted that in real-life applications, the quantification of the actual value of may often be difficult, inasmuch as it would require the comparison of alternative (some $\min\{\sum_{j=1}^{2} C_i^{jR}(f_1, f_2)\}$ of which merely hypothetical) states of the world. This would exacerbate the difficulties of implementing the subsidiarity principle in an objective way, preventing it from becoming an instrument of political manipulation.

With respect to these final results, one might conclude observing that the incorporation of the principle of mutual recognition in the subsidiarity test could provide a more effective constraint to the forces of progressive centralization identified in this chapter. When viewed in a dynamic setting, subsidiarity becomes a weak, and possibly self-defeating, principle. Mutual recognition and rule competition become important corollary principles to counterbalance the possible biases of dynamic subsidiarity. These conclusions, however, need to be qualified in light of the underlying trust in a market for rules. If the mechanisms of rule competition are affected by externalities, which trigger a race to the bottom rather than to the top, then the subsidiarity test may drive the system toward full centralization. As argued above, this might not always be the preferred solution. But it could nevertheless be seen as a second-best solution, and a preferred alternative to a malfunctioning system of rule competition.

PART II

Lawmaking through Adjudication
Judge-Made Law

FIVE

Lawmaking through Adjudication
An Introduction

JUST AS ECONOMISTS STUDY the efficiency properties of the market, law and economics scholars have extensively studied the efficiency properties of the common law. Public choice and law and economics scholars have contrasted statutes and common law sources, focusing on the advantages of common law rules over legislation and statutory law (Rubin 1982; Easterbrook 1983; Rowley 1989; Wagner 1998). In the literature, the efficiency of the common law is further explained by making reference to the evolutionary process that emerges out of the interaction of judges, juries, lawyers, and litigants (Ehrlich and Posner 1974; Priest 1977; Rubin 1977; Posner 1981; and several others). The common law, it is often argued, evolves through a natural selection mechanism. Theories of evolution of judge-made law offer an account of how law develops. These theories do not inform us about the content of any judicially created rule but explain why the law develops as it does.

Understanding the process of common law adjudication is an essential step to identify the forces that drive the evolution of judge-made law. In the following three chapters we consider some of the peculiar characteristics of lawmaking through adjudication. We address issues effecting legal evolution ranging from doctrine of precedents to parties' decisions whether to bring a claim in the first place.

% 1. The Efficiency of the Common Law Hypothesis

An important premise of law and economics is that judge-made law leads to efficient outcomes. According to this premise—known as the efficiency of the common law hypothesis—judge-made laws enjoy a comparative advantage over legislation and statutory law in creating efficient outcomes, because of the evolutionary selection of common law rules through adjudication and the gradual accretion of precedent. Several important contributions provide the foundations for this claim. However, the scholars who have advanced theories in support of the hypothesis often disagree on a conceptual level.

There are two general strands in the literature.[1] The first strand focuses on the role of litigants and their "demand" for efficient precedents. The second strand focuses instead on the role of judges and their "supply" of efficient precedents.

1.1. Demand-Side Explanations

The demand-side explanations of the efficiency of the common law hypothesis common law frequently involve the concept of case selection. Case selection is simply the idea that parties will choose whether or not to fully litigate (as opposed to settling or not bringing a claim at all) a given dispute based on their individual interests.

Several early contributions provide the foundation for demand-side explanations of the efficiency of the common law. The early work of Landes (1971) first hinted at this premise, considering the amount of litigation in a society as a function of how public court services were administered. The demand-side explanations were later extended by Rubin (1977), Priest (1977), and later revisited by Priest and Klein (1984). Rubin (1977) argues that efficiency of the common law is best explained by noting that parties will more likely litigate inefficient rules than efficient ones. The pressure for common law to evolve to efficiency, he argues, rests on the desire of parties to create precedent because they have interest in future similar cases. Rubin thus considers three basic situations: (1) where both parties are interested in creating precedent; (2) where only one party is interested in creating precedent; (3) and where neither party has such an interest. When both parties have interest in future similar cases, and when the current legal rule is inefficient, Rubin claims that the party held liable has an incentive to force future litigation. Parties will continue to use the courts until the rule is changed. If the current rule is efficient, however, there is no incentive to change it, so it will remain in force. Where only one party has interest in future similar cases, the incentive to litigate depends on the allocation of liability. If liability falls on the party likely to face similar cases in the future, litigation likely occurs, whereas the other party has no incentive to litigate further. As a result, precedents evolve in the interested party's favor, whether or not the rule is efficient. In the event that neither party is interested in precedents, the legal rule—whether efficient or not—remains in force, and parties settle out of court because they lack incentive to change the current rule. Rubin thus concludes that common law becomes efficient based on the utility maximizing decisions of litigants, rather than on judges' desires to maximize efficiency.

Rubin's analysis was extended by Priest (1977), who articulated the idea that common law tends to develop efficient rules independent of judicial bias in decision making. Priest asserts that efficient rules develop even in the face of potential judicial hostility toward efficient outcomes. He parts with Rubin, however, on the source of the tendency toward efficiency, rejecting Rubin's conclusion that this tendency occurs only where both parties to a dispute have an interest in future similar cases and therefore have incentive to litigate. He asserts instead that litigation is driven by the costs of inefficient rules, rather than the desire for precedent.

According to Priest's analysis, inefficient rules impose greater costs on the parties than do efficient rules, thereby making the stakes in a dispute greater. Where the stakes are greater, litigation becomes more likely than settlement. Consequently, disputes arising under inefficient rules tend to be litigated and relitigated more often than disputes arising under efficient rules. This means that efficient rules tend to be uncontested. Because efficient rules are less likely to be reviewed, especially by judges hostile to efficient outcomes, they tend to remain in force. Further, as inefficient rules are reviewed, judges may discard those rules in favor of more efficient variants that, in turn, are less likely to be reviewed. Thus, the legal system perpetuates selection of efficient legal rules.

An important component of the theories advanced by Rubin and Priest are the criteria for selecting which disputes will be litigated. Only disputes that are actually litigated are capable of generating legal precedents. Disputes that do not lead to a filing or that are settled before a final judgment have no impact on the law. Priest and Klein (1984) develop a model of the litigation process that explores the relationship between disputes that are litigated and those that are settled. Priest and Klein show that the set of disputes selected for litigation, rather than settlement, constitutes neither a random nor a representative sample of the set of all disputes. They then derive a selection hypothesis: when both parties have equal stakes in the litigation, individual maximizing decisions of the parties create a strong bias toward a success rate for plaintiffs at trial (or appellants on appeal), regardless of the substantive law.

Several other contributions have added important insights into the economics of judge-made law. Cooter and Kornhauser (1980) model legal evolution as a Markov process and find that evolution does not necessarily lead to an evolutionary selection of efficient rule, but always to some equilibrium of better and worse rules. According to Cooter and Kornhauser (1980) there is no automatic mechanism to guarantee that the common law will converge toward economically efficient equilibria, even if we allow for a higher rate of litigation of economically inefficient rules and allow judges to replace inefficient rules with efficient rules. Cooter and Rubinfeld (1989) look at common law dispute resolution from an informational perspective. They review economic models of legal dispute resolution, attempting to synthesize a model that provides a point of reference necessary to both an understanding of the courts and legislative deliberation over proposed changes in legal rules. Using a unified model of suit, settlement, and trial, Cooter and Rubinfeld examine the incentives parties face as they proceed through the litigation process, and make predictions based on the decisions available to the parties, with a discussion of some of the concerns that arise from the pursuit of efficiency which pervades normative economic analysis. The theories of Landes, Rubin, Priest, Klein, and to a great extent Cooter and Rubinfeld, all contain the premise that cost analysis by the litigating parties plays a role in shaping the efficiency of the common law.

When considering the role of litigation in the development of legal rules, it is important to note that the private costs and benefits to litigating parties are not necessarily in line with the social costs and benefits. This creates a divergence between the private and social incentives that may undermine the optimal evolutionary path of judge-made law. Shavell (1982) argues that in some types of suits a party's private benefits from litigating are high but the social costs of such litigation are also high while the social benefits may be low. In other types of suits the potential social benefits of litigation may be high, but a party's private costs will be too high, preventing them from bringing suit. Menell (1983) challenges Shavell's second conclusion, that divergent costs and benefits will chill some forms of litigation, arguing instead that because parties bear only private costs (not social costs) of litigation, the general trend will be a high rate of litigation, likely in more cases than are socially optimal. Menell argues, however, that this effect may be overridden by a defendants' ability to influence the outcome of litigation. Kaplow (1986) revisits the work of both Shavell and Menell and finds that despite the fact that Menell's arguments are persuasive, Shavell's theory on the divergence between social and private costs and benefits of litigation remains intact. Further, Kaplow bolsters Shavell's argument that the efficiency problems caused by such divergence would be very difficult, if not impossible, to cure through lawmaking. Rose-Ackerman and Geistfeld (1987) argue that Menell's and Kaplow's theories only hold in special cases, and that with a change in policy (such as the adoption of the English loser-pays rule in litigation), Shavell's divergence problem could be corrected. Shavell (1997 and 1999) revisits his original hypothesis and finds that it would continue to hold also in those scenarios: because parties do not take social costs or potential social benefits into account when deciding whether to litigate, the private and social incentives to litigate (or to settle a case) are divergent. This divergence is difficult to remedy.

1.2. Supply-Side Explanations

Supply-side theories that support the efficiency hypothesis are best captured by Posner's (1994) interesting work on judicial behavior. Posner rejects the theory that the common law evolves toward efficiency is because of the good judge's work to promote the public interest. Although it might explain the decisions of a few judges, these benevolent preferences cannot be assumed across the board for all individual judges, and it would be an error to build a theory on such a weak assumption. Although it is often believed that judicial systems are structured in such a way as to protect judges' autonomy and to remove them from economic incentives, Posner develops a positive economic theory of the behavior of federal appellate judges, using a model in which judicial utility is primarily a function of income, leisure, and judicial voting. He argues that appellate judges are ordinary, rational people whose behavior is difficult to evaluate in terms of objective quality (neutral "justice"). Judges probably derive utility in judging from something besides money and leisure. Posner believes that judges derive positive utility from good reputation in the profession, popularity, and prestige and derive disutility from reversals by higher courts. Most importantly, Posner believes that voting on cases is a critical source of judicial utility due to the deference judges' opinions receive by lawyers and the public. Judges consumption value in deciding cases is obviously balanced by the preference for leisure. Among other things, Posner suggests that the balancing between the consumption benefits and the opportunity cost of decision making explains why judges adhere to *stare decisis*, although not rigidly. The function of judges was considered again by Posner (2006) who points the role of judges as political actors motivated by the dual desires of making the world a better place and playing the "judicial game." Posner concludes that if emotions and judicial views are subjectively colored and have an impact on judicial decision making, there are strong reasons to promote a diverse judiciary. Zywicki (2003) considers additional variations of the supply-side theories, providing an institutionally based explanation of the supply of efficient common law rules. The three conditions set by Zywicki include (1) the doctrine of "weak precedent" under the common law, (2) the polycentric legal order of the formative years of the common law, and (3) the emphasis on private ordering, including freedom of contract and accepted custom. These supply-side conditions no longer characterize the judicial decision making in the current era.

The following three chapters build on this literature, considering with particular attention the possible interaction between demand-side and supply-side theories. The combined consideration of demand and supply of legal precedents discloses the possibility of biases in the equilibrium paths of legal evolution. These results suggest that, in addition to the deviations already identified in the literature, there are additional biases that may affect the efficient evolution of judge-made law.

2. Legal Evolution: Judicial Path Dependence under Different Doctrines of Precedent

Legal evolution, changes in the law over time, under a system of judge-made law depends upon a number of factors. An important factor in legal evolution is judicial path dependence. Judicial path dependence is the idea that the decisions of judges in cases will affect judges decisions in future cases involving the same, or similar, legal issues. Doctrines of precedent are the mechanism through which judicial path dependence is created. Simply put, doctrines of precedent are legal doctrines under which judges hold past case decisions to be persuasive legal authority on cases currently before them. Doctrines of precedent vary widely in the degree and manner in which earlier case decisions are persuasive or binding on judges' decisions. Two common doctrines of precedent are *stare decisis* and *jurisprudence constante*. As previously discussed, the legal doctrine of *stare decisis* (literally to stand by things that have been settled) implies that courts should adhere to past legal precedent on issues of law when deciding pending cases. *Jurisprudence constante* doctrines instead hold that judges should only consider themselves bound to follow a consolidated trend of decisions. Judicial decisions do not become a source of law until they mature into a prevailing line of precedents

(Lambert and Wasserman 1929; Dainow 1974; Dennis 1993). It is important to note that these doctrines are not discrete, but rather should be thought of as points on the spectrum of possible doctrines of precedent, at one side of which a single earlier decision would be fully binding on a judge, and at the other side of which earlier decisions would not be binding at all.

Despite their varying dependence on judge-made law, doctrines of precedent are present in both civil law and common law systems, and some historical background is helpful to understanding the role of such doctrines. The principle of precedent can first be identified at the end of the 16th century when English courts started to adhere to previous custom in matters of procedure and pleading (Berman and Reid 1996: 446). However, it was not until the 17th and 18th centuries that a substantive rule of precedent developed in common law systems. In that period, courts were entrusted with the task of "finding" the law, rather than "making" the law. According to Blackstone (1764), the function of common law, which consists of the original common custom and the role of courts, was to find and declare such custom and to provide persuasive evidence of its content and existence. The presence of several cases recognizing the same legal principle increased the persuasive force of judicial findings: precedents became more authoritative when they were reaffirmed by a sequence of consistent decisions over time. In Hale's (1713) view, "a line of judicial decisions consistently applying a legal principle or legal rule to various analogous fact situations is 'evidence' of . . . the existence and the validity of such a principle or rule" (Berman and Reid 1996: 448). During the late eighteenth and early nineteenth centuries, under Bentham's positivist influence, the doctrine of *stare decisis* moved from practice to principle, giving rise to the common law notion of binding authority of precedent. By the end of the 19th century the concept of formally binding rules of precedent was established (Evans 1987: 36–72). The system of precedents was no longer viewed as persuasive evidence of the law, but itself became a primary source of law (Depoorter and Parisi 2003).

Most civil law systems underwent quite a different evolution, relegating case law to the rank of a secondary legal source. Codes and special legislation were recognized as the only primary source of law. In France, the "only legitimate source of the law is 'the law'" (Troper and Grzegorczyk 1997: 107). The law consists of the statutes created by the legislature and codified in the code. The "principle [of the code being the sole source of law] was formerly established by the law of 16–24 August 1790, [and] forbid[s] the courts to make rules or interfere with legislation" (Troper and Grzegorczyk 1997: 117).

In nineteenth-century Europe the doctrine of the separation of powers was understood to imply that "[t]he role of the courts is to solve disputes that are brought before them, not to make laws or regulations" (David 1972: 180–81). This strict historical conception of separation of powers was due to general distrust of courts that were manipulated by the king before the French revolution. The ideals of certainty and completeness in the law implied that legislative provisions had to be formulated and interpreted as mathematical canons to avoid any room for discretion or arbitrary decisions in the judiciary (Parisi 1992). After the French revolution "the judicial function was conceived as a mere application of statutes, by way of syllogisms" (Troper and Grzegorczyk 1997: 103). These protections "enclosed [the judgment] within a constitutional framework which is intended to prevent it from ever becoming a rule of law" (Carbonnier 1969: 95–96).

However, European jurists gradually developed a healthy skepticism concerning the ideals of certainty and completeness in the codified law. A prominent European legal theorist, commenting on the notion of legal logic, cynically wrote: "I have to confess that, as time passes, my distrust for legal logic increases" (Calamandrei 1965: 604). Calamandrei's distrust resurfaces in a number of recent legal analyses discussing the difficulties encountered in applying codified legal rules to an ever-changing pattern of factual circumstances. As memories of the abuses of prerevolution regimes began to fade, ideological concerns over the judiciary's role were assuaged. In their own judicial practices, civil law jurisdictions gradually adhered to a system of informal precedent law, where a sequence of analogous case decisions acquired persuasive force as a source of law. This judicial practice emerges as a way to promote certainty, consistency, and stability in the legal system that codifications had failed to achieve, while minimizing the costs of administering justice.

This path of legal development gave rise to *jurisprudence constante*, the doctrine under which a court is required to take past decisions into account only if there is sufficient uniformity in previous case law (i.e., differing decisions within a jurisdiction about the same legal issue). According to the *jurisprudence constante* doctrine, "the practice of the courts does not become a source of law until it is definitely fixed by the repetition of precedents which are in agreement on a single point" (Lambert 1929: 14). No single decision binds a court and no relevance is given to split case law. Once uniform case law develops, courts treat precedents as a persuasive source of law, taking them into account when reaching a decision. The higher the level of uniformity in past precedents, the greater the persuasive force of case law.

Considerable authoritative force therefore stems from a consolidated trend of decisions on any given legal issue. Under French law, this doctrinal construction, also known as *arret de principe*, holds that a series of decisions, all in accord, give bearing to an established rule of law (Depoorter and Parisi 2003).

In modern legal systems, the doctrine of *jurisprudence constante* is followed in France (Troper and Grzegorczyk 1997), Germany (Dainow 1974), Louisiana (Carbonnier 1969; Dennis 1993), and other mixed jurisdictions (MacCormick and Summers 1997). In France, precedents that consolidate into a trend or a "persisting jurisprudence" (*jurisprudence constante*) become a source of law. There is no judicial practice of citing or expressly referring to a specific precedent, but a continuous line of precedents becomes a relevant, and often decisive, factor in judicial decision making (Troper and Grzegorczyk 1997). "[C]ourts as well as scholars tend to recognize the existence of [a case] rule and the character of '*arrêt de principe*' of the precedent when it has been followed by a line of others" (Troper and Grzegorczyk 1997: 130).

Along similar lines, Louisiana law provides that a precedent becomes a source of law when it has become "settled jurisprudence" (*jurisprudence constante*). As pointed out by Louisiana Supreme Court Justice James Dennis, when a prevailing trend of cases forms a stream of uniform and homogeneous rulings with the same reasoning, the doctrine accords the prevailing jurisprudence persuasive authority. The doctrine of *jurisprudence constante* allows future courts to take into account past jurisprudential trends and to justify reliance on such precedents in deciding future cases (Dennis 1993). Likewise, Germany has adopted the notion that a line of decisions on a certain subject creates a sort of judicial custom. A prevailing line of precedent that has been standing for some time is referred to as "permanent adjudication" (*staendige Rechtsprechung*) (Dainow 1974). These examples are representative of a general tendency to accord persuasive force to a dominant trend of court decisions within civil law jurisdictions. This background will provide an important framework for the analysis of doctrines of precedent in Chapters 7 and 8.

3. Legal Evolution through Adjudication: The Economics of Judge-Made Law

In the chapters that follow, we expand on the existing law and economics literature on the economics of judge-made law. In Chapter 6 we analyze an often overlooked precondition of litigation and set out the circumstances under which different patterns of legal change may occur. We consider a model of legal evolution in which judges have varying ideologies and propensities to extend the domain of legal remedies and causes of action. Parties bring a case to court if the expected net return from the case is positive. The net expected value of the case depends on the objective merits of the case, the state of the law, and the ideological propensity of the judge. Because plaintiffs have full control over whether to bring a case to court, case selection generate a monotonic upward trend in the evolution of legal rules and remedies. The combined presence of differences in judges' ideology and plaintiff's control of the decision to file may explain how certain areas of the law have been granting increasing levels of remedial protection and recognition of plaintiffs' actions.

In Chapter 7 we explicitly revisit the role that litigation and case selection play in the process of legal change. We examine the effect of judicial path dependence on the consolidation of liability rules and legal remedies. We suggest that the selection of disputes for litigation is biased by the parties' range of choices. We examine the role of case selection and litigation in the evolution of legal remedies. If judges differ in their ideological or policy views and parties have some knowledge of such views prior to the final decision, judicial path dependence may lead to gradual consolidation or contraction of legal remedies. Increases in win-loss ratios (i.e., the amount a party expects to gain if they succeed through litigation versus the amount they expect to lose if they do not) signal to plaintiffs that cases can be rationally filed also when the probability of success is fairly small. The result is that a large number of negative precedents—denying a new cause of action or restrictively interpreting an existing remedy—may be produced. Conversely, in other instances an initial judicial innovation may be followed by gradual consolidation of legal precedents. A small fraction of early favorable decisions could lead to wider acceptance and eventually consolidate into a binding doctrine. In the presence of judicial path dependence, the private incentives of individual plaintiffs may diverge from the incentives of future plaintiffs: the filing of suits in low probability cases may have a negative impact on the likelihood of success of future similar cases. Our analysis sheds light on the process of legal evolution and provides the basis for further research on legal change under different doctrines of precedent. These results are consistent with the recent empirical evidence recently presented by Niblett, Posner, and Shleifer (2008), who examine whether the common law actually does converge toward efficiency in commercial areas, observing patterns of legal evolution that are in many respects at odds with the conventional predictions.[2]

In Chapter 8 we use a model to describe the dynamics of judicial decision making in civil law systems. Unlike the common law systems, civil law jurisdictions do not adopt a *stare decisis* principle in adjudication. In deciding any given legal issue, precedents serve a persuasive role. Civil law courts take past decisions into account, however, when there is a sufficient level of consistency in case law. Generally speaking, when uniform case law develops, courts treat precedents as a source of "soft" law, taking them into account when reaching a decision. The higher the level of uniformity in past precedents, the greater the persuasive force of case law. Although civil law jurisdictions do not allow dissenting judges to attach a dissent to a majority opinion, cases that do not conform to the dominant trend serve as a signal of dissent among the judiciary. These cases influence future decisions in varying ways. Judges may also be influenced by recent jurisprudential trends and fads in case law. The evolution of case law under civil law doctrines of precedent is described, showing the conditions under which we are likely to observe the consolidation or corrosion of legal remedies and the permanence of unsettled case law. This analysis offers a benchmark for the comparative analysis of different doctrines of precedent and provides insights to the institutional design of judicial lawmaking and the importance of giving optimal weight to precedent in a variety of dynamic settings.

SIX

Litigation and the Evolution of Legal Remedies*

IN THIS CHAPTER WE CONSIDER an often-overlooked ingredient of the creation of legal precedents and revisit the role of litigation in the evolution of judge-made law. As discussed in Chapter 5, a well-known result in the literature is that the process of case selection in legal disputes plays a fundamental role in the process of legal evolution. Here, we address one important observation made by Posner (2006), who observed that judicial opinions and emotions play a relevant role in case decisions—a subjectivity that may render it desirable to promote an (ideologically) diverse judiciary. In this chapter we examine the extent to which an increase in judges' diversity will actually avoid biases in the evolution of the common law. Our results in this respect are not very encouraging. We formulate an adverse selection theory of litigation, suggesting that the tendency toward increasing expansion of legal remedies, and more generally the entire process of creation and change of legal precedent in civil cases, is driven by a pervasive adverse selection mechanism. In our model parties have symmetric stakes in the case and judges differ ideologically from one another. Plaintiffs decide whether to file suit based on the likelihood of success in a specific court. As shown in our model, an ideologically diverse and balanced judiciary is not sufficient to generate unbiased case law. The resulting choices of the plaintiffs create a strong bias toward filing in pro-plaintiff jurisdictions. New legal precedents will be created on the basis of the resulting subset of litigated cases, with a greater opportunity for pro-plaintiff judges to create new legal precedents.

---

* This chapter is based on an article previously published as Fon, Vincy, and Francesco Parisi, "Litigation and the Evolution of Legal Remedies," in *Public Choice* 116: 419–33 (2003).

1. Case Selection and Legal Evolution

According to the efficiency of the common law hypothesis, discussed in Chapter 5 above, common law rules attempt to allocate resources efficiently, typically in a Pareto or Kaldor-Hicks efficient manner. Common law rules enjoy a comparative advantage over legislation in fulfilling this task because of evolutionary selection through adjudication and the gradual accretion of precedent.[1] The foundation of the efficiency of the common law thesis is the evolution of legal rules by the common law tradition of *stare decisis*. Rubin argued that the efficiency of the common law is best explained by the fact that parties will more likely litigate inefficient rules than efficient ones. The pressure for the common law to evolve to efficiency rests on the desire of parties to create precedent because they have interest in future similar cases. Priest (1977) articulates a similar idea, suggesting, however, that the common law tends toward efficiency in the absence of repeat litigation also, because litigation is driven by the costs of inefficient rules, rather than the desire for precedent. As a sort of survival-of-the-fittest argument, Priest suggests that efficient rules are less likely to be reviewed and thus tend to remain in force. Priest and Klein (1984) develop a model of litigation focusing on the criteria for the selection of disputes for litigation and derive a selection hypothesis: where both parties have equal stakes in the litigation, the individual maximizing decisions of the parties will create a strong bias toward a success rate for plaintiffs at trial (or appellants on appeal).[2]

The theories of Rubin, Priest, and Priest and Klein provide the essential ingredients for our theory of adverse selection in litigation. Our model, however, parts from those examined above in several important respects. Unlike Rubin, our results do not rely on the parties' incentives to create precedents. In our model, litigation is driven exclusively by the attempt to maximize returns from the case, rather than by the desire for precedent. Plaintiffs are rational and decide to bring a case to court whenever the expected net return from the case is positive. This implies that one-time as well as repeat litigants contribute to the process of legal evolution. Our model also differs from Priest's. Inefficient rules, we concede, impose greater costs on the parties subject to them than do efficient rules, and thus may be litigated more often than disputes arising under efficient rules. However, avoidance of inefficient rules is only a small factor in the parties' cost-benefit calculation. The opportunity to file a case in the first place is controlled by the plaintiff, creating an opportunity for adverse selection. As in Priest and Klein, the set of disputes selected for litigation constitutes neither a random nor a representative sample of the set of all disputes. As stressed by Hadfield (1992), judges can, of course, only rule on litigated cases. Our selection hypothesis, however, differs from Priest and Klein's and Hadfield's. Along the lines of Rubin and Bailey (1994), we develop an alternative model of legal evolution, which takes into account some important public choice components. Unlike Rubin and Bailey, who focus on the role of lawyers in changing the law, we consider the role of judges. In our model judges have different ideological views and plaintiffs decide whether to file suit based on the likelihood of success in the specific court. As shown in our model, the parties' rational decisions create a strong bias toward filing in liberal (i.e., typically pro-plaintiff) jurisdictions. This means that liberal judges have a greater opportunity to create new legal precedents than conservative (i.e., typically pro-defendant) judges.

2. An Adverse Selection Model of Litigation and Legal Evolution

This section provides an adverse selection model of legal evolution to explain the gradual expansion of legal remedies, and the resulting tendency of legal systems to grant ever-increasing levels of relief for plaintiffs' claims. We analyze a stylized fact in comparative legal history: an increasing number of civil claims that were once not recognized in law and were without remedy are now granted legal protection and effective legal remedies (Parisi 1992). We suggest that the tendency toward increasing expansion of liability in case-based legal systems results from the process of creating legal precedent.

We consider an adverse selection model of civil litigation.[3] Parties to a dispute face symmetric stakes. We assume that plaintiffs are rational and decide whether to bring a case to court, and that cases are filed whenever the expected net return from the case is positive. The expected value of the case is affected by the current state of the law and, for some marginal cases, by ideological views of the judge. We assume that judges have different policy perspectives and have different propensities to expand the scope of legal remedies and to recognize new causes of action. Judges recognize the binding force of law and of past precedents, but their policy views can affect outcomes in new or borderline cases.[4] Following Priest and Klein, we assume that potential litigants form rational estimates of likely decisions, whether based on legal precedent or ideological bias. Plaintiffs (and their lawyers) estimate judges' policy views and take such ideological components into account when evaluating expected returns from their cases.[5] Given rational choices, plaintiffs are unlikely to bring marginal cases that are not supported by current case before a conservative or pro-defendant court but may bring such cases before a liberal or pro-plaintiff court.[6]

2.1. Marginal Cases and Judicial Discretion

Marginal cases are often outside the domain of past rules, and emerge out of novel or borderline legal issues. In these situations, the court's evaluation of the case is influenced by subjective policy considerations: precedents only serve as persuasive sources of law, leaving a greater degree of freedom to judges in interpreting and applying precedential rules (Posner 1994; Depoorter and Parisi 2003).[7] Unavoidably, judges exercise such flexibility according to their ideologies. This process of legal evolution has dynamic effects. Marginal cases, once adjudicated, affect the future state of the law. Later cases are adjudicated according to new standards set forth by past marginal precedents. Over time this changes the liability threshold r_t necessary for a plaintiff to obtain judicial relief.

The asymmetric predisposition of conservative and liberal judges toward marginal cases should not be misinterpreted. Ideological decision making is not an attribute peculiar to liberal, as opposed to conservative, judges. In fact, all judges would likely push the threshold of liability closer to their ideal point, when given an opportunity to do so.[8] Liberal judges, however, have a greater opportunity to create pro-plaintiff precedents than conservative judges have to create pro-defendant precedents. This is not due to a different willingness to change the boundaries of the law, but rather to the judges' different opportunities to adjudicate marginal cases.

Let x be an index representing the objective legal merit of a potential suit. It is randomly distributed with probability density function $f(x)$ and cumulative distribution function $F(x)$.

For simplicity, let r be the ruling variable, or more precisely, an index of the legal system's willingness to recognize plaintiffs' claims. Such ruling variable is a representation of the existing stock of precedents. With an increase in legal precedents recognizing new claims and causes of action, the ruling boundary r decreases, because a lower objective legal merit would be necessary for a case to be decided in favor of the plaintiff. At each time period, let r_t be the "current" state of case law in period t which sets the minimum level of objective legal merit necessary for a suit to be ruled in favor of plaintiffs. We will refer to r_t as the liability threshold at time t.

Given a case of objective legal merit x that is brought to the court, the expected outcome of the case depends not only on the merit of the suit but also on the ideological inclination of the judge. Let i be a representation index of the ideological inclination of a judge, where the higher the index i, the more liberal the judge. Let $\kappa_i(x)$ represent the expected ruling of the court. In particular, $\kappa_C(x)$ represents the expected ruling function of a pro-defendant or conservative judge and $\kappa_L(x)$ represents the expected ruling function of a pro-plaintiff or more liberal judge.[9]

It is assumed that $\partial \kappa_i / \partial x > 0$. That is, the greater the level of the objective legal merit of the case, the more the plaintiff can expect the court to find in his favor, given the ideological inclination of the judge. This is because a claim with greater objective legal merits can be supported by a larger body of legal precedents, rendering a decision in favor of the plaintiff more likely for any type of judge. Meanwhile, our assumption that a liberal judge is more likely to rule in favor of a suit means that $\kappa_C(x) < \kappa_L(x)$.

Because κ_i is an increasing function, the inverse function of κ_i exists. The inverse of the expected ruling curve will be denoted by x_i. Hence,

$$\kappa_i(x) > r \Leftrightarrow x > x_i(r)$$

Further,

$$\kappa_C(x) < \kappa_L(x) \Leftrightarrow x_C(r) > x_L(r)$$

Figure 6.1 shows two inverse expected ruling curves $x_C(r)$ and $x_L(r)$. We will refer to these curves simply as the expected ruling curves. Note that

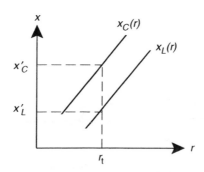

FIGURE 6.1 Expected Ruling Curves for Conservative and Liberal Judges

both expected ruling curves are upward sloping. This property reflects the fact that the greater the objective legal merit of the case filed, the more the plaintiff rationally expects the court to find in his favor.

Note that the expected ruling curve for a typical conservative judge $x_C(r)$ is higher than the expected ruling curve for a more liberal judge $x_L(r)$. This implies that for any stock of precedents r_t, the level of objective legal merit required for a case to be decided in favor of the plaintiff varies between conservative and liberal judges. A more conservative judge imposes a more stringent standard on the suit, bringing the "conservative" decision standard x'_C above the "liberal" decision standard x'_L.

Because the expected ruling curve for a conservative judge $x_C(r)$ is above the expected ruling curve for a liberal judge $x_L(r)$, the set of suits decided in favor of the plaintiff is smaller than that ruled on by a more liberal judge. To see this, consider a liability threshold r_t. All suits of merit x greater than or equal to x'_C are ruled in favor of the plaintiff by the conservative judge in question. Likewise, all suits of merit x greater than or equal to x'_L are ruled in favor of the plaintiff by the liberal judge.

2.2. Adverse Selection and the Decision to Litigate

Plaintiffs (and their lawyers) have some ability to identify policy views of the court, and know that when filing marginal cases the likelihood of winning increases with the judges' liberal propensities. Given r_t, the current period's liability threshold, consider what happens to a party who has a claim of objective legal merit x. If he is subject to the jurisdiction of a conservative court, he faces the expected ruling curve $x_C(r)$ when he brings a suit to the court. Hence, if the merits of the case are large, say much larger than x'_C, based on current law he can safely expect a favorable ruling and would file suit. On the other hand, for cases with merit x lower than x'_C, the plaintiff knows that the chances of success under current law are fairly limited. As it will be discussed below, plaintiffs may decide not to file claims in such cases. Therefore, the set $\{x/x \geq x'_C\}$ represents the suits that are likely to be filed and ruled in favor of the plaintiff in a conservative court.[10]

Plaintiffs subject to a liberal jurisdiction would rationally file suit if $x > x'_L$, even if the objective legal merit x falls below the standards necessary to succeed in a conservative court, $x < x'_C$. This is true because they know that they face a more favorable environment than their peers subject to a more conservative jurisdiction. Hence, the range of cases filed in a liberal court is broader than that filed in a conservative court. In particular, the set $\{x/x \geq x'_L\}$ represents all suits filed in a liberal court, if potential plaintiffs and their lawyers expect the decision standard to be x'_L. Hence, in general the range of suits filed in a liberal court is broader than the range of suits filed in a conservative court. This is illustrated in Figure 6.1. Note that the types of suits filed in a liberal court are all points above x'_L, and all points lying above x'_C represent the types of suits that would also be filed in a conservative court.

Let us start with a median judge's interpretation of the current liability threshold r_t implied by the stock of precedents at time t, $x^*(r_t)$. Such an interpretive standard is referred to as x^*. Liberal and conservative judges are characterized by ideological departures from policy views of the median judge. Both types of judges are willing to let their ideology influence their decision of marginal cases, pushing the threshold of liability closer to their ideal policy, toward more permissive or restrictive standards.

The interpretive standards of liberal and conservative judges depart in opposite directions from the policy views of the median judge x^*. We can think of l and c as the interpretive discretion of the liberal and conservative judges. Judges have different reservation values, intended as the minimum legal merit of cases that they are willing to decide in favor of the plaintiff. From now on, we think of $x^* - l$ and $x^* + c$ as the boundaries of cases for which outcomes depend on the ideology of judges. These values represent the bounds on the judges' discretion when applying and interpreting the current body of law r_t.

All suits with merit x such that $x > x^* + c$ are decided in favor of the plaintiff by all judges, even the most conservative ones. Likewise, all suits with merit x such that $x < x^* - l$ are decided against the plaintiff by all judges, even the most liberal ones.

In a liberal jurisdiction a judge is more willing to adjudicate a case in favor of the plaintiff than a judge in a conservative jurisdiction. Litigants have rational expectations reflecting such differences among courts. However, litigants cannot observe the actual view of the judge on the specific case at bar. Now consider a suit of merit x where $x^* - l < x < x^*$ that is in front of a liberal judge. Because $x < x^*$, the judge cannot use the current stock of precedents to decide his case. Because $x^* - l < x$, the case falls in the range where ideological and policy views of the judge can influence the outcome of the case. Even in the absence of past precedents and legal authorities, the liberal judge may rule in favor of the plaintiff. Cases with high values of x such that $x^* - l < x$ are likely to be filed, because rational plaintiffs expect that such cases will be decided in their favor.

When a liberal judge adjudicates in favor of the plaintiff for a suit with merit greater than $x^* - l$ and less than x^*, the judge is setting a newer and more liberal precedent.

The impact of liberal decision making on the state of the law finds no countervailing force from conservative courts. Consider a suit of merit x where $x^* < x < x^* + c$ that is in front of a conservative judge. Although $x^* < x$ means that a median judge may rule for the plaintiff, a conservative judge would want to rule in favor of the defendant, because $x < x^* + c$. However, because $x^* < x$, the judge would not be able to do so by merely invoking the current stock of precedents. When deciding according to his views, the judge would create a more restrictive legal precedent. Knowing this, a rational plaintiff would typically decide not to bring the case or to terminate any pending litigation. This takes away the opportunity for conservative judges to render a decision in marginal cases. Hence, the countervailing force of conservative decision making will rarely be at work. Cases with values of x such that $x < x^* + c$ are unlikely to be filed in conservative courts, because rational plaintiffs expect such cases to be decided in favor of defendants. This leads to a higher rate of adjudication of marginal cases in liberal courts and to the possibility for a biased flow of new liberal legal precedents.

Finally, note that interpretive standards for all types of judges are a function of the current stock of precedents. The biased flow of precedents in favor of liberal decision making will over time affect the interpretive standards of future judges, liberal or conservative. This makes legal boundaries moving targets, given the dynamic effects considered next.

2.3. Legal Precedent and the Expansion of Legal Remedies

Even though liberal and conservative judges are equally willing to be influenced by their ideology when deciding marginal cases, if litigants have equal stakes in the case, only one subset of marginal cases will be brought to court. Namely, a marginal suit is filed only in liberal jurisdictions when the merit of the case x is such that $x^* - l < x < x^*$. Thus, let M_t represent the set of "marginal suits filed" in period t. These are the marginal suits where $x < x^*$, such that the legal merit of the case falls below the median judge's interpretive standard. They are filed in liberal courts: only suits filed there have a chance of a ruling in favor of the plaintiffs. Without loss of generality, assume that the lowest limit of all suits filed by plaintiffs has objective legal merit $x^* - \Delta$, where Δ is the plaintiff's estimate of l. That is, the set of marginal suits filed is $M_t = \{x/x^* - \Delta < x < x^*\}$.

Here we treat Δ as an estimate of the liberal judge's ideology. There are several environmental factors that may influence Δ. Ideological litigation by special interest groups, symbolic litigation for purposes of political persuasion, cases that enjoy public visibility and mass media attention, cases that may advance current political views of the government, and other environmental factors may influence the degree with which marginal suits are filed. These factors affect the filing rate of marginal suits because they similarly affect the degree to which judges are free to interpret the current stock of precedents in light of their policy or ideological views.[11]

To better understand the model, make the simplifying assumption that x is uniformly distributed on $(0, A)$ for some A. The probability that new precedents are set for the plaintiffs is then given by the following:

$$\Pr\{new\ precedents\} = \min\left\{\Pr(x^* - l < x < x^*),\ \Pr(x^* - \Delta < x < x^*)\right\}$$

$$= \min\left\{\frac{l}{A}, \frac{\Delta}{A}\right\}$$

Hence, new precedents in favor of plaintiffs are likely as long as there are ideological differences between judges and there are plaintiffs willing to file marginal suits.

Because the probability of setting new precedents is positive, the probability that the next period's liability threshold falls below the current period's threshold is positive. Hence, when r_{t+1} *does* fall below r_t, the liability threshold is relaxed. This affects the stock of precedents under which both liberal and conservative judges adjudicate. Therefore, in the next period, even the most conservative judge would likely rule in favor of the plaintiff when confronted with a suit that falls below r_t but above r_{t+1}. Over time, new precedents enter the established body of law. Suits that previously would have been decided in favor of the defendant by a conservative court are now decided in favor of the plaintiff as a result of the change in law. Figure 6.2 illustrates this possibility.

At any point in time, assume the current period's liability threshold to be r_t and the median judge's interpretive standard to be x^*. Liberal judges will be adjudicating cases in the range $x^* - l < x < x^*$ in favor of plaintiffs. Over time, the flow of those new liberal precedents may lead to a change in the law. The median judge's interpretive standards would in turn be affected by such change in the law, with a likely shift from r_t to r_{t+1}. Thus, suits that

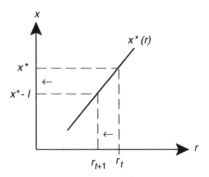

FIGURE 6.2 Effect of Past Decisions on Current Cases

would have previously been decided in favor of the defendant would now be decided in favor of the plaintiff.

As time goes on, when the liability threshold is relaxed, additional suits with an even lower legal merit x will be filed in liberal courts. Over time, then, the range of cases brought before courts broadens, including new situations that previously lacked legal remedies.

It is interesting to note what happens if l does not change (fall) over time. Suppose liberal judges do not become more liberal and relax their critical value l over time. In this case, the probability that new precedents are set approaches zero. When this happens, the liability threshold r_t will stabilize.

The assumption driving this final result obviously begs the empirical question as to whether ideology is absolute or is itself shifting over time. Are the ideological views of yesterday's liberal judges less progressive, compared with the liberal standards of today (or tomorrow)? Different answers are likely to be found in different settings. A self-reinforcing effect of liberal judicial intervention is plausible in some situations, given that what constitutes an "extreme" decision is a relative matter that depends on the presence (or lack thereof) of similarly progressive and innovative precedents in the current law. This suggests that the interpretive standards of liberal judges may become more liberal over time and that the critical value l may consequently be routinely relaxed over time.

3. Rethinking the Evolution of the Common Law

Legal and economic scholars have often noticed the gradual expansion of legal remedies, and the tendency of legal systems to grant ever-increasing levels of relief for plaintiff's claims. Situations that were once considered outside the domain of compensable harm are gradually granted protection in the law. Interestingly, this process of evolution seems to be characterized by a monotonic expansion of legal remedies. In this chapter we have built on the existing literature on the well-known efficiency of the common law hypothesis, suggesting that the stylized fact of ever increasing availability of legal remedies may be explained by an adverse selection theory of litigation and legal evolution.

As is well known in the literature (e.g., Priest and Klein 1984), the selection of disputes for litigation is biased by the parties' strategic litigation choices. The litigation process generates decisions on cases that are neither random nor a representative sample of the set of all disputes. We build on this insight by considering litigants facing symmetric stakes in a case and allowing judges to differ in their ideological or policy views. We assume that policy views of the judges are irrelevant in most cases, because current law and objective legal merits of the case determine the outcome. In some cases, however, we allow policy views of judges to affect the outcome. Plaintiffs are rational and decide whether to file suit based on the likelihood of success in the specific court. These rational decisions of the parties create a strong bias toward filing marginal cases in pro-plaintiff jurisdictions. This means that progressive judges have a greater opportunity to create new legal precedents than conservative judges.

In our illustration, this generates a potential monotonic increase of remedial protection in the legal system. More generally, pervasive adverse selection mechanisms may affect the entire process of creating and changing legal precedent.

Although we used an illustration where parties have equal stakes and plaintiffs control the initial filing, the essence of the model is agnostic on the actual direction of legal evolution. Depending on the initial environmental conditions, the adverse selection mechanism may bias legal evolution toward expansion or contraction. With the appropriate parameters, this may explain different trends in the evolution of legal remedies. For example, our model can explain expansion of remedial protection in several areas of the law where the filing of new marginal cases and the adjudicating jurisdiction are asymmetrically controlled by one or the other group of litigants (e.g., tort plaintiffs decide whether to bring a new case to court; contract defendants determine the place of jurisdiction).[12] The model presented in this chapter predicts that in the more frequent case of plaintiffs having better control over whether and where to file claims, the stock of precedents will increasingly expand the scope of remedial protection. In the more unusual case where defendants have better control of the jurisdiction, such adverse selection mechanisms may be undermined and, at the limit, the opposite outcome may be observed, with the gradual shrinking of remedial protection. In Chapter 7 we extend this analysis to consider the combined effects of adverse selection and asymmetric stakes in litigation on the dynamic process of legal evolution. In Chapter 8 we consider alternative doctrines of precedent to examine how they affect legal evolution.

SEVEN

Judicial Path-Dependence and Legal Change*

DUE TO THE VERY NATURE of common law, the boundaries of legal remedies and the domain of legal protection have changed over time. A large number of situations that were outside the domain of existing legal remedies have been granted remedial protection over time. Following different doctrines of precedent, such as *jurisprudence constante*, similar processes of evolution have affected the boundaries of legal rules and remedies in civil law systems. For example, causes of action in torts have historically increased in number and scope of application under both common law and civil law systems (Lawson 1955; Lawson and Markesinis 1982; Parisi 1992). Yet in other areas of the law, the domain of legal remedies has not experienced similar expansion. Current theories of legal evolution are unable to explain these changes, let alone predict conditions that may induce changes to legal rules and to the scope of remedies.

In this chapter we consider the dynamic process of case selection and its role in generating the different patterns of change of legal remedies in various areas of the law. We consider the importance of the win-loss ratios (essentially, what a plaintiff stands to win if litigation is successful versus what he stands to lose if it is not) and the prospect of success of legal claims for the resulting process of legal change. Section 1 briefly assesses existing explanations of the process of legal change and reviews the seminal papers that evaluate the process of selection of disputes as an ingredient of the efficient evolution of legal rules. These contributions, while compelling, fail to provide a framework that can explain or predict the different outcomes of litigation that impact legal change. Section 2 proposes a model that evaluates the impact of case selection on legal evolution in different litigation contexts, highlighting the interaction among selection of disputes, litigation stakes in

---

* This chapter is based on an article previously published as Fon, Vincy, Francesco Parisi, and Ben Depoorter, "Litigation, Judicial Path-Dependence, and Legal Change," *European Journal of Law and Economics* 20: 43–56 (2005).

the case, and litigation costs, as well as their impact on legal change. The model of path-dependence in the law suggests the rate of recognition of legal claims brought by plaintiffs in past cases affects the state of the law in the future. In this precedential system a prevailing rate of negative judgments on a specific legal issue reduces the likelihood that such a claim will be successful in future cases.[1] Likewise, a high rate of success for claims and recognition of new types of causes of action increase the probability that similar claims will be recognized and expanded in future cases. In a path-dependent system, evolution of the law is affected by the rate of positive and negative judgments, which in turn depends on the relationship between some critical parameters of the dispute. More specifically, we investigate how the processes of creation and change of legal precedent are affected by litigation stakes, the probability of success of plaintiffs' claims, and the institutional weight attached to past precedents. Section 3 concludes with a few summary considerations and suggestions for applications and future extensions.

1. Legal Evolution and the Changing Boundaries of Remedies and Liability

We frame our analysis in the context of the existing literature on dispute selection and legal evolution. A well-known result of the efficiency of the common law hypothesis is that judge-made law attempts to efficiently allocate resources. This claim has generated extensive research in law and economics. According to the hypothesis, first intimated by Coase (1960) and later systematized and greatly extended by Ehrlich and Posner (1974), Rubin (1974), Priest (1974), Posner (1981), and several others, judicially created law enjoys a comparative advantage over legislation in generating efficient rules because of evolutionary selection through adjudication and the gradual accretion of precedent.[2] Several important contributions provide the foundations for this claim, though scholars who have advanced theories in support of the hypothesis often disagree as to their conceptual basis.

As discussed in Chapter 5, the doctrines of precedent such as *stare decisis* and *jurisprudence constante* are fundamental ingredients of the evolution of judge-made law. As discussed in Chapter 6, Rubin's (1977) main argument is that the pressure for case law to evolve to efficiency rests on the desire of parties to create precedent, because of their interest in future similar cases. Given this incentive, parties are more likely to litigate inefficient rules than efficient ones. Priest (1977) similarly articulates the idea that common law tends to develop efficient rules even in the face of potential judicial hostility toward efficient outcomes. In Priest, however, we see the argument that litigation is primarily driven by the costs of inefficient rules, rather than the desire for clear precedent. According to Priest's analysis, inefficient rules impose greater costs on the parties than do efficient rules, thereby making the stakes in a dispute higher. When the stakes are greater, litigation becomes more likely than settlement. Consequently, disputes arising under inefficient rules tend to be litigated more often over time than disputes arising under efficient rules. The corollary is that efficient rules tend to be uncontested, and through this mechanism the legal system fosters the selection of increasingly more efficient rules.[3]

As discussed earlier, the criteria by which parties choose whether to litigate a given dispute are important ingredients of the efficiency hypothesis. Only disputes that are actually litigated are capable of generating legal precedents. Priest and Klein (1984) show that when both parties have equal stakes in the litigation, individual maximizing decisions of the parties create a strong bias toward a success rate for plaintiffs at trial (or appellants on appeal), regardless of the substantive law.[4]

In Chapter 6, we built upon existing literature on the evolution of judicially created law, considering a model of legal evolution in which judges have varying ideologies and propensities to extend the scope of legal remedies and to create causes of action. In our model presented in Chapter 6, plaintiffs decide whether to file suit based on the likelihood of success in the specific court. Given differing judges' ideology, the parties' rational decisions create a strong bias toward filing in liberal jurisdictions. This means liberal judges have a greater opportunity to create new legal precedents than conservative judges.[5] This model departs from the previous literature in several important ways. Unlike Rubin (1977), the result does not rely on the parties' incentives to create precedents. The selection of which disputes to litigate (i.e., case selection) is not based upon parties' asymmetric interests in future similar cases and the fact that parties therefore have incentives to avoid unfavorable precedents. Instead, litigation is exclusively driven by the attempt to maximize returns from a case. The net expected value of the case depends on the objective merits of the case, the state of the law, and the ideological propensity of the judge. When the policy views of judges are capable of affecting decisions in marginal cases, case selection might create a strong bias toward filing marginal cases in pro-plaintiff jurisdictions (i.e., forum shopping). This means that liberal judges have a greater opportunity to create new legal precedents than conservative judges, with a potential increase of remedial protection in the legal system. This selection mechanism was shown to have a potentially adverse effect on the process of legal change. More specifically, the combined presence of differences in judges' ideology and plaintiff's case selection was shown to generate a steady trend in the evolution of legal rules and remedies toward the creation more remedial protection.

Although much emphasis has been placed on the failed-settlement condition in the decision to bring a claim, this chapter highlights the importance of an often overlooked condition: for a threat of litigation to be credible, the expected net judicial award should be positive. This chapter follows the previous literature, assuming that the opportunity to file a case is initially controlled by the plaintiff, creating an occasion for case selection. We thus assume that cases that may lead to litigation have a positive expected net return, and concentrate on the effect of this overlooked "precondition" for the emergence of a relevant legal dispute on the evolution of precedents.

2. Case Selection and Legal Evolution

In this section we consider the impact of different litigation stakes and litigation costs on parties' selection of which disputes to litigate and on the resulting process of legal evolution. After considering the potential role of judicial path-dependence under the doctrine of precedent, *jurisprudence constante*, we consider litigation and case selection under conditions of costless litigation and litigation with positive litigation costs. These elements provide the building blocks for a general understanding of the conditions that may lead to consolidation (i.e., the establishment and entrenchment of a law such that availability of causes of actions and remedial protection expand) or contraction of legal precedents and judicial remedies.

2.1. Precedents, *Jurisprudence Constante*, and Judicial Path-Dependence

We consider the impact of case selection on the formation of legal precedents, and study the role of precedents under *jurisprudence constante* doctrines, where a judge does not consider himself bound in any way by a single previous decision. Rather, as discussed above, under *jurisprudence constante* considerable authoritative force stems from a consolidated trend of decisions on a certain point, and the earlier judicial decisions do not become a source of law until they mature into a prevailing line of precedents (Lambert and Wasserman 1929: 14).

Under this doctrine of precedent, if the rate of positive judgments with respect to some new legal issue or interpretation of existing causes of action falls above a critical threshold π (a threshold that is institutionally determined by the legal system), the recognition of such legal claims in future disputes will be increased with an increase in the presence of legal authority. This creates path-dependence in the process of legal evolution, because past jurisprudential rulings affect the likelihood that such rules will be perpetuated in future case law.[6] New legal issues presented to a court will have a rate of success that, for any given merit of the case, also depends on litigation stakes and the litigation costs. Different combinations of parameters will generate different choices of case selection, and consequently different probabilities of positive versus negative leading precedents.

The following discussion will be framed in the context of a *jurisprudence constante* regime, looking at the percentage of positive versus negative precedents, rather than at the probability of positive versus negative leading cases. We thus assume that when past litigation generates a percentage of positive precedents that falls above π, legal evolution induces a gradual consolidation of new remedies and causes of action. The following analysis contemplates a threshold $\pi = \frac{1}{2}$, which implies that a majority of precedents on a given legal issue would be regarded as persuasive authority, increasing the chances of success for future similar cases. In other institutional settings a threshold different from the value of $\pi = \frac{1}{2}$ would mean that more than a simple majority of past decisions is necessary to influence decisions on future similar cases.

2.2. Case Selection: Two Necessary Conditions for Litigation

In our model of civil litigation, litigants face a dispute where p is the probability of litigation success for the plaintiff. Following Priest and Klein (1984) and Fon and Parisi (2003a), we assume that potential litigants form rational estimates of the probability of success in litigation and take them into account when evaluating expected returns from their cases. The parties' expectations, although unbiased, have some margin of error, which explains why some disputes are litigated, rather than settled before trial.[7] When a judge decides in favor of the plaintiff the judicial award is W. In the case of a ruling in favor of defendant, the plaintiff suffers a prejudice equal to L. This prejudice can be interpreted as the net present value of the loss from litigation in future similar cases (as in Rubin 1977) or the immediate cost imposed on plaintiffs or any other liability imposed by the court such as court sanctions or defendant's counterclaims.[8] Plaintiffs face direct litigation costs C (e.g., filing fees, attorneys' fees, and other costs of bringing the action). These costs are not recovered once litigation is carried out and a final judgment is rendered.[9]

Plaintiffs are rational in deciding whether to pursue litigation. There are two necessary conditions that need to be satisfied before a potential plaintiff files a legal.[10] First, the expected judicial award should be greater than the nonrecoverable portion of litigation costs. That is to say, the expected net judicial award should be positive. Second, the expected net judicial award should exceed any settlement amount offered by the defendant.

Although much emphasis has been given to the latter condition in the literature (Posner 1973; Priest and Klein 1984; Shavell 1993; Kobayashi 1996), the first condition plays an important role in the litigation choice. In fact it is only when the first condition is fulfilled that the second condition becomes relevant. If the expected net recovery falls below the litigation costs, the expected net recovery is negative and no threat of litigation can be credibly made. As a result, the defendant will not offer settlement.

We thus concentrate on the effect of this often overlooked "precondition" for the litigation of a dispute and its effect on legal evolution. Given the presence of the two necessary conditions for litigation, cases that will ultimately lead to a judicial precedent will be a subset of such cases. The existing literature, focusing on the filing versus settlement decision, has shown that common law precedents tend to evolve toward efficiency. We complement the existing literature by showing how the "positive expected net return condition" may create a bias in the evolution of case law.

As mentioned above, the condition for a plaintiff's credible threat of litigation is that a case, if filed, should yield a positive expected net judicial award.[11] The net expected return of the litigant is given by the following:

$$R = p \cdot W - (1-p) \cdot L - C \qquad\qquad 7.1$$

Whenever the value R is negative, the plaintiff's threat of litigation would not be credible and no filing or judicial ruling would take place. To clarify the impact of the magnitude of litigation stakes on the decision problem, we highlight the win-loss ratio W/L and concentrate on the normalized expected return function by rewriting equation (7.1):

$$\frac{R}{L} = p \cdot \left(\frac{W}{L} + 1\right) - \left(\frac{C}{L} + 1\right)$$

7.2

Our analysis proceeds by considering the relevance of litigation costs and litigation stakes on the process of legal evolution.

2.3. Costless Litigation

We first consider the simple case of costless litigation $C = 0$. This will serve as a useful stepping-stone for understanding the more realistic cases of costly litigation. Without loss of generality, our attention will be limited to the more realistic case of $W > L$. Similar analysis could be applied to the complementary case of $W < L$.

Figure 7.1a shows the expected return curve as a function of the probability of winning p. Figure 7.1b shows the filing decision, where the dotted curve represents zero expected return for the case with no litigation cost, indicating potential substitutions between different win-loss ratios and probabilities of winning on break-even litigations.[12] Point B in Figure 7.1a

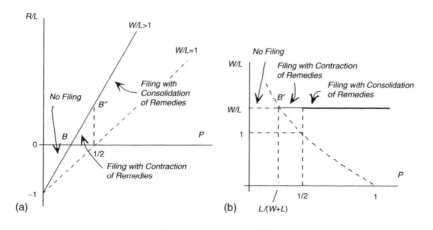

(a)

(b)

FIGURE 7.1a Expected Return with $C = 0$ FIGURE 7.1b Filing Decision with $C = 0$

and point B' in Figure 7.1b correspond to zero expected return when p is equal to $\frac{L}{W+L} = \frac{1}{1+W/L}$. For all cases corresponding to $p < \frac{1}{1+W/L}$, the expected return from litigation is negative, and the plaintiff rationally avoids filing suit. These cases are also represented by points to the left of B' in Figure 7.1b.[13] For cases corresponding to $p > \frac{1}{1+W/L}$, the plaintiff files suit because the expected return from litigation is positive.

In order to understand the impact of litigation stakes on the process of legal evolution, it is important to realize that a case may be rationally filed even when the probability of success is less than 50 percent. However, although privately rational, the filing of suits in low probability cases may have a negative impact on the likelihood of success for future similar cases. When past litigation generates a flow of negative precedents that outweighs the positive precedents, the percentage of positive precedents falls below the critical threshold $\pi = \frac{1}{2}$, and the process of legal evolution generates a gradual contraction in the scope of remedies. In our model, cases that are filed but which would lead to contraction of remedies are represented by points between B and $B"$ in Figure 7.1a. These cases are also represented by the lighter portion of the solid W/L line in Figure 7.1b.

For all cases corresponding to $p > \pi = \frac{1}{2}$, the probability of success for litigation is above the relevant threshold and consolidation of jurisprudential rules would likely occur. This is true because more positive precedents will be generated with resulting path-dependence in the evolution of case law. These conditions foster consolidation in the scope of remedies and legal protection.

2.4. Costly Litigation

We next turn our attention to the case with positive litigation cost, considering the impact of such costs on the process of case selection and evolution. Figure 7.2 shows the zero-expected-return curve for positive litigation cost (represented as the darker hyperbola marked as $C > 0$) along with the zero-expected-return curve for zero litigation cost (represented as the lighter hyperbola marked as $C = 0$).[14] Three different win-loss ratios are presented in Figure 7.2. As before, for any given win-loss ratio, all points to the left of the zero-expected-return curve correspond to cases with negative expected returns. Rational plaintiffs would not file suits in this region. Hence, for example, in the case of win-loss ratio W^1/L and positive litigation cost, no filing would take place in the region between the vertical axis and point F.

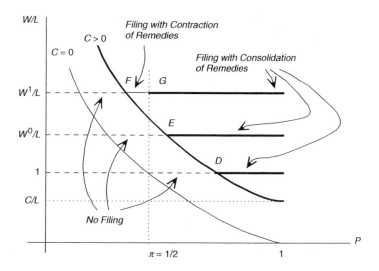

FIGURE 7.2 Filing Decision with $C > 0$

On the other hand, for any given win-loss ratio, all points to the right of
the zero-expected-return curve correspond to cases with positive expected
returns. These cases are potential candidates for filing by rational plaintiffs.
In such region of positive expected returns, if the probability of winning is
greater than the critical threshold $\pi = \frac{1}{2}$, consolidation of jurisprudential
rules obtains. When past litigation generates a percentage of positive
precedents that falls above π, legal evolution induces a gradual consolidation
of legal rules and remedies. For example, given the intermediate win-loss
ratio W^0/L in Figure 7.2, the region to the right of point E is characterized
by gradual consolidation. Here the probability of success required to
induce litigation also suffices to induce consolidation of judicial precedents,
fostering a consolidation of judicial remedies and legal protection.

Meanwhile, for all suits with probability p falling to the right of the
zero-expected-return curve but to the left of the critical threshold $\pi = \frac{1}{2}$,
cases would be filed. However, the small percentage of positive precedents
would lead to a contraction of remedies. For example, given the high
win-loss ratio W^1/L in Figure 7.2, the region between points F and G
would be characterized by active litigation but contraction in the scope of
remedies and legal protection. This is true because the probability of success
sufficient to generate positive litigation falls below the threshold π and
contraction follows as a consequence of the high rate of negative precedents
generated overtime.

2.5. Litigation and Legal Change

Consider a doctrine of precedent where past decisions are taken into account by courts only when there is a sufficient level of consistency in case law, similar to *jurisprudence constante*. Following Fon and Parisi (2004), we assume that no single decision binds a court, and no weight is given to split jurisprudence in this system. Although a judge is not bound by a single decision in a single previous instance, authoritative force stems from a consolidated trend of decisions on a given legal issue. We further continue to assume that litigants form rational and unbiased estimates of their probabilities of success in litigation. This ensures a correspondence between the litigants' estimated winning probabilities and the percentage of cases actually upholding plaintiffs' claims. Thus ex ante win probabilities can be treated as ex post fractions of positive precedents.

If the fraction of positive judgments (or the fraction of negative judgments) with respect to a legal issue exceeds the threshold, then recognition of such legal claims in future disputes will be facilitated (or made more difficult) by the presence of such consolidated case law. This creates path-dependence in the process of legal evolution, because a consolidated trend of past jurisprudential rulings affects the likelihood that such rulings will be perpetuated in future case law. In the face of any legal claim presented in court, a *jurisprudence constante* regime can therefore evolve in two possible ways. A claim may be accepted by a sufficiently large percentage of cases, giving rise to a dominant "positive" jurisprudence. Positive precedents become persuasive authority when their density in past cases exceeds the critical threshold. Alternatively, a claim may be negated by a sufficiently large percentage of cases, establishing a dominant "negative" jurisprudence. Negative precedents influence future decisions when the density of positive precedents falls short of the critical threshold.[15]

Figure 7.2 also brings together our findings for different litigation stakes, when litigation involves a positive litigation cost C and a fixed loss L. All points to the southwest of the zero-expected-return curve (i.e., break-even litigation curve) correspond to cases that generate negative expected payoffs and are thus not filed.[16] All cases to the northeast of the zero-expected-return curve correspond to cases that generate positive expected payoffs and are thus candidates for filing. Within this filing region, the area to the left of the critical threshold $\pi = \frac{1}{2}$ represents the region of contraction in the scope of remedies, whereas the area to the right of $\pi = \frac{1}{2}$ represents the region of gradual consolidation of positive judicial precedents and legal remedies.[17]

With high win-loss ratios, cases can be rationally filed even when the probability of success is small. As a result, the number of negative precedents may outweigh the number of positive precedents. When the percentage of positive judgments falls below π, the filing of the first cases leads to consolidation of negative authority. This process of judicial path-dependence may induce a gradual contraction in the scope of remedies. Conversely, if the probability of positive judgments falls above π, initial filings may be followed by a gradual consolidation of remedies. Figure 7.2 depicts some of the relevant trade-offs in this process of legal evolution: an increase in the win-loss ratio renders less disputes worthy of litigation. This increases the region characterized by contraction of remedies. It is also easy to see that given a fixed win-loss ratio, an increase in litigation costs requires a higher probability of success to justify litigation. This, in turn, may decrease the region with a gradual contraction of remedies.

As cases are filed over time, the distribution of p changes depending on where the case falls relative to the critical value π. This will change the parties' expected success rate and consequently their decision to litigate future similar cases. Thus, the likelihood of success of a given claim changes over time depending on what happened in a previous period.[18] Finally, Figure 7.2 shows that the relative size of the regions with consolidation versus contraction critically depends on the institutional choice of π. More generally, a change in the institutional weight of past precedents may have a substantial impact on (1) the domain of the region characterized by stable remedies; and (2) the direction that the process of legal evolution may take. For example, an increase in the level of case consistency required for an emerging jurisprudential trend to become binding case law may reduce the likelihood of gradual consolidation of available causes of action and remedies.

3. Path-Dependence and Legal Evolution

As is well known in the literature, the selection of disputes for litigation is biased by the parties' litigation choices. Following previous work by Fon and Parisi (2003a), in this Chapter we examined the role of case selection and litigation in the evolution of legal remedies. In Chapter 6 we considered legal evolution when judges differ in their ideologies. The results of the present chapter do not rest on judges' ideological decision making. Rather, all judges, regardless of their ideology, give deferential weight to past decisions, when the weight of authority falls above a threshold determined exogenously by the legal system. Our analysis reveals that the consolidation and increase in the scope of remedies is not necessarily a consequence of adverse selection in litigation. In many ways, the results complement those reached in the earlier literature and serve as building blocks for studying the more complex interaction between ideological judicial intervention and path-dependence in judicial action.

This analysis reveals that judicial path-dependence may lead to gradual consolidation or contraction of legal remedies. Increases in win-loss ratios imply that cases can be rationally filed also when the probability of success is fairly small. The result is that a large number of negative precedents—those affirmatively denying the recognition of a new cause of action or restrictively interpreting the scope of application of an existing remedy—may be produced. When the percentage of positive judgments falls below the level of support that the legal system in question considers necessary before widespread judicial recognition occurs, an initial wave of filing may be followed by a gradual implosion. Conversely, in other instances an initial judicial innovation may be followed by gradual consolidation of legal precedents. A small fraction of early favorable decisions could lead to wider acceptance and eventually consolidate into a binding doctrine.

It is noteworthy that in all such cases parties' private choices have public consequences on the future state of the law. In the presence of judicial path-dependence, the private incentives of individual plaintiffs may diverge from the incentives of future plaintiffs. This may be for either of two reasons. In cases with a low probability for success in litigation, bringing a claim may be privately rational but detrimental to the interest of future similar plaintiffs: the filing of suits in low probability cases may have a negative impact on the likelihood of success of future similar cases. On the other hand, the filing of a case with high probability of success may not be privately rational due to high litigation costs or low win/loss ratio, although filing would increase the probability of success for future similar cases. In both cases, the presence of externalities cannot be fully internalized by current private parties. For the collective well-being of present and future plaintiffs, this may lead to too much or too little litigation. But, unless we assume that success rates systematically reflect the social desirability of the remedy, the intertemporal externalities created by current plaintiffs toward future similar plaintiffs are not necessarily socially relevant and no normative conclusions should be drawn.

In this chapter we have analyzed an often overlooked precondition of litigation and set out the circumstances under which different patterns of legal change may occur. We considered the relevance of litigation stakes, the presence of positive litigation costs, and the weight of precedents on the process of legal evolution. Our analysis sheds light on the process of legal evolution and provides the basis for further research on legal change under different doctrines of precedent. It offers a benchmark for the comparative analysis of different doctrines of precedent and provides insights to the institutional design of judicial lawmaking and the importance of giving optimal weight to precedent in a variety of dynamic settings. An extension of our model of case selection should verify if a similar process of legal evolution could be at work under a common law system of precedents. A modified version of our model could be applied to the *stare decisis* doctrine of precedent inasmuch as the probability of generating a positive rather than a negative leading case depends on the parameters considered.

In this chapter we implicitly assumed that positive precedents (i.e., those granting a remedy or recognizing a cause of action) have equal weight as negative precedents (i.e., those denying a remedy or cause of action). Legal systems, however, may give greater weight to a minority view, when it recognizes a new cause of action or expands the scope of existing remedies (in many ways, leading cases in a traditional common law system may be regarded as examples of this category). In such situations, the threshold marking the boundary between situations of consolidations of legal remedies and contraction of legal remedies may change. In the context of our model, different positioning of the threshold may explain the different trends of evolution of tort liability in different legal systems. For example, the stylized fact that expansion of tort remedies is less pronounced in Europe than in the United States (Tellinghast et al. 1995) can be explained by the fact that the precedential threshold in civil law jurisdictions is shifted to the right of the standards of precedential value accepted in common law jurisdictions, because no single leading case or limited set of leading cases constitute binding authority under civil law. In Chapter 8, we extend our analysis to consider different procedural settings and evaluate the effect of positive and negative precedents.

EIGHT

Theories of Legal Precedent

Stare Decisis and *Jurisprudence Constante**

THE DOCTRINES OF PRECEDENT of *stare decisis*[1] and *jurisprudence constante*[2] are fundamental ingredients of legal evolution. Although much attention has been given to the evolution of the common law under a *stare decisis* principle (Heiner 1986; Kornhauser 1989; von Wangenheim 1993), legal evolution under alternative doctrines of precedent remains an open theoretical issue. In this chapter we consider how legal rules may evolve under the precedential doctrine of *jurisprudence constante* in civil law.

Current theories are unable to explain why, in spite of emphasis on legal certainty and stability, the practice of civil law systems in certain areas of the law is often characterized by instability and uncertainty. Traditional explanations focus on the lack of *stare decisis* (Mattei 1988), different judicial cultures, political instability, and different levels of separation of powers (Merryman 1969). The following analysis provides an explanation based on the dynamic process with which judicial precedents evolve.

We consider legal change under civil law doctrines of precedent, contemplating different patterns of consolidation or corrosion of legal remedies in the law. Legal rules granting rights and legal protection may evolve over time and gradually consolidate into established legal entitlements. On the other hand, legal protection may be subject to gradual corrosion and certain forms of legal protection may be abandoned.[3] Finally, legal entitlements may enjoy a mixed level of recognition and such level of mixed protection may persist over time. We focus on conditions that may determine these alternative patterns of legal evolution.

After briefly introducing the theory of legal precedent from comparative and historical perspectives, we focus on one modern-day product of

---

* This chapter is based on an article previously published as Fon, Vincy, and Francesco Parisi, "Judicial Precedents in Civil Law Systems: A Dynamic Analysis," in the *International Review of Law and Economics* 26: 519–39 (2006).

such evolution: the doctrine of *jurisprudence constante*. Although developed in a system that emphasizes certainty and stability, we suggest that this doctrine of precedent potentially leads to quite contrary results. In Section 1, we introduce a model that evaluates the impact of *jurisprudence constante* on legal evolution in different litigation contexts. It highlights the interaction between established precedents and judicial fads in shaping future case law. It also explains the possible impact of exogenous shocks in the legal system on the evolution and stability of the law. We formulate a simple model of path dependence in the law in which the rate of legal claims brought by plaintiffs in past cases affects the future state of the law. This formulation considers a legal system that specifies a minimum level of uniformity in case law. Any set of precedents that falls below such level of consistency is regarded as "split" case law and inconclusive as a source of law. Precedents that reach or surpass the required level of consistency become a persuasive source of law, affecting decisions for future similar cases. In this way, a large fraction of affirmative precedents on a specific legal issue (e.g., cases that recognize a new type of claim or cause of action) increases the probability that similar claims will be recognized in the future and a prevalence of negative precedents reduces the likelihood of a successful claim in future cases. In such a system, the state of the law is determined by the stock of established legal precedents and the flow of recent decisions.[4] We elaborate on this simple framework to analyze features of legal evolution under different parameters of the problem. Most importantly, we show that the stability and change of legal precedent are affected by the institutional threshold of *jurisprudence constante* and the weights attached to established precedents and recent jurisprudential trends. Section 2 concludes with a few summary considerations and suggestions for applications and future extensions.

Our model concentrates on the evolution of precedent within a unitary judicial system, a system in which precedents have an intrajurisdictional effect rather than an interjurisdictional effect across different judicial branches.[5] This analysis is thus applicable to doctrines of precedent for decisions of a multipanel Supreme Court within a typical civil law jurisdiction, where past decisions issued by other divisions of the Court are persuasive if they are sufficiently uniform, but where departures remain possible and are often observed in the presence of exogenous shocks. The model provides a testable hypothesis to explain the varying levels of consistency in case law in civil law systems.

※ 1. Legal Evolution under *Jurisprudence Constante*

As more extensively discussed in Chapter 5, there are substantial historical and conceptual differences between the doctrines of precedent in common law and civil law traditions. Both legal traditions regard legal precedent as the presence of a sequence of consistent decisions in similar cases over time. However, these principles operate differently in the two traditions. In the following, we model the evolution of case law under the doctrines of precedent of *jurisprudence constante* and *stare decisis*, considering the possibility for consolidation, corrosion, and instability of legal rules. It will become clear how different variations of civil law doctrines of precedent, in requiring different levels of consistency in past decisions, affect the evolution of the legal system.

Law and economics scholars have formulated a variety of models to study the creation of precedents and evolution of the common law. To review from the previous chapters, demand-side theories formulated by Rubin (1977), Priest (1977), Priest and Klein (1984), Cooter and Rubinfeld (1989), and Fon, Parisi and Depoorter (2005), hypothesize that cost analysis by the litigants influences legal change over time.[6] Similar results were reached by other scholars who focused on the supply-side of legal decision making. Coase (1960), Ehrlich and Posner (1974), and Posner (1994) concentrated on the role of the judiciary in shaping efficient common law rules.[7] Subsequent work by Fon and Parisi (2003a) looked at the combined effects of these variables, studying the role of ideology and adverse selection in legal evolution. In their model, this selection mechanism was shown to potentially affect legal rules and remedial protection in the legal system.[8]

Our model adds a dynamic view to existing supply-side models, looking at ways in which the dynamics of legal evolution may differ under civil law doctrines of precedent. Whether courts' past decisions were affected by parties' case selection or judges' preferences, past precedents affect future decisions. We thus study how the more gradual and softer impacts of precedents in civil law jurisdictions affect the evolution of the law.

We consider how the degree of consistency in past case law and the likelihood of success in litigation can induce changes in legal systems. These factors explain some of the different patterns of evolution in the levels of remedial protection and the gradual consolidation or corrosion of legal principles. In examining *jurisprudence constante* doctrines, we look at two types of legal precedents. Negative precedents—those denying recognition to a filed claim or restrictively interpreting the scope of application of an existing statute—may consolidate into a negative jurisprudential rule that eliminates legal protection with respect to the legal issue. Positive precedents—those recognizing a filed claim or expansively interpreting the scope of application of an existing statute—may consolidate into a positive jurisprudential rule that grants legal protection in such a situation.

As mentioned above, under *jurisprudence constante* doctrines a judge is not bound by a single decision in a single previous instance.[9] Authoritative force stems from a consolidated trend of decisions on a certain point. The practice of the courts becomes a source of law when it matures into a prevailing line of precedents. Under variations of this doctrine of precedent, if the fraction of positive judgments (or the fraction of negative judgments) with respect to a legal issue exceeds a threshold, then recognition of similar legal claims in future disputes will be more likely (or less likely) by the presence of such consolidated case law.[10] This creates path dependence in the process of legal evolution, because a consolidated trend of past jurisprudential rulings affects the likelihood that such rulings will be perpetuated in future case law. We denote the threshold as π. Its value is greater than or equal to one-half and is institutionally determined by the legal system. In most legal systems of the world such determination of the threshold π is generally established by statutes and bylaws governing judicial bodies and occasionally covered by constitutional provisions. The choice of the value of the threshold π reflects the specific conception of separation between legislative and judicial powers and the relative weight attached to the needs for stability and flexibility in the legal system.

In the face of any legal claim presented in court, a *jurisprudence constante* regime can therefore evolve in three possible ways. A claim may be accepted by a sufficiently large percentage of cases, giving rise to a dominant "positive" jurisprudence. A claim may be negated by a sufficiently large percentage of cases, establishing a dominant "negative" jurisprudence. Finally, if there is insufficient consensus in courts' decisions, jurisprudence is "split" and precedents do not influence future courts' decisions.

Even in the presence of *jurisprudence constante*, minority cases play an important informational role in civil law decision making. Unlike common law systems, civil law systems generally do not allow judges to attach dissenting opinions to majority decisions. Minority cases, cases decided against a prevailing trend of decisions, thus become the main way in which judges can express views that are contrary to the prevailing jurisprudential trend. Minority cases therefore convey information that would otherwise remain buried under the opaque majority decision of the court.[11] Although not directly applicable as a source of law, cases that do not conform to the dominant trend serve as a signal of emerging dissent among the judiciary. Although minority cases typically lose on appeal, we allow for these cases to play a signaling role, informally influencing future decisions.

Some literature (von Wangenheim 1993; Daughety and Reinganum 1999; and Levy 2005) has examined judicial behavior with a microeconomic analysis of judges' incentives. In this chapter we look at the dynamic macroeconomic impact of court decisions on the evolution of legal rules, focusing on how established case law and recent jurisprudential trends exert some persuasive influence over the decision of pending cases.[12]

We now consider a model of civil litigation. Litigants face a dispute where p is the probability of success for the plaintiff. In our terminology, this corresponds to the probability that a positive judgment is rendered. At period $t-1$, let p_{t-1} be the probability for a plaintiff to see his claim recognized on grounds of law on a specific legal issue. In the next period t, we assume that the previous period probability has been realized and becomes the fraction of cases that recognized a given category of legal claims *during the last period*. That is, at time t, p_t is the current flow of cases that recognized a given category of claims. Let L_t represent the fraction of total cases that recognized a given category of legal claims *in all past periods*. Thus, L_t is the stock (in fraction) and p_t is the flow (in fraction) of case law affirming remedies at time t.

Changes in the stock of affirmative case law in the future period depend on L_t and p_t. In particular, assume that

$$\dot{L_t} \begin{cases} < 0 & \text{if } L_t > p_t \\ = 0 & \text{if } L_t = p_t \\ > 0 & \text{if } L_t < p_t \end{cases} \qquad 8.1$$

When $L_t = p_t$, the recent cases recognizing a given category of legal claims (positive case law) are generated in the same proportion as the current stock of case law. When the fraction of flow for positive case law continues at the same rate as the fraction of current stock, there is no change in the future stock value L_{t+1}. When $L_t > p_t$, the flow falls below the current stock, decreasing the resulting fraction of positive cases in the future stock of case law. This is much like the interaction between a marginal value and an average value. When the flow p_t (the marginal) is less than the stock L_t (the average), the future fraction of positive case law (the new average) declines. Likewise, when $p_t > L_t$, the fraction of flow exceeds the fraction of stock for positive case law, and the future fraction of stock for positive case law increases.

In modeling the effect of *jurisprudence constante*, we allow judges to be influenced by both established case law (tradition) and recent jurisprudential trends and fads (fashion). Recent case law can depart from past case law in response to a variety of exogenous factors, such as changes in the regulated environment and the evolution of values in society, as well as trends generated by endogenous factors or possible changes in judges' incentives.

We assume that change in the probability of success of any given category of legal claims is affected by the fraction of similar claims that successfully received relief in court in both recent and older case law, p_t and L_t. On the other hand, we also assume that past negative cases that rejected a legal claim presented to the court are important elements for reaching decisions in future similar cases as well. In other words, judges are also influenced by negative precedents that did not grant relief to the legal claim—both the flow and the stock of cases $1 - p_t$ and $1 - L_t$.

The likelihood that a plaintiff receives a positive judgment does not directly depend on the flows of positive and negative case law p_t and $1 - p_t$. Instead, the relative impact of these flows is most important. Thus, let αp_t represent the *impact* from positive recent case law and $\beta(1 - p_t)$ represent the *impact* from negative recent case law. The *relative* impacts of positive and negative recent case law $\alpha p_t - \beta(1 - p_t)$ then directly influence the probability that the plaintiff obtains recognition of a filed claim. The force of this relative impact represents the degree of influence of recent jurisprudence. If the influence of $\alpha p_t - \beta(1 - p_t)$ on the probability of success for new decisions becomes larger (the magnitude of change is larger), it indicates a stronger judicial trend or fashion. Following this interpretation, it is convenient to refer to this relative impact variable as a judicial fashion variable F_t. That is, $F_t = \alpha p_t - \beta(1 - p_t)$.

Unlike the rather informal influence of judicial fashion F_t, the impact of past cumulative case law is a formal legal effect that does not depend simply on L_t and $1 - L_t$. Under *jurisprudence constante*, past cases do not become a source of law until they mature into a prevailing line of precedents. If the rate of positive judgments L_t (or negative judgments $1 - L_t$) with respect to a legal issue is above the institutionally determined threshold π, the recognition (or rejection) of such legal claims will be affected by the presence of legal authority. The effect of past cumulative case law thus depends on differences of L_t and $1 - L_t$ from the judicial threshold π. As in the previous case of recent case law, we postulate that it is the relative impact of the positive and the negative cumulative case law that directly influences the probability of receiving remedies for a case. Letting $\gamma(L_t - \pi)$ and $\delta((1 - L_t) - \pi)$ represent the *impacts* of existing positive and negative case law respectively, the *relative* impact is $\gamma(L_t - \pi) - \delta((1 - L_t) - \pi)$. This relative impact directly influences the probability of success for new cases filed. A larger influence of the relative impact of positive and negative cumulative case law $\gamma(L_t - \pi) - \delta((1 - L_t) - \pi)$ on the probability of success for future similar cases indicates that the legal system gives more deference to established jurisprudential tradition. For convenience, we refer to this relative impact of past case law as the jurisprudential tradition variable T_t. That is, $T_t = \gamma(L_t - \pi) - \delta((1 - L_t) - \pi)$.

Specifically, we assume that changes in the probability of obtaining recognition of a filed claim are a function of the judicial fashion variable and the jurisprudential tradition variable with the following property:

$$\dot{p}_t = g(\alpha p_t - \beta(1 - p_t), \gamma(L_t - \pi) - \delta((1 - L_t) - \pi))$$
$$= g(F_t, T_t)$$

8.2

where

$$\begin{cases} g(F_t, T_t) > 0 \text{ if } & F_t > 0 \text{ and } T_t > 0 \\ g(F_t, T_t) < 0 \text{ if } & F_t < 0 \text{ and } T_t < 0 \\ g(F_t, T_t) = 0 & \text{otherwise} \end{cases}$$

8.3

To understand the logic behind our model, first consider the case where positive case law dominates, $L_t \geq \pi$. Here, the number of cases that recognized a given category of legal claims substantially outweighs the number of cases that denied recognition to such claims. The dominance of positive precedents satisfies the institutional threshold π. In this situation, we postulate that the impact of positive case law is greater than the impact of negative case law $\gamma(L_t - \pi) > \delta((1 - L_t) - \pi)$, and the jurisprudential tradition variable T_t is positive. Meanwhile, we assume that a judicial fashion that develops in line with a preexisting jurisprudential tradition reinforces the rule and is given greater weight than a wave of cases that could develop against such established tradition. When cumulative positive case law dominates, recent positive cases also have a larger influence than recent negative cases, $\alpha p_t > \beta(1 - p_t)$, and the judicial fashion variable F_t is positive as well.

Thus, when $L_t \geq \pi$, the model specifies that the first branch of g is valid, that $g(F_t, T_t) > 0$, and that $\dot{p}_t > 0$. Intuitively, under a system of *jurisprudence constante* with dominant positive case law, judicial tradition acquires persuasive force as a secondary source of law. When this happens, judicial trends backed by such legal tradition give courts the additional benefit of being part of a growing fashion. Judges can at the same time be fashionable and comply with their judicial obligation by following established tradition. This would not be the case for waves of cases that go against an established tradition, as a conflict would develop between the attraction of fashion and the legal force of tradition. It is thus reasonable to expect judicial fashion to follow and reinforce judicial tradition in the case of dominant positive case law.

Consider next the other extreme case of dominant negative case law with $1 - L_t \geq \pi$. Here, the number of cases that denied recognition to a given category of legal claims substantially outweighs the number of cases that recognized such claims. The fraction of negative precedents satisfies the institutional threshold, $1 - L_t \geq \pi$. In this situation, the impact of negative case law is greater than the impact of positive case law so that $\gamma(L_t - \pi) < \delta((1 - L_t) - \pi)$ and $T_t < 0$. Likewise, the impact from recent negative cases exceeds the impact from recent positive cases such that $\alpha p_t < \beta(1 - p_t)$ and $F_t < 0$ hold. Note that $1 - L_t \geq \pi$ is equivalent to $1 - \pi \geq L_t$. Thus, when $1 - \pi \geq L_t$, the model specifies that $g(F_t, T_t) < 0$ and that $\dot{p}_t < 0$. This is intuitive, because a negative judicial tradition, like a positive judicial tradition, can acquire force as a secondary source of law. Negative judicial trends that are consistent with such a legal tradition allow courts to be part of a fashion, without violating their obligation to follow established precedents.

Lastly, consider the case of "split" case law where neither positive case law nor negative case law is sufficiently dominant to satisfy the institutional threshold. This is equivalent to the case where both $L_t < \pi$ and $1 - \pi < L_t$ hold. That is, the split case law region is characterized by $1 - \pi < L_t < \pi$. In this region of split case law, the doctrine of *jurisprudence constante* is not applicable and courts are free to decide a case anew without being bound by past precedents. In our model, this means that the impact of negative cumulative case law versus the impact of positive cumulative case law is unknown. The absence of a dominant jurisprudential tradition further implies that courts have greater freedom to follow positive or negative jurisprudential trends. Positive and negative trends can be influential in this region, as neither conflict with established case law. Hence, when $1 - \pi < L_t < \pi$, we postulate that $g(F_t, T_t) = 0$ and that $\dot{p}_t = 0$.

To summarize our specification of the dynamic behavior of the probability p_t to obtain recognition of a new filed claim qualitatively, we have the following:

$$\dot{p_t} \begin{cases} > 0 & \text{if} & \pi \leq L_t \\ = 0 & \text{if} & 1 - \pi < L_t < \pi \\ < 0 & \text{if} & L_t \leq 1 - \pi \end{cases} \qquad 8.4$$

Now consider the dynamic behaviors of L_t and p_t with the help of the phase diagram in Figure 8.1. From the dynamic equation (8.1) for L_t, if $L_t = p_t$, then $\dot{L_t} = 0$. Along the 45° line on the $L_t - p_t$ space, L_t does not change over time. When $L_t > p_t$, then $\dot{L_t} < 0$: below the 45° line L_t decreases and moves to the left over time. Likewise, when $L_t < p_t$, then $\dot{L_t} > 0$: above the 45° line L_t increases and moves to the right over time. Thus, only a point on the 45° line can become a steady state, although not all points on the 45° line are steady states.

Next consider the dynamic behavior of p_t given in (8.4). In the region of dominant positive case law where $L_t \geq \pi$, $\dot{p_t}$ is positive and the probability of obtaining judicial recognition of a similar claim increases. Thus, p_t moves upward and increases until it can no longer do so when it reaches 1. When this happens, p_t stabilizes. In other words, the set of potential steady states where $\dot{p_t} = 0$ is represented by the horizontal line at $p_t = 1$. In Figure 8.1, this is represented by the darker portion on $p_t = 1$ from $L_t = \pi$ to $L_t = 1$. Combining with the dynamic behavior of L_t, the steady state in this region of dominant positive case law is then the intersection of the 45° line and the darker portion on $p_t = 1$. It is represented by the point $(L_t = 1, p_t = 1)$,

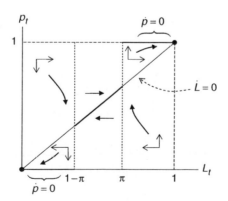

FIGURE 8.1 The Dynamics of *Jurisprudence Constante*

a point where legal remedies have evolved and consolidated reaching a point of stability.

In the split case law region where neither positive case law nor negative case law dominates and $1 - \pi < L_t < \pi$, $\dot{p}_t = 0$ everywhere. Everywhere in this region, p_t does not increase nor decrease and it does not move over time. Along with the dynamic behavior of L_t, we observe that the steady states are numerous in this region of split case law. They are represented by all points on the portion of the 45° line between $L_t = 1 - \pi$ and $L_t = \pi$ (the darker portion on the 45° line). In this region, split precedents and unsettled case law can persist in the long run.

Lastly, in the region of dominant negative case law with $1 - L_t \geq \pi$ or $L_t \leq 1 - \pi$, $\dot{p}_t$ is negative and the probability of obtaining judicial recognition of a filed claim decreases as time passes. Thus, p_t decreases until it can no longer do so when it reaches 0. In other words, the set of potential steady states ($\dot{p}_t = 0$) in this region is represented by the horizontal line at $p_t = 0$. It is given by the darker portion on $p_t = 0$ from $L_t = 0$ to $L_t = 1 - \pi$ in Figure 8.1. Combining with the dynamic movement of L_t, the steady state in this region of dominant negative case law is the origin ($L_t = 0$, $p_t = 0$), a point where negative precedents have entirely corroded preexisting legal remedies.

With the help of Figure 8.1, it is now easy to see that starting from a point in the region of dominant negative case law below the 45° line, over time the dynamic path will approach the steady state located at the origin. Likewise, starting from a point in the region of dominant positive case law above the 45° line, over time the dynamic path will approach the steady state located at (1,1). Also, starting from a point where both past and recent precedents are unsettled, with L_t and p_t between $1 - \pi$ and π, the dynamic path will approach a steady state in the middle portion of the 45° line with a persistent split in case law.

To further understand possible dynamic paths of case law under a doctrine of *jurisprudence constante*, take as a starting point A in Figure 8.2 in the region of dominant positive case law. Courts are influenced by a positive line of precedents and the probability of obtaining recognition of a claim increases. Point A, however, lies below the 45° line. This means that the fraction of positive decisions in recent cases falls below the fraction observed in the past cumulative case law, and the new fraction of cumulative case law falls. Fashion is moving away from tradition. This occasions a short-term movement toward the northwest. In spite of such short-term movement, positive case law continues to accumulate and eventually the fashion fades out until the path intersects the 45° line. From that point on fashion and tradition become self-reinforcing and the positive recognition of legal claims stabilizes at point (1,1).

The consolidation of positive precedents can also be reached when the originating point is outside the region of dominant positive case law. Take for example point B (in Figure 8.2) in a region of dominant negative case law where courts are influenced by a negative line of precedents. The probability of obtaining recognition of a claim decreases over time. Point B, however, lies substantially above the 45° line. This means that the fraction of positive decisions in recent cases is substantially higher than the fraction observed in past case law. The new fraction of cumulative case law L_t thus increases quickly, approaching $1 - \pi$. A short-term movement toward the southeast is created. Due to this short-term movement, the fraction of negative precedents $1 - L_t$ is gradually lowered until it crosses the institutional threshold π. (In Figure 8.2, this is read as the path originating from point B approaches and crosses $L_t = 1 - \pi$.) At that point, the previously dominant negative case law is transformed to split case law. Courts are no longer constrained by past jurisprudential tradition and can decide cases anew, following their good judgment and the information conveyed by other recent decisions. While the path from point B is in the intermediate region, the trajectory is always above the 45° line. This implies that positive cases continue to be created, gradually raising the fraction of positive cumulative case law. This process continues until the path crosses the institutional threshold π. Here the trend was able to generate a dominant mass of positive precedents to acquire the force of positive *jurisprudence constante*.

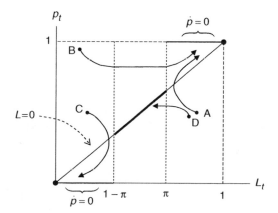

FIGURE 8.2 Some Possible Dynamic Paths in Civil Law Precedents

Even though the paths originating from points B and A start from different and remote regions, both lead to the same equilibrium and the positive recognition of legal claims stabilizes in point (1,1).

The path originating from point C also starts from the region of dominant negative jurisprudence, but proceeds in quite a different direction. In this region, courts are influenced by negative precedents, decreasing the probability of obtaining recognition of a claim over time. Point C also lies above the 45° line. The fraction of positive decisions in recent cases is greater than the fraction observed in past cumulative case law, increasing the new fraction of positive cumulative case law over time. Similar to the movement of the path originating from point B, the two forces occasion a short-term movement leading path C toward the southeast. However, in spite of this short-term trend, negative case law continues to accumulate. Eventually the path intersects the 45° line, at which point the negative judgments start consolidating toward the origin (0,0).

The path starting from point D shows a different trajectory in which a situation previously governed by positive case law eventually stalls in a region of split and unsettled case law. In the initial phase, courts are influenced by a dominant positive case law, increasing the probability of obtaining recognition of a claim over time. Point D, however, lies below the 45° line. This means that the fraction of positive decisions in recent cases falls below the fraction observed in the past cumulative case law, and the new fraction of positive cumulative case law falls. The joint forces occasion movement toward the northwest, similar to the initial movement of the path starting from point A. However, in this case, the fraction of positive precedents gradually declines until it crosses the institutional threshold π. At that point, tradition is corroded and the previously dominant positive case law turns into split case law. Courts are no longer constrained by past jurisprudential tradition.

The path starting from point D bears some similarity to the path originating from point B. In both cases, judicial fashion corrodes an established tradition. In the path starting from point D, however, the forces of judicial fashion are not sufficiently strong to push the path away from the intermediate region of split and unsettled case law. The trajectory ends when it reaches the darkened portion of the 45° line. The split in judicial decisions is likely to persist until an exogenous shock triggers new jurisprudential trends that can eventually consolidate into positive or negative case law.

Our analysis further reveals that the domain of the regions with consolidation versus corrosion critically depends on the institutional choice of π.

More generally, a change in the institutional choice of *jurisprudence constante* may have a substantial impact on the domain of the region characterized by expansion and subsequently on the direction that the process of legal evolution may take. Consider for example the effect that an increase in the level of case consistency required for *jurisprudence constante* would have on path A. Given a high enough π, path A would cross the $L_t = \pi$ line, leading to split jurisprudence on a point along the darkened portion of the 45° line. More generally, an increase in π broadens the intermediate region of split and unsettled case law. This is intuitive because an increase in π means that greater consistency in past decisions is required before cases acquire precedential value. A higher consistency threshold implies that more situations would be deprived of the guidance of past case law. Thus, an increase in the institutional threshold increases the intermediate region of split jurisprudence, and the likelihood of reaching certainty on a legal issue through the consolidation (or corrosion) of a past jurisprudential tradition decreases. This reveals an interesting paradox. Greater institutional demand for consistency (higher threshold values of B) may lower the actual consistency in adjudication.[13]

It is interesting also to note what would happen in the presence of some exogenous shocks to the system. For example, assume that under the current case law the probability of obtaining recognition of a given claim is represented by point A in Figure 8.2. Some random event occurs, propelling the current status quo from point A to point D in Figure 8.2. A real-life example could be found in the exogenous shock occasioned by terrorist attacks on the judicial protection of privacy. As Figure 8.2 illustrates, even a minor disturbance moving the current state from point A to D may have a very large impact on the evolution of the law. Over time, the shock produces uncertainty and split case law (the path approaches the 45° line) instead of stabilized positive recognition of legal claims (in the absence of exogenous shocks, the path would have approached the northeast corner). A small disturbance leads to long-term uncertainty. Returning to our real-life example, this may indeed be the case in the future judicial developments of the law of privacy.

Now imagine what could happen if a similar shock took place under a different institutional setting with a lower *jurisprudence constante* threshold. In this setting, the intermediate region of split jurisprudence would be represented by a narrower band surrounding $1/2$.[14] A shock that catapults the current status quo from point A to point D may not lead to split case law. When the region of uncertainty $(1 - \pi < L_t < \pi)$ is small, the dynamic path originating from point D could resemble the path originating from point A in Figure 8.2. In this case, a random shock may eventually delay stability of the positive recognition of legal claims, but would not prevent it.

※ 2. Legal Stability and the Evolution of Judge-Made Law

The adoption of institutional constraints that foster stability in judge-made law may be desirable to promote stable expectations, but at times, such constraints may hinder the opportunity for judicial experimentation and gradual consensus formation. In this chapter we have considered legal change under different doctrines of precedent, focusing on conditions that may determine consolidation or corrosion of legal remedies. We have intentionally refrained from developing normative conclusions based on the positive results of this chapter, because correlation between consistency and efficiency may work in different ways.

In our model of precedents, the stability and change of legal rules is affected by the stock of established legal precedents, the flow of recent decisions, the institutional threshold of *jurisprudence constante,* and the weights attached to established precedents and recent jurisprudential trends. We highlighted the relevance of the institutional threshold in the face of exogenous shocks, inasmuch as different dynamic paths may be produced by a similar shock under different precedent regimes.

Civil law doctrines of precedent require varying degrees of consistency in past case law. Consistent decision making does not necessarily imply efficiency, and the social value of consistency may vary over time and under different circumstances. Certain aspects of contemporary law may have stabilized, while others are in a state of flux. For more traditional legal issues consistency may be desirable to promote certainty and facilitate the formation of parties' legal expectations. For new legal issues and in the presence of volatile environments, requiring consistency may be detrimental, inasmuch as it precludes experimentation with diverse legal solutions, offering the possibility to tailor legal rules to changing circumstances overtime. The institutional variable, interacting with other exogenous variables, generates different patterns of evolution. Interestingly, our model suggests that higher thresholds (i.e., greater demand for consistency) actually lower the consistency in adjudication. This chapter implies the testable hypothesis that unsettled jurisprudence noticeably characterizes civil law countries, insofar as they adopt higher thresholds. Future research should test this hypothesis in a cross-country comparison.

Future extensions could integrate more factors to enrich the model. For example, a time weight variable may be added, allowing for more recent cases to be more (or less) influential than older cases. This could allow fashion to outweigh tradition more (or less) often. For example, greater weight to recent cases may be given in situations where technological advances or other changes in the regulated environment render traditional values outdated. Alternatively, in situations where social values and tradition are at stake greater deference may be paid to older leading cases. Another extension may incorporate the idea that as law approaches certainty, litigation fades out. The final stages of consolidation or corrosion may thus slow down. It would also allow a surge of fashion to have a greater impact in a low litigation environment. Another strand of extension would concentrate on the relevance of the role of precedent in more complex systems. For example, the model can be extended to consider multiple courts with different propensities to follow judicial fashion and established tradition when deciding a case. The model could also be extended to study the impact of percolation theories, to study the effect of legal precedents across different jurisdictions or judicial bodies. Finally, our analysis does not commit to any specific view on the determinants of courts' substantive choices. In reality, the cases that reach a final judgment often constitute a biased subset of the relevant disputes. Past decisions are affected by parties' case selection and judges' ideological preferences. The study of the effect of alternative doctrines of precedent on the evolution of the law can thus be valuably extended to consider possible interactions between the identified dynamics and other potential determinants of case adjudication.

PART III

Lawmaking through Practice
Customary Law

NINE

Lawmaking through Practice
An Introduction

IN THE FOLLOWING THREE CHAPTERS we consider the process of formation and evolution of customary law. Legal theorists define customary law as a practice that emerges outside of legal constraints and which individuals, organizations, or states spontaneously follow in the course of their interactions, out of a sense of legal obligation. The legal system eventually adopts and enforces rules that individual, group, or state actors have embraced. Unlike mere social norms, customary laws are then treated by some legal systems as proper sources of law and enjoy the centralized enforcement and adjudication generally reserved to legislation, judge-made law, or binding international treaties.

The process of formation of customary law is quite unique and different from the process of formation of the other sources of law thus far examined in Parts I and II of this book. By voluntarily adhering to emerging behavioral standards, individual members contribute to the development of rules that govern their social interaction. The subjects of the law, rather than their representatives (legislation) or third-party decision makers (judge-made law), contribute directly through their own actions and practices to the process of formation of customary law. This process, which we may think of in terms of "direct legislation through action," differs from traditional lawmaking processes in that the resulting rules emerge gradually through the independent and spontaneous adherence of community members to customs rather than through political deliberation or adjudication.

In the following chapters we discuss custom in the context of individuals acting within one community as well as in the context of state actors on an international level.

❦ 1. Custom Defined: What Custom Is

Those legal systems that grant direct legal force to customary rules, including international law, regard custom as a primary, although not exclusive, source of law. In such legal traditions, courts enforce customary rules as if they had been enacted by the proper legislative authority.[1] There are relatively few principles that govern the formation of customary law. As mentioned above, the theory of customary law defines custom as a practice that emerges outside of legal constraints, and which individuals and organizations spontaneously follow in the course of their interactions out of a sense of legal obligation. Gradually, individual, group, or state actors embrace norms that they view as requisite to their collective well-being.

According to traditional theories, an enforceable custom emerges from two formative elements: (1) a quantitative element consisting of a general or emerging practice; and (2) a qualitative element reflected in the belief that the norm generates a desired social outcome.

1.1. The Quantitative Element

The quantitative requirements for the formation of customary law concern both the length of time and the universality of the emerging practice. Regarding time, there is generally no universal minimum duration for the emergence of customary rules. Customary rules have evolved from both immemorial practice and single acts. Still, French jurisprudence has traditionally required the passage of forty years for the emergence of an international custom, whereas German doctrine has generally required thirty years (Tunkin 1961; Mateesco 1947). Naturally, the longer the formative stage of custom, the less likely it is for custom to effectively provide a viable substitute for formal law or treaty agreements, and to adapt to changing circumstances over time. Regarding the condition of universality, international legal theory is ambivalent. Charney (1986) suggests that the system of international relations is analogous to a world of individuals in the state of nature, dismissing the idea that unanimous consent by all participants is required before binding customary law is formed. Rather than universality, well-accepted restatements of international law refer to consistency and generality (D'Amato 1971; Brownlie 1990). Where it is impossible to identify a general practice because of fluctuations in behavior, the consistency requirement is not met. Similarly, more recent cases in international law restate the universality requirement in terms of increasing and widespread acceptance, allowing special consideration for emerging general norms (or local clusters of spontaneous default rules) that are expected to become widespread over time. With regard to rules at the national or local level, the varying pace at which social norms are transformed suggests that no general time or consistency requirement can be established as an across-the-board condition for the validity of a custom. Some variance in individual observation of the practice should be expected because of the stochastic origin of social norms. A flexible time requirement is particularly necessary in situations of rapid flux, where exogenous changes are likely to affect the incentive structure of the underlying relationship. In Chapter 11 we will consider these issues for the appropriate design of customary processes, providing guidance in the judicial task of adjudicating customary rules, with respect to both issues of timing and sufficient consistency of application.

1.2. The Qualitative Element

The second formative element of a customary rule is generally identified by the phrase *opinio iuris ac necessitatis*, which describes a widespread belief in the desirability of the norm and the general conviction that the practice represents an essential norm of social conduct. This element is often defined in terms of necessary and obligatory convention (Kelsen 1939 and 1945; D'Amato 1971; Walden 1977). The traditional formulation of *opinio iuris ac necessitatis* is problematic because of its circularity. It is quite difficult to conceptualize that law can be born from a practice which is already believed to be required by law. The traditional requirement that the states involved must believe in the normative principle embedded in the emerging practice (*opinio iuris*) may be appraised as a belief of social obligation, arising in response to game inefficiencies, to support behavioral rules that avoid aggregate losses from strategic behavior.[2]

2. Custom in Practice: How Custom Works

Judicial recognition of spontaneous norms amounts to a declaratory, as opposed to a constitutive, function that treats custom as a legal fact. The legal system finds the law by recognizing social norms, but does not create the law. The most notable illustration is the system of international law, where, absent a central legislative authority, custom stands next to treaties as a primary source of law. Specifically, Article 38(1) of the Statute of the

International Court of Justice and the Restatement § 102 of the Foreign Relations Law of the United States support this notion.[3]

Whenever they are granted legitimate status in a legal system, customary rules are usually given the same effect as other primary sources of law. Although often subordinate to formal legislation, customary rules derive their force from the concurrence of a uniform practice and a subjective belief that adherence to them is obligatory (*opinio iuris*), without necessarily being formally incorporated into any written body of law (Walden 1977). In this setting, they are usually classified as "immaterial" sources of law (Brownlie 1990). This notion implies that custom remains the actual source of law even after its judicial recognition. For this reason, the judicial decisions that recognize a custom offer only persuasive evidence of its existence and do not themselves become sources of law. In turn, this prevents the principle of *stare decisis* from crystallizing customary law.

Modern legal systems generally recognize customary rules that have emerged either within the confines of positive legislation (*consuetudo secundum legem*) or in areas that are not disciplined by positive law (*consuetudo praeter legem*). Where custom is in direct conflict with legislation (*custom contra legem*), the latter normally prevails. In some instances, however, a custom supersedes prior legislation (*abrogative custom*), and some arguments have been made in support of emerging practices that conflict with obsolete provisions of public international law (*desuetudo*, or abrogative practice) (Parisi 1998 and 2000).

2.1. Articulation

As discussed above, custom is generally formed through the actions of individuals, groups, or states. Statements and expressions of belief of, however, can also play a role in the formation of custom. Theories under which statements and expressions of belief play a role in custom formation are called articulation theories. These theories apply in the context of international law. D'Amato (1971 and forthcoming) considers articulation as a formative element of international customary law. In D'Amato, this element operates in conjunction with state practice and abstention.

According to articulation theories, in the process of ascertaining the qualitative element of *opinio iuris*, the states' statements and expressions of belief should be attentively considered. In the process of custom formation, individuals and states can signal which rules they intend to follow by articulating norms that they would agree to be bound by. Articulation gives some tangibility and objectivity to the otherwise subjective and intangible element of *opinio iuris*, allowing belief to be expressed before or in conjunction with customary action. To avoid the effect of biased articulations, these theories suggest that greater weight should be given to beliefs that have been expressed prior to the emergence of a conflict. In the model discussed in Chapter 11, articulation provides a way for states to precommit to the content and interpretation of an emerging custom. The binding effects and enforceability of the custom would depend on the development of state practice, but articulation would provide a focal point facilitating the coordination of states on a given emerging practice. We will discuss articulation theories and their impact on custom formation in much greater depth in Chapter 11.

2.2. Change in Custom: The Persistent Objector and Subsequent Objector Doctrines

Although custom can create binding rules on all participants, exceptions to the universality rule are present in the process of customary law formation. States may attempt to gain exemption from rules of general customary law by opposing a custom. What is the effect of a custom that is not universally followed by the relevant set of individuals or states? There are two legal doctrines that address these situations: the persistent objector and subsequent objector doctrines.

The persistent objection doctrine is the result of claims brought by states arguing that persistent objection to an emerging rule of customary law should provide objector states an opportunity to gain an exemption from the rule. These claims led to the recognition of a principle known as the persistent objector doctrine, which gives objecting states an opportunity to avoid, partially or entirely, the binding force of an international norm by objecting to it. Much of the recent international law literature attempts to limit the scope of the persistent objection doctrine. The analysis in Chapter 12 shows that states that face high costs in complying with custom can control level of custom formation. These results may provide a rationale for a qualified application of the persistent objection doctrine, consistent with the position held in the recent literature, to avoid that a relatively small number of high costs states may block the emergence of custom.

The subsequent objection doctrine applies when states attempt to depart from an already established rule of customary law, as opposed to objecting to the rule during its emergence, as in the persistent objector case. Under the subsequent objector doctrine, states can gain an exemption to depart from an existing rule of customary law by securing the acquiescence of other states. The effect of the subsequent objector doctrine on the process of formation and evolution of customary law will be discussed in great depth in Chapter 12. As it will be seen, many different outcomes are possible under this doctrine.

⅏ 3. The Economics of Customary Law

Customary law has been the object of study in both the economic and philosophical literature. Recent scholarship has addressed this topic building on the foundations of institutionalism. These contributions assume that states rationally pursue their own interests in their international relations, interests that often require international cooperation. Abbott (1989) considers the "demand" for international cooperation, analyzing the benefits that international rules and organizations provide. On the "supply" side, the mechanisms of custom and treaty formation provide important instruments through which beneficial international cooperation can be achieved.

In the law and economics literature, one important discussion concerns the proper domain of custom among the sources of legal order. In academic discussions, customary law has many supporters but also many critics. Besides the commonly criticized problems of inaccessibility and inelegant fragmentation, critics often denounce the limited reach of customary rules in a modern world with heterogeneous players. Most notably, Goldsmith and Posner deviate from institutionalism primarily in their skepticism about the role of law in international cooperation. With respect to customary law, Goldsmith and Posner (1999 and 2005) have questioned the notion of *opinion iuris* and the resulting circular explanation of the binding nature of customary law, providing a more complex formulation of the factors that lead states to adhere to international custom. According to Goldsmith and Posner, customary law is a relevant source of international law to the extent that it creates state reliance. The reasons for state compliance with custom, however, should be searched elsewhere. Goldsmith and Posner explain compliance with custom by considering a number of factors that are consistent with their view of states' interest-oriented behavior—factors that range from coercion to states' mere coincidence of interests. The analysis carried out in Chapter 10 considers the extent to which coincidence of interests (or lack thereof) affects the formation of customary law in a number of possible scenarios. Kontorovich (2006) is also skeptical of the ability of customary international law to generate efficient rules when a large number of heterogeneous states are involved. There are many factual scenarios, it is suggested, that remain outside the possible reach of spontaneous norms of customary law. The analysis carried out in Chapter 12 considers some of the rules that are used in public international law to reconcile the needs and partially inconsistent practices of states and shows how custom may emerge in a heterogeneous world.

Supporters of customary law address the public choice dimension of the process of customary law formation. Customary rules can be regarded as an implied and often nonverbalized exercise of direct legislation by the members of society. Rules of customary law, similar to social norms, originate from decentralized processes determining their content and scope of application (Ellickson 1991). A fundamental insight of the economic analysis of law is the notion that legal sanctions are "prices" set for given categories of legally relevant behavior. One common objection to such sanction-as-prices metaphor is that legal systems cannot set efficient prices, because there is no market process that generates them. From a law and economics perspective, customary law can be viewed as a process for generating legal rules that is analogous to a price mechanism in a partial equilibrium framework (Cooter 1994b).

In the following three chapters we contribute to this literature, considering three fundamental moments in the process of emergence and evolution of customary law. In Chapter 10 we discuss the formative conditions of customary law. We consider the roles played by role-reversibility and stochastic ignorance in the formation of custom. These conditions are shown to minimize the strategic bias of individual choice on social cooperation. Under role-reversibility, each participant in a process of customary law formation maximizes his expected payoff, knowing the status quo at the time of the action as well as the ex ante probabilities about his what role he will play in future time periods. In contrast, under stochastic ignorance, players make their choices under a veil of uncertainty. Without the role-specific context influencing the judgment of the individual, cooperative customs emerging under stochastic ignorance are more likely to be close to first-best than are customs chosen under conditions of role-reversibility.

In Chapter 11 we model the process of customary law formation under different regimes. We start by considering a traditional model of customary law where legal rules emerge out of past practice. Once established by practice, legal customs enjoy reciprocal application. Our model reveals the limits of the process of custom formation when choices are sequential and players know their roles at the time of strategy selection. After studying the effect of reciprocity, we examine the effects of "articulation" theories, which allow players to commit publicly to a strategy before their respective roles are unveiled. The welfare analysis of the alternative mechanisms of custom formation reveals the advantages and limits of the various processes of customary law formation.

In Chapter 12 we discuss the process by which customary rules can change over time. Although customary law is capable of creating universally binding rules, the rules that govern its formation allow parties to gain an exemption from emerging norms of customary law by remaining persistent objectors. This form of objection requires the objecting parties to take express action to oppose an emerging practice by making its objections widely known before the practice solidifies for others into a binding rule of custom. After the custom is formed the opportunity to express an objection or depart from the custom produces different effects. An exemption from the binding custom is obtained only to the extent to which the prospective beneficiaries of the rule acquiesce to the departure. We model the effects of persistent objector and subsequent objector doctrines in the formation and change of customary law when heterogeneous parties are involved. By noting the ability of low cost states to block changes in custom already in place, our analysis partially supports those who worry about the inertia of custom in a world of technological change (McGinnis and Somin 2007), advocating a qualified application of the persistent and subsequent objection doctrines.

TEN

Fostering the Emergence of Customary Law*

NOTABLE SCHOLARS HAVE CONSIDERED the conditions under which principles of justice can emerge spontaneously through voluntary interactions and exchanges between members of a group. As in a contractarian setting, customary law formation relies on a voluntary process through which members of a community develop rules that govern their social interactions by voluntarily adhering to emerging behavioral standards. Ullmann-Margalit (1977) suggests that optimal social norms emerge under conditions of "role-reversibility." Harsanyi (1955) and Rawls (1971) suggest that optimal social norms emerge through the interaction of individual actors with "impersonal" preferences. The impersonality requirement for individual preferences is satisfied given "stochastic ignorance" about the future—decision makers have an identical chance of finding themselves in any one of the possible initial social positions, and each rationally chooses a set of rules to maximize his expected welfare.[1]

Although earlier work has considered the emergence of norms and customs for coordination problems (Young 1993 and 1998; Bowles and Gintis 2001), much remains to be done to understand the conditions that foster the emergence and sustainability of efficient custom for cooperation problems. Recent scholarship has reached widely divergent conclusions as to whether custom is capable of generating welfare-enhancing rules. Some argue that custom should be held presumptively efficient, and that courts should recognize and adjudicate such practices (Cooter 1994b and 1996). Others recognize the potential limits of customary law, identifying the conditions under which customs may be welfare-enhancing (Parisi 1995 and 1998). Still others reach less optimistic conclusions respecting the ability of customary law to generate efficient, binding rules (Goldsmith and Posner 1999).[2]

---

* This chapter is based on an article previously published as Fon, Vincy and Francesco Parisi, "Role Reversibility, Stochastic Ignorance, and Social Cooperation," *Journal of Socio-Economics* 37: 1061–1075 (2008).

In this chapter, we compare custom formation in the specific context of a cooperation problem, under the alternative environments of role-reversibility and stochastic ignorance. The quantitative element of a custom is given by a behavioral pattern that emerges through the independent or interdependent actions or statements of individuals, each of whom pursues his self-interest. We focus on the optimal choices of individuals under two perspectives, role-reversibility and stochastic ignorance, in the absence of preexisting customs or social structure. Individual choices concur to the formation of shared behavioral patterns and constitute the ingredients of emerging custom. Once a behavioral regularity is observed in the face of a cooperation problem, parties' expectations are shaped accordingly. The emerged behavioral standard becomes at that point the expected response in future similar circumstances. Along with the existing literature, we assume that, once emerged, custom operates as an effective constraint on behavior.[3]

In this context, we consider a scenario in which parties initially choose their course of action in the absence of preexisting customs. Parties know that their behavior or statements in the initial stage may lead to customs that bind future behavior. Parties thus select actions that incorporate the discounted flow of costs and benefits triggered by their initial actions. Under conditions of role-reversibility, the status quo is known to each agent at the time of the action, but the actual roles in future time periods are known only on a probabilistic basis. Actors maximize their expected payoffs based on their ex ante probabilistic information about future interactions. Under conditions of stochastic ignorance, players make their choices under a Harsanyi-type veil of uncertainty. Each agent decides what to do before knowing the status quo and without knowing which role he will play in the future. Rather, he maximizes his expected payoff based on his ex ante probabilistic information about possible future roles. We examine the conditions under which the privately rational choices of individual parties approach the social optimum.

The regimes of role-reversibility and stochastic ignorance are both capable of reducing the strategic bias of parties' choices by separating decision makers from the immediate consequences of their actions. However, stochastic ignorance and role-reversibility impact the parties' effort and participation incentives differently. Parties are more likely to endorse and commit to follow a cooperative custom when choosing under stochastic ignorance than when choosing under role-reversibility. Also, under stochastic ignorance, parties are willing to accept a higher compliance burden than they would accept under role-reversibility. This suggests that stochastic ignorance is more effective than role-reversibility in fostering compliance efforts and participation in cooperative customs.

We further discuss the effect of group size on the emergence of custom and show that variations in group size have different effects upon the two regimes of stochastic ignorance and role-reversibility. Under both regimes cooperative customs are more likely to emerge when individuals interact in smaller groups, but stochastic ignorance and role-reversibility induce different effort levels.

1. Formation of Custom

As mentioned above, the social processes that produce customs and social norms rely on the voluntary participation of the members of a community. By voluntarily adhering to emerging behavioral standards, individual members contribute to the development of rules that govern their social interaction. These social processes of rule formation differ from traditional lawmaking processes in that the resulting rules emerge gradually through the independent and spontaneous adherence of community members to customs, rather than through political deliberation.

The literature on customary law focuses on noncontractual mechanisms and considers situations that are more easily governed by spontaneous law. In an environment characterized by perfect incentive alignment, contracts and relationships are self-enforcing (Klein 1996). In such an environment, cooperation results both in one-shot settings and in repeated settings in which players are faced with high discount factors. With perfect incentive alignment, no one has any reason to challenge emerging cooperative customs ex ante or to violate such customs ex post, and there is no need for legal enforcement.

When incentives are not aligned but parties face symmetric payoffs, customs that promote cooperation and maximize group welfare also maximize individual expected payoffs. Ex ante, parties will not withhold support for cooperative customs, for these customs maximize the expected well-being of all group members.[4] Each individual has an incentive to agree to a set of rules maximizing his expected share of wealth, such that the aggregate welfare of the group is maximized.[5] In this context,

Cooter (1994a and 1994b) suggests that customs will evolve successfully when the ex ante individual incentives are aligned with the collective public interest. Cooter (1994b: 224) calls this proposition the "alignment theorem."

The same alignment of private and social cooperation incentives is believed to be present when parties reverse their future roles or when they choose a course of action under a veil of stochastic ignorance. We analyze this claim and verify the extent to which an alignment of private and social incentives is present. The analysis partially supports the conventional wisdom, stressing that strategic behavior may undermine incentive alignment and cooperative outcomes when customs necessitate costly compliance efforts.[6]

In the presence of asymmetric players, difficulties arise ex ante, when players must decide whether to endorse emerging customs and to participate in emerging customary practices. Traditionally, strategic preference revelation is viewed as a hindrance to the spontaneous emergence of cooperation. This problem is believed to be minimized in situations of role-reversibility or stochastic ignorance with asymmetric players (Parisi 1995). With respect to role-reversibility, Fuller (1969: 24) observes that frequent role . . . changes foster the emergence of mutually recognized and accepted duties. Fuller points out that "in a society of economic traders . . . the members of such a society enter direct and voluntary relationships of exchange. . . . Finally, economic traders frequently exchange roles, now selling, now buying. The duties that arise out of their exchanges are therefore reversible, not only in theory but in practice."[7] Similarly, stochastic ignorance is believed to induce each member to agree to a set of rules that benefits the entire group, thus maximizing an individual member's expected share of the wealth. Conditions of role-reversibility and stochastic ignorance, coupled with behavioral standards that generate disincentives to adopt opportunistic double standards,[8] are therefore believed to foster the emergence of optimal custom via spontaneous processes.[9]

In the following, we formally analyze these claims, giving separate treatment to the two conditions of role-reversibility and stochastic ignorance.

2. Optimal Customs for a Cooperation Problem

In our stylized setting, cooperative customs impose costs on certain groups of individuals and create benefits for others. We adopt the Benthamite criterion of welfare and define efficient custom as that which maximizes the social welfare function, that is, the sum of all players' payoffs for all time periods. Our choice of a framework of aggregate payoff maximization—rather than some social welfare function using multiplicative or weighted utilities—is driven by the desire to isolate the effects of strategic behavior in the formation of custom. Because aggregate payoffs for all players is what matters for a Benthamite social problem, the relative frequency with which each player is on the receiving side rather than on the giving side of the interaction is unimportant. Not all efficient custom is likely to enjoy the support and compliance of all members of society, given the possible uneven distribution of costs and benefits across different members of the group. We therefore examine the conditions under which efficient customs hold among a group of players.

Consider the problem of a cooperative custom in the absence of a preexisting rule. At any time, voluntary participation in the cooperative custom imposes costs on some parties while conferring benefits on others. For illustration, imagine the case of a customary rule of rescue: one party faces an emergency while other parties face a decision whether to voluntarily rescue the party in need. We assume that rescues yield a net social gain, such that the cost of the rescue activity is lower than its benefit. This ensures that rescues are socially desirable.

In each future period the cooperative custom becomes relevant, as one party requires rescue by the others. Let e be the level of effort expended by others in fulfillment of the customary rule of rescue. Assume that ae^2 is the total social cost of rescue borne by all giving parties and that be is the total benefit enjoyed by the single receiving party. Hence, $be - ae^2$ is the social net benefit in each period.

Given N parties in each period, and assuming that only one party needs help, the probability of an individual party being on the receiving side is $1/N$. As the sole beneficiary of the customary rule of rescue, a party receives benefit be. Thus the probability is $1 - 1/N$ that a party is called to undertake the rescue in fulfillment of the custom. All $N - 1$ members of the rescue mission share the cost of rescue ae^2 equally, each paying $ae^2/(N - 1)$.

We assume that all parties are risk-neutral. Given the individual participant's effort e under the rescue rule, the social net benefit (i.e., the benefit to the rescued individual net of the total costs faced by the rescuers) in each period becomes

$$SNB = be - ae^2$$

Because the Benthamite social welfare function sums the expected payoffs for all players for all time periods, the probabilities of each individual being on the receiving or giving side become irrelevant in the social problem. The use of ex post frequencies instead of ex ante probabilities or expectations would not change the solution to the social problem.

Assume that the cost and benefit functions are the same in every period from now till infinity, and that the social discount rate is r^S. Then the total discounted value of social payoffs from future periods is

$$P^S = \sum_{t=0}^{\infty} \frac{1}{(1+r^S)^t}(be - ae^2) = \frac{1+r^S}{r^S} \cdot (be - ae^2) \qquad 10.1$$

It is readily seen that the social optimal level of effort e^S is determined by equating social marginal cost and marginal benefit in each period. That is, the socially optimal level of effort for each participant is given by

$$e^S = \frac{b}{2a} \qquad 10.2$$

3. Formation of Custom under Role-Reversibility

The emergence of customs relies on the independent participation choices made by members of the community. Individual group members decide whether to engage in a custom-creating activity and, if they do engage, how much effort to expend toward such activity. When some members comply with a custom-creating activity, other members of the group benefit.

The fact that compliance with a given cooperative custom creates total benefits exceeding total costs does not guarantee that the cooperative custom will be followed by the relevant individual decision maker. We therefore consider parties' private incentives in order to identify the conditions under which efficient custom can emerge through the voluntary interaction of members of society.

Under conditions of role-reversibility, players engage in actions knowing that future time periods may hold a reversal of roles with other players. The status quo is known to each agent at the time of the action, but the actual role in a future time period is known only on a probabilistic basis. Actors maximize their expected payoffs based on their ex ante probabilistic information about future roles. Because the choice of action in compliance with the cooperative custom rests exclusively with the active player, we concentrate on the actions of those who are called to uphold the cooperative custom by exerting effort in the current period.

3.1. The Private Problem under Role-Reversibility

Assume that each of N parties has the discount rate r, $r > 0$. In period 0, consider a representative of the $N - 1$ parties who are called upon to exert effort to rescue a single party in need of help. A representative rescuer assumes that all parties participate and share the social marginal rescue cost equally.[10] Hence, assuming joint participation in the rescue by all others, the individual rescuer bears cost $ae^2/(N - 1)$ while the receiving party derives benefit be.

After period 0, periods 1 to infinity include the possibility of role reversal. Previous rescuers may need help from others and vice versa. Looking at the uncertain future, each party estimates the probability that he will benefit from the emerging customary rule of rescue. We assume that given uncertainty, heterogeneous parties face homogeneous ex ante expectations. In spite of the possible ex post differences in frequency of rescue, each individual estimates the ex ante probability based on group size. This allows us to concentrate on the impact of group size on the emergence of custom.

In a group of size N, the party reasons that the ex ante probability of his benefiting from the emerging cooperative custom is $1/N$. When he is the beneficiary, he enjoys the social benefit be. The current rescuer may also be called upon to rescue again in the future, with ex ante probability $1 - 1/N$. When this happens, the giving party again shares the social cost of rescue equally with all other rescuers, facing cost $ae^2/(N - 1)$.

Hence, in each future period, the party's expected payoff is given by

$$\frac{1}{N}be - \left(1 - \frac{1}{N}\right)\frac{ae^2}{N - 1} = \frac{1}{N}(be - ae^2) \qquad 10.3$$

With the discount rate r, each of the $N - 1$ parties will choose an effort level to maximize total expected payoffs over all periods. This total payoff includes the cost incurred in the current period and the total discounted value of expected payoffs from future periods:

$$\max_{e} P = -\frac{ae^2}{N - 1} + \frac{1}{r} \cdot \frac{1}{N}(be - ae^2) \qquad 10.4$$

The optimal level of effort e^R under conditions of role-reversibility is then

$$e^R = \frac{(N-1)b}{2a(rN+N-1)} \qquad 10.5$$

For a party confronting the choice of whether to participate in the rescue with an initial cost in period 0, if he chooses to participate in the rescue, his private optimal level of effort is e^R.

To investigate whether the party should participate in the rescue, consider the participation constraint. In our example, the participation constraint for the rescue rule is the payoff that the party would obtain if living in a world where no rescue rules existed. More generally, the participation constraint represents the status quo value prior to the establishment of a cooperative custom.

Substituting the optimal level of effort e^R in (10.5) into the objective function P^R in (10.4) provides P^R, the optimal participation payoff for the party:

$$P^R \equiv P(e^R) = \frac{b^2(N-1)}{4arN(rN+N-1)} \qquad 10.6$$

In order for the party to partake in the venture, the participation constraint $P^R \geq k$, for some k, should be met. Thus, the higher the value of P^R, the more likely the party is to participate in the rescue venture. This means that customary rules of rescue that impose lower participation costs (a) are more likely to attract initial participation.[11] Likewise, when the potential benefits (b) from the rescue rule are high, participation will be more likely. The party's discount rate (r) is also relevant for the participation constraint. A lower discount rate means that the initial rescuer attaches greater value to the benefit of potential rescues in the future, making her more willing to join the group.

A change in group size (N) has two countervailing effects. First, a larger group size lowers the immediate cost of participation by spreading the initial cost among more people. This encourages participation. Second, in larger groups there is a greater probability that the initial rescuer will be involved again on the giving side of a rescue before enjoying the benefits of a potential rescue in his favor. This discourages participation. The second effect dominates the first.[12] Thus, when the number of potential participants increases, it is less likely that a potential rescuer will join the group.

3.2. The Efficiency of Custom under Role-Reversibility

To evaluate the efficiency of custom emerged under initial conditions of role-reversibility, compare the privately optimal effort level e^R from (10.5) to the socially optimal level e^S from (10.2) and get

$$e^R = \frac{(N-1)b}{2a(rN+N-1)} < e^S = \frac{b}{2a}$$

This is true because $N-1 < rN+N-1$. Thus, the privately optimal level of effort e^R under role-reversibility is a fraction of the socially optimal level of effort e^S.

4. Formation of Custom under Stochastic Ignorance

The paradigm of choice under stochastic ignorance has often been examined in conjunction with the emergence of social norms and principles of justice. Harsanyi's (1955) "veil of uncertainty" and Rawls's (1971) "veil of ignorance" both suggest that optimal social norms can emerge through the interaction of individual actors with "impersonal" preferences. The impersonality requirement for individual preferences means that all decision makers have an equal chance of finding themselves in any one of the initial social positions. In such an environment, to maximize their own expected welfare, individuals will rationally choose a set of rules that also maximizes the well-being of society at large. In the following section, we examine the process of cooperative custom formation in which individuals can endorse a custom before knowing whether the custom will first benefit or burden them at the time its application becomes necessary.

In the following exercise, the paradigm of stochastic ignorance differs from the previously examined paradigm of role-reversibility in that the choice takes place before the cooperative custom is applied in practice. In our rescue example, individuals have an opportunity to discuss and reach a consensus on the appropriate rescue custom within the group. Hence, under the paradigm of role-reversibility, parties know their current role when participating in the process of custom formation without full knowledge of their roles in each of the future periods. Under stochastic ignorance, however, individuals articulate their preferred cooperative custom without yet knowing which role they will be playing when the custom is first applied or which role they will be playing in future periods.

4.1. The Private Problem under Stochastic Ignorance

The notions of role-reversibility and stochastic ignorance have been treated extensively by philosophers and political theorists. Our analysis focuses on the informational differences between these two paradigms. The stochastic ignorance in our model takes the form of a Harsanyi-type "veil of uncertainty," where each agent chooses before knowing which role she will play in the future. Agents maximize their expected payoffs based on their ex ante probabilistic information about future roles.

Agents acting in a role-reversibility situation know a bit more than those acting under stochastic ignorance. Once the veil of ignorance is lifted, informational differences disappear. In our model, the differences between role-reversibility and stochastic ignorance are captured by a representative first-period difference between the two maximization problems. The formulation of the stochastic ignorance problem is similar to the previous role-reversibility problem except that there are no current period costs or benefits, as parties adhere to a cooperative custom chosen ex ante. As before, each party assumes the ex ante probability of being a receiving party to be $1/N$ and the probability of being on the giving end to be $1 - 1/N$. When the party is on the receiving end, the benefit gained is be, and a party on the giving end shares the rescuing cost with all other parties equally, facing cost $ae^2/(N - 1)$.[13]

The expected payoff of each party equals the expression given in (10.3). Discounting future payoffs with a discount rate r, the problem confronted by the party is

$$\max_{e} P = \frac{1}{r} \cdot \frac{1}{N}(be - ae^2) \qquad \text{10.7}$$

The optimal level of effort e^I under stochastic ignorance is given by

$$e^I = \frac{b}{2a} \qquad \text{10.8}$$

Substituting e^I into the objective function of the maximization problem (10.7) gives the optimal expected payoff P^I, where

$$P^I \equiv P(e^I) = \frac{b^2}{4arN} \qquad \text{10.9}$$

Consider the participation constraint $P^I \geq k$ for some k. From (10.9) it is easy to see that P^I increases when b increases, or when $a, r,$ or N decreases.

Thus, the qualitative impacts of these parameters on the issue of participation in the case of stochastic ignorance are similar to that in the case of role-reversibility. Further, because the party does not face an up-front compliance cost under stochastic ignorance, it is easier for the participation constraint to hold when choices are made under the veil of uncertainty, ceteris paribus. Comparing the optimal participation payoff under role-reversibility P^R in (10.6) and the optimal participation payoff under stochastic ignorance P^I in (10.9), it can be seen that $P^R < P^I$. In our example, this means that it is more likely that the party will adhere to a customary rule of rescue, if decided ex ante under stochastic ignorance, than to join in an actual rescue venture with the expectation of future role-reversibility.

4.2. The Efficiency of Custom under Stochastic Ignorance

The above results confirm the conventional wisdom that ex ante choices made under stochastic ignorance are socially optimal. Comparing the privately optimal level of effort chosen under stochastic ignorance e^I in (10.8) with the social optimal level of effort e^S in (10.2), we see that they are identical. Given the uncertain future and the absence of immediate costs, parties are willing to articulate cooperative customs that maximize their expected well-being; by doing so, they maximize the well-being of society at large. This convergence of private and social incentives was not obtained under conditions of role-reversibility, except in the limited case in which parties had zero discount rates.

These results shed light on an important difference between the frameworks of role-reversibility and stochastic ignorance examined in this chapter. When a cooperative custom is applied, it imposes costs on certain groups of individuals and creates benefits for others. Although efficient cooperative customs yield benefits exceeding the costs that they generate, under role-reversibility not all such customs would induce widespread support and compliance by members of society, given the uneven initial burden of costs across members of the group. As shown in our model, no such strategic withholding of participation occurs when parties choose under conditions of stochastic ignorance, for the stochastic ignorance scenario avoids the hold-up problems that are present in the first period of the role-reversibility framework.

These differences have important implications for designing institutions that foster the emergence of efficient custom. Whenever feasible, consensus on given customs should be promoted ex ante, rather than when a situation requiring the application of the cooperative custom is imminent. Likewise, if third parties who are not involved in the current period may later be affected by the custom, their opinions on a given issue may be valuable indicators of truthful social preferences. This is because the position of third-party spectators is very similar to those who choose under stochastic ignorance. Policy design should assign greater weight to the opinions of current neutral spectators, because the views of those directly involved on the giving or receiving sides of the cooperative custom are likely biased or short-sighted.

5. The Relevance of Group Size, Coordination Problems, and Discount Rates

The sociological and experimental literature emphasizes group size and how closely knit the community is when studying conditions for the emergence of customs.[14] We thus use our results to study further the sensitivity of the role-reversibility and stochastic ignorance equilibria with respect to group size.

5.1. The Case of Stochastic Ignorance

Recall that the social optimum and the private optimum for the stochastic ignorance case were identical: $e^I = e^S = b2a$. An increase in the number of parties has no impact on the privately optimal level of effort e^I. That is, group size does not matter for determining the optimal effort level under the stochastic ignorance case. In our rescue example, this means that parties would be inclined to articulate efficient rules of rescue regardless of group size. However, when the parties face an opportunity cost while endorsing a cooperative custom, group size may affect the participation decision. In other words, although group size may affect willingness to participate in the emerging custom, it does not affect the choice of effort after joining the emerging custom. From the optimal value P^I given in (10.9), we see that as group size increases, it is less likely that the participation constraint will be satisfied. Hence, the more parties there are, the less likely it is that parties will endorse an emerging cooperative custom. These findings are consistent with the established wisdom in the sociological and anthropological literature, according to which small and close-knit communities are more fertile environments for the emergence of custom under conditions of stochastic ignorance.

5.2. The Case of Role-Reversibility

A similar investigation can be carried out respecting the effect of group size when parties choose custom under conditions of role-reversibility. Recall that the privately optimal level of effort e^R under role-reversibility is a fraction of the socially optimal level of effort e^S. Differentiating e^R in (10.5) as regards the number of parties N, we have

$$\frac{\partial e^R}{\partial N} = \frac{2abr}{4a^2(rN + N - 1)^2} > 0$$

As the number of parties involved increases, the optimal level of effort chosen under role-reversibility increases. Larger groups allow more spreading of the initial cost, thereby minimizing the strategic behavior of initial participants and making them willing to undertake a higher effort level. Furthermore, it is easily shown that

$$\lim_{N \to \infty} e^R = \frac{b}{2a(r+1)} < e^S$$

This suggests that the impact of group size on effort level is limited and that, no matter how large the group, the effort level e^R falls short of the socially optimal e^S.

Finally, although group size plays a favorable role in the effort choice, it decreases the likelihood of participation to the emerging cooperative custom.[15] Hence, as the number of participants becomes larger, it becomes less likely that a party will join the group. This is because the probability of becoming a beneficiary of the emerging custom decreases with group size, and, given an opportunity cost in participation and the presence of immediate compliance costs, this may bring participation below the threshold of convenience. However, a party who decides to join the group is willing to expend more effort in compliance with the cooperative custom, for compliance costs are spread among more participants.

5.3. Group Size and the Emergence of Custom

The previous analysis reveals that an increase in group size is generally detrimental to the formation of custom. That is, custom formation is harder in large groups. These findings are consistent with well-known results from the public good literature. Our results improve understanding of the traditional literature, revealing that the environments of role-reversibility and stochastic ignorance have different degrees of sensitivity to increases in group size, creating different effort and participation incentives. Comparing optimal effort and participation under role-reversibility and stochastic ignorance, we see that

$$e^R < e^I \quad \text{and} \quad P^R < P^I$$

Participation constraints are more likely satisfied and effort levels are higher under stochastic ignorance than under role-reversibility. This suggests that for the purpose of fostering greater compliance efforts and broader participation in custom, stochastic ignorance provides a more fertile environment than role-reversibility.

Similarly, group size has different effects in the two regimes of stochastic ignorance and role-reversibility.[16] Under both stochastic ignorance and role-reversibility, it is easier to encourage custom participation when individuals interact in smaller groups than larger ones. Group size, however, has a different impact on effort levels in the two regimes. Compliance efforts in regimes of role-reversibility are sensitive to changes in group size. No such impact is visible in regimes of stochastic ignorance, in which the willingness to expend effort is invariant to group size.

5.4. Coordination Problems and Evolutionary Traps in the Formation of Customs

The effect of group size should be revisited to consider possible coordination problems in the emergence of customs. The desirability of participation in an emerging custom depends on the expected participation by other group members. If the rescuer cannot rely on the support and widespread participation of other rescuers, the above results concerning the effects of group size on the participation constraint may be altered, given the lack of sharing of the initial cost in the first round. For example, if an initial rescuer must face the entire cost of the rescue in order to provide a good example, she may be less willing to undertake the rescue or may select a suboptimal level of effort to minimize the up-front cost.

To understand the boundaries of the first-mover participation problem, consider the limiting case in which the initial rescuer acts alone, with no opportunity to count on the support and cost-sharing of other community members. The initial rescuer may engage in the rescue to set a good example, with the expectation that such an example will be followed by others in subsequent time periods, yet at the time of rescue she incurs the full cost of the rescue mission. In this case, the problem of the party can be formulated as

$$\max_e P = -ae^2 + \frac{1}{r} \cdot \frac{1}{N}(be - ae^2)$$

The privately chosen level of effort $\tilde{e}$ is

$$\tilde{e} = \frac{b}{2a(rN+1)}$$

Clearly $\tilde{e}$ is less than e^S. In this case, group size has a detrimental effect on both the effort level and the participation constraint. As group size N increases, the privately optimal effort level $\tilde{e}$ goes down and it is harder to satisfy the participation constraint, for group size affects future benefits without reducing current cost.

This suggests that in the absence of a prior consensus on the desirability of a cooperative custom, those who wish to be pioneers in establishing a new custom face an initial private cost. Players are willing to face an initial cost in the expectation of a future benefit and would rationally undertake a rescue to avoid establishing a no-rescue custom that may harm them in the future. However, even in the face of desirable rescue customs, coordination problems may arise. With imperfect coordination, each member of the group might be willing to join the rescue if she could count on the participation of others but may withhold participation if uncertain about others' choices. This may lead to suboptimal effort and participation in establishing new custom. Another way to look at the issue is to think of it in terms of externalities. The action of the first-mover, if not supported by the immediate participation of others, would impose a private cost to and generate a social benefit partially internalized by the decision maker. The larger the initial cost and the less group sharing of such cost, the greater the amount of externality not internalized. The presence of externalities means that the initial action to establish a new cooperative custom is undertaken at a suboptimal level.

5.5. Discount Rates in the Formation of Custom

Our model of role-reversibility reveals that when a private party discounts the future less, the future expected benefits from the cooperative custom become larger to compensate for the cost faced in the current period. As the private discount rate approaches zero, the gap between private and social incentives closes: $e^R \to e^S$ if $r \to 0$. Hence the private optimum approaches the social optimum. A discrepancy between private and social optima may be exacerbated by an increase in the private discount rate, given the discounting of future benefits by private actors and the irrelevance of discount rates for the social problem. This result sheds light on the difficulties of generating optimal customary practices when individuals interact under role-reversibility and have limited time horizons and/or internalize only partially the benefits of current customs on subsequent generations.

In the case of stochastic ignorance, private discount rates play no role in the individual determination of effort level. This reveals that stochastic ignorance outcomes are much more robust to the presence of myopic agents. As a normative corollary, when myopic decision-making is likely to occur, it may be desirable to make agents choose under conditions of stochastic ignorance. Such a condition operates as a shield, insulating agents from their own myopic bias.

6. The Limits of Custom Formation

Existing literature shows that although the process of custom formation is often capable of supporting cooperative behavior by participating parties, individual participants may systematically fail to behave optimally. In addition, role-reversibility and stochastic ignorance are regarded as instrumental in facilitating the formation of efficient customs. In this chapter, we developed a model of custom formation to compare the environments provided by stochastic ignorance and role-reversibility, where each is designed to foster participation and optimal compliance to custom.

The results revealed the importance of timing with respect to a player's endorsement of an emerging cooperative custom relative to the time in which compliance with the custom becomes necessary. The main differences between the effects of role-reversibility and stochastic ignorance lie in the fact that role-reversible processes require a "first-mover" to trigger formation of the custom, which can take place only in a context where action is necessary. In such settings, actors' preferences and resulting actions are biased by the immediacy of the situation; thus, any cooperative custom that begins in such a context is unlikely to be first-best. In contrast, customs chosen under conditions of stochastic ignorance can be articulated in the abstract, outside the context of an imminent action. The parties are separated from the type of role-specific context that clouds and biases formation of custom among heterogeneous parties. Consequently, customs formed when parties face uncertainty about their future roles are, through expression of belief, more likely closer to first-best, and more likely to satisfy parties' participation constraints at any given time, than are customs chosen through initial action under conditions of role-reversibility. The economic model shows that the strength of both processes of custom formation depends on several environmental parameters.

We identified important differences between role-reversibility and stochastic ignorance. Several factors may limit the ability of these conditions to yield socially optimal custom. Among these factors, attention was given to the effect of group size, cost and benefits of custom participation, and private discount rates on the formation of custom. We examined the sensitivity of role-reversibility and stochastic ignorance to changes in group size. Participation in emerging customs is negatively affected by an increase in group size under both regimes. Compliance efforts, although negatively affected by group size in regimes of role-reversibility, are not affected when parties choose in regimes of stochastic ignorance. Role-reversible processes depend more crucially on the studied parameters than custom formation under stochastic ignorance and are thus less conducive to the emergence of efficient customs.

Next, in Chapter 11, we consider the role of articulation theories in addressing the identified problems of custom formation under uncertainty. Although parties do not know who will benefit first from the custom, they could face different expectations and probabilities of being on the giving or receiving side of the relationship. The analysis will unveil the relevance of different degrees of heterogeneity among members of a group for the emergence and evolution of efficient custom. We build on these results to consider conditions for sustainability of existing customs when group size increases and when groups become more heterogeneous.

Appendix

The problem facing a representative rescuer with role-reversibility is given as

$$\max_e P = -\frac{ae^2}{N-1} + \frac{1}{r} \cdot \frac{1}{N}(be - ae^2)$$

Note that the first-order necessary condition that defines the optimal level of effort $e^R = [(N-1)b]/[2a(rN+N-1)]$ is

$$\frac{-2ae}{N-1} + \frac{1}{rN}(b - 2ae) = 0$$

This condition can be rewritten as

$$\frac{1}{rN}(b - ae) = \frac{2ae}{N-1} + \frac{ae}{rN} \tag{10.10}$$

Hence, the optimal level of effort e^R must satisfy equation (10.10). Next, the optimal value function is found by substituting e^R in the objective function P:

$$P^R = P(e^R) = -\frac{ae^{R2}}{N-1} + \frac{1}{r} \cdot \frac{1}{N}(be^R - ae^{R2})$$

The envelope theorem then implies the following:

$$\begin{aligned}
\frac{\partial P^R}{\partial N} &= \frac{ae^{R2}}{(N-1)^2} - \frac{1}{rN^2}(be^R - ae^{R2}) \\
&= \frac{ae^{R2}}{(N-1)^2} - \frac{e^R}{N}\left(\frac{1}{rN}(b - ae^R)\right) \\
&= \frac{ae^{R2}}{(N-1)^2} - \frac{e^R}{N}\left(\frac{2ae^R}{N-1} + \frac{ae^R}{rN}\right)
\end{aligned}$$

The last equality holds because e^R is the solution to the first-order condition (10.10). Simplifying the last expression yields

$$\frac{\partial P^R}{\partial N} = ae^{R2}\left(\frac{1}{(N-1)^2} - \frac{2}{N(N-1)} - \frac{1}{rN^2}\right)$$

$$= \frac{ae^{R2}}{(N-1)^2 N^2 r}\left(Nr(2-N) - (N-1)^2\right) < 0$$

The last inequality holds because there are at least two parties involved: $N \geq 2$. Thus, the fewer parties there are in the group, the higher the optimal payoff from participating in the custom.

ELEVEN

Customary Law and Articulation Theories*

IN THIS CHAPTER WE EXTEND the analysis of Chapter 10 to consider new theories of customary law formation, with special emphasis on the role of articulation.[1] Under traditional customary law, a tenet of international law becomes a viable custom only when it is both (1) widespread in practice and (2) individually rational for each member in the relevant community to follow.

In the search for a rational choice theory of international law, legal scholars have recently criticized the traditional explanations of customary law for being tautological, nondescriptive of actual practice and unable to provide meaningful normative guidance in the adjudication of customary rules. Most recently, Goldsmith and Posner (1999 and 2000) and Kontorovich (2006) have critiqued traditional theories of customary law, suggesting in a number of ways that compliance with international law results from a variety of factors and that customs are followed out of a coincidence of interest, rather than a sense of legal obligation.[2] We begin considering the extent to which the coincidence of the states' normative interest is sufficient to yield efficient rules of customary law. In modeling the formation of customary rules, we pay close attention to the role played by a state's articulation of belief and the critical timing of articulation and action.

Through articulation, practice can be accompanied or even preceded by an expression of intent, which may let states signal how they might wish the custom to develop before any specific incidence of conflict takes place. The articulation component comes in the form of an "announcement" by states of their intentions—announcements that may take place by means of unilateral statements, as well as through bilateral or multilateral informal understandings. Under both versions of custom formation—those formed

---

* This chapter is based on an article previously published as Fon, Vincy, and Francesco Parisi, "International Customary Law and Articulation Theories: An Economic Analysis," *International Law and Management Review* 2: 201–33 (2007).

through articulation and those not—compliance with emerged norms is sustained, albeit imperfectly, by reputational constraints.

Within this setting, in this chapter we will see that while customs formed without articulation are often capable of supporting cooperative behavior by participating states, the content of such customs may systematically fall short of what might be obtainable through articulated customs. The key reason is that customs necessarily require a "first mover" for formation, and that can only take place in a context where action is necessary. In such settings, individuals' preferences (and resulting actions) are already biased by the immediacy of the situation, and thus any custom that begins in such a context is unlikely to be first best. In contrast, an articulated custom can commence in the abstract, outside of the context of an imminent emergency. States are thus separated from the type of role-specific context that can cloud and bias the formation of customs formed with and individual, rather than a state, as the "first mover." Consequently, articulated customs are much more likely to be closer to first-best, and are more likely to satisfy states' participation constraints at any given time than are nonarticulated customs. The economic model confirms that the strength of both types of custom depend on environmental parameters with predictable effects (such as the costs of custom compliance relative to the benefits obtained when other states' comply with the custom, discount rates, the number of participants, time delays, and uncertainty). Further, customs formed without articulation tend to depend more crucially on these parameters, and thus are much harder to support than are articulated customs.

The chapter is structured as follows. In Section 1, we present the traditional doctrines of customary law and model the traditional process of custom formation for the case of bilateral custom. In Section 2, we extend the bilateral custom model to the case of multilateral custom, and to situations of uncertainty and delay in the formation and recognition of an emerging custom. We assess how the participation and effort incentives of states are affected by the presence of such conditions. Participation and effort incentives assume particular importance for identifying the limits of the traditional customary processes in real-life conditions.

We revisit these limits in Section 3, examining the potential role of alternative doctrines and processes of customary law formation in mitigating the shortcomings of traditional customary law theory. Here, we introduce a variation in the process of custom formation, by allowing states to express their consensus over emerging rules of custom prior to the time of their action through practice (i.e., articulation). We model the process of custom formation under such alternative doctrines and identify the respective limits and advantages of such frameworks in different environmental settings.

1. A Model of Customary Law Formation

Although much is known about what types of outcomes are sustainable as a norm of behavior, much remains to be done to understand how such behavioral regularities emerge. In the following we address this issue, modeling the process of customary law formation under different legal doctrines and regimes.

According to the theory of customary law discussed in Chapter 9, a formative element of a customary rule is given by the qualitative element *opinio iuris ac necessitates*. This Latin phrase refers to the need that the customary practice (quantitative element) be followed out of a belief of legal, social, or moral obligation (qualitative element). Those who follow the custom should do so believing that it represents a necessary and obligatory convention (Kelsen 1939 and 1945; D'Amato 1971; Walden 1977). This formulation of *opinio iuris* has been criticized because of its circularity: customary law can be born from a practice only if the practice is already believed to be required by law. In this chapter we consider Goldsmith and Posner's (1999 and 2000) critique of *opinio iuris*, according to which rules of customary law emerge out of a coincidence of interest, rather than a sense of legal obligation. We build on this insightful critique to verify the extent to which the coincidence of the states' normative interest may indeed be sufficient to yield efficient rules of customary law.

Customary rules emerge from past practice. Prior to the consolidation of a practice into a binding custom, states engage in actions on a purely voluntary basis.[3] There are two main factors that influence an individual (or state) actor's choice to engage in a given action: (1) the immediate costs and benefits of the action (i.e., *circumstantial interest*); and (2) the interest that they may have in establishing a customary rule, which would bind for the future (i.e., *normative interest*).

What distinguishes an emerging custom from a mere usage is the expectation that the current practice may lead to a binding customary rule. Compliance with emerged norms of customary law is sustained by reputational constraints. Unilateral departures from established rules of custom impose reputational costs on the departing states. The expectation of reciprocal compliance contributes to influence the states' actions.

In the following analysis, we initially assume that compliance is ensured by these reputational constraints and later relax this assumption to allow for uncertainty and imperfect compliance. This allows us to concentrate on the "content" of the emerging norms under different mechanisms of custom formation.

The relative importance of circumstantial and normative interests in influencing a given action obviously depends on the specific situation. In some cases, the circumstantial interest is of decisive importance: states engage in a specific action due to their immediate interest (e.g., it is in their self-interest to do so at the present time), regardless of the expectation that such action may generate a binding rule for the future. In other cases, the normative interest dominates: states engage in a certain activity in order to establish a binding custom that will govern future interactions.[4]

Although in some situations the motives of action may converge, in other cases there is a possible tension between circumstantial and normative interests.[5] In the presence of such a conflict, the process of formation of customary law poses a cooperation problem. In this chapter we investigate the process of customary law formation in this group of situations. We assume that at each moment in time, the circumstantial interest of one state is in conflict with the commonly shared normative interests of all the states. More specifically, we consider the case of customary practices that, at each instance of practice, create costs on one state, while generating benefits to others. Such customary practices are desirable because the total benefits exceed the total costs incurred by the various states. We start considering the case of bilateral practices and will later extend the analysis to multilateral practices.

In each period, a state can expend a level of effort e to generate some benefit for another state. The social net payoff is the sum of costs and benefits for all states. Thus, the social net benefit from e is:

$$SNB = -ae^2 + be \qquad 11.1$$

Here, it is assumed that the marginal cost of effort is increasing: $MC = 2ae$ is an increasing function of e. The marginal benefit of effort is assumed constant and independent of e: $MB = b$. In each period, the social optimal level of effort e^S is determined by equating social marginal cost and marginal benefit. That is, the social optimum is given by:

$$e^S = \frac{b}{2a}. \qquad 11.2$$

We shall now consider the extent to which customary law processes are capable of approaching such social optimum. We shall start with a standard bilateral custom problem.

1.1. Formation of Custom: Bilateral Case

Consider the case of two states faced with a voluntary participation problem in the absence of an existing custom. Voluntary participation in a new practice would impose costs on one state while conferring benefits on another. As an illustration, it is useful to think of one state facing an emergency, and the other state facing the decision of whether to voluntarily rescue the other. For a rescue that nets some degree of success, the marginal cost of the activity is lower than the social benefit, thus ensuring that rescues are socially desirable.

In period 0, a state is confronted with the need to exert some effort to rescue another state. If he undertakes the rescue, he would bear cost ae^2 while the other state would receive benefits be. These immediate costs and benefits are the states' circumstantial interests. Note that the circumstantial interests of the states have different signs. In our example, the circumstantial interest of the rescuer is negative, $-ae^2 < 0$, while the rescued state faces a positive circumstantial interest, represented by benefit $be > 0$. In our example, the choice of action is in the hands of the rescuer, not the rescued state, who is a passive recipient of the benefit. It is thus sufficient to consider the participation and incentives of the state that faces negative circumstantial interests.[6]

The states are engaged in repeat interaction. After the initial time period 0, starting from period 1 to infinity, the states alternate roles (role reversal). Their future roles (as rescuers or rescued, in our example) are only known on a probabilistic basis. In each period, there is probability π that a given state will be the beneficiary of other states' activities (in our example, this represents the probability of being rescued). On the other hand, there is a probability of $1 - \pi$ that a given state will continue to be on the giving side (in our example, that would be the probability that the state would again need to rescue others).

We start considering the case in which socially desirable practices are followed, subject to reciprocity. Reciprocity extends both to the participation in the emerging practice and to the quality or effort level of the reciprocating conduct. This starting point allows us to identify with greater clarity, the extent to which the acting state's normative interest may lead to action and customary practice. In doing so, we assume that whatever the level of effort chosen by the state, it can expect that the effort will be reciprocated when he needs to be rescued.[7] Hence, in each of the future periods, the state's expected payoff is given by

$$\pi be - (1 - \pi)ae^2.$$

Assuming that the state has a discount rate r, $r > 0$, then the total discounted value of expected payoffs from future periods is[8]

$$\sum_{t=1}^{\infty} \frac{1}{(1+r)^t}(\pi be - (1 - \pi)ae^2) = \frac{1}{r} \cdot (\pi be - (1 - \pi)ae^2).$$

The problem facing the individual state who is confronted with the responsibility of being the rescuer in period 0 while in some future period may become the rescued or the rescuer is then given by the following:

$$\max_{e} P = -ae^2 + \frac{1}{r}(\pi be - (1 - \pi)ae^2). \tag{11.3}$$

The optimal level of effort e^C is easily seen to be given by the following:

$$e^C = \frac{\pi b}{2a(r + 1 - \pi)}. \tag{11.4}$$

Substituting the optimal value of e^C into the objective function of the state gives the following maximal payoff:

$$P^C \equiv P(e^C) = \frac{\pi^2 b^2}{4ar(r + 1 - \pi)} \tag{11.5}$$

1.2. Participation Constraint

Given these premises, we can consider the extent to which the acting state's circumstantial and normative interests may lead to action and participation in the emerging customary practice. In our specific example, in order for the state to be willing to participate in the rescue venture, we should verify whether the participation constraint is satisfied. In particular, $P^C \geq k$ must hold for some k. From equation (11.5) it is easy to see that the following comparative statics hold:

$$\frac{\partial P^C}{\partial a} < 0, \frac{\partial P^C}{\partial b} > 0, \frac{\partial P^C}{\partial r} < 0, \frac{\partial P^C}{\partial \pi} > 0.^9$$

Thus, *ceteris paribus*, the participation constraint is less likely to be satisfied when the cost of the activity is higher, as represented by a larger a. Likewise, an increase in the state's discount rate, r, renders the participation constraint less likely to be satisfied. These results are fairly intuitive if we consider that participation to our emerging customary practice imposes a present cost for the expectation of a future benefit, a benefit whose present value is reduced by higher discount rates. On the other hand, the participation constraint is more likely to be satisfied if the benefit from reciprocal cooperation, b, is greater, and if the probability of being on the benefiting side in future time periods, π, is higher.

1.3. Incentive Problem

The fulfillment of the participation constraint represents a necessary condition for the emergence of a custom. But efficient customary norms also require that the participating states undertake optimal levels of effort in the specific activity. In this section we investigate whether the process of customary law formation creates optimal incentives for the participating states.

From the optimal effort level (11.4), first observe the following:

(i) If $\pi = 0, e^C = 0$.
(ii) If $\pi = 1, e^C = b/2ar$.

These extreme cases are intuitive. When the probability of benefiting from the emerging custom is null (e.g., the rescuing state knows that it will never need rescue from others in the future), expending any effort now would impose a cost with no corresponding future benefit; thus the state will rationally choose zero effort level: $e^C = 0$. This is true in spite of the assumed reciprocity. Reciprocity is vacuous in this case, because the acting state will never be in a position to benefit from reciprocation in the future.

On the other hand, the benefits from reciprocal behavior are at their highest when there is certainty that the acting state will be on the receiving side of the emerging custom in the future. In this case, the state's best action is to set a higher standard of conduct in the present time, in expectation of the higher obtainable benefits. The optimal conduct will balance current payoff versus discounted future payoff: $e^C = b/2ar$. The optimal level of effort critically depends on the state's discount rate.[10]

Comparing the social optimal level of effort (11.2) and the private optimal level of effort (11.4), we note the following.

$$e^C < e^S \Leftrightarrow \pi < \tfrac{1}{2}(1+r) \qquad \qquad 11.6$$

$$e^C = e^S \Leftrightarrow \pi = \tfrac{1}{2}(1+r) \qquad \qquad 11.7$$

In order for the private and the social optimal levels of effort to be identical, whenever π is less than or equal to ½, the discount rate r must be less than or equal to zero. But, in the realistic case of positive discount rates, the private optimum will not be the same as the social optimum unless $\pi > \tfrac{1}{2}$. Thus, symmetric states with positive discount rates will not have optimal incentives under the traditional process of custom formation with role-reversibility. Symmetric states with π approaching ½ will undertake socially optimal effort only in the limit case of r approaching 0. Only in this limited instance will the private optimum under classical customary law and the social optimum coincide. Also, when $\pi = 1$, r must be 1 for the private and the social optima to be the same.

Returning to the privately optimal level of effort given in (11.4), it can easily be seen that the following comparative static results hold:

$$\frac{\partial e^C}{\partial a} < 0, \ \frac{\partial e^C}{\partial b} > 0, \ \frac{\partial e^C}{\partial r} < 0, \quad \text{and} \quad \frac{\partial e^C}{\partial \pi} > 0.\text{[11]}$$

Thus, *ceteris paribus*, the states' level of effort in the formative stage of the customary rule will be lower when the cost of the activity is higher, as represented by a larger a. On the other hand, the privately optimal level of effort will increase if the benefit from reciprocal compliance, b, increases and if the probability of being on the benefiting side of the customary practice in future time periods, π, increases. Further, from the fact that $\frac{\partial^2 e^C}{\partial \pi^2} > 0$, we deduce that, given a fixed discount rate r, the optimal effort curve increases at an increasing rate in terms of the probability π of being a beneficiary of the emerging custom in the future.[12] Likewise, $\frac{\partial e^C}{\partial r} < 0$ indicates that as the discount rate falls, the optimal level of effort increases and the optimal effort curve shifts up. This is intuitive if we consider that effort spent toward an

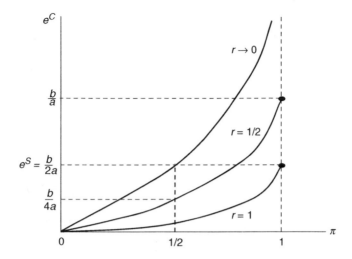

FIGURE 11.1 Optimal Effort Curves under Traditional Customary Law

emerging customary practice imposes a present cost for the expectation of a future benefit (whose present value is increased by lower discount rates).

Figure 11.1 presents a few optimal effort curves. Recall that when $\pi = 0$, $e^C = 0$, and when $\pi = 1$, $e^C = b/2ar$. Thus all optimal effort curves start from the origin and end at $b/2ar$ when $\pi = 1$. In the figure, the lowest optimal effort curve corresponds to $r = 1$. Note that when $r = 1$, future payoffs are discounted at 100% in each period, and the total discounted value of *all* future payoffs is weighted equal to the current period (period 0) payoff. In order for the state to be willing to expend the socially efficient level of effort, it must be assured that it will be the one who is rescued in the future, because it must expend its effort up front in the current period to rescue others. That is, when $r = 1$, $e^C = e^S$ can only occur when $\pi = 1$.

As the discount rate falls to, say $r = \frac{1}{2}$, the optimal effort curve shifts upward. In this case, in order for the private optimum to coincide with the social optimum, a lower probability of becoming a beneficiary of the emerging custom is required. In Figure 11.1, it is easy to see the tradeoff between the various parameters of our customary law problem under efficiency. For any given effort level, lower discount rates r necessitate lower probabilities π to achieve efficiency. For example, the intersection of the $r = \frac{1}{2}$ optimal effort curve and the $e^S = b/2a$ line is found at the left of the intersection of other effort curves corresponding to higher discount rates. As the discount rate approaches zero ($r \to 0$), the optimal effort curve approaches the highest curve shown. Hence, as $r \to 0$, the required probability of being the beneficiary of the custom in future periods approaches $\pi = \frac{1}{2}$ for a social optimum.

Note that earlier, as illustrated in (11.7), we have shown that in order for the private and the social level of effort to coincide, $\pi = \frac{1}{2}(1 + r)$ must hold. The optimal effort curves shown in Figure 11.1 are consistent with this condition. From the figure, it can be seen that in order for the state to undertake the socially optimal level of effort, an increase in the discount rate must be accompanied by an increase in the probability of becoming the beneficiary of the custom in future time periods. This is intuitive. Because discounting the future more heavily indicates caring for future benefits less and given the fact that participation to the customary practice imposes a present cost for the expectation of a future benefit, a socially optimal effort level can be privately rational only if the acting state has a more than a fair chance of being on the receiving side of the customary practice in the future.

2. Multilateral Customs, Uncertainty, and Delayed Recognition

In this section we extend the above analysis to the more general case of multilateral custom. We consider the impact of uncertainty and time lags in the process of formation and recognition of customary law. We verify how the previously discussed participation and incentive constraints are affected by the presence of such conditions. These extensions acquire particular importance when the circumstantial and normative interests of the states are not perfectly aligned. This analysis will thus help identify the limits of traditional customary processes in real-life conditions.

The analysis unveils situations in which the states are unable to generate Pareto superior customs through their own practice. In Section 3, we use these findings to investigate whether the adoption of alternative doctrines of customary law formation can mitigate the shortcomings of traditional customary law processes.

2.1. Multilateral Custom and The Problem of Large Number Participation

In the previous section we considered the stylized case in which the states are always involved in the process of custom formation. In our illustration, we assumed that the states would always be involved, in one role or the other (e.g., as victims or rescuers), in future time periods. This is an appropriate and realistic assumption for the case of bilateral customs, but one that would hardly be applicable to the case of multilateral customs.

There are reasons to extend our basic model to situations where the participants to a customary practice (e.g., those in need of rescue and their rescuers, in our example) are randomly drawn from a larger population. Not every individual state is actively or passively involved in the custom-generating practice. At each time, a positive number of nonparticipants observe others' activities without participating. We can think of the nonparticipating individuals as acquiescing spectators of an emerging custom.

Consider the case in which the probability of being a participant in a rescue venture depends on the number of states available. Let N ($N \geq 2$) be the number of states involved. Then there is a $1/N$ probability that the state will be the rescuer, and likewise there is a probability of $1/N$ that the state will need assistance from other states. This means that there is a residual probability of $1 - 2/N$ that the state is just a bystander in each period in the future. Then the problem of the state becomes:

$$\max_{e} P = -ae^2 + \frac{1}{r} \cdot \frac{1}{N}(\pi be - (1 - \pi)ae^2).$$

Note that N plays a similar role to r in the state's optimization problem. Hence, similar to the comparative static results $\partial e^C / \partial r < 0$ and $\partial P^C / \partial r < 0$ found before, $\partial e^C / \partial N < 0$ and $\partial P^C / \partial N < 0$ now also hold. When the number of potential participants increases, the probability of a state's involvement decreases. The decrease in the probability of involvement leads to a decrease in the optimal level of effort expended by the state. Likewise, as more participants become involved, it becomes harder to satisfy the participation constraint, and it is less likely for the state to take part in the customary practice. Both results are related to the fact that the choice of initial participation imposes a present and sure cost on the states, whereas the probability of future involvement with the emerging custom, and the resulting net benefits, may decrease with the number of participants.

These results are consistent with the empirical findings of sociologists and anthropologists according to which close-knit environments and small communities of players provide the most fertile environments for the emergence of efficient customs (Ullmann-Margalit 1977; Parisi 1998; Ellickson 2001). This result further supports Goldsmith and Posner's

(1999 and 2000) skepticism about reciprocity explanations of international cooperation involving more than two states. Finally, these results have important implications for the adjudication of customs. Given the greater ease with which efficient rules may emerge in such environments, courts should give full attention and enforcement to customs emerged in small or close-knit communities. Local, regional and special customs should likewise enjoy as much recognition, or even greater recognition, than the more general and widespread customary practices.

2.2. Introducing Uncertainty in the Formation of Custom

Thus far, our model of custom formation assumed that later participants to the custom always followed the initial practice with reciprocal behavior. This allowed us to isolate the effects of strategic participation and effort choices of the states from the effects of uncertainty concerning the participation and future compliance of other states. In real-life settings, however, initial participants to a customary practice have no guarantee that their action will actually lead to a binding custom. Thus, an initial effort may not always be met with reciprocity, which may undermine the motivation of the initial action, frustrating the expectation of reciprocal behavior from others. In our working example, if the potential rescuer has no assurance that his effort will be met with like behavior when fortunes are reversed, his incentives to offer voluntary rescue may be compromised.

Here, we consider the conditions under which optimal practices will emerge when there is uncertainty as to whether a binding rule of custom will emerge from the states' initial efforts (i.e., the initial participants have no assurance that reciprocal customary practices will be followed by others). We do so by extending our basic model to include the possibility of uncertainty in custom formation. In particular, we assume a probability β $(0 < \beta < 1)$ that in the future others will follow the practice undertaken by the state in question. The private optimization problem then is adjusted accordingly:

$$\max_{e} P = -ae^2 + \frac{1}{r}(\beta \pi be - (1 - \pi)ae^2).$$

Because the probability β plays a role similar to that of b in the optimization problem, the comparative static results are also similar: $\partial e^C / \partial \beta > 0$ and $\partial P^C / \partial \beta > 0$ hold. As intuition suggests, when the states have higher expectations that their behavior will successfully consolidate into a binding custom, they will be more likely to participate in the practice and their initial action will be characterized by higher effort level.[13] Likewise, as the probability of reciprocal customary behavior increases, higher efforts will likely characterize the behavior of the initial participants.

2.3. Introducing Time Lags in the Formation and Recognition of Custom

In this last extension of our basic customary law model, we consider the effects of time lags in the process of emergence and recognition of the custom. In our basic model, time lags and delays in the recognition of custom affect the time in which the initial participants are able to capture the benefit of the custom, when roles are reversed. The delays can be determined by the type of practice, such as events of rare occurrence (e.g., a rescue in the outer space or on the high seas), or action in the legal system (e.g., some legal systems require a long-standing practice of 20 or 30 years before the usage is recognized and enforced as a binding customary rule). Let T be the number of periods after the initial action before the practice consolidates into a binding custom and reciprocal benefits can be expected. From period T onward, the states will act under a reciprocally binding rule of custom, such that one state may obtain the benefit of the rule or face the burdens of such rule, with probabilities π and $(1-\pi)$, respectively. In this case, the present discounted value of the future expected payoff is given by:

$$\sum_{t=0}^{\infty} \frac{1}{(1+r)^{t+T}}(\pi \, be - (1-\pi)ae^2) = \frac{(\pi \, be - (1-\pi)ae^2)}{r(1+r)^{T-1}}$$

Thus, the problem confronting the state becomes:

$$\max_{e} -ae^2 + \frac{(\pi \, be - (1-\pi)ae^2)}{r(1+r)^{T-1}}$$

Comparing the current problem with the basic problem formulated in (11.3), r is replaced by $r(1+r)^{T-1}$. From the basic model, we know that $\partial e^C/[\partial(r(1+r)^{T-1})] < 0$ is true. Because $[\partial r(1+r)^{T-1}]/\partial T > 0$, we now have $\partial e^C/\partial T < 0$. That is, the longer the delay in the process of formation or recognition of the custom, the lower will be the level of effort rationally exerted by the initial participants. The presence of delays and time lags in the formation of the custom also affects the participation constraint. From the fact that $\partial P^C / [\partial (r(1+r)^{T-1})] < 0$, we have $\partial P^C / \partial T < 0$. This implies that some practices that would have successfully evolved in the normal case would not be undertaken, if the effects were delayed. In sum, when states have a positive time preference and their circumstantial and normative interests are not aligned, delays in the formation and recognition of the custom may have negative participation and incentive effects. The above results further suggest that customary settings that entail infrequent states' actions should require a lower number of observations, and thus a shorter waiting period, before the practice is allowed to consolidate into a binding rule. Given the infrequency of action and delay in custom formation, the states would otherwise heavily discount the benefits of future applications of the custom. Such discounting would negatively affect both the participation and the incentives of the states.

3. Belief and Action in Custom Formation: The Relevance of Timing and Articulation

In Section 2 we have shown that, in all situations where the circumstantial and normative interests of the states are not aligned, the following factors may have negative effects on the states' participation and incentives: (1) increases in the number of participants, (2) uncertainty in the future development of the custom, and (3) delays in the formation and recognition of the custom. These findings have important implications for the assessment of alternative mechanisms of customary law formation. In this section we examine the role of alternative processes of customary law formation in mitigating the above shortcomings of the traditional approach.

We proceed considering an important variation in the process of custom formation, which we refer to as articulation theory. As discussed above, this variant of traditional customary law processes allows states to express their consensus over potential rules prior to the time of their action through practice. Custom emerges when states undertake action consistent with the expression of a belief contained in their prior or concurrent articulations.[14] We model the process of custom formation under such alternative doctrines and identify the respective limits and advantages of the alternative frameworks of custom formation in different environments.

3.1. Normative and Circumstantial Interests in Custom Formation: The Role of Articulation

Notable scholars have considered the conditions under which principles of justice can emerge spontaneously through the voluntary interaction and exchange of individual members of a group. As in a contractarian setting, the reality of customary law formation relies on a voluntary process through which members of a community develop rules that govern their social interaction by voluntarily adhering to emerging behavioral standards.[15] In the law and economics literature, recent work has contributed to the understanding of the relationship between law and social norms—a relationship that bears some analogies but cannot be identified with the issues raised under customary law.[16]

As discussed above, this process of custom formation becomes problematic when the circumstantial and normative interests of the states are not aligned. Legal theorists and practitioners have addressed this issue in the context of customary law, considering the requirement of *opinio iuris*.[17] Legal theorists have proposed to look past the notion of *opinio iuris* concentrating on the element of articulation. Articulation theories capture two important features of customary law: (1) customary law is voluntary in nature; and (2) customary law is dynamic. According to these theories, in the process of ascertaining the qualitative element of *opinio iuris*, the states' statements and expressions of belief should be attentively considered. Individuals and states articulate desirable norms as a way to signal that they intend to follow and be bound by such rules. In this way, articulation theories remove the guessing process from the identification of *opinio iuris* and allow expressions of belief to be manifested before or in conjunction with customary action.

We consider a hypothetical scenario in which articulation determines the content of emerging customs. In this context, articulation may be a way for states to precommit to the content and interpretation of an emerging custom. The consolidation and enforcement of the custom would remain contingent upon the development of future state practice, but articulation would facilitate the coordination of states with respect to the emerging practice. Further, articulation can be viewed as a way for states to recognize an emerging norm of international law even in the absence of concurrent state practice.[18]

Consistent with the predicament of the economic models, articulation theories suggest that greater weight should be given to beliefs that have been expressed prior to the emergence of a conflict.[19] When states face a tension between their circumstantial and normative interests, this would imply that relevance should be given to statements of belief (i.e., articulations) expressed by the states, even when articulations are not accompanied by actual practice.

Before the contingent circumstances of the matter are known, states articulate rules that are consistent with their ex ante normative interests. They have incentives to articulate and endorse rules that maximize their expected welfare. This rule may not necessarily correspond to the ex post circumstantial interest of the states in the specific case and may fail to maximize their actual payoff when roles and circumstances are unveiled to the states. Thus, timing of relevant action is important to both participation and effort incentives. To illustrate the point, it is useful to consider again our working example of mutual rescue. Given some degree of uncertainty as to the future course of events, the states' normative interests are easily aligned. If a rule of mutual rescue maximizes the expected welfare of the international community at large, states are likely to endorse such a rule. If asked in the abstract whether their society should be bound by a norm of mutual rescue, they would thus likely agree to be bound.

As previously seen in Section 2, this may not necessarily be the case under traditional processes of customary law formation. When individuals and states have an opportunity to manifest their belief only in conjunction with their action, participation and incentive constraints may be undermined. At the time of action, states have biased strategic incentives and this may fail to induce optimal participation and efficient incentives under the circumstances. More generally, once the future is disclosed to them, states will tend to articulate rules that best fulfill their circumstantial interests and welfare, rather than the normative interest and expected welfare to be derived from an uncertain future. In our working example, those in need of rescue may reclaim too much effort; those called to provide it, may undersupply it. In the absence of a previously agreed standard of conduct, mutual assistance is likely to be withheld or undersupplied. In this situation, if adjudicators were asked to choose between the behavioral standards articulated ex ante by the potential participants and the standards advocated ex post by the states, they should favor the adoption and enforcement of the ex ante standards of conduct.

3.2. A Model of Custom Formation with Articulation

In this section we will build on the above intuition to consider the incentive properties of customary law processes that rely on ex ante articulations. We consider a setting similar to that considered in Section 1, where the states do not have to actively engage in the customary practice in the initial time period. In period 0, the states are allowed to choose a rule by means of articulation. In our working example, imagine that the states are allowed to express their beliefs on the norm of rescue before their respective roles are unveiled. The future horizon for the states is unchanged. Like before, in future periods, we assume that the states will benefit from the rule with probability π and are burdened by such rule with probability $1 - \pi$. Assuming a discount rate r, the problem confronting the state is to maximize the present discounted value of the total expected payoff:

$$\max_{e} \tilde{P} = \frac{1}{r}(\pi b e - (1 - \pi)ae^2) \qquad 11.8$$

We can now compare this problem to the basic customary law problem considered in (11.3). The objective of the current maximization has one less negative term, because the endorsement of a hypothetical rule by means of articulation requires no practice or effort expenditure. The optimal level of effort e^A is then given by the following:

$$e^A = \frac{\pi b}{2a(1 - \pi)}. \qquad 11.9$$

Substituting the optimal value of e^A into the objective function $\tilde{P}$ gives the following maximal payoff P^A:

$$P^A \equiv \tilde{P}(e^A) = \frac{\pi^2 b^2}{4ar(1 - \pi)}. \qquad 11.10$$

3.2.1. Participation Constraint

Articulation processes allow states to pursue their normative interests avoiding any potential conflict with their circumstantial interests. In a traditional customary law case, in order for the participation constraint to be satisfied, a payoff $P^C \geq k$ had to be expected from the participation to the customary practice. Participation constraint in the articulation case is also checked against a fixed number, k. Comparative statics show that the participation constraint $P^A \geq k$ is more or less likely to be satisfied as the following parameters change: $\partial P^A / \partial a < 0$, $\partial P^A / \partial b > 0$, $\partial P^A / \partial r < 0$, and $\partial P^A / \partial \pi > 0$. That is, *ceteris paribus*, the participation constraint is less likely to be satisfied when it is more costly to undertake the activity, as signified by a greater a, or the state's discount rate, r, are higher. On the other hand, the participation constraint is more likely to be satisfied when the benefits from reciprocal cooperation, b, or the probability of being on the benefiting side in the future, π, are higher.

3.2.2. Incentive Problem

From the optimal level of effort under articulation given in (11.9), we have the following results: $\partial e^A / \partial a < 0$, $\partial e^A / \partial b > 0$, $\partial e^A / \partial r = 0$, and $\partial e^A / \partial \pi > 0$.[20] Comparing these sensitivity results with those obtained in the case of traditional customary law, an important qualitative difference is revealed. Under articulation theory, the states' discount rate has no impact on the optimal level of effort. However, we have previously learned that, even under articulation theory, the discount rate does have an impact on the participation constraint. The higher the discount rate, the less likely it is for the participation constraint to be satisfied, and the less likely it is for the state to join the custom-generating articulation (in our working example, it will be less likely that the state will advocate a rule of rescue in contemplation of future contingencies). The interesting point here is that, even though higher discount rates may undermine participation, if participation is fulfilled, optimal effort levels will be chosen and optimal rules will be advocated. This is a substantial improvement over traditional customary law processes. The improvement is due to the fact that articulation processes, unlike traditional processes of custom formation, eliminate the incentives to understate the states' true normative interests by letting states commit to a customary rule before the specific circumstantial interests are unveiled.

3.3. Private Versus Socially Optimal Articulation

Comparing the privately optimal effort e^A identified in (11.9) with the socially optimal level e^S in (11.2), it is readily seen that the two can be identical only

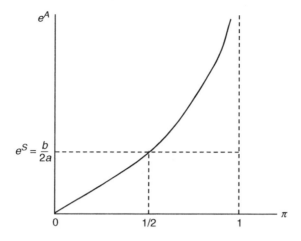

FIGURE 11.2 Optimal Effort Curve under Articulation Theories

if the probability of being a beneficiary of the emerging rule is $\pi = \frac{1}{2}$. This means that homogeneous states or unbiased role-reversibility are important prerequisites of processes of custom formation, even under articulation theories.

Figure 11.2 shows the optimal effort curve under articulation: $e^A = \pi b/[2a(1-\pi)]$ as a function of π. Note that as $\pi \to 1$, $e^A \to \infty$. As the probability of becoming a beneficiary of the rule approaches certainty, the state articulates a larger cooperation effort. Figure 11.2 also shows that when probabilities are fairly distributed, $\pi = \frac{1}{2}$, the privately optimal effort e^A equals the social optimum, e^S.

In our working example, when the probability of being rescued equals the probability of becoming a rescuer in the future, the two states will face incentives to articulate efficient rescue rules. This is so because the states will give equal weights to the expected costs and benefits of future rescue missions. This is not so when the states face asymmetric probabilities of being rescuers or victims. With asymmetry, the private and social incentives diverge and the resulting articulations will be affected by the diverging interests of the states.

The lack of alignment between private and social incentives is due to the fact that a privately optimal effort level is obtained by balancing the expected private marginal cost and benefits. Such privately optimal balancing takes into account the individual probabilities of receiving a benefit or being burdened by a cost. For a social optimum, no such discounting should be made. The social marginal cost and marginal benefit for the states should be balanced, but no weighing would enter the calculation or a social optimum, because the ex post distribution of costs and burdens between the states is irrelevant. Thus, the private optimum and the social optimum will only coincide when the probabilities are uniform for all players.

3.4. Articulation and the New Boundaries of Customary Law

We now consider the different attributes of the processes of custom formation, evaluating the ability of articulation processes of custom formation to correct the shortcomings identified in Section 2 with respect to traditional customary processes. We shall proceed to inquire which formative process is more likely to facilitate the formation of custom. We do so by first comparing the effect of articulation processes on the participation constraint and then consider the impact on the states' incentives.

We compare the participation constraint under articulation theories $P^A = \pi^2 b^2/[4ar(1-\pi)] \geq k$, as implied by (11.10), and the participation constraint under customary law $P^C = \pi^2 b^2/[4ar(r+1-\pi)] \geq k$, as implied by (11.5). We see that the denominator of P^A is smaller than the denominator of P^C, because the former has one less term than the latter. Hence P^A is larger than P^C. This implies that the participation constraint is more easily satisfied in the articulation case than in the traditional customary law case. Allowing potential participants to announce ex ante their participation to the emerging custom and to articulate the level of effort that they consider appropriate and desirable for such activity thus facilitates the formation of customary law.

A similar inquiry can be undertaken with respect to the content of the emerging custom, as symbolized by the chosen effort level. We can do so by comparing the privately optimal effort that states would advocate under articulation theories, as derived in (11.9), $e^A = \pi b/[2a(1-\pi)]$, with the privately optimal level of effort chosen under customary law, as derived in (11.4), $e^C = \pi b/[2a(r+1-\pi)]$. By inspection, we see that the denominator of e^A is smaller than the denominator of e^C because $r > 0$. Hence $e^A > e^C$. That is, the optimal effort that states would rationally choose under articulation is greater than the effort that those same states would choose under traditional customary law processes.

3.5. Articulation and the Problem of
Multilateral Custom

As before, we extend the basic articulation model to consider situations where the participants to a customary practice (e.g., those in need of rescue and their rescuers, in our example) are randomly drawn from a larger population. Also in this case, we assume that not every individual is actively or passively involved in the custom-generating practice. At each time period, a positive number of nonparticipants observe others' activities without participating: the probability of being an active participant depends on the number of states involved. In our illustration, imagine that the probability of being a participant in a rescue venture depends on the number of states N ($N \geq 2$) available. In particular, in each period, let the probability of being either a rescuer or a rescued be $1/N$ and the probability that the state is a bystander be $1 - 2/N$. Then the private problem becomes

$$\max_{e} \tilde{P} = \frac{1}{r} \cdot \frac{1}{N}(\pi be - (1 - \pi)ae^2).$$

Because N plays a similar role to r in the state's optimization problem, the comparative static results are qualitatively similar to $\partial e^A/\partial r$ and $\partial P^A/\partial r$. That is, we have $\partial e^A/\partial N = 0$ and $\partial P^A/\partial N < 0$.

Comparing these results with those obtained in the case of traditional customary law, we note an important difference. Under articulation, a change in the number of potential participants has no impact on the optimal level of effort expended by a state. An increase in the number of states, however, reduces the probability of a state's involvement in the articulation process (in our example, it would make it less likely for the state to articulate the rescue rule). However, even though an increase in the number of states may render participation less likely, once participation occurs, the states will undertake optimal effort levels and advocate optimal rules. This is a substantial improvement over traditional customary law processes that, as seen above, are affected by pervasive strategic problems in multilateral settings.

3.6. Uncertainty and Articulation in the Formation
of Custom

In Section 2 we considered the conditions under which optimal practices would emerge when there is uncertainty as to whether a binding rule of custom will evolve from the states' initial efforts (i.e., participants have no assurance that reciprocation by others will follow their articulation and subsequent customary practice). We now consider the effect of such uncertainty in the case of articulation processes. As in the customary law case, we extend our basic model by assuming that others will follow the practice in question with a probability β $(0 < \beta < 1)$ in the future. The problem of the state thus becomes:

$$\max_{e} \tilde{P} = \frac{1}{r}(\beta \pi be - (1 - \pi)ae^2).$$

Note that the probability β plays a role similar to that of b in the private optimization problem, in that it amounts to a multiplier of the future benefits. Hence the comparative static result for β is qualitatively similar to the comparative static result for b. Hence, $\partial e^A/\partial \beta > 0$ and $\partial P^A/\partial \beta > 0$. An increase in the probability of custom formation β increases the state's willingness to expend effort and it has a positive impact on the willingness of the state to advocate customary norms by means of articulation. The probability of custom formation thus affects both participation and incentives under articulation.

3.7. Time Lags and the Formation of Custom Through Articulation

The last extension of our basic articulation model considers the effects of time lags in the process of emergence and recognition of the custom. In Section 2 we observed that time lags and delays in the recognition of custom affect the time in which the initial participants are able to capture the benefit of the custom, when roles are reversed. Such delay can undermine both the participation and the effort incentives in the traditional customary law case. Thus, if custom aims at regulating events of rare occurrence, traditional customary law processes may be ineffective. Likewise, if legal systems delay the process of custom formation by requiring the finding of long-standing practices, participation and effort incentives may be undermined.

We shall now consider whether the same problems occur under articulation processes of custom formation. Let T be the number of periods after which the prior articulation consolidates into a binding custom and reciprocal benefits can be expected. In this case, the private optimization problem becomes

$$\max_{e} \frac{(\pi b e - (1 - \pi)ae^2)}{r(1 + r)^{T-1}}.$$

Comparing this problem with the basic articulation case without time lags, as formulated in (11.8), we can see that r is replaced by $r(1+r)^{T-1}$. From the basic model, we know that $\partial e^A/[\partial(r(1+r)^{T-1})] = 0$ and $\partial P^A/[\partial(r(1+r)^{T-1})] < 0$ hold. Because $[\partial r(1+r)^{T-1}]/\partial T > 0$, by chain rule we have $\partial e^A/\partial T = 0$ and $\partial P^A/\partial T < 0$. Hence the presence of time lags negatively affects the participation choice under articulation theories as well as traditional processes of custom formation: the longer the delay before any enforcement of the articulated rule takes place, the less likely that the state will actively engage in the articulation process. However, this delay has no impact on the qualitative standards advocated by the states and the resulting rules of custom. These results can be explained by considering that delays in the implementation of the rule decrease the present discounted value of the future payoff, thereby weakening the incentives to participate in the articulation venture. On the other hand, delays in future events do not alter the balance between expected benefit and expected cost in the future. Consequently, if the participation constraint is fulfilled, there is no reason for the state to alter its choice of optimal effort no matter how long the delay is. Also in this case, articulation processes of custom formation improve upon the traditional processes with respect to the states' incentives and the resulting qualitative content of the emerging custom.[21]

4. The Limits of Customary Law

In this chapter we developed a model of custom formation and identified some of the strengths and weaknesses of customary law formation processes. Customary law is in many respects an effective source of law that generates rules on the basis of the revealed choices of the participating actors. Some settings are more congenial than others to the evolution of customary rules. We have identified some of the conditions that undermine the effectiveness of customary law. Among such conditions, the following have been shown to have negative effect on the states' participation and incentives: (1) increases in the number of participants, (2) uncertainty in the future development of the custom, and (3) delays in the formation and recognition of the custom.

We extended our analysis to model articulation doctrines. According to these doctrines, custom emerges when states formulate like-minded articulations prior to or in conjunction with customary practice. Our analysis identified the potential benefits and residual limitations of this alternative mechanism of custom formation. Most notably, customary rules would more easily emerge if prior articulation were made possible. Likewise, articulation processes of custom formation, while still leaving room for the emergence of suboptimal customs under asymmetric settings, always improves the effort incentives for the participating states, compared to traditional processes.

These findings call for further reflection on the respective advantages of these sources of customary law vis-à-vis other sources of law. Articulated norms share with treaty law the fact that rules can be formulated prior to any instance of practical implementation. This eliminates the first-mover problem that affects typical custom formation. Articulated norms share with traditional customary law the avoidance of the costly and difficult process of treaty negotiation and ratification. As seen in our analysis, however, both articulated norms and traditional customary law can diverge from first best, even when the first best is otherwise feasible. As it will be discussed in Part IV of this book, under treaty law, full-fledged bargaining between states can take place, and this may lead to first best outcomes even when asymmetric state preferences are involved.

A significant advantage of articulated customs over traditional customary law is the ability for states to form consensus on a given norm, without having to wait for a sufficiently large number of state actions to be recognized as uniform practice. This allows a shortening of the time of formation of the norm, a benefit that is potentially sizeable, when the frequency of the states' actions is intrinsically low (e.g., to continue our rescue examples, imagine a hypothetical norm of rescue of vessels in the outer space). A possible shortcoming of the articulation approach that is not combined with state practice is the risk of miscoordination. Under an articulated norm approach, initial coordination problems may arise. For example, if states make inconsistent initial articulations, it is not obvious that states will coordinate with one another on what the resulting norm should eventually be. Traditional customary law, by looking at actual practice, avoids such risk. Under traditional customary law, the initial actions of first movers become a focal point for the action of subsequent movers. This eventually evolves into a customary norm, where the observed practice reveals to participating states what is expected of them in the future. In the presence of such coordination problems, articulation processes may be unable to effectively expedite the process of custom formation.

These findings have important policy implications for the design of optimal mechanisms of customary law formation, revealing the respective advantages and limits of the alternative regimes in different environments. In Chapter 12 we extend this analysis to persistent and subsequent objector doctrines in order to identify the best rules to foster efficient evolution of customary law.

Stability and Change in Customary Law*

THE PROCESS OF CUSTOM formation has struggled with the vexing question of how to promote stability and reliance on customary law, while preserving the voluntary support of customary law in the fluid environment of international relations. The balance between stability and change in international customary law becomes particularly complex in the face of diverse preferences and changed circumstances over time. The rules that govern the formation and application of customary law have themselves been the product of customary evolution. The process of custom formation is capable of creating universally binding rules. At the same time, this process contemplates ways for unwilling states to gain exemption from emerging or existing rules of customary law.

In this chapter we consider two legal doctrines that allow states to avoid the binding force of international customary law: the persistent objector and subsequent objector doctrines. The first doctrine gives objecting states an opportunity to avoid, partially or entirely, the binding force of an international norm by objecting to it. Under the subsequent objector doctrine, states can gain an exemption to depart from an existing rule of customary law only by securing the acquiescence of other states. This chapter considers the effects of these two doctrines when heterogeneous states are involved. The economic model reveals that the persistent and subsequent objector doctrines minimize the impact of strategic objections and departures from customary law, while maintaining the flexibility necessary for adapting custom to changed circumstances over time. By doing so, these international law doctrines effectively balance opposing needs

---

* This chapter is based on an article forthcoming as Fon, Vincy, and Francesco Parisi, "Stability and Change in International Customary Law," *Supreme Court Economic Review* (2009). An earlier draft of this paper was awarded the 2004 Garvin Prize in Law & Economics for Best Workshop paper by the University of California at Berkeley.

for stability and change in the evolution of custom, while preserving the voluntary basis of international customary law.

Section 1 provides a stylized explanation of the rules that govern the formation of international customary law and the role of the persistent objector doctrine in the formation of custom. Section 2 models custom formation when states have an opportunity to opt out of emerging customs by invoking the persistent objector doctrine. Section 3 considers the role of the subsequent objector doctrine in custom formation. Section 4 extends the model to examine the workings of the subsequent objector doctrine. Section 5 compares the effects of the two doctrines on custom formation.

1. International Customary Law and Persistent Objector Doctrines

As discussed in Chapter 9, when resolution of a dispute requires application of international customary law, an international tribunal verifies the presence of two formative elements of a custom. These elements are generally referred to as the "quantitative" element of practice, and the "qualitative" element of *opinion juris*. When both elements are present, the international practice gains the status of international customary law and states are considered bound by the resulting custom.

With respect to the first formative element, the emergence of an international customary law requires the presence of a stable and fairly uniform international practice with which many states have consistently complied. A time limit for compliance is not defined; however, a long duration helps to establish that compliance with the practice was consistent, and also helps to clarify the context and meaning of the practice.[1] Further, the practice should emerge from the spontaneous and uncoerced behavior of states. Restatements of international law refer to the consistency and generality of the customary practice. The consistency requirement is not met if it is impossible to identify a general practice because of fluctuations in behavior.[2] More recent cases in international law restate the uniformity requirement in terms of increasing and widespread acceptance, allowing special consideration for emerging norms (or local clusters of multilateral practice) that are expected to become widespread over time.

As also discussed in Chapter 9, the second formative element is generally identified by the phrase *opinio juris ac necessitatis*, which describes the requirement that the customary action be perceived by states as fulfilling an essential norm of social conduct.[3] According to the *opinion juris* requirement, states must act with the belief that the applied practice is undertaken to fulfill an underlying legal obligation, and that the practice is not followed by the state out of convenience or diplomatic courtesy during a certain period of time. This requirement is aimed at insuring that customary law results from a general consensus of states, rather than from an occasional and unqualified convergence of state practice.[4]

In a multilateral setting, the formative elements of a custom may be present only for a subset of states, or only for a limited portion of the international practice. International law has developed legal doctrines that govern the workings of customary law when states have different levels of participation in a customary practice or when states have outright opposed an emerging custom. Although customary law is capable of creating universally binding rules, for a fuller understanding of the process of international customary law formation, it is important to consider the possibility that some states may attempt to gain exemption from emerging rules of general customary law by fully opposing a nascent custom or may trigger a special bilateral custom by partially opposing the nascent custom and complying with a lower behavioral standard.

Some states have successfully argued that if they persistently object to an emerging rule of customary law, if and when a rule is formed it cannot be applied to them. These claims led to the gradual recognition of a principle known as the persistent objector doctrine, allowing states to opt out of a new and otherwise universal rule of international customary law by remaining persistent objectors (Brownlie 1990; Kontou 1994; Stein 1985; Wolfke 1993).[5] Objection to an emerging custom may be full or partial. Full objection signifies that the state does not accept and does not wish to become bound by any part of the emerging custom. A partial objection implies acceptance of some part of the custom. Partial objection is generally found when states object by articulating or implementing a different rule, which they consider preferable to the emerging custom. Full persistent objection leads to a complete exemption from the emerging custom, while partial objection leads to a partial exemption. Once the custom solidifies, the portion of the custom that was not objected to binds the partial persistent objector.

Feasibility of the persistent objector doctrine was explicitly supported by two well-known cases decided by the International Court of Justice. In *Columbia v. Peru*, the Columbian embassy granted political asylum to a Peruvian national who was a leader of a military rebellion in Peru.

The Peruvian government argued that the grant of asylum violated both a 1911 extradition treaty and a rule of customary law. The court ruled in favor of Peru, stating that Colombia failed to establish existence of a custom which permits the state granting diplomatic asylum to unilaterally define an offense as political. The court stated that because Peru did not ratify the treaty in question and specifically repudiated the asylum provisions, it would only be bound by international customary law. The customary rule governing asylum was, however, found not enforceable against Peru, because Peru persistently objected to such custom during its formative stage.[6] Similarly, in *United Kingdom v. Norway*, the court ruled that because the government of Norway had consistently opposed the territorial fishing zone regime, Norway was a persistent objector and therefore not bound by such customs.[7]

To successfully invoke the persistent objector doctrine two elements must be met. First, the objecting state must oppose an emerging customary practice by making its objections widely known before the practice solidifies into a binding rule of custom. Thus, the state must clearly object to the law from the moment of its conception or from the moment the state learns about any relevant practice or declaration that may lead to the establishment of a custom. The objection can be expressed in the form of statements, votes, or protests or can be implied by "abstaining from practice or adhering to a different practice" (Viller 1985: 15).[8] Second, the objection to a practice must be consistent. Thus, the state must clearly object to the law from the beginning and continue to do so throughout its formation and beyond (Loschin 1996). A state may not adhere to a practice on some occasions and object to the practice on other occasions. A consistency requirement allows other states to rely on the position of the objecting state and prevents the objecting state from benefiting from ambiguities in its own course of action.

Two additional principles govern applicability of the persistent objector doctrine. The first excludes application of the persistent objector doctrine to international norms that are peremptory. A state may not invoke the persistent objector doctrine if the customary law has achieved the status of *jus cogens* or imperative law.[9] The second principle provides new states an opportunity to opt out of an existing rule of international customary law. New states, and states that achieved independence after formation of a custom, can obtain exemption from a previously arisen custom if they object within a reasonable period of time.[10]

Traditionally, influence of the persistent objector doctrine on formation of international customary law was quite limited (Stein 1985). In the past the doctrine was rarely applied; states that did not want to follow a rule simply attempted to refute its existence. Recent decades have seen a growing amount of official documentation concerning the existence and content of customary law (judgments of international courts, writing of publicists, or declaratory treaties). With increased awareness by the international community and nongovernmental organizations of existing international customs, states cannot easily confute an existing customary rule and invoke the persistent objector doctrines to avoid the binding force of existing custom.

The greater accessibility and verifiability of general customary law has thus given momentum to the persistent objector doctrine in the practice of international law (Loschin 1996). The persistent objector doctrine offers a dissenting state a way to avoid being bound by specific emerging customs, while reaffirming the legitimacy of the underlying customary law process at the same time.

▓ 2. The Formation of Custom with Persistent Objectors

In the recent law and economics literature, attention has been devoted to the emergence, sustainability, and change of international customary law (Goldsmith and Posner 1999 and 2000; Kontorovich 2006; Fon and Parisi 2006). This section wishes to contribute to that literature analyzing the impact of the persistent objector doctrine on the process of custom formation when heterogeneous states are involved. As discussed above, customary rules emerge from past practice. Prior to the solidification of a practice into a binding custom, states engage in actions on a purely voluntary basis, taking into account the costs and benefits of the action and their interest in establishing a customary rule that would bind for the future.[11] After the initial period, from period 1 to infinity states alternate roles on a probabilistic basis and engage in repeated interaction. Each state i confronts probability α_i that once the custom is established, it may receive a benefit from other states' compliance with the custom, and probability β_i that state i may be called upon to fulfill obligations created by the custom.[12]

Consider the emergence of a multilateral custom among M heterogeneous states. A level of participation effort e characterizes the content of the customary rule.[13] Effort to comply with the custom imposes costs on the performing state and benefits on the receiving state. A state i that participates in the custom with level of effort e_i faces compliance costs ae_i^2

and generates benefits be_i to other states. Once the custom is established, the state can rely on reciprocal conduct from other states. Assuming that the state has a discount rate $r(r > 0)$, the ideal level of custom participation for state i is identified by solving the following problem:[14]

$$\max_{e_i} \; P_i = \frac{1}{r}(\alpha_i be_i - \beta_i ae_i^2)$$

12.1

The ideal level of custom participation chosen by state i is thus

$$e_i = \frac{\alpha_i b}{2\beta_i a}$$

12.2

and the payoff achievable under the custom for state i is

$$P_i(e_i) = \frac{\alpha_i^2 b^2}{4\beta_i a r}$$

12.3

Note that if states are homogeneous, so that each state faces the same probabilities, costs, benefits, and participation constraints, then the interests of all states converge. Each state desires the same custom level $e_i = \alpha b/2\beta a$, and no state has an incentive to become a persistent objector.

The presence of heterogeneous states implies that participating states may have different views on the desirability and content of the custom. The persistent objector doctrine provides a mechanism through which the different actions and objections of the states are brought together to generate a rule of custom.[15]

When a typical heterogeneous state i chooses not to participate in the emerging custom, the alternative for the state is to continue its undertakings in the absence of a recognized rule. In many instances the no-custom regime implies adopting a "self-help" approach. In the absence of custom, the state faces the cost of its own effort each time it seeks to obtain a benefit for itself, and the probabilities of supplying and receiving help thus equal α_i.[16]

Generally speaking, we assume that the costs faced by the state in a no-custom regime are $\bar{a}_i e_i^2$, which differ from costs faced by the state under the custom.[17] We assume that the benefit received is the same and equals be_i. Given these assumptions, the custom-participation problem faced by state i depends on solving the following problem.

$$\max_{e_i} \; \bar{P}_i = \frac{1}{r}\alpha_i(be_i - \bar{a}_i e_i^2)$$

12.4

The optimal choice of effort for the no-custom regime is $\bar{e}_i = b/2\bar{a}_i$. The optimal payoff obtainable by the state in the absence of the custom is given by the following:

$$\bar{P}_i(\bar{e}_i) = \frac{\alpha_i b^2}{4\,\bar{a}_i\,r} \qquad\qquad 12.5$$

State i's best obtainable payoff in the no-custom regime, $\bar{P}_i(\bar{e}_i)$, determines state i's participation in the custom. State i chooses to participate in the custom when the best obtainable payoff under the custom is higher than $\bar{P}_i(\bar{e}_i)$.

States may gain an exemption from customary law by persistently objecting to an emerging customary practice. Objection can be full or partial. Objection is full when a state is altogether unwilling to join the custom, whatever its content. Objection is partial when a state is willing to join the custom, but prefers a level of effort lower than that required by the emerging custom.[18] Consider the behavior of two groups of states. The first group of states desires a lower level of obligation than that required by the custom. Conversely, the other group of states prefers a higher level of obligation than the emerging custom would deliver.

First, take the case in which the ideal level of custom participation e_i for state i is less than the emerging custom obligation level e^C. Should state i decide to join the custom, it would never choose full participation, given the opportunity to obtain partial exemption via the persistent objector doctrine. This is true because the payoff obtainable at the privately optimal e_i is higher than that obtained by full adherence to the custom e^C. Thus, state i either joins the custom partially by becoming a partial persistent objector, or opts out of the custom altogether by raising full objection. In either case, state i takes advantage of the opportunity to be a persistent objector. The choice between full and partial objection is driven by the relative magnitudes of $P_i(e_i)$ and $\bar{P}_i(\bar{e}_i)$. If $\bar{P}_i(\bar{e}_i)$ is greater than $P_i(e_i)$, the payoff under the no-custom regime is higher than the payoff from joining the custom. State i therefore fully objects to the custom. Substituting the values found in (12.3) and (12.5) for $\bar{P}_i(\bar{e}_i)$ and $P_i(e_i)$ and simplifying, we see that state i fully objects if $1/\bar{a}_i > \alpha_i/\beta_i\,a$. Thus, when the cost of not joining the custom $\bar{a}_i$ is relatively small and/or the probability ratio α_i/β_i is small, the persistent objector state i fully opposes the emerging custom.[19] On the other hand, when the cost of not joining the custom is rather large and/or the probability ratio α_i/β_i is large, the persistent objector state i partially opposes the emerging custom.

Next, consider the case in which the ideal level of custom participation e_i for state i is greater than the emerging custom obligation level e^C. Although state i prefers the emergence of a custom with a higher level of obligation, persistent objector states cannot force a level of customary obligation higher than the emerging custom. Thus, the state's benefit from joining the custom is given by the payoff at the custom obligation level e^C: $P_i(e^C)$. The participation constraint now requires a comparison between the payoff obtained under the no-custom regime $\bar{P}_i(\bar{e}_i)$ and $P_i(e^C)$. If $P_i(e^C)$ is greater than $\bar{P}_i(\bar{e}_i)$, there is full participation in the custom and state i does not become a persistent objector. If $\bar{P}_i(\bar{e}_i)$ is greater than $P_i(e^C)$, state i is better off opting out of the custom altogether by becoming a full persistent objector.

The above analysis brings to light some interesting results. First, different categories of states may choose to opt out of an emerging custom. Full objection is a rational strategy not only for states that consider the emerging custom excessively burdensome, but also for states that like the custom but want more of it. Some states agree with the spirit of the custom but are not satisfied with the emerging rule because they would like a custom with a greater level of obligation. Some of these states may be better off opting for a no-custom regime and addressing the issue on their own. The payoff in a no-custom regime represents the opportunity cost of custom participation identified in (12.5). This opportunity cost will likely be larger for stronger states that face lower cost, $\bar{a}_i$, and which may have greater opportunities to stand alone and generate benefits for themselves in the absence of international cooperation. For those states customary cooperation is less indispensable than for other states that have less opportunity to address the underlying need by acting on their own. Given the lower payoff obtainable in a no-custom regime, weaker states facing higher costs may be more willing to go along with an emerging custom that does not correspond to their ideal level.

Second, the likelihood of participation in a less than ideal custom depends on the ratio of the probabilities of being on the receiving side versus the giving side of the customary relationship in future time periods. States that are more likely to benefit from the custom than to be burdened by it are more likely to participate in the custom, even though the custom does not correspond to their ideal optimum.

Finally, the level of objection would differ if states had to formulate objections at the time they were called upon to comply with the custom. In this model we do not include the initial cost of custom compliance because the persistent objector doctrine requires the objection to be "consistent" (i.e., states' objections should be formulated ex ante, rather than when states are called upon to perform a custom obligation). The legal requirement of "consistency" is thus instrumental in avoiding manipulation of the content of the custom by a state's myopic strategic objection. If allowed to formulate objections when compliance is due, states might be tempted to corrode the mutual long-term benefits of the custom to avoid immediate compliance costs. This would compromise the ability of the custom process to generate desirable levels of legal obligations.

3. Subsequent Objector Doctrines in International Customary Law

According to traditional international law, states can object to a norm of international customary law only during its emergence. The persistent objector doctrine requires a timely reaction of states to emerging customs. If a state waits to object until after the practice becomes a binding rule of international customary law, the state cannot claim exemption from it. Subsequent departures of a state from an established custom would constitute an international wrong, unless other states acquiesce to the state's late departure. A state cannot *unilaterally* depart from a customary rule once it has become bound by it.[20]

This traditional approach provides an opt-out opportunity during the formative phase of a custom but provides no flexibility for subsequent adaptation of custom to the changing needs of the international community over time. In the context of multilateral customs, international law practice has gradually developed doctrines to avoid excessive rigidity of international customary law. One such doctrine, resulting from the application of the long-standing principle of *rebus sic stantibus* to customary law, allows states to depart from international law in the face of fundamental changes in the state of affairs that led to the original legal obligation (Kontou 1994).[21] Given their limited verifiability, changes to individual states' costs and benefits are not covered by the *rebus sic stantibus* principle. Likewise, states are not allowed to invoke changes in internal laws or policies as a justification for a unilateral departure from international customary law.[22] Departures from customary law that are not supported by the *rebus sic stantibus* principle may nevertheless find limited accommodation in the *subsequent objector doctrine* (Brownlie 1990).

The subsequent objector doctrine addresses situations where a state (the "subsequent objector" state) objects or departs from a customary rule after its formation, as opposed to objecting to the rule during its emergence, as in the persistent objector case.[23] The effects of a state's departure from a previously recognized custom are determined by the speed and spread of the process of defection. Many different outcomes are possible under this doctrine. One limiting case occurs if a substantial number of states depart from an old custom. If the momentum of widespread defection is accompanied by general acquiescence by the remaining states, a new rule may result. Thus if events unfold rapidly, one state's departure from an existing custom may trigger the emergence and widespread adoption of a new custom. The other limiting takes place when the subsequent objector's departure from customary law is met with general opposition by other states. In this case the subsequent objector's action, far from generating a new custom, is construed as a breach of international customary law. The subsequent objector doctrine in fact does not allow unilateral departures from existing custom.

The subsequent objector doctrine provides rules to govern the array of possibilities contained between these limiting cases. Specifically, when defection is not widespread and it is not possible to identify a new emerging general custom, the effects of the subsequent objector's actions depend on specific relationships with the opposing states. The subsequent objector doctrine specifies that in the face of a unilateral departure from an existing custom, a subsequent objector can only gain an exemption from a rule of customary law if, and to the extent that, its departure is not opposed by other states. Because the reactions of the other states may differ from one another, application of the subsequent objector doctrine leads to the creation of "a network of special relations based on opposability, acquiescence, and historic title" (Brownlie 1990: 5). For example, the relationship between a subsequent objector and a fully acquiescing state is governed by a bilateral obligation consistent with the norm advocated by the objector state. The relationship between a subsequent objector and an opposing state remains governed by the preexisting custom. Finally, when the departure is only partially opposed, the content of the rule governing the bilateral relation between the departing state and the partially objecting state changes according to the extent of the latter state's acquiescence.

The above process implies that when one state departs from a preexisting custom and another state acquiesces to such departure the subsequent objector doctrine allows the rule to be modified between these parties.[24]

The change in customary law affects only the relations between these states. Other states must choose between becoming parties to a new or amended custom that may affect their rights under the preexisting customary rule, or continue to adhere to the old regime and demand compliance with the preexisting custom by the departing state. Even in the face of a third state's opposition, the change in the customary law between the departing state and the acquiescing state will take place.[25] In practice, this process often fragments a previously uniform rule of custom into a network of bilateral relations, where the content of each bilateral relation is determined by the extent of one state's departure and the other state's acquiescence.[26]

4. Custom with Subsequent Objectors: Theoretical Considerations

In the subsequent objector doctrine, the objection to a custom takes the form of a departure from an established and already binding rule of custom. To highlight and separate the subsequent objector's problem from the persistent objector's problem, we start with a group of homogeneous states acting under an established custom. This stylized simplification ensures that when the custom emerges, no state has an incentive to become a persistent objector. In particular, each state faces the same probability of receiving benefit α, the probability of being burdened by the custom obligation β, the same discount rate r, and the same benefit and cost from participation in the custom, be and ae^2. Thus, each homogeneous state i is confronted with the forward-looking problem before the practice consolidates to a custom:

$$\max_{e} \; P_i = \frac{1}{r}(\alpha\, be - \beta a e^2), \qquad\qquad 12.6$$

and each state chooses the following effort level:

$$e^* = \frac{\alpha b}{2a\beta} \qquad\qquad 12.7$$

Given homogeneity of the states, the effort level e^* characterizes the content of the states' respective obligations under customary law.

Given an existing rule of customary law, there are many reasons why a state may become a subsequent objector.[27] Some reasons are merely strategic: a state may object to an existing rule of customary law to avoid the cost of fulfilling its obligations under that rule. Other subsequent objections are driven by changes in the costs and benefits of the custom. For example, if the cost a of complying with the custom has increased or if the probability α of receiving a benefit from other states' compliance has decreased, a state may develop different views on the desirable content of the custom.[28]

To understand how other states react to a subsequent objector's departure from existing custom, it is useful to separate states into three groups. The first group consists of first-party states that have reasons to become subsequent objector states. The second group of states comprises second-party states that would benefit from the subsequent objector's fulfillment of the customary obligation. Finally, third-party states neither expend effort to fulfill the customary obligation nor receive any direct benefit from the subsequent objector's compliance in the current period.

Just as a state may become a subsequent objector for various reasons, different factors influence the reactions of second-, third-, and other first-party states to a proposed departure of a subsequent objector.[29] We first consider the case of no exogenous changes in the circumstances of all states. Then we assume uniform changes in the circumstances of all states. Finally, we study the subsequent objector doctrine given asymmetric changes in the circumstances of all states.

4.1. Strategic Departures, Subsequent Objector Doctrine, and Opposition from Other States

Consider the case in which probabilities, benefits, and costs associated with the expected long-term participation in the custom do not change for any state. A first-party state may still become a subsequent objector for strategic and myopic reasons. In one period, the first-party state confronts its turn to fulfill the obligations under customary law. The need to incur an immediate cost for compliance with the custom may induce the first-party state to invoke a standard different from the existing customary law and to become a subsequent objector. Due to the immediate performance costs the first-party state faces a somewhat different yet myopic problem from before:

$$\max_{e} P_1 = -ae^2 + \frac{1}{r}(\alpha be - \beta ae^2) \qquad 12.8$$

The privately optimal effort of the first-party state now differs from the existing customary obligation:

$$e_1 = \frac{\alpha b}{2a(r + \beta)}$$ 12.9

Because $\alpha/(r + \beta) < \alpha/\beta$, from (12.9) and (12.7) we see that $e_1 < e^*$. The first-party state wishes to depart from the existing rule of custom and is willing to lower the future customary obligations for all participants in light of its current situation. Although e_1 is first-best for the subsequent objector state, any value less than the original customary rule e^* is better than e^*, as long as it is greater than e_1. Thus, in proposing a departure from the existing custom, the subsequent objector effectively puts a lower bound on the acceptable level of custom at e_1.

If the subsequent objector state could have its own way, custom would evolve to a lower level, with a partial erosion of the preexisting customary rule. But the subsequent objector's proposed departure is not necessarily acceptable to other states.[30] When another state does not oppose (acquiescence) the subsequent objector's departure from an existing custom, the content of the custom changes from the original value e^* to e_1 for both the subsequent objector and the acquiescing states. When another state opposes (no acquiescence) the subsequent objector's departure from an existing custom, the content of the custom between the subsequent objector and the nonacquiescing state remains at the original value e^*. In the intermediate case in which departure is partially opposed (partial acquiescence), the content of the custom between the two states changes from the original customary value e^* to the lower value acquiesced by the other state.

A typical third-party state acquiesces to the first-party state's departure from an existing custom only if the resulting change to the custom yields a total payoff that exceeds the payoff obtainable under the current rule. Because there is no obligation to comply in the current period, there are no immediate benefits to be gained, and no change occurred, the third-party state's problem does not change. That is, the problem confronting the third-party state is again given in (12.6) and the existing customary level of effort given in (12.7) remains optimal to the third-party state. The third-party state continues to find the existing custom obligation privately optimal:

$$e_3 = e^*.$$ 12.10

This means that in the absence of changes to the exogenous variables, a third-party state opposes the subsequent objector state's departure.

Similar to a third-party state, a second-party state acquiesces to another state's departure from an existing custom only if the resulting change in custom yields a total payoff at least as large as the payoff obtainable under the current custom. Although there are no changes to the circumstances of the second-party state, this state derives an immediate benefit from the subsequent objector's fulfillment of the customary obligation in the current period. Thus, the problem confronting the second-party state is no longer given by (12.6). Instead, it is the following:

$$\max_{e} \; P_2 = be + \frac{1}{r}(\alpha be - \beta ae^2) \qquad\qquad 12.11$$

This means that the desired custom for the third-party state is characterized by effort level:

$$e_2 = \frac{(r+\alpha)b}{2a\beta}. \qquad\qquad 12.12$$

Given the expectation of an immediate benefit from the other state's compliance with the custom, the second-party state desires a level of effort e_2 that is larger than the one required by existing customary law $e^* = \alpha b / 2a\beta$. The second-party state opposes the subsequent objector state's departure to a level lower than e^*.

Affected by strategic and myopic considerations, a second-party state opposes more strongly an objector's departure than does a neutral third-party bystander, as can be seen from the fact that $e_2 > e^* = e_3$. These results suggest that in the absence of any change in circumstances for all states, the subsequent objector doctrine effectively constrains departures from existing customary law driven solely by the attempt to avoid immediate costs of compliance. Any such strategic attempts to depart are always met with opposition by second- and third-party states.

4.2. Strategic Nonacquiescence and the Inertia of Customary Law

After the formation of a custom, there may be changes to exogenous factors affecting the behavior of states. We next concentrate on a uniform change to all states that gives the first-party state an additional reason to depart from the custom. Without loss of generality, assume that the cost of performing increases from a to a' for all states. Updating the problem confronting the first-party state and adjusting the effort level from (12.9), the first-party state now chooses to depart from the existing customary level e^* to effort level e_1' where e_1' satisfies the following:[31]

$$e_1' = \frac{\alpha b}{2a'(r+\beta)} < e_1 < e^* \qquad 12.13$$

In addition to the immediate compliance cost issue, the first-party state now incurs a higher cost to fulfill its obligations under the custom. This provides an additional reason for the first-party state to become a subsequent objector.[32] Indeed, comparing effort level e_1' for this case and effort level e_1 in (12.9) when there are no exogenous changes in performance cost, the first-party state now has an incentive to depart from the custom by adopting a lower level than it would adopt in the absence of an increase in performance cost.

Given the rise in performance cost, the third-party state is also inclined to adopt a lower level of custom than before. Updating the optimal level of effort in (12.7), the third-party state now desires e_3' where

$$e_1' < e_3' = \frac{\alpha b}{2a'\beta} < e^* \qquad 12.14$$

Thus, induced by higher cost the third-party state consents to a change in custom by partially acquiescing to e_3'. The customary obligations of two states toward one another can only be modified by the extent to which both implicitly agree to the change. Partial acquiescence by the third-party state to the subsequent objector therefore leads to a partial change in customary law. The content of the custom between the two states changes from the original customary value e^* to e_3'.

For the second-party state, the problem is similar to that considered previously, with an immediate benefit term. This time, however, the second-party state faces the same exogenous cost change faced by the other states. Adjusting (12.12) to the higher-cost parameter a', the optimal level of effort for the second-party state becomes

$$e_2' = \frac{(r+\alpha)b}{2a'\beta} \qquad 12.15$$

Comparing the level of effort in (12.15) with the existing customary level $e^* = \alpha b/2a\beta$, it is not clear whether e_2' or e^* is larger; the immediate benefit has a positive impact on the level of effort while the increase in future performance cost has a negative impact. When e_2' is greater than or equal to e^*, the second-party state opposes the subsequent objector's departure. This prevents any change in the custom governing the relationship between the first- and second-party state. When e_2' is less than e^*, given that e_2' in (12.15) is greater than e_1' in (12.13), the second-party state only partially opposes the subsequent objector's departure. Hence, the content of the custom between the two states changes from the original customary value e^* to e_2'.

To conclude, when all states face a uniform increase in performance cost, there is a partial convergence of interests between the subsequent objector and the third-party state. The subsequent objector's departure from the current custom is motivated by the attempt to reduce the burden of immediate compliance and to minimize the impact of higher compliance costs in the future. The third-party state shares the motive to reduce the impact of higher compliance costs in the future. Thus the subsequent objector has incentives to depart more extensively from the existing custom than the third-party state would likely allow.

For the second-party state, the net effect of an exogenous change in costs depends on whether the presence of an immediate benefit for the second-party state is offset by the increase in future performance cost. If the impact of immediate benefit dominates, the second-party state is either content with the current customary rule or wants a level of custom higher than the current level. The second-party state opposes any departure by the subsequent objector from the current custom, and the relationship between the two states remains governed by the existing customary rule. If the impact induced by the increase in future performance cost dominates, the second-party state's private optimum falls below the existing customary law. Still, the second-party state's private optimum is greater than the level preferred by the subsequent objector. In this case a partial convergence between the interests of the subsequent objector state and the second-party state takes place. The second-party state forgoes part of the immediate benefit from the custom by providing partial acquiescence. The custom governing the relationship between the two states changes from the existing customary law to the level desired by second-party state.

The above analysis reveals a potential factor of inertia in the process of custom formation. When exogenous changes affect the states' ideal levels of customary law, the adaptation of customary law to such changes in circumstances may be hindered by opposition from second-party states. Second-party states may oppose the subsequent objector's departure not so much because they value the current custom, but because they are attracted by the immediate benefit from custom compliance. This further justifies the workings of the subsequent objector doctrine, allowing the bilateral obligations of first- and third-party states to adapt to changed circumstances in spite of second-party states' opposition.

4.3. The Adaptation of Custom to Changed Circumstances

We end our analysis of the subsequent objector doctrine by considering the case of asymmetric exogenous changes for the states involved. Start by assuming that the subsequent objector chooses a level of departure effort e_1'' less than existing customary law e^*, either for strategic reasons or for reasons induced by environmental changes.[33]

In the face of the subsequent objector's departure from current custom, the problems confronting a second-party state and a third-party state are similar, except for the extra immediate benefit factor enjoyed by the second-party state. Without loss of generality, we only consider the specific problem confronting a third-party state in detail. With primes indicating new values for the parameters, the problem confronting the third-party state is

$$\max_{e} \; P_3 = \frac{1}{r'}(\alpha' b' e - \beta' a' e^2). \tag{12.16}$$

The optimal level of effort for the third-party state is given by

$$e_3'' = \frac{\alpha' b'}{2a' \beta'} \tag{12.17}$$

Recall that a state acquiesces to another state's departure from an existing custom if the resulting change to the custom yields a total payoff that is higher than the payoff obtainable under the current rule. In this section, because the problem is more general, we introduce the concept of acquiescence constraint to help identify the changing relationship between a state's departure and another state's acquiescence. Given that e^* is the existing customary level of effort, the third-party state acquiesces to a different and lower level of effort e (perhaps different from e_3'') only if it satisfies the acquiescence constraint:[34]

$$\frac{1}{r'}(\alpha' b' e - \beta' a' e^2) \geq \frac{1}{r'}(\alpha' b' e^* - \beta' a' e^{*2}) \tag{12.18}$$

Note that e_3'' maximizes the left hand side of inequality (12.18). Thus, if the exogenous changes in the third-party state are such that e_3'' is greater than the existing customary law e^*, the third-party state would like to raise the content of the custom obligation to its privately optimal value e_3''. But this is not an option for the third-party state. When faced with the departure of a state from current customary law, the third-party state can either acquiesce or oppose such departure but cannot induce a change of the custom toward an even higher level e_3''. The acquiescence constraint thus implies that the lowest acceptable value for the third-party state is the current customary value e^*. In this case, the third-party state does not acquiesce.

Next consider the case in which the exogenous changes in the third-party state induce an effort level e_3'' less than the existing customary law e^*. Like the subsequent objector, the third-party state also desires a lower level of effort for the custom. Clearly e_3'' is the most desirable among all customary rules that are acceptable to the third-party state. Departures from the customary obligation that fall between e_3'' and e^* satisfy the acquiescence constraint (12.18) and all changes of the customary rule between e_3'' and e^* improve the payoff to the third-party state over the status quo. In particular, the closer the custom level to the private optimum e_3'' the better off the third-party state will be. On the other hand, although there are levels of effort below e_3'' that satisfy the acquiescence constraint, these levels of effort are inferior to e_3'' for the third-party state. Hence, there is no reason for the third-party state to acquiesce to any change in current custom that brings the level of customary obligation below its privately optimal value e_3''. Thus, similar to the subsequent objector, the third-party state has a lower bound on the acceptable level of custom: e_3''.

Given that the third-party state is willing to accommodate any proposed change in custom as low as e_3'', when the subsequent objector's desired level e_1'' is larger than e_3'', the third-party state provides full acquiescence. In this case, e_1'' becomes the content of the bilateral custom that governs the relationship between the first-party state and the third-party state. When the subsequent objector's desired level e_1'' is less than the desired level e_3'' for the third-party state, the third-party state is only willing to provide partial acquiescence. In this case, e_3'' characterizes the bilateral custom between the third-party state and the subsequent objector.

At this point, we adopt a slightly more general notation. Let e_O represent the effort level adopted by the subsequent objector state. We refer to any state confronted with the subsequent objector state's departure and facing the acquiescence problem as state A. Further, assume that e_A is the privately

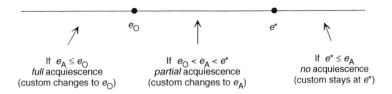

FIGURE 12.1 The Subsequent Objector Doctrine

optimal level of effort for state A. We generalize the results found in the previous analysis to show that the combined effects of the subsequent objector's departure from current customary law and the other state's acquiescence may lead to various possible changes in the custom between the two states. Such change is given by max $\{e_O, e_A\}$ when $e_A < e^*$. According to the subsequent objector doctrine, if max $\{e_O, e_A\} = e_O$, there is full acquiescence and the bilateral custom evolves to the subsequent objector's preferred level e_O. If max $\{e_O, e_A\} = e_A$, there is partial acquiescence, and the bilateral custom governing the relationship between the two states instead evolves to the choice of the partially acquiescing state e_A. No change in customary law takes place when $e_A \geq e^*$.

Figure 12.1 maps the different scenarios. In the figure, the value chosen by the subsequent objector e_O and the current customary rule e^* are held constant.

Figure 12.1 identifies three regions. In the first region, $e_A \leq e_O$ indicates that state A wants a level of custom less than or equal to the level proposed by the subsequent objector. In this case, application of the subsequent objector doctrine implies that the relationship between state A and the subsequent objector state is governed by a bilateral customary rule e_O.

The second region, $e_O < e_A < e^*$, is characterized by partial convergence between the interests of state A and the subsequent objector state. Although both states are dissatisfied with current custom, state A wants a level of custom above the level proposed by the subsequent objector. In this case, application of the subsequent objector doctrine leads to a more limited change, from e^* to e_A, in the custom governing the relationship between the two states.

In the third region, $e^* \leq e_A$, state A is either content with the current customary rule, $e^* = e_A$, or wants a level of custom which is higher than the current level, $e^* < e_A$. In this case, state A opposes any attempted departure of the subsequent objector from the current custom. This lack of acquiescence implies that the relationship between the two states remains governed by the existing customary rule e^* and that any departure from the rule is treated as a breach of international customary law.

%% 5. Change and Stability in Customary Law

The economic models of custom formation presented in this chapter illustrate how existing legal principles are instrumental to securing consensus in the formation and transformation of custom. Customary rules cannot be enforced against states that have opposed a given custom from its inception. Similarly unilateral departures from existing customary law can exempt from legal obligations only with the acquiescence of other states.

The significance of the persistent and subsequent objector doctrines can be fully appreciated in the case of heterogeneous states. Widely accepted customary principles may acquire different forms when implemented in the practice of heterogeneous states. The content of some customary rules may prove very undesirable for high-cost states. In this chapter we have explored the important intuition of Goldsmith and Posner (1999) according to which universal norms of international customary law are the result of pairwise state interactions. This exploration contributes to this line of research by studying the specific role of persistent and subsequent objector doctrines in the process of custom formation and change. These doctrines avoid the dangers associated with imposing a new rule or transforming an existing rule on a sovereign nation that has ostensibly opposed the new rule or transformation. Any attempt to force changes in the customary law against nonconsenting states would open the doors to a potential "tyranny of the majority," in that any large number of states could impose a costly customary obligation on a minority of nonconsenting states.[35] This would undermine the legitimacy of custom as a source of public international law in a world of sovereign nations.

As a result of these voluntary mechanisms of custom formation, customs emerge only if the resulting rule is at least weakly preferred to the status quo. Dissenting states can opt out of emerging regimes of customary law. Likewise, changes in existing customary law can only take place with respect to states that suffer no prejudice from the change. Opposing states can continue to invoke the older rule against departing states.

Both doctrines assure that any new rule of customary law or any change to existing customary law only affects states for which the new rule or the change in existing rule constitutes a Pareto improvement. A state facing a net prejudice from a newly emerging custom can opt out from that rule by persistently objecting. Likewise, any state facing a prejudice from a departure from an existing custom can oppose the departure and enforce the current rule. There are, however, limits to custom formation when heterogeneous states are involved. Through application of the persistent objector doctrine, high-cost states effectively constrain the emergence of new custom in their relationships with other states. The resulting level of custom formation may be suboptimal compared to the alternative scenario in which high-cost and low-cost states effectively bargain with one another for the choice of a value-maximizing customary effort. The subsequent objector doctrine creates the opposite problem. By allowing acquiescence of other states to serve as constraints, this doctrine may yield excessive customary obligations to outlive the circumstances that justified their emergence. In the presence of heterogeneous states, these persistent and subsequent objector doctrines allocate control over the resulting level of customary law on different states. By doing so, these doctrines promote stability in customary relations but may fail to induce first best social optima obtainable via compromise solutions. These results are consistent with the traditional wisdom according to which custom is an effective source of international law when homogeneous states are involved, but that alternative sources such as treaty law may be better instruments for the pursuit of first best outcomes when heterogeneous parties are involved.[36]

A comparison between the results achieved under persistent objector and subsequent objector regimes reveals that when acting in a timely fashion, high-cost states have an advantage over low-cost states. Persistent objectors can gain a partial or full exemption from an emerging custom. High-cost states can effectively control the level of custom formation, at least with respect to their networks of bilateral relations with other states. In the face of a persistent objection, low-cost states can only invoke the general principle of reciprocity in international law, allowing them to adopt the same customary level against the objecting state when roles are reversed. In this context, the persistent objector doctrine constitutes an example of weak reciprocity, given that the reciprocal level of customary obligations corresponds to the lower level unilaterally desired by the persistent objector.

Opposite results hold when the objecting state fails to manifest its dissent in a timely fashion. In this case, high-cost states can legitimately depart from custom only if the departure is accepted by low-cost states through express endorsement or tacit acquiescence. Low-cost states thus control change in the custom by having an opportunity to oppose other states' departure from a binding rule of customary law. In this context, the subsequent objector doctrine constitutes an example of strong reciprocity, because customary obligations are kept high by states that prefer higher levels and oppose the departure of the subsequent objector state.

It is generally believed that the more restrictive conditions of the subsequent objector doctrine promote stability and reliance in customary law. The economic model reveals that the subsequent objector doctrine also avoids strategic departures from existing custom motivated by myopic attempts to avoid the immediate costs of compliance with existing customary law. Absent such restrictions the sustainability of customary law would be severely undermined. The general functionality of this doctrine, however, reveals its shortcomings when states that derive an immediate benefit from the custom are myopic and act strategically, opposing departures from existing custom. This may result in the survival of customs that no longer correspond to the values of the international community at large.

⁂ 6. Conclusions

Given the absence of a world legislature and the cost involved with forming and ratifying multilateral treaties, customary law has played a fundamental role in governing relationships between sovereign states in both historical and modern settings. Although customary law is capable of creating universally binding rules, the persistent and subsequent objector doctrines provide ways for states to gain exemptions from emerging or existing rules of customary law. According to the persistent objector doctrine, a state can gain an exemption from emerging norms of customary law by opposing an emerging customary practice. The subsequent objector doctrine additionally allows a state to gain an exemption from a binding custom when its departure from the custom is met with acquiescence by other states.

The persistent and subsequent objector doctrines acquire particular importance when heterogeneous states are involved, because they provide criteria for determining the content of the binding custom when states advocate different customary rules in the course of their interactions. The economic analysis has shown that these processes of custom formation effectively discourage strategic objections and opportunistic departures from customary law, while leaving room for objections and departures that reflect differences in state preferences or changes in costs and benefits of custom compliance. These mechanisms, which are themselves the product of spontaneous evolution, provide flexibility for the gradual adaptation of custom to changing circumstances over time.

Numerous related issues exist which we have not explicitly considered in the present analysis. For instance, reputational costs may influence the formation of customary norms. Objector states may face reputational costs when objecting to customary law, and second- and third-party states may also face reputational costs when opposing another state's departure from an existing custom. The practice of customary law is heavily affected by considerations of diplomatic and political expediency, and such costs may create frictions and biases in the process of custom formation that are worthy of consideration. Further, if reputational costs differ from state to state, this may create a systematic advantage for states that place less weight on reputation. The process of custom formation is further affected by free-riding and opportunistic behavior by second- and third-party states, none of which fully internalizes the benefit of monitoring other states' compliance with custom. Thus when states face a private cost in opposing departures from customary law and generate a public benefit for the international community a public good problem may arise. As a result states may fail to oppose other states' departures more often than is desirable for the world community as a whole. Future research should verify the relevance of this analysis for understanding other social and legal settings where social norms or customary rules are created through the spontaneous interaction of parties in society.

PART IV

Lawmaking through Agreement
Treaty Law

THIRTEEN

Lawmaking through Agreement
An Introduction

IN THE FOLLOWING THREE CHAPTERS we consider the role of treaties among the sources of law, with special attention to the rules governing their formation and process of evolution. Treaties are a unique source of law and are difficult to analogize to any of the other sources of law considered thus far in this book.

A critical feature of this form of lawmaking is its consensual nature. The formation of treaty law is governed by notions of privity. Unlike other sources of law capable of exerting their effect on individuals that did not participate (or did not agree) to their formation, treaty law is binding only on parties that affirmatively agreed to be bound by it.

※ 1. Treaties Generally

Treaties are agreements between international actors, such as states and international organizations, capable of having lawmaking effects for the participating parties. According to Buergenthal and Maier (1990), "[t]reaties perform a variety of functions on the international plane that in domestic law are performed by many different types of legal acts and instruments, including constitutions, laws of general applicability, contracts, deeds, trust agreements, corporate charters, etc." When treaties perform their function as sources of law they are referred to as *lawmaking treaties*, that is, lawmaking by means of an agreement between two of more nations creating legally binding rules for them (Brownlie 1990).

Treaties can be classified according to the number of initial participants as bilateral, plurilateral, and multilateral agreements. Bilateral agreements are generally concluded via negotiations between the foreign ministries with the occasional involvement of other representative organs. Drafts are prepared and exchanged until an agreement on a final version is reached. Plurilateral treaties, involving a relatively small number of participants, are concluded similarly. The process of negotiations for multilateral treaties, involving a large number of states or organizations, is quite different. Diplomatic delegations negotiate the terms of the prospective treaty, usually with the creation of drafting committees and the support of legal advisors. There is an abundance of preparatory work, working papers, draft proposals, amendment, and revisions that makes multilateral negotiations costly and difficult to administer. Further, the rate of successful formation and implementation of multilateral international agreements is generally lower, given the obvious difficulties of reaching a unanimous consensus among participants that come to the bargaining table with different views and expectations. Treaties enter into force when the parties indicate their intention to be bound by the agreement, subject to the ratification requirements specified by the states' domestic constitutional rules.

A state may become part of a treaty in one of two ways, (1) by being one of the original signatories to a treaty, or (2) by acceding to an existing treaty.

2. Treaties under the Vienna Convention

The rules that govern the formation and effects of international treaty law are largely customary in origin but have now been codified by the U.N. Convention on the Law of Treaties, which was signed in Vienna on May 23, 1969 (Vienna Convention). The Vienna Convention itself represents a combination of codification of customary international law and creation of new legal norms through progressive development, although the line between the two is not necessarily clear. In this part of the book, we largely analyze treaties as they would be created, acceded to, and ratified under the Vienna Convention. As such, some background on the Vienna Convention will be helpful.

2.1. Treaty Creation and Accession under the Vienna Convention

As discussed above, states can become part of a treaty by either being an original signatory to the treaty or by acceding (i.e., joining) a treaty that has already been created. This is true under the Vienna Convention, as it was under customary international law.

The Vienna Convention also addresses how and when nonsignatory states may accede to a treaty, thereby assenting to be bound by that treaty.

Article 15 of the Vienna Convention establishes three ways such accession is possible: (1) The treaty itself provides that states may accede to it; (2) it is otherwise established by the states negotiating the treaty that states may accede to the treaty; or (3) all signatories to the treaty have agreed that a state may accede.[1]

When signatories to a treaty elect the first option and places no further restrictions on accession, the treaty is referred to as "open." When they elect the third option, thereby requiring unanimous consent for accession, the treaty is referred to a "closed." Signatories to a treaty also sometimes adopt an intermediate option, for instance allowing accession only if a majority of signatories approve. Treaties with such rules are referred to as "semi-open."

Treaty creation and accession will be discussed in greater detail in Chapter 14.

2.2. Treaty Ratification and Reservations under the Vienna Convention

Ratification is the means by which states officially approve the entry into a signed treaty, thereby binding the ratifying state. When ratifying a treaty, states can introduce reservations about specific provisions of a treaty, attempting to exclude themselves from some of the obligations arising from the treaty. Unlike the prior customary rules governing the formation of treaties, which required the unanimous consent of all parties to change the legal effect of a treaty through reservations, the Vienna Convention allows states who ratify or accede to a treaty to introduce reservations on specific provisions via unilateral statements. By making a reservation, a state can modify or exclude the applicability of certain treaty provisions, thus excluding itself from the legal effect of such terms. The effects of treaty reservations will be discussed in Chapter 15 and dealt with in greater depth in Chapter 16.

3. Lawmaking through Agreement: The Economics of Treaty Law

The following provides a brief outline of Chapters 14, 15, and 16, which address different aspects of the economics of treaty law. In Chapter 14 we develop a stylized model of international treaty formation and analyze the different ways states can become part of an international treaty according to the procedures set forth by the Vienna Convention on the Law of Treaties. We consider the rules governing accession to international treaties, distinguishing between three situations: (1) treaties for which acceptance of a new member requires unanimous approval of the signatory states with an amendment of the original treaty agreement (closed treaties); (2) treaties where acceptance of a new member is made possible through the approval by a majority of the existing member states (semi-open treaties); and (3) treaties where the original member states have agreed to leave the treaty open for accession by other states (open treaties).

In Chapter 15 we consider the process of treaty reservation. The difficulties that characterize the formation of multilateral treaties explain the special attention given by the 1969 Vienna Convention to the preservation of multilateral treaties at the stage of ratification. To help facilitate multilateral agreements coming into force when signatory states introduce reservations at the time of accession or ratification, the Vienna Convention originated a more liberal approach to treaty reservations, as introduced above. The new regime introduced by the Convention allows states to formulate reservations, as long as the signatory states did not agree otherwise and as long as the reservations are not contrary to the general objectives of the treaty. When allowed to do so, states can introduce reservations when signing, ratifying, accepting, approving, or acceding to a treaty. Reservations purport to exclude or to modify the legal effect of certain provisions of the treaty in the reserving State. Article 21 of the Vienna Convention creates a matching-reservations mechanism, according to which a reservation modifies the treaty not only in favor of the reserving state but also in the relationships between the reserving state and the other nonreserving parties. We identify some of the strengths and weaknesses of the reservations mechanism introduced by the Vienna Convention. When states face asymmetric incentives, the rules introduced by the Vienna Convention may not discourage all reservations. We also analyze the welfare properties of the outcomes likely to be generated when such asymmetric incentives are at work. We show that the rules set forth by the Vienna Convention provide an effective solution to the danger of strategic behavior by states attempting to gain unilateral benefits through the mechanism of reservations. However, the current reservations regime does not always induce socially optimal levels of ratification. We will show that a social optimum is achieved only in the limited subset of cases where signatory states have homogeneous payoff functions, or when all states prefer full ratification, despite the differences in the incentives that they face.

The strengths of the reservations regime discussed in Chapter 15 become particularly obvious in complex multilateral treaties, where significant negotiating (and renegotiating) cost savings can be achieved by allowing minor deviations through reservations. It is in these settings, however, that the reciprocity mechanism reveals its shortfalls. In Chapter 16 we unveil an interesting effect of the process of treaty ratification introduced by the Vienna Convention. Behind the apparent neutrality of the reciprocity principle, reservations under Article 21 create a strategic advantage for developing countries and, more generally, for states that face higher costs or receive lower benefits from treaty implementation and compliance. This strategic advantage in turn can potentially affect the content of treaty law. As it will be discussed, the source of the bias is found in the unequal opportunity of high-cost and low-cost states to introduce reservations. A state who gains less from the treaty relative to other states has the opportunity to reduce its international treaty obligations via unilateral reservations. No symmetric opportunity is given to other states who desire to add provisions to a treaty or to raise the content of a treaty obligation under an existing provision. This strategic advantage may in some occasions favor poorer and developing nations that face higher cost-benefit ratios in treaty implementation, whereas in other situations it may create an advantage for larger and powerful nations, whose well-being depends less critically on international cooperation.

Formation and Accession to Treaties*

TREATIES ARE INSTRUMENTS of international cooperation. Although states can pursue some goals in isolation, international cooperation through treaties may provide an opportunity to more effectively achieve such goals. In this chapter we begin the analysis of treaty law by considering the initial steps through which treaties come to life.

As discussed in Chapter 13, states can become part of an international treaty in two basic ways: (1) being among the original signatory states of a treaty; and (2) acceding to an existing treaty. Original signatory states often face substantial costs in the process of treaty negotiation and drafting, whereas the costs of acceding to an existing treaty are generally lower. However, there are benefits in being part of the original group of signatory states, rather than acceding to the treaty at a later stage. For example, the founding states influence the content of the treaty. In this chapter we analyze the process of treaty formation in light of the possibility that nonsignatory states may be given an opportunity to join an existing treaty through accession. Under what conditions is it desirable for the original states to leave a treaty open for accession? What are the likely characteristics of these treaties?

In this chapter we develop a model of international treaty formation to analyze the different modalities by which states can become party to an international treaty. We analyze the advantages original signatory states have over acceding states that justify undertaking the initial treaty negotiation costs. Section 1 starts by describing the main categories of treaty accession: (1) closed treaties; (2) semi-open treaties; and (3) open treaties. Section 2 considers the process of treaty formation under these categories.

* This chapter is based on an article previously published as Fon, Vincy, and Francesco Parisi, "Formation of International Treaties," *Review of Law and Economics* 3: 37–60 (2007).

Section 3 discusses some variations of the basic model and draws conclusions.

🦓 1. Formation and Accession to International Treaties

The Vienna Convention on the law of treaties allows the original parties to an international treaty to determine if and how nonsignatory states may subsequently join the treaty agreement. Article 15 of the Vienna Convention authorizes a state to consent to be bound to a treaty by accession when

(a) the treaty provides that such consent may be expressed by that State by means of accession;

(b) it is otherwise established that the negotiating States were agreed that such consent may be expressed by that State by means of accession; or

(c) all the parties have subsequently agreed that such consent may be expressed by that State by means of accession.[1]

International law thus requires prior or subsequent consent of the signatory states for an applicant state's accession to an existing treaty. As discussed in Chapter 13, above, when signatory states preauthorize accession of applicant states at the time of signing the original treaty, the treaty is described as "open" for accession. Conversely, if no such preauthorization is given in the original treaty, the subsequent consent by all signatory states is necessary for an applicant's accession and the treaty is "closed." The intermediate case of "semi-open" treaties leaves admission of a new applicant in the hands of a majority of the signatory states.

The default rule dictates that a treaty is closed unless its terms provide for open or semi-open accession (Bishop 1971). Signatory states must unanimously consent to a new state's accession unless they have included an open or semi-open accession clause in the treaty. This insures that the existing parties approve changes in membership, so their rights and obligations are not disturbed without their consent (Starke 1989). The International Law Commission has advocated changing the default rule to make all multilateral treaties open for accession unless otherwise stated. A similar change was advocated in plurilateral treaties, when a state invited to participate in negotiations to become a founding state declined to join the treaty at that time. The treaty would be left open for such states that subsequently applied for accession. Signatory states that disapproved of the accession could hold the treaty inoperative between themselves and the acceding state.

The International Law Commission's modifications were expressed through draft articles on the laws of treaty that have not been adopted.[2] The analysis in Section 2 shows that the prevailing default rule favoring closed-form treaties may be justified. States face incentive problems when confronted with treaty participation. Because treaty negotiation is costly, leaving all multilateral treaties open for accession by default could undermine incentives to invest in the initial negotiations and drafting of treaty agreements.

1.1. Closed Treaties

According to Article 15(c), some treaties are closed treaties in which acceptance of a new member requires unanimous approval by the current signatory states. Most bilateral treaties are closed because they concern a relationship between two entities. Although closed treaties do not allow automatic accession, with unanimous consent the existing signatory states can amend the original treaty to allow accession of a nonsignatory state. For example, the Association of Southeast Asian Nations Treaty (ASEAN) was amended several times to allow the accession of Brunei Darussalam, Vietnam, Laos, Myanmar, and Cambodia. However, it was not amended to permit the accession of Papua New Guinea (Chinkin 1993).[3]

A closed treaty may serve a purpose that requires exclusivity. For example, the Treaty on the Non-Proliferation of Nuclear Weapons, signed in 1968, extended special privileges to states that manufactured and detonated nuclear weapons before 1967.[4] These states became "nuclear weapons states."[5] In an effort to limit the number of states that hold special privileges with regard to nuclear weapons, similar privileges were not later extended to other states that manufactured explosive nuclear devices after the effective date of the treaty (Beemelmans 1997).

Some closed treaties are open or semi-open to specific groups of countries, but closed to the world-at-large. For instance, the General Act of Arbitration of 1928 contained a clause which stated, "[t]he present General Act shall be open to accession by all the Heads of States or other competent authorities of the Members of the League of Nations and the non-Member States to which the Council of the League of Nations has communicated a copy for this purpose."[6] This act was initially open to most nonsignatory states, who were members of the original League. However, the treaty became more closed over time as more states came into existence after the treaty was formed. Some interesting questions were raised concerning Pakistan and India, which both gained independence from British India in 1947. Pakistan claimed authority under the treaty in a legal dispute against India before the International Court of Justice in 2000.[7] India claimed that it was not bound to the treaty because it never specifically provided its consent to be bound and in fact manifested its explicit intent not be bound in 1974.[8] Further, India argued that Pakistan could not invoke the treaty because it was not the "continuator of British India" and therefore could not accede to the treaty due to its closed nature.[9] The Court found India's prior manifestation of not-to-be-bound intent sufficient, and denied application of the General Act.[10]

1.2. Semi-Open Treaties

Semi-open treaties are treaties where acceptance of a new member depends on approval by a majority of the existing signatory states. These treaties invite accession, but require a majority of the signatory states to approve specific acts of accession. Although semi-open treaties generally specify the conditions for accession in the terms of the treaty, the need for specification is less critical than under the case of open treaties, given that the majority of signatory states must review and accept accession terms.

A traditional example of a semi-open treaty is the 1974 Agreement on an International Energy Program, which promotes the secure acquisition of oil.[11] The treaty sets up a Governing Board which includes representatives of the participating states but with a balance of power among the original signatories. The accession clause of this agreement states that a country seeking to enter by accession must gain approval of a majority of the Governing Board.[12]

One variant of a semi-open treaty is the 1993 Center for International Forestry Research Treaty, which "established a Center for International Forestry Research (CIFOR) which will be concerned with forestry research that benefits developing countries."[13] The treaty was left open for "original" signatories for two years, after which states seeking accession must receive approval from a majority of members of CIFOR Board of Trustees.[14]

Another variant of the semi-open treaty comes from the Treaty of Rome establishing the European Economic Community (EEC 1951).

Although the only formal criterion for membership in the Community was a state's "European identity," member states have used various unwritten requirements to weigh the eligibility of new entrants. This leaves great political discretion to current member states on whether to allow accession to new applicants. Although treaty amendments require the consent of every incumbent state, accession negotiations take place between candidate members and the Commission, which is a representative organ deliberating on a majority basis.[15]

Although our analysis in Section 2 concentrates on semi-open treaties where accession of new states is contingent on approval by a simple majority of states, some semi-open treaties require more than a simple majority. One such treaty is the General Agreement on Tariffs and Trade: Multilateral Trade Negotiations Final Act Embodying the Results of the Uruguay Round of Trade Negotiations (GATT 1994) which established the World Trade Organization (WTO). Its accession clause provides that states seeking accession to the treaty (and membership into the WTO), must gain the approval by two thirds of the present WTO membership.[16] The clause also states that the Ministerial Conference may negotiate terms of agreement with the state seeking accession, creating an opportunity for negotiation for those states that may initially lack two-thirds support (Karasik 1997).[17]

The majoritarian principle, at work in the admission of new states, highlights the difference between consent to be bound in the formation of a closed treaty and consent in the case of semi-open treaties. Part II, Section I of the Vienna Convention on the Law of Treaties refers to the process by which parties officially manifest their consent to be bound to one another by the specified terms of the treaty. However, as pointed out by Kelsen (1966), in the case of semi-open accession, an original signatory agrees to be bound to a treaty knowing that treaty participation and content can subsequently be modified by a majority of signatory states. A minority signatory state may later disagree with changes brought about by the accession of a new state, but is nevertheless bound to the treaty as modified by the majority.

1.3. Open Treaties

Open treaties contain clauses under which the original member states grant a right of accession to all states that are willing to agree to the terms of a treaty, though sometimes subjecting the right to some general limitations. Open accession clauses are common in multilateral treaties, particularly those of general concern that promote cooperation and foster dispute resolution between states.[18] For instance, the Vienna Convention on Diplomatic Relations (1961) states in Article 50 that the Convention "shall remain open for accession" to all states, United Nations members, parties to the statute of the International Court of Justice and other states invited by the UN General Assembly to join the Convention.

Many treaties have no original signatories in the technical sense, but rather require all states who wish to join the treaty do so through accession (Perry et al. 1996). The treaty may take effect once a specific number of states ratify it (Starke 1989). Being party to the original group of signatory states only provides the advantage of being able to influence the treaty content. Some treaties remain open for original signatures for a set time period after which states must enter through accession.

Open treaties do not require affirmative action by the original signatories for an additional state to accede. Such treaties are more rigid in their content formulation, because all conditions for treaty accession must be specified ex ante. For example, the Convention on Combating Bribery of Foreign Public Officials in International Business Transactions, December 18, 1997 (also known as the OECD Convention), is open to "non-members which become full participants in the OECD Working Group on Bribery in International Business Transactions."[19] By formulating the conditions and prerequisites for accession, the original signatory states avoid the necessity for a formal renegotiation of the treaty, thus permitting expansion without a simultaneous alteration of treaty content. Although amendments of treaty content are possible through unanimous consent in an open treaty, original states can, de facto, achieve a greater protection of their own interests and the integrity of the treaty, while at the same time securing the freedom of entry that open accession clauses provide.

2. Formation of International Treaties: An Economic Analysis

In deciding whether to participate in a treaty, rational states compare the net payoff without international cooperation with that obtainable through international cooperation in pursuit of a given goal. We think of the payoff obtainable by states in the absence of international cooperation as the "self-help" payoff. The highest self-help payoff represents the opportunity cost that states face when contemplating participation in an international treaty. States may be more or less equipped to pursue specific goals in the absence of international cooperation and may derive different net benefits from such pursuits. That is, states face different opportunity costs in treaty participation. The payoff for state i, obtainable without treaty participation, is $V_i^1(s)$ when undertaking an effort level s, where V_i^1 is assumed to be strictly concave. The superscript signifies that the state is not cooperating with other states (only 1 state is involved, the state itself). The maximum payoff obtainable for each state without participating in a treaty is $\hat{V}_i^1$, the state's opportunity cost in treaty participation.

By engaging in international cooperation, states may exceed their opportunity costs. This may be due to economies of scale in the pursuit of the common goal, the presence of gains from trade, or benefits from coordination and network effects. International treaties may serve to secure these benefits. In an N-state treaty, $\pi(s_{NT}, N)$ represents the benefit enjoyed by *each* state participating in the treaty. The benefit from treaty participation π is an increasing function of s_{NT}, the effort level mandated by the treaty (hereinafter referred to as treaty content), and N, the number of participants in the treaty. The treaty variable s has two subscripts: the variable subscript N refers to the number of treaty participants and the fixed T signifies that it is the treaty content.[20] A treaty agreement with no substantive content generates no benefit: $\pi(0, N) = 0$. Similarly, no benefit can be derived from a treaty without other states: $\pi(s_{1T}, 1) = 0$. Further, states obtain nonincreasing marginal benefits from more substantive treaty content: $\pi_{SS} \leq 0$.

We consider both complementarity and substitution between treaty content and participation. Complementarity may characterize international agreements for adopting new technological standards with network externalities, or situations distinguished by weakest-link problems, such as the fight against terrorism. In these cases, the treaty effort level and the number of participants are complements: $\pi_{SN} > 0$. In other situations such as environmental cleanup or financial contributions to fight hunger in third world countries, one state's increase in effort can make up for another state's reduction. The treaty effort level and the number of participants are then substitutes: $\pi_{SN} < 0$.

The *total* payoff of state i, when participating in an N-state treaty with content s_{NT}, is $V_i^N(s_{NT}) = V_i^1(s_{NT}) + \pi(s_{NT}, N) - c_i$. Here V_i^1 represents the state's *direct* net benefit from undertaking the effort specified by the treaty: if state i undertakes effort level s_{NT} by itself without joining a treaty, then its benefit is $V_i^1(s_{NT})$. Once the state joins the treaty, π is the *additional* benefit from undertaking the effort in the company of other participating states, and c_i represents the costs of negotiating and drafting the treaty, as well as the political cost of joining the treaty. The superscript for V refers to the number of treaty participants, where 1 indicates payoff without participating in a treaty. A superscript greater than 1 represents the state's total net payoff, including gains from cooperation and negotiation costs. We simplify notation by assuming that the negotiation cost for a state is constant and independent of the number of states involved in negotiating a treaty. To ease the notational burden further, the negotiation cost is the same whether the state negotiates to form a treaty with other states or requests accession to an existing treaty, although we expect that the former exceeds the latter. It is possible that both the payoff V_i^1 and the benefit from treaty-participation π are present discount values of future benefits. The negotiation cost to a treaty is borne only once. Any costs suffered in future periods—for example, minor political consequences—can be subsumed as part of the payoff V_i^1.

2.1. Setting the Stage: Initial Treaty Formation

As discussed above, states can join an international treaty as original signatory states or by acceding to an existing treaty. Accession to a treaty presupposes the existence of a treaty formed by a group of founding states. To set the stage for analyzing treaty accession, first consider the process of treaty formation by a group of states. Founding states become the incumbent states that control entry of new states applying for accession according to rules set forth in the initial treaty agreement.

Without loss of generality, consider the simplifying case of two states forming a treaty. When two states form a treaty with content s_{2T}, each state's payoff from participating in the treaty becomes $V_i^2(s_{2T}) = V_i^1(s_{2T}) + \pi(s_{2T}, 2) - c_i$. We consider the negotiation of the treaty content s_{2T} by a Nash bargaining game. The bargaining powers for the two risk-neutral states, state 1 and state 2, are θ and $1 - \theta$ respectively. Recall that $\hat{V}_1^1$ and $\hat{V}_2^1$ are the opportunity costs of treaty participation that each state can obtain through its own effort without participating in a treaty. These are their threat points in the bargaining problem or their best alternatives to a negotiated agreement. The Nash bargaining solution to the 2-state treaty negotiation, s_{2T}, is the solution to the problem:

$$s.t. \ \ V_1^2 \geq \hat{V}_1^1, \ \ V_2^2 \geq \hat{V}_2^1 \qquad\qquad 14.1$$

This Nash bargaining solution can vary with different scenarios. We highlight the importance of different factors in determining the outcome of the bargaining solution.

(A) We should stress the importance of the magnitudes of the benefit from treaty participation π and the bargaining and negotiating costs c_i. High benefits from international cooperation and low bargaining costs are required before states will agree to international cooperation. Otherwise, bargaining room for states to achieve acceptable treaty content may be lacking and no treaty will be signed.

As a simple example, consider the payoff $V_i^1(s) = b_i s - a_i s^2$ and the benefit from joining the treaty $\pi = \alpha s$, where dependence of B on the number of treaty participants is suppressed. Then $b_1/2a_1 = \arg\max V_1^1$ and $(b_1 + \alpha)/2a_1 = \arg\max V_1^2$. The optimal level $b_1/2a_1$ is chosen by state 1 in the absence of a treaty. The level $(b_1 + \alpha)/2a_1$ is the desired treaty content for state 1, without considering the other state's constraint or any bargaining issues. The desired treaty content is greater than the optimal effort without joining the treaty, because higher effort leads to higher mutual benefit from treaty-participation. Also, the opportunity cost for state 1 with no treaty is $\hat{V}_1^1 = b_1^2/4a_1$. Under a treaty, the best payoff that state 1 can hope for is $\tilde{V}_1^2 = [(b_1 + \alpha)^2/4a_1] - c_1$. State 1 will participate in a treaty only if $[(b_1 + \alpha)^2/4a_1] - c_1 > b_1^2/4a_1$. This means $\alpha(2b_1 + \alpha)/4a_1 > c_1$. Thus, the higher the benefit from international cooperation α and/or the lower the cost of negotiation c_1, the more likely the inequality holds. It then becomes more likely for state 1 to participate in a treaty formation. This matches our intuition exactly.

Note that a high potential benefit from cooperation and a low transaction cost to participate in a treaty only provide the backdrop for a state's willingness to join a treaty. Whether a state indeed participates in the formation of a treaty rests on the negotiation process and treaty content. Thus, in the following, we assume that it is beneficial for a state to participate in treaty formation, and turn to the outcome of the Nash bargaining process itself.

(B) Consider the case of *homogeneous* states with identical preferences and costs of negotiation and drafting, and the same gains to cooperation $(V_1^2(s) - \hat{V}_1^1 = V_2^2(s) - \hat{V}_2^1)$. State bargaining powers do not matter here because their interests coincide exactly. The treaty content, $\arg\max V_i^2(s) - \hat{V}_i^1 = (V_i^1(s) + \pi(s, 2) - c_i - \hat{V}_i^1)$, maximizes net payoff for each state, and a treaty is formed.[21] Convergence of the interests of homogenous states leads to the best outcome possible. In general, when states have similar preferences and similar negotiation and drafting costs, there is little disagreement concerning treaty content, and a treaty will be formed. This explains why many regional treaties are formed among rather homogeneous states.

(C) Next consider *heterogeneous* states with *diametrically opposite bargaining strengths*. The states' preferences V_i differ and one state, say state 1, has overwhelming bargaining strength. In the limiting case where state 1 has all the bargaining power, the bargaining solution must satisfy max $V_1^2 - \hat{V}_1^1$ s.t. $V_2^2 \geq \hat{V}_2^1$. Thus, due to its superior bargaining power, state 1 realizes most, if not all the gains from cooperation. The treaty content maximizes state 1's net payoff, while the less persuasive state 2 remains close to its threat point. An extreme example involves a state with little potential gain being strong-armed into signing a treaty.[22]

(D) Now turn to the case of *heterogeneous* states with different preferences but very *similar bargaining powers*.[23] Not surprisingly, the tension created by different payoff patterns but equal bargaining power to pull and push the treaty content would be greatest under this circumstance. In particular, when states are even in bargaining power, at the optimal treaty content, the net payoff from treaty-participation of one country is increasing while that of another country is decreasing. This is because the treaty content must satisfy $(V_1^2(s) - \hat{V}_1^1) \cdot \partial V_2^2 / \partial s + (V_2^2(s) - \hat{V}_2^1) \cdot \partial V_1^2 / \partial s = 0$. Because the coefficients in the equation represent gains to each state from joining the treaty and are positive, the two partials in the equation must be opposite in sign. That is, when the treaty content is increased, the state with the positive partial gains while the other state loses. We submit that many treaties signed by "equal-partner" countries, for example, the 1951 Treaty establishing the European Coal and Steel Community, the 1956 treaty establishing the European Atomic Energy Community, and the 1957 Treaty of Rome establishing the European Economic Community, fit the description of this case.

The analysis of these different cases clarifies the resulting formation of treaties with different countries. The first important criterion for the formation of an international treaty is a substantial gain in cooperation and reasonable bargaining cost for each participating state. Beyond that, we observe that homogeneous states are most likely to form an international treaty to cooperate. In such cases we surmise that the treaty would likely be open or semi-open. Any state willing to join the open treaty, accepting treaty content as is, would be welcomed by the signatory states. Likewise, acceptance by a majority of signatory states of the accession of a new state to a semi-open treaty means that interests in all other states with similar preferences are well served.

In the case of heterogeneous states with an overwhelming bargaining strength for one party, the strong-armed state enjoys most of the benefit of cooperation. The weaker state gains little. We surmise that the treaty would most likely be closed, because the stronger state may refuse to give away any stake resulting from the negotiation advantage that it enjoys. In the more general case, a very strong state may sustain a closed treaty with a few weaker states. For example, the old Soviet Union may have forced other countries to join their version of NATO. On the other hand, if a group of weak states is capable of extracting concessions from a strong state while negotiating a treaty, then the strong state would have preferred to sign many separate treaties with individual weaker states.[24]

When states are heterogeneous but have fairly even bargaining powers, in order for a treaty to be formed, the range of effort level with potential gain from cooperation must be large for all participating states. Otherwise, there is insufficient bargaining room for the states to negotiate. If one state desires high treaty content while another wants low content, the resulting treaty content is typically a compromise. With any change in treaty content, stakes change for some parties. Thus, there is little reason for founding states to be amenable to new treaty content. However, if additional treaty membership with no alteration of treaty content creates large additional gains for every state, then an open treaty may be in order. This is especially true if the founding states anticipate a pool of future accession applicants who are amenable to existing treaty terms.

Not only does the expected number of potential entrants matter, but the typology of states expected to request accession may also matter. Founding states may prefer not to accept an accession application from one state while accepting an application from another state. For example, the founding states accept accession applications from states willing to increase the content of the treaty undertaking, but not from others. These factors can also help determine whether the treaty is closed or left open for accession.

Thus far, we have concentrated on treaty formation and on the interests of the founding states. Once the treaty is formed, the interests of a potential newcomer state and interactions between the newcomer and the signatory states become important. In our notation, after a treaty is formed, the payoffs of the two states are denoted $\hat{V}_1^2$ and $\hat{V}_2^2$. With this as a starting point, we now turn to the accession process.

2.2. Treaty Accession

Once a treaty is formed, nonsignatory states may wish to join the treaty. The accession process through which third states may join an existing treaty is generally set out in the original treaty agreement. The three accession types are discussed separately.

2.2.1. "Closed" Treaties: Unanimous Consent

Suppose a new state applies to join an existing treaty where expansion of the treaty requires unanimous consent of the signatory states and an amendment to the treaty. Consider the region where increased treaty participation generates increasing benefits for all states ($\pi_N > 0$). In the limiting case where the new state has preferences identical to those of the incumbent signatory states, incumbents welcome accession, as more states joining the treaty increases the benefit from treaty participation without modifying treaty content. The more problematic case emerges when a third state desiring different treaty content applies to join the treaty.

In a closed treaty where unanimous agreement of the incumbent states is required, either state would veto the proposed entry if expansion necessitates a treaty amendment that lowers its payoff compared to the original treaty agreement. Thus, incumbent states approach an application for new entry by first calculating whether an additional participant in the treaty is beneficial, assuming that the entrant accepts the treaty content (possibly amended from the previous content) proposed by them:

$$\max_{s} (V_1^3 - \hat{V}_1^2)^\theta (V_2^3 - \hat{V}_2^2)^{1-\theta} \quad s.t. \quad V_1^3 \geq \hat{V}_1^2, V_2^3 \geq \hat{V}_2^2 \qquad \text{14.2}$$

Setting aside the interest of the new state, state 3, for the moment, this treaty amendment problem is similar to the bargaining problem that states 1 and 2 faced when negotiating the original treaty agreement. One difference is that the opportunity costs faced by the original signatory states have changed since they joined the original treaty. When considering the application for entry by a third state, the incumbent states look at the higher payoffs generated by the original treaty ($\hat{V}_1^2$ and $\hat{V}_2^2$) as their opportunity costs, rather than the lower optimal self-help payoffs ($\hat{V}_1^1$ and $\hat{V}_2^1$). Although admitting a third state creates additional value-enhancing opportunities for both states, new negotiations may entail new costs similar to those at the formation stage of the original treaty. If treaty expansion offers no Pareto

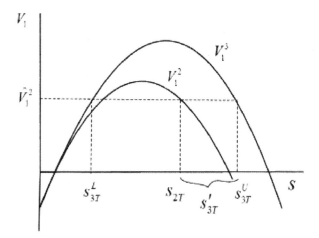

FIGURE 14.1 Agreeable Treaty Content for Incumbent Signatory State

superior treaty content for the incumbent states, then the current treaty arrangement is preferable and accession by the third state is denied.

On the other hand, high increases in benefits from more states participating in the treaty and low renegotiation costs could produce a range of Pareto superior treaty arrangements involving admission of the third state. Let s'_{3T} be a solution to the Nash bargaining problem (14.2) in the enlarged treaty environment. More treaty participants increase the net payoff from joining the treaty and the range of agreeable treaty obligations widens for an individual incumbent state. Figure 14.1 illustrates this for state 1. The existing treaty content between states 1 and 2 is given by s_{2T}, making $\hat{V}_1^2$ state 1's payoff derived from the original 2-state treaty. With a third state joining the treaty, the general net payoff function for state 1 shifts up from V_1^2 to V_1^3.[25] The range of treaty content that makes state 1 at least as well off as in the original treaty spans s_{3T}^L to s_{3T}^U. Any proposed treaty amendment that lies in this region would be agreeable to the incumbent signatory state. The solution to the incumbents' bargaining problem generates the *proposed* treaty terms for the third state applying for admission.

Treaty amendments made in contemplation of membership expansion may increase or reduce substantive treaty obligations. Whether the existing states propose a treaty amendment s'_{3T} containing higher or lower treaty obligations than the original treaty content, s_{2T}, depends on whether the number of treaty participants and the treaty content are complements or substitutes. In general, setting aside any bargaining problems and constraints imposed by other states wishing to join a treaty, consider the first-best payoff maximization problem for an existing state in an N-state treaty: say $\max_s V_1^N$ for state 1. The first-best treaty content desired by the state, s_T^*, must meet the condition that net marginal payoff is zero. Simple comparative static results show that $ds_T^*/dN > 0$ if the treaty content and the number of treaty participants are complements, and $ds_T^*/dN < 0$ if they are substitutes.[26] If treaty content and the number of treaty participants are complements, an increase in the number of states joining the treaty raises the marginal impact of efforts on payoff. Individual states would prefer a higher treaty obligation (more effort level) when more states join the treaty. Thus, when treaty content and the number of treaty participants are complements, treaty content proposed by the incumbents falls in the region identified by a brace in Figure 14.1 (the opposite would hold for substitutes).

Assume complements so that each participating state is willing to undertake higher treaty obligations when more states join the treaty. When confronted with the prospect of treaty expansion brought about by a third state's application for entry, both states wish to raise the level of treaty obligation and to amend the treaty to allow for admission. In this case, the bargaining outcome between the incumbent states must end with a proposal for amendment that contains higher treaty obligations than the original treaty. In our notation, the proposed treaty content s_{3T}' is greater than the existing treaty content s_{2T} for the two incumbent states (opposite results obtain in the case where treaty participation and treaty content are substitutes).

When the treaty amendment s_{3T}' is proposed to state 3, state 3 needs to verify whether the obligations imposed by the proposed treaty amendment provide an opportunity to improve upon its status quo payoff. For a third party state without alternative treaty opportunities, the status quo payoff coincides with the opportunity cost obtainable in the absence of treaty participation. State 3 must consider whether $V_3^3(s_{3T}') \geq \hat{V}_3^1$. If so, state 3 joins the original signatory states, and the original treaty content is amended to $s_{3T} = s_{3T}'$. On the other hand, if $V_3^3(s_{3T}') < \hat{V}_3^1$, the proposed treaty amendment generates a payoff for state 3 lower than its opportunity cost, and state 3 is not willing to join the treaty under those terms. In this case, state 3 may have the opportunity to make a counteroffer to the incumbent states, proposing different terms for the amended treaty.

Recall that the proposed treaty amendment, s_{3T}', was the solution to the bargaining problem between the incumbent states. However, in additional to the specific proposed treaty content s_{3T}', the possibility of entry by state 3 generates a range of Pareto superior alternatives for states 1 and 2. Thus the lack of acceptance of the proposed treaty content s'_{3T} by state 3 may still leave a range of potentially acceptable alternative terms for the two incumbent states. That is, a counteroffer by state 3 may not be in vain. Figure 14.2 focuses on the choice of the newcomer state. It illustrates cases in which the third party state finds the initially proposed terms s'_{3T} unacceptable and makes a counteroffer, with a request for concessions from the incumbent states. The third-party state's rejection of the initial proposal is inevitable when the payoff under the proposed terms $V_3^3(s'_{3T})$ is less than its opportunity cost $\hat{V}_3^1$. In turn the incumbent states need to entertain and evaluate the counteroffer.

2.2.1.1. Subcase A: Third State Applies for Entry Requesting Minor Concession

In Figure 14.2 the graph on the left illustrates the case where the third state applies for entry asking for a minor concession. The incumbent states' proposed treaty terms, s'_{3T}, call for an increase over obligations undertaken in the original treaty, s_{2T}. This proposed amendment is unacceptable to state 3, because it would generate lower payoffs for this state than those obtainable without treaty participation. To generate a positive return from joining the treaty, state 3 should propose an alternative treaty content less than s''_{3T}. In fact, any treaty content less than s''_{3T} and greater than s_{2T} benefits the acceding state as well as all incumbent states. We use s''_{3T} as the proxy for this mutually beneficial treaty modification, and abstract from further bargaining problems between acceding and incumbent states. The counteroffer s''_{3T} provides treaty obligations above those of the original treaty, s_{2T}, but lower than those of the initial proposed amendment. Because states 1 and 2 prefer

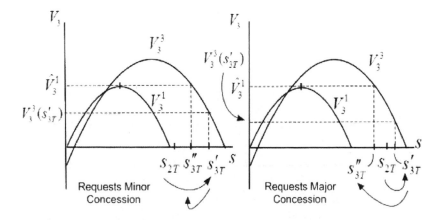

FIGURE 14.2 Third-Party State Requests Concessions at Time of Accession

a higher level of treaty content given more participants, they find this minor request for concession acceptable and allow entry by state 3. In this case, a 3-state treaty is formed with treaty obligations set at $s_{3T} = s''_{3T}$.

2.2.1.2. Subcase B: Third State Applies for Entry Requesting Major Concession

The graph on the right panel of Figure 14.2 illustrates the situation when the third-state applicant requests a more substantial concession. The initial treaty amendment s'_{3T} proposed by incumbent states again imposes higher obligations than those in the original treaty, s_{2T}. This proposed amendment is unacceptable to state 3. In order to make it worthwhile to participate in the treaty, state 3 makes a counteroffer proposing lower treaty obligations s''_{3T}. This not only constitutes a departure from the proposed treaty amendment, s'_{3T}, but also lowers the treaty obligation below the original treaty value s_{2T}. This counteroffer by state 3 represents a major concession request from the incumbent states, because they prefer raising treaty content in concert with an expansion of membership.

Whether the original signatory states are willing to make this larger concession depends on the circumstances of the case. In the relevant range where expansion of membership brings large positive benefits, admitting state 3 brings potential benefits that may lead incumbent states to compromise on the treaty terms. That is, although the incumbent states prefer to increase treaty obligations as membership increases, they are willing to compromise treaty content to promote membership expansion as long as the payoffs from the treaty enlargement are greater than the payoffs from the original treaty. That is, concessions are made by the incumbents if $V_1^3(s''_{3T}) \geq \hat{V}_1^2$ and $V_2^3(s''_{3T}) \geq \hat{V}_2^2$. When these conditions hold, the original treaty is amended and the states form a 3-state treaty with treaty obligations set at $s_{3T} = s''_{3T}$.

On the other hand, if $V_1^3(s''_{3T}) < \hat{V}_1^2$ or $V_2^3(s''_{3T}) < \hat{V}_2^2$, then state 1, state 2, or both object to the proposed treaty amendment s''_{3T}. No treaty content is agreeable to the incumbent states and the newcomer state. In this case, the application of the third state for entry is rejected and no treaty expansion takes place.

Given multiple incumbents in an N-state treaty, similar considerations drive the process of treaty amendment in contemplation of entry of a new party state. We make two additional observations at this point. First, a state may apply for membership to a treaty even though the applicant state is unwilling to accept the current treaty content. This may be so because the third-party state knows that incumbent states would benefit from membership expansion, and that its application for accession opens the opportunity for renegotiating the existing treaty terms. Even in a closed-treaty regime where any state may veto entry of a new state, the net benefits of treaty expansion may be high enough to induce each incumbent state to compromise its own position in order to promote entry of the third state.

Second, when multiple states are interested in applying for admission, the positions of third-party states may be strengthened if they apply as a block, rather than sequentially. Notwithstanding the increase in bargaining power of the new block, the gain in payoffs may make a difference. Major concessions may be unacceptable to one or more incumbent states if proposed by a single applicant. When multiple third-party states apply for admission as a block, the greater magnitude of the benefit from large-scale expansion may justify a larger concession on treaty content. This may explain the stylized fact that treaty expansions for EU membership include several new states at each time of enlargement.

2.2.2. Semi-Open Treaties: Consent by Median-Voter State

For semi-open treaties, entry of a new member state requires approval by a majority of the existing signatory states. We assume that the process of treaty expansion is carried out through majority vote. Thus, an application of the Median Voter theorem makes the impact on the welfare of the median voter state, state m, the focus of attention in our analysis (Downs 1957; Black 1958).[27] Given that the content of the treaty obligation is the critical variable, the median voter state has median preferences with respect to the treaty content, s. In an application for entry by a newcomer state, the median state decides whether the application is accepted, leading to an expansion of the treaty from N to $N+1$ participants. In reaching this decision, the median state confronts the following problem:

$$\max_s V_m^{N+1}(s) = V_m^1(s) + \pi(s, N+1) - c_m \quad s.t. \quad V_m^{N+1} \geq \hat{V}_m^N$$

Similar to the previous case of a closed treaty, we assume that negotiations on treaty content take place when states apply for accession and incumbent states have discretion whether to grant admission. Incumbent states may use this opportunity to modify the level of treaty obligations specified in the treaty and newcomer states may ask for concessions. Assume that $s'_{(N+1)T}$

is the proposed treaty content offered to the newcomer, state $N + 1$. State $N + 1$ compares the payoff under the prospective treaty arrangement to the payoff obtainable without joining the treaty. If the treaty payoff is higher than its opportunity cost, state $N + 1$ accedes. A treaty with $N + 1$ states is formed with $s_{(N+1)T} = s'_{(N+1)T}$ as the treaty content.

On the other hand, if the proposed treaty terms are unacceptable to state $N + 1$ it may request concessions. The outcome of the deliberation concerning the proposed accession would reflect the preferences of the median state m, according to the Median Voter theorem. If the concessions requested by the acceding state $N + 1$ are acceptable to state m, the application for entry is approved and an enlarged treaty with $N + 1$ states is formed. Otherwise, no expansion of the existing treaty occurs.

2.2.3. Open Treaties: Take It or Leave It

Treaties with open accession provide an open invitation (at times, subject to limitations) to nonsignatory states to join the original treaty signed by the founding states. There is no need for negotiations between incumbent and newcomer states at the time of accession. Although open accession clauses are more common in multilateral treaties promoting international cooperation between states, we examine the simple case of two founding states. There are two aspects to the problem. First, the founding states start negotiating to see if both states benefit from forming a treaty, assuming that the treaty will not be open. Let the proposed closed treaty content be the bargaining solution to (14.1), leading to payoffs $\hat{V}_1^2$ and $\hat{V}_2^2$ for the two states. Next, if the founding states expect future applications for accession to the treaty, they are confronted with another bargaining problem. They may adjust the treaty content, leaving the treaty open to reflect their expectations for enlargement and easing the cost of future negotiation. Let's say that N^E is the expected number of states that will apply for accession. The founding states will bargain to reach a level of treaty obligation that maximizes their expected gains under the enlarged treaty. In particular, the bargaining problem with an open treaty becomes:

$$\max_{s} (V_1^{N^E} - \hat{V}_1^2)^{\theta} (V_2^{N^E} - \hat{V}_2^2)^{1-\theta} \quad s.t. \quad V_1^{N^E} \geq \hat{V}_1^2, \; V_2^{N^E} \geq \hat{V}_2^2 \qquad 14.3$$

Note that the incumbent states' default position in this second Nash bargaining problem is given by the best payoff under the alternative 2-state closed treaty. Only when the prospect for treaty enlargement increases both incumbents' expected payoffs do the founding states leave the treaty open for accession while setting treaty content in expectation of such enlargement. If no treaty content satisfies (14.3), then the incumbent states do not support treaty expansion and consequently settle for a closed treaty structure. This may happen in situations where the states perceive that a bilateral or plurilateral treaty creates an advantage for the member states, and that such an advantage will vanish if the treaty is expanded through accession of third states.

On the other hand, if s_{NET} is the solution to (14.3), then an open treaty is formed with treaty content specified as s_{NET}. The founding states' decision to leave the treaty open for accession allows newcomer states to join the treaty as originally specified without the need to negotiate entry or to obtain approval from incumbent states. Entry is granted when the acceding state agrees to be bound by the original treaty. If the terms are not acceptable, the newcomer state can still apply for entry, requesting that the terms of the treaty be modified. But such modification should be carried out through treaty amendment, as if the treaty were closed.[28]

3. Form and Substance in Treaty Law

In this chapter we have developed a stylized model of treaty formation and accession to study the effect that the choice of treaty form can have on the substantive content of the treaty. We have considered three modalities with which states can become party to an international treaty according to the procedures set forth by the Vienna Convention on the Law of Treaties: (1) closed treaties for which treaty membership expansion requires the unanimous approval of the existing signatory states; (2) semi-open treaties where treaty expansion can be approved by a majority of signatory states; and (3) open treaties that offer third-party states the option to accede by expressing their intent to be bound to the existing treaty terms.

Our analysis can easily be extended to include variations such as having the most favored nation clause incorporated into the original treaty, under which both signatories agree that if state 2 makes another relevant treaty with a third state, the terms of the second treaty apply to state 1 as well. If similar treaty content for the second treaty would also increase its payoff, state 1 would like to be guaranteed the same extra benefit created by the new alliance between states 2 and 3. The most favored nation clause can also reduce the temptation of state 2, making it more difficult for state 3 to seduce state 2 to create a new treaty that bypasses the prior agreement made in their original treaty. These pressures make it advantageous for the original signatory states to insist on a closed treaty that includes a most favored nation clause. A more stringent form of closed treaty helps a state protect itself against future unpleasant surprises and increases its bargaining power when a third nation attempts to steer one of the signatories away from cooperation.

Bilateral investment treaties (BITs) have become important instruments for attracting foreign investment by many emerging economies. Often, investors in a (home) country are not confident about the investment environment of a potential host country. A potential host country believes that it would benefit from signing a treaty, conceding to favorable investment conditions that set a stable and advantageous framework for foreign direct investment deals in the host country. In BITs, the signatories agree to a set of rules governing investments by investors from the home country in the jurisdiction of the host country. Our analysis can help explain why there is a growing number of BITs but few multilateral investment treaties. Consistent with the predictions of our model, BITs are typically not open to accession by other states, as they are often concluded among relatively heterogeneous states (an advanced economy and a less-developed country). Because the more developed nation has dominant trading and negotiating power, treaty content favors the dominant nation. Dominant states tend to duplicate the terms of BITs, using the same treaty content with different partners in different bilateral treaties. The advantage of many BITs over a multilateral treaty is that the dominant state is not outvoted by many less developed countries. It does not have to make concessions, and can maintain its dominant power and dictate the terms of each BIT.

In practice, when states face the prospect of a multilateral international agreement, two interrelated choices need to be made. First, states must decide whether to be among the promoters of the international treaty, engaging in the negotiations for its drafting and signature. Second, signatory states have to decide whether to leave the treaty open for accession to other states and if so under what conditions. Our analysis reveals the effect of the choice of treaty form on evolution of treaty content given the different expansion mechanisms set forth by the various regimes. In turn, these findings help predict when states may join the original founding states and when they instead prefer to wait and accede to a treaty at a later time.

Our analysis further unveils an important interrelationship between the chosen form of treaty and its substantive content. When a treaty is left open and accession of other states is expected, treaty content is set optimally on the basis of the incumbent states' expectation of treaty enlargement. This may alter treaty content from that which would be chosen under other treaty forms or if no expansion was expected. Open treaties simplify the expansion process, but impose uncertainty costs on incumbent states. Founding states calibrate treaty content on the basis of their expectations of enlargement, but such expectations may not be fulfilled, or may be fulfilled with delay. In this context, time-preference may become a relevant factor, determining the timing of treaty participation for given states.

Another interesting insight is the paradoxical result that closed treaties may at times be conducive to greater expansion than open treaties. Although expanding a closed treaty through treaty amendment imposes greater transaction costs, it allows tailored negotiations that may render the treaty acceptable to a newcomer state that might not have been acceptable under the original terms, if the treaty had been left open for accession.

Further work should be carried out to collect data and test our results beyond the anecdotal evidence offered in this chapter. In order to carry out such empirical testing in the context of multilateral treaties it would be useful to focus on specific types of treaties where the international obligations created by the treaties are limited to one narrow and well-defined sphere of activity (e.g., extradition, mutual recognition of medical degrees, mutual access to territorial waters, freedom of movement for unskilled workers). A quantitative analysis in the context of broader treaties such as the WTO, the Treaty of Rome and subsequent European treaties, might be less illuminating, inasmuch as the multiple dimensions of cooperation are confounded, making it difficult to ascertain the degree of "homogeneity" or "heterogeneity" of the participating states. The empirical analysis of specific areas of international law would allow the use of data to support or refute the predictions of our model.

In Chapter 15 and 16 we proceed to consider the dynamics of endogenous treaty participation. There is an unavoidable tradeoff between treaty content and participation. With heterogeneous states, an increase in the number of states increases network and coordination benefits for all participating states, but exacerbates diversity, making it harder to select treaty content that reflects each state's ideal. Our results may provide a basis for understanding when to expect universal multilateral treaties and when to expect formation of multiple treaties among homogeneous states with more limited participation. Adjustments to treaty content and participation may lead to a gradual clustering of states, with the formation of many different treaties that optimally balance the benefits of expansion with the costs brought about by increased heterogeneity in participation.

FIFTEEN

Ratification and Reservations

The Effects of Reciprocity*

IN THIS CHAPTER WE STUDY the second important step in the process of treaty formation: treaty ratification. As discussed in Chapter 13, ratification is the act that gives official sanction or approval to a signed treaty. In the process of ratifying a treaty, states can introduce reservations, purporting to exclude or modify the legal obligations and the effects of the treaty on the reserving state. The study of reservations in multilateral treaties reveals a striking paradox. The number of reservations attached to international treaties is relatively low in spite of the fact that the rules governing reservations set forth in the Vienna Convention create a natural advantage in favor of the reserving state (Gamble 1980; Greig 1994; Parisi and Sevcenko 2003). In search of a possible explanation for this phenomenon, this chapter investigates the possible role played by the legal regime governing treaty reservations set forth by Articles 19–21 of the Vienna Convention.[1]

In this chapter we develop a simple game-theoretic model of treaty ratification to understand the efficacy and the limits of Articles 19–21 of the Vienna Convention in promoting cooperation through international treaty agreements. Under the rules governing treaty reservations introduced by the Vienna Convention, after a treaty has been signed, states have an opportunity to attach reservations to it before ratification. For example, a U.S. treaty signed by the secretary of state will not become effective unless ratified by the Senate, and reservations to the original treaty can be introduced at the time of ratification. In the absence of constraints dictated by political or diplomatic expediency, individual states may have incentives to utilize the ratification process to introduce reservations that create a unilateral advantage. These dominant strategies may undermine the effectiveness of multilateral treaties, creating a prisoner's dilemma for all states.[2]

---

* This chapter is based on an article forthcoming as Fon, Vincy, and Francesco Parisi, "The Economics of Treaty Ratification," *Journal of Law, Economics and Policy* (2008).

We analyze the rules governing treaty ratification and reservations under the 1969 Vienna Convention.[3] We formalize the intuition put forth in the previous literature, according to which the matching-reservations mechanism introduced by Article 21 provides an effective solution to such a prisoner's dilemma. A state that wants to exempt itself from a treaty obligation must permit other nations to escape that same burden (Parisi and Sevcenko 2003). States know that the matching-reservations mechanism will make their sought-after advantage automatically available to others. When states enter into negotiations with symmetrical incentives, they have no reason to attach merely strategic reservations to the treaty. In such settings, the matching-reservations constraint set forth by Article 21 leads to socially optimal levels of treaty ratification. Recent game theoretic models, however, raise some doubt about the effectiveness of matching constraints (such as those set forth by Article 21) when states face asymmetric incentives (Fon and Parisi 2003b).

We develop an economic model of treaty ratification to study the role of Article 21 of the Vienna convention in promoting optimal levels of treaty ratification when states with potentially asymmetric incentives are involved. Given that states likely anticipate the reservation strategies of other signatory states, the results of this chapter shed light on the process of treaty formation, which reflects states' subsequent ratification strategies. This may help explain why the number of reservations attached to international treaties is relatively low in spite of the natural advantage of reserving states which will be more extensively discussed in Chapter 16.

1. The Vienna Convention on Treaty Reservations

The purpose of the 1969 Vienna Convention on the Law of Treaties was to articulate the framework for international treaty making, codifying a comprehensive set of principles and rules governing significant aspects of treaty law. The treaty came into force in 1980 as the result of international efforts which began in 1949. As mentioned in Chapter 13 above, the Vienna Convention mostly codifies established international practice on how to conclude, apply, and interpret treaties. On some issues, however, the Vienna Convention brings about a change in the rules governing treaty formation. Although the line between the two sets of rules is often unclear, it is commonly accepted that the specific provisions governing treaty reservations (Articles 19–23) depart from preexisting customary law. The innovative nature of these provisions is revealed by the drafting history and the animated debate that surrounded the issue of reservations during negotiations of the Vienna Convention. In this respect, the Vienna Convention breaks away from the previously followed rule of unanimous acceptance of reservations as articulated by the International Court of Justice in the *Genocide Convention* (Sinclair 1984).[4]

The new regime in the Vienna Convention was chosen to foster the coming into force of multilateral treaties in the face of occasional impediments by signatory states to full ratification. To inject greater flexibility into multilateral treaty making, the Vienna Convention introduces a relatively liberal approach which draws on the concept of reciprocity, one of the basic eta-principles of international law.[5]

Article 21(1)(d) of the Vienna Convention defines a reservation as "a unilateral statement, however phrased or named, made by a State when signing, ratifying, accepting, approving or acceding to a treaty, whereby it purports to exclude or to modify the legal effect of certain provisions of the treaty in their application to that State."[6] In breaking away from the older unanimity rule, Article 19 of the Vienna Convention allows states to include reservations in their acceptance of treaty obligations, unless the treaty itself expressly forbids reservations, or the reservation is incompatible with the object and purpose of the treaty.[7] Although it is possible to object to a state's reservation, an objection to a reservation does not preclude entry into force of the treaty between the two states.[8] Rather, Article 21 tailors the relations between reserving and nonreserving states through a mechanism of matching reservations. If a state does not object to a reservation, it modifies the treaty relations between the two states according to the scope of the reservation, and the limitation imposed by the reserving state applies equally to both parties. If a state objects to the reservation, then the entire provision does not apply between the two parties. The objecting state may also declare the entire treaty not in force between the two countries.

Although the more liberal approach to reservations introduced by the Vienna Convention might make one anticipate many reservations appended to multilateral treaties, few states actually attach reservations to their accession to a treaty (Parisi and Sevcenko 2003).[9] One argument is that states care more about the integrity of the treaty than promoting their particular interests through the use of reservations. We propose an alternative and more plausible explanation for the fact that the more liberal approach to treaty reservations has caused no explosion in the number of reservations to treaties. In the following section we develop a model of treaty ratification, to verify the suggestion of previous literature according to which the matching-reservations mechanism of Article 21 deters strategic reservations, because other signatory states would also gain an exemption from treaty obligations to the extent of the reservation. The matching-reservations effect of Article 21 is likely accounted for by signatory states that anticipate the reservation strategies of other signatory states and adjust the treaty terms accordingly. We study the extent to which such constraint is effective in the presence of states with asymmetric interests.

🏛 2. A Model of Ratification of International Treaties

As discussed above, Articles 19–21 of the Vienna Convention regulate the effect of a state's reservations in a multilateral treaty setting. The multiplicity of bilateral effects created by unilateral reservations to a treaty makes it necessary to study how reservations affect interactions between two states. We thus proceed to model the impact of unilateral reservations between two representative states who are parties to a multilateral treaty.

   We consider two states whose payoffs are interdependent upon each other's treaty ratification levels, and who are facing a prisoner's dilemma problem. The degree of treaty ratification indicates the states' willingness to invest in international cooperation. Such ratification levels for states 1 and 2 are denoted s_1 and s_2 respectively, where s_1, $s_2 \in [0, 1]$. When both $s_i = 0$, there is no ratification of the treaty and when both $s_i = 1$, there is full ratification. Intermediate levels $0 < s_i < 1$ indicate cases of partial ratification where state i introduces reservations limiting its obligations under the treaty. In the case of a two-state treaty, the payoff function for state 1 depends on the treaty ratification choices of state 1 and state 2, $P_1(s_1, s_2) = -as_1^2 + bs_2$ and the payoff function for state 2 can be similarly written as $P_2(s_1, s_2) = -cs_2^2 + ds_1$. Note that greater levels of treaty ratification undertaken by one state impose a cost upon the ratifying state while creating a benefit for the other state. Although treaty ratification problems need not necessarily reflect this property, it is safe to assume that states generally receive a benefit from other states' compliance with the treaty, and do not receive any direct net benefit from their own compliance. If they could take advantage of other states' fulfillment of the treaty obligations, without fulfilling their own, they would happily do so.

This characteristic of the treaty ratification problem leads to a potential prisoner's dilemma. In the absence of other constraints both states face dominant nonratification (defection) strategies. Whatever ratification strategy s_2 is chosen by state 2, state 1 prefers to avoid investing in international cooperation and chooses $s_1 = 0$. To generate such a prisoner's dilemma and ensure that the strategy of no ratification is dominant for both states we assume that $a > 0$ and $c > 0$. Further, prisoner's dilemma prescribes that the payoff of a state from full mutual treaty ratification (that is, $P_1(1, 1) = -a + b$ and $P_2(1, 1) = -c + d$) is greater than the state's payoff when both states fail to ratify the treaty (that is, $P_1(0, 0) = 0$ and $P_2(0, 0) = 0$). Hence $-a + b > 0$ and $-c + d > 0$ are also assumed. Combining these requirements, in order to capture the essence of the prisoner's dilemma where the Nash equilibrium of joint defection ($s_1 = 0, s_2 = 0$) is inefficient, we assume that $0 < a < b$ and $0 < c < d$.

Under these assumptions, neither state is willing to invest in international cooperation. Yet states can enjoy positive payoffs only through cooperation. For example, in an ideal world in which the willingness of state 1 to undertake a certain ratification level s_1 induces state 2 to undertake an equal ratification level so that $s_2 = s_1$, then the matching-reservations payoff function of state 1 becomes $P_1(s_1, s_2) = P_1(s_1, s_1) = -as_1^2 + bs_1$. Consequently, the marginal benefit of ratification in a matching-reservations regime for state 1 is b, and the corresponding marginal cost of ratification is $2as_1$. This is the best scenario that state 1 can expect. Less desirable instances involve situations where state 2 undertakes lower levels of ratification.

Thus, both states can induce and internalize some benefit through mutual cooperation. Under the best scenario from the viewpoint of the individual states, b and d are the marginal benefits of ratification when ratification is matched by the other state, whereas $2a$ and $2c$ are the corresponding marginal costs at full treaty ratification level ($s_i = 1$). The marginal-benefit/marginal-cost ratios of state 1 and state 2 with matching ratification can thus be denoted as $b/2a$ and $d/2c$ respectively. Without loss of generality, we assume that state 1 has a lower benefit-cost ratio: $b/2a < d/2c$. For simplicity we refer to state 1 as the high-cost cooperator, as it obtains a lower net benefit from cooperation. Because state 1 is the high-cost cooperator, its desired level of matching treaty ratification (which happens to be $b/2a$) is lower than that of state 2 ($d/2c$). Under the rules set forth by the Vienna Convention, this lower level of ratification of state 1 becomes the de facto level of treaty ratification for both states, as will be clarified below. We now turn to the different matching-reservations equilibria and the possible social optima.

2.1. Matching-Reservations Equilibrium

Under the regime set forth by Article 21 of the Vienna Convention, each state knows that, within the limits of mutually agreeable levels of cooperation, the lesser level of treaty ratification chosen by any two given states becomes the *de facto* level of international cooperation under the ratified treaty. The impact of such a constraint on the ratification and reservation strategies of the two states and the subsequent equilibrium will be investigated. Before that, we look at individual ratification payoffs incorporating the matching requirement for each state. As indicated above, the model focuses on the degree of ratification. The highest level of ratification $s = 1$ indicates that the state accepts the treaty obligations in full, without reservation. When states introduce a reservation, treaty obligations are only partially ratified with $s < 1$.

The matching-ratification payoff function for state 1 is given by
$\pi_1(s_1, s_2) = \begin{cases} -as_1^2 + bs_1 \ if \ s_1 \leq s_2 \\ -as_2^2 + bs_2 \ if \ s_1 > s_2 \end{cases}$. In the upper branch, state 1 is assumed
to desire a degree of treaty ratification that state 2 is willing to undertake. In this case, state 1 does have a choice on the degree of treaty ratification and it chooses $s_1 = b/2a$, as this ratio maximizes state 1's payoff $\pi_1(s_1, s_1) = -as_1^2 + bs_1$. This choice of treaty ratification by state 1 then becomes binding for both states. In the lower branch, state 1 desires a higher level of treaty ratification than state 2, but this is not feasible as the degree of agreeable treaty ratification by state 2 is binding. All state 1 can do is to match state 2's degree of treaty ratification s_2. Along this branch, state 1's payoff is $\pi_1(s_2, s_2) = -as_2^2 + bs_2$. Likewise, the matching-ratification payoff
function for state 2 is given by $\pi_2(s_1, s_2) = \begin{cases} -cs_2^2 + ds_2 \ if \ s_2 \leq s_1 \\ -cs_1^2 + ds_1 \ if \ s_2 > s_1 \end{cases}$. In the
upper branch where state 1 is more than willing to match any level of treaty ratification desired by state 2, state 2 chooses $s_2 = d/2c$ to maximize its payoff and this choice becomes the effective treaty obligation for both states. In the lower branch where state 1's ratification choice binds as an upper limit on the effective treaty obligation, state 2 can only take advantage of the matching effects of Article 21 and go along with the lower ratification level determined by state 1. State 2's payoff thus becomes $\pi_2(s_1, s_1) = -cs_1^2 + ds_1$.

It is clear that when the marginal benefit-marginal cost ratios from ratification for both states exceed one ($1 \leq b/2a \leq d/2c$), both states are willing to ratify the treaty in full under Article 21. In this case, it does not matter which state's desired degree of treaty ratification is binding, as the preferences converge at or beyond full treaty ratification.[10] Full treaty ratification becomes the equilibrium strategy for both states ($s_1^* = 1$, $s_2^* = 1$).

Such convergence of preferences is not likely to be found in the case of asymmetric states. In spite of the reciprocal effects of reservations under Article 21, asymmetric states may nevertheless prefer different levels of treaty ratification. The ratification choice favored by one state under Article 21 may not be matched by an equal willingness to ratify by the other state. Clearly, the most desirable partial cooperation levels $b/2a$ and $d/2c$ for states 1 and 2 are the maximum levels of treaty ratification they are willing to undertake. The value of each maximum agreeable treaty ratification level depends on how the marginal benefit under matching reservations compares with the marginal cost at full ratification. Assuming that the states desire partial treaty ratification, we now need to analyze individual reactions of the two states.

Consider how state 1 reacts to state 2 when the most desirable level of treaty ratification of state 1 is less than full: $b/2a < 1$. If state 2's expected level of treaty ratification s_2 is less than $b/2a$, state 1 cannot choose $b/2a$ in spite of its preference. State 1 is forced to go along with state 2's level of treaty ratification: $s_1 = s_2$. On the other hand, if state 2's level of treaty ratification is expected to exceed or equal $b/2a$, state 1 is free to settle on its privately optimal partial treaty ratification level; it would react by choosing $s_1 = b/2a$.[11]

Next consider how state 2 reacts to state 1 when the most desirable level of treaty ratification of state 2 is less than full: $d/2c < 1$. When state 1's expected level of treaty ratification is less than $d/2c$, state 2 must match state 1's level of treaty ratification ($s_2 = s_1$), in spite of its preference. However, if state 1's expected level of treaty ratification is greater than or equal to $d/2c$, state 2 is free to react and to choose $s_2 = d/2c$, its privately optimal partial ratification level.[12]

Thus, assuming that the other state is willing to cooperate and that the individual state is able to select its desired level of ratification, state 1 chooses $b/2a$ while state 2 chooses $d/2c$. Given the asymmetry of the two states, the privately optimal values of ratification do not coincide for the two states except in very special cases.[13] Given the matching effects of reservations under Article 21, the two states are only bound to undertake treaty obligations to the lesser level of treaty ratification desired by the two states. Because state 1 is the high-cost state and $b/2a \leq d/2c$ is assumed, the maximum agreeable ratification level chosen by state 1, $b/2a$, becomes the binding strategy for both states. Hence the matching-reservations equilibrium strategies are $s_1^* = b/2a$, $s_2^* = b/2a$.

To recap the matching-reservations equilibrium, if $1 \leq b/2a \leq d/2c$, both states desire full ratification and both states afford the maximum ratification possible ($s_1^* = 1$, $s_2^* = 1$). The payoffs for the two states are both positive ($\pi_1^*(1,1) = b - a > 0$ and $\pi_2^*(1,1) = d - c > 0$). If $b/2a < 1$, then the partial ratification level chosen by the high-cost state (state 1) becomes binding for the other state as well. In this equilibrium induced by the reciprocal effects of Article 21, the partial ratification level desired by state 1 becomes the mutually binding ratification level for both states ($s_1^* = b/2a$, $s_2^* = b/2a$). In this case, the payoffs for the two states are also positive as well.[14]

These matching-reservations outcomes should be contrasted to the alternative Nash equilibrium. Absent a matching-reservations constraint, the Nash equilibrium strategies are $s_1 = s_2 = 0$ and the payoffs for the two states fall to $P_1(0,0) = P_2(0,0) = 0$. Thus, the existence of the matching constraint set forth by Article 21 of the Vienna Convention induces states to undertake higher levels of treaty ratification than they would without any constraint, and this leads to a substantial improvement over the payoff under Nash equilibrium. In this respect Article 21 constitutes a valuable instrument to promote international cooperation through treaty formation, while providing the desired flexibility for the necessary ex post reservations of signatory states.

2.2. Social Optimum

Next we turn our attention to the social problem in which the joint payoffs of the two states is maximized, assuming feasible ratification levels:

$$\max_{s_1, s_2} \overline{P}(s_1, s_2) = \overline{P}_1(s_1, s_2) + \overline{P}_2(s_1, s_2) = (-as_1^2 + bs_2)$$

$$+ (-cs_2^2 + ds_1) \ s.t. \ 0 \leq s_1 \leq 1, 0 \leq s_2 \leq 1$$

Find the social optimum by comparing, say, the marginal cost of strategy of one state s_1 ($MC_1 = 2as_1$), with the social marginal benefit enjoyed by another state ($MB_1^S = d$), not with the private marginal benefit under matching-reservations of the first state ($MB_1^R = b$).[15] Thus, without considering feasibility, the socially desirable levels of treaty ratification are given by the social marginal benefit-marginal cost ratios $d/2a$ (for state 1) and $b/2c$ (for state 2). Clearly, these two benefit-cost ratios may not coincide and they may not be feasible (either benefit-cost ratio can exceed one). If either or both marginal benefit-cost ratios are not feasible, then one or both states are required to undertake full treaty ratification.

Thus, depending on the relative magnitudes of the social marginal costs and benefits of the treaty, the social optimum may be characterized by one of the following. (1) There is full treaty ratification from both states: $\bar{s}_1 = 1, \bar{s}_2 = 1$. (2) There is partial treaty ratification from one state and there is full treaty ratification from the other state: $\bar{s}_1 = d/2a < 1$ and $\bar{s}_2 = 1$, or $\bar{s}_1 = 1$ and $\bar{s}_2 = b/2c < 1$. (3) There is partial treaty ratification from both states: $\bar{s}_1 = d/2a < 1$ and $\bar{s}_2 = b/2c < 1$. It is noteworthy that state 1 may be required to undertake full ratification while state 2 undertakes partial ratification (the second case in [2] above), in spite of the fact that state 1 is the high-cost cooperator. This can happen only when the social marginal benefit of s_1 is much higher than the private marginal benefit of s_1.

Given that alternative socially optimal strategies exist under different situations, the relationship between matching-reservations equilibrium and social optimum also varies, depending on the costs and benefits of treaty ratification for the states.

2.3. Article 21 and Socially Optimal Treaty Ratification

Thus far the economic model confirms the general intuition that the reciprocal effects of unilateral treaty reservations created by Article 21 provide a viable solution to prisoner's dilemma problems. The matching effects of treaty reservations always induce states to adopt levels of treaty ratification higher than those that they would otherwise adopt in Nash equilibrium. But, while improving on the Nash equilibrium, to what extent is Article 21 also capable of generating socially optimal levels of treaty ratification?

First and foremost, given asymmetry between the two states, the social optimum calls for equal levels of treaty ratification from both states only in the unlikely case where the social marginal benefit-marginal cost ratios $d/2a$ and $b/2c$ are the same, or in the more plausible case where both states need to undertake full treaty ratification in order to maximize their joint surplus from the treaty. Thus, if the social optimum requires asymmetric levels of treaty ratification from the two states, the presence of a binding matching constraint, as required by Article 21 and leading to equal levels of treaty ratification, would obviously prevent the achievement of such an ideal optimum. For the matching-reservations equilibrium outcome to be socially optimal, it is then necessary that identical levels of treaty ratification for the two states be required under a social optimum. This means that the effectiveness of a matching-reservations constraint to induce socially optimal strategies may be impaired when heterogeneous states are involved. The equilibria induced by Article 21 may be second-best in a world of strategic players, but they are not necessarily first-best outcomes when asymmetric incentives are at work.

There are two ways in which the matching-reservations constraint set forth by Article 21 will lead to socially optimal outcomes. First, if all private and social marginal benefits are large enough so that the social marginal-benefit marginal-cost ratios ($d/2a$ and $b/2c$) as well as the private marginal-benefit marginal-cost ratios for individual states ($b/2a$ and $d/2c$) are greater than or equal to one, then both the social optimum and the matching-reservations equilibrium are characterized by a full treaty ratification level. In this case, the benefit is so great that even though both states may desire different amounts greater than what is feasible, full treaty ratification is all that can happen in practice.

Second, as intimated earlier, convergence of preferences is not likely in the case of partial treaty ratification. Even with the assurance of matching treaty ratification, the high-cost state, state 1, will prefer a lower level of treaty ratification ($b/2a$). This lower level of treaty ratification will *de facto* characterize the mutual treaty obligations in the regime set forth by Article 21 of the Vienna Convention. In order for this matching-reservations equilibrium level of partial treaty ratification to be socially optimal, it must equal the two social marginal benefit-marginal cost ratios ($d/2a$ and $b/2c$) as well. This implies that $b = d$ and $a = c$ must hold. In other words, if the equilibrium partial treaty ratification induced by the matching-reservations constraints are socially efficient, the states must be homogeneous.

This is an important result: if the social optimum requires partial levels of treaty ratification for the two states, such equilibrium is obtainable under a matching-reservations rule only if the players have symmetric payoff functions. In the case of asymmetric states when the privately optimal level of treaty ratification for at least one state falls short of full treaty ratification, the matching-reservations levels induced by Article 21 will not coincide with the social optimum. Thus, with asymmetric players, partial treaty ratification will always be dictated by high-cost states. The resulting equilibrium treaty obligations under Article 21 will be privately optimal only for these states and would never be privately optimal for the low-cost states or socially optimal for the international community as a whole.

3. The Effects of Article 21 of the Vienna Convention on Treaty Ratification

In this chapter we have studied the effects of Article 21 of the Vienna Convention on states' ratification incentives. The economic model of treaty ratification identified the strengths and weaknesses of the matching-reservations mechanism introduced by Article 21. The incentives for unilateral reservation are substantially reduced because the matching-reservations effect created by Article 21 basically transforms a situation of unilateral reservation into one of reciprocal reservation. When states have symmetric incentives, optimal treaty obligations are likely included in the original treaty agreement. Strategic unilateral reservation matched by others would occasion mutual losses for all states involved and would thus not be introduced. States refrain from introducing strategic unilateral reservations as a way to maximize their expected return from the treaty relationship.

When states face asymmetric incentives, the rules introduced by the Vienna Convention may not discourage all reservations. In such cases, some states may introduce unilateral reservations in spite of the matching-reservations effect of Article 21. Erosion of the original treaty content may be inevitable, unless the signatory states opt out of the regime set forth by Article 21, by precluding reservations in the treaty itself.

We also examined the welfare properties of the matching-reservations outcomes generated by Article 21, starting with states that have different payoff functions. Specifically, we considered two asymmetric states with payoff functions that engender a prisoner's dilemma in their ratification choices. We identified the matching-reservations equilibrium—equilibrium in which states introduce reservations knowing that Article 21 allows other, nonreserving states to invoke equal levels of reservations to their advantage—and showed that Article 21 provides quite an effective solution to the prisoner's dilemma problem. However, the matching-reservations equilibrium does not always induce socially optimal levels of ratification. The model shows that a social optimum is achieved under Article 21 only in the limited subset of cases where signatory states have homogeneous payoff functions, or when all states prefer full ratification, despite facing different incentives.

Real-life examples can be analyzed though the framework of this chapter to assess the effectiveness of matching-reservations mechanisms vis-à-vis explicit exclusions of reservations in the original treaty agreement. Consider for example a reservation to a free trade treaty, restricting trade for a specific category of products (e.g., sugar). States that are likely to introduce such reservations are net importers, attempting to protect their domestic industries. The matching effects of such reservations give little benefit to the nonreserving states. States that are large producers of sugar would in fact gain little advantage from a restriction on imports of those products from reserving states, because such kinds of imports would be unlikely to begin with. As it will be extensively discussed in Chapter 16, our analysis of asymmetric states brings to light the limits of the matching-reservations mechanism in these real-life scenarios.

These results should be evaluated in conjunction with the findings discussed in Chapter 14, considering the impact of such expected ratification strategies in the earlier stage of treaty negotiations. For example, when asymmetries between states render unilateral reservations likely under the regime set forth by Article 21, it is natural to expect that states will anticipate future reservation strategies and adjust and/or react accordingly. In this respect, the results of this chapter may provide the basis for a more complete understanding of a treaty formation process, in both its formation and ratification stages.

SIXTEEN

The Hidden Bias of Treaty Law*

AS DISCUSSED IN THE PREVIOUS CHAPTER, the regime governing treaty accession, ratification, and reservations, introduced by the 1969 Vienna Convention, represents a change in international law. Prior to the Vienna Convention, unilateral reservations introduced by states at the time of accession or ratification had to be accepted by all signatory states in order to become effective. To help facilitate multilateral agreements coming into force when signatory states introduce reservations at the time of accession or ratification, the Vienna Convention originated a more liberal approach to treaty reservations. If a state introduces a reservation, the treaty relationship between that state and any nonreserving state is modified according to the scope of the reservation: the exception or limitation claimed by the reserving state applies equally to both states.[1]

For reasons discussed in Chapter 15, in spite of this approach to reservations in the Vienna Convention, relatively few reservations are appended to multilateral treaties. One such reason, discussed in prevailing literature, is that states value the integrity of the treaty more than their ability to tailor the agreement to their needs through the use of reservations.[2] In this chapter we shall suggest that in spite of the apparent neutrality of the reciprocity principle, a hidden bias of the Vienna Convention creates a systematic advantage for states with high costs and low benefits. The analysis sheds light on the troubled evolution of Article 21 of the Vienna Convention, and explains why, at times, economically disadvantaged states favored the reciprocity principle adopted by the Vienna Convention.

Section 1 of this chapter discusses the rules governing the process of treaty reservation and the change brought about by the Vienna Convention on the Law of Treaties. Section 2 presents an economic model of treaty reservations

---

* This chapter is based on the paper, Fon, Vincy, and Francesco Parisi, "The Hidden Bias of the Vienna Conventions on the International Law of Treaties," presented at *The American Law and Economics Association Annual Meetings*, Paper No. 21 (2004).

to reveal the latent bias created by heterogeneous states under Article 21 of the Vienna Convention. Section 3 summarizes the main findings.

⅛ 1. Reservations under the Vienna Convention of the Law of Treaties

As previously discussed, the Vienna convention mainly codifies preexisting customary practice governing the formation, entry into, and interpretation of treaties, as well as the procedural rules for treaty administration.[3] However, on the specific issue of treaty reservations, the Vienna Convention introduces a new regime which substantially changes preexisting international customary law—a change that was far from unproblematic as revealed from the preparatory work of the Vienna Convention. In the following, we search for an explanation for the strong positions held by states on this issue, by investigating the effects brought about by this progressive development in the international law of treaties.

1.1. Reservations to a Treaty under Prior Customary International Law

A fundamental premise of international law is that a state cannot be bound to a treaty rule without its consent. The traditional unanimity rule requires all states to adopt the text of a multilateral treaty. This ensures that no state participating in treaty negotiations is bound by any treaty or part of a treaty that it finds unacceptable. Further, any treaty coming into force has the clear backing of all its constituent parties, laying a strong foundation for compliance. Until the late nineteenth century, this consent principle also strictly applied to the process of treaty accession, ratification, and reservation.[4] The rule governing unilateral reservation closely followed the principles of private contract law adopted by most legal systems. A state reservation to a treaty was construed as a unilateral amendment of the original agreement which should not bind other parties without their consent. Unanimous consent for the admissibility of treaty reservations was then regarded as the logical corollary of the unanimous consent requirement for treaty formation.

   Strict application of the unanimity rule gradually started to lose support in the post–World War I era. Under this regime a state not wishing to ratify a particular treaty provision had the limited choice of accepting the treaty as a whole or not being a party to the entire agreement. The leading European nations continued to support the rule that a state cannot attach a reservation to a treaty unless all parties agree to it. Other nations, however, began to recognize that the unanimity principle for treaty reservations could become unworkable in a world characterized by broader participation of international actors, such as that which followed World War I and the establishment of the League of Nations. Multilateral agreements involved growing numbers of nations, thus increasing the difficulties and costs of treaty negotiation. This brought about a need for more flexible rules that could facilitate the formation of multilateral agreements even in the face of reservations in the ratification of treaties by signatory states. An important event that opened the door to the modern formulation of Article 21 is India's 1959 request for accession to the Inter-Governmental Maritime Organization, which it originally submitted in 1948. The Secretary General wanted to apply the unanimity rule.[5] India's specific case was resolved in the General Assembly's Resolution 1452 (XVI). The Indian addendum to its ratification was labeled a "policy declaration," avoiding a clash with the unanimity rule.[6]

There was no easy solution to the problem of reservations to international treaties. Although some leeway for reservation was recognized as necessary, the question was left open on how to limit its scope. The ability to introduce unilateral reservations without requiring consent from other states would unfairly tip the balance in favor of reserving states. In turn, this would trigger a strategic and frequent use of reservations, which would undermine the stability of treaty agreements. On the other hand, the very existence of a treaty agreement should not be discouraged by excessively strict rules on reservations. International rules on treaty formation should foster treaty preservation and avoid situations where a minor disagreement over some technical provision undermines the treaty as a whole.

1.2. The Origins of Article 21 of the Vienna Convention

One of the most difficult issues to resolve during negotiations of the Vienna Convention was finding an appropriate balance between flexibility and stability in treaty formation.[7] While remaining faithful to the general principle of *pacta sunt servanda* (agreements must be kept), the Vienna Convention (Articles 19–23) addressed unilateral reservations by moving away from the unanimity principle and appealing to the concept of reciprocity, a basic and universally accepted principle of international law.[8] This effectively balanced the conflicting needs for flexibility and integrity that surfaced during the previous reservations regime.[9] The argument for a more liberal regime rested on the possibility that most reservations would not incorporate substantive changes to treaties, but would be triggered by incompatibilities of procedural or jurisdictional provisions of the treaty with constitutional or administrative rules of the signatory states. Allowing reservations in such cases would allow states to participate in certain multilateral treaties where they otherwise would not.

Articles 19–23 of the Vienna Convention, concerning reservations, represent an innovation over preexisting international customary law. They define a reservation as "a unilateral statement, however phrased or named, made by a State when signing, ratifying, accepting, approving or acceding to a treaty, whereby it purports to exclude or to modify the legal effect of certain provisions of the treaty in their application to that State." Article 19 allows states to include reservations in their acceptance of treaty obligations, unless the treaty itself expressly forbids reservations, or the reservation is incompatible with the object and purpose of the treaty. Article 20 outlines the circumstances under which reservations must be accepted by the other parties; if a state does not object to a reservation from another state within a set amount of time, its silence is construed as tacit acceptance. An objection to a reservation does not, however, preclude entry into a binding treaty between two states. Rather, Article 21 allows states to tailor relations between them through the mechanism of reciprocity.

The reciprocal effects of unilateral reservations provide protection against strategic reservations. As discussed in the previous chapter, unilateral reservations under Article 21 become a "double-edged sword," as other states are also exempt from treaty obligations to the extent of the reservation. Given reciprocal effects of reservations against the reserving state and the applicability of the original treaty obligation between nonreserving states in their relations with one another, Article 21 often transforms a multilateral treaty obligation into a network of fragmented bilateral treaty obligations.

1.3. Treaty Reservations under the Vienna Convention

Under Article 14 of the Vienna Convention, a treaty subject to ratification does not become binding until after it is approved by the legislature.

Under Article 15 accession is the means by which a state becomes a party to an existing treaty to which it is not an original signatory. The Vienna Convention allows states who ratify or accede to a treaty to introduce reservations on specific provisions via unilateral statements. With a reservation, a state can omit or modify treaty provisions, thus excluding itself from certain terms of the treaty or varying the legal effect of such terms. The treaty, as modified by the reservation, enters into force between the reserving state and states that do not object to the reservation. As for states who do not accept the reservation, neither the reserving state nor the nonreserving states are bound by *omitted* provisions. The objecting state may also declare the entire treaty not in force between the two countries. Further, nonreserving states remain bound to the original treaty provision in their relations with one another. Similarly, *modified* provisions apply to all bilateral relations of the reserving state with a nonreserving state, while the original treaty provision governs the relations among nonreserving states.

Although not explicitly specified in the Vienna Convention, the mechanism of treaty reservation should permit more than one state to introduce reservations to the treaty. In a stylized setting in which several states can introduce reservations to the same treaty provision with a single dimension of commitment, the effects of the states' reservations should be distinguished as follows: (1) reserving states are bound to the treaty as modified by their respective reservations in their relations with nonreserving states; (2) reserving states are bound to the treaty as modified by the greater of the reservations in their relations with one another; and (3) nonreserving states are bound by the original treaty in their relations with one another.[10]

2. Treaty Reservations among Heterogeneous States

Articles 19–21 of the Vienna Convention consider the effect of a state's reservations in a multilateral treaty setting.[11] As discussed earlier, when a state introduces a reservation to a treaty at the time of accession or ratification, it creates multiple bilateral implications and transforms the unilateral reservation into multiple bilateral changes in treaty content. The treaty is modified by the reservation between the reserving state and nonreserving states. Between the reserving state and another reserving state, the treaty is modified by the lower level of ratification agreed to by these two states. Lastly, unilateral reservations do not prejudice application of the original treaty provisions among nonreserving states.

The multiplicity of bilateral effects created by unilateral reservations to a treaty makes it necessary to first study how reservations affect interactions between two states, taking the underlying treaty as exogenous. Consider the impact of unilateral reservations between any two states who are parties to a multilateral treaty. This serves as a building block for subsequent analysis of the multilateral effects of unilateral reservations, where more than one state introduces reservations.[12] We consider heterogeneous states facing different cost-benefit ratios from treaty implementation. These different cost-benefit ratios can be interpreted as the states' respective comparative advantage in international cooperation. For example, poorer or developing nations may face higher cost-benefit ratios in treaty implementation, or the well-being of large and powerful nations may depend less critically on international cooperation.

2.1. Bilateral Interaction between States H and L

To study the bilateral effects of unilateral reservations in a multilateral treaty, consider two representative states H and L. Each state benefits from the other state's acceptance and ratification of the treaty, and incurs costs when ratifying the treaty and undertaking obligations toward the other state. Although the Vienna Convention applies to both accession and ratification of treaties, we refer to the ratification choice as a strategy variable and denote it as s, where $s \in [0, 1]$. Ratifying states can accept treaty obligations in full or introduce limitations in the form of unilateral reservations. Higher levels of s imply greater willingness of the state to ratify and undertake treaty obligations. A reservation creates a discrepancy between the original treaty obligation and the ratified treaty obligation. A larger reservation (indicated by a smaller value of s) implies a lower level of ratification of the treaty. The level of ratification strategy extended from state H (L) to state L (H) is denoted by s_H (s_L).

The benefit enjoyed by state H from s_L, the ratification level of the treaty by state L, is $b_H s_L$.[13] The cost incurred by state H for its chosen level of ratification s_H is $a_H s_H^2$. The payoff for state H from entering into a treaty relationship with state L is then given by $P_H^L = b_H s_L - a_H s_H^2$.[14] We assume that $b_H > a_H$ so that some positive level of treaty ratification is preferred to no treaty ratification. Likewise, the payoff for state L when entering into a treaty relationship with state H is $P_L^H = b_L s_H - a_L s_L^2$ where $b_L > a_L$.

For now, assume that state H chooses a level of ratification expecting *unconditional reciprocity* from state L through the treaty. That is, state H expects state L to ratify the treaty at the same level: $s_L = s_H$. Confronted with the problem to maximize $b_H s_H - a_H s_H^2$, state H chooses ratification level $s_H' = b_H / 2a_H$. Likewise, assuming that state H reciprocates the level of ratification, state L chooses $s_L' = b_L / 2a_L$ to maximize $b_L s_L - a_L s_L^2$. Thus, if both countries assume unconditional reciprocity the optimal levels of ratification are:

$$s_H' = b_H / 2a_H \quad \text{and} \quad s_L' = b_L / 2a_L \tag{16.1}$$

If states were allowed to introduce unilateral reservations without the reciprocity effect created by Article 21, they could choose any ratification level lower than the existing treaty obligation. Each state is tempted to reduce the level of treaty ratification and take advantage of the other state's compliance with higher levels of treaty obligations. The resulting level of ratification for state H is $s_H = 0$ because $s_H = 0$ maximizes $P_H^L = b_H s_L - a_H s_H^2$ given any s_L. Likewise, the level of ratification for state L is $s_L = 0$ given any s_H. Thus, without the reciprocity constraint imposed by Article 21, the Nash equilibrium is ($s_H = 0$, $s_L = 0$). This constitutes a prisoner's dilemma because both states would benefit by settling on a positive level of treaty ratification.

The reservation mechanism set forth by the Vienna Convention has two important characteristics. One is reservation itself—a state may ratify or accede to a treaty while choosing a level of obligation lower than that specified in the original treaty. The second is that reservations have reciprocal effects under Article 21. Combining these two factors, consider the *conditional reciprocity* problem that a state confronts. If the level of ratification of the other state is below the treaty obligation s_T, given reciprocity, a state expects that the smaller level of ratification chosen by the two states becomes the binding level of reservation.

In particular, assume that state L introduces a reservation level of ratification less than the treaty obligation: $s_L \leq s_T$. The problem confronting state H, given the reciprocal effects of the introduced reservation, depends on whichever state chooses the smaller ratification level:

$$\max_{s_H} \pi_H^L = \begin{cases} b_H s_H - a_H s_H^2 & \text{if } s_H \leq s_L \\ b_H s_L - a_H s_L^2 & \text{if } s_H \geq s_L \end{cases} \quad \text{given } s_L \leq s_T \tag{16.2}$$

Recall that the optimal level of treaty ratification with unconditional reciprocity is s_H'. Suppose that state L chooses a level of ratification s_L that is less than the privately optimal s_H' for state H. Although state H desires a higher level of mutual treaty obligation, the best it can do is to take advantage of the reciprocal effect of state L's reservation and invoke the same level of reservation. If instead state L chooses a level of ratification s_L greater than the privately optimal s_H' for state H, then state H is better off choosing s_H' and will not agree to a ratification level higher than s_H'. Hence, given the ratification level s_L and reciprocity induced by Article 21, the reaction function of state H can be written as follows:

$$s_H = \begin{cases} s_L & \text{if } s_L \leq s_H', \ s_L \leq s_T \\ s_H' & \text{if } s_H' \leq s_L, \ s_L \leq s_T \end{cases} \qquad 16.3$$

Likewise, assuming $s_H \leq s_T$ and given the ratification level s_H, the reaction function of state L under reciprocal reservation is given in the following:

$$s_L = \begin{cases} s_H & \text{if } s_H \leq s_L', \ s_H \leq s_T \\ s_L' & \text{if } s_L' \leq s_H, \ s_H \leq s_T \end{cases} \qquad 16.4$$

Assume that state H is the high-cost state, with a cost-benefit ratio higher than the low-cost state L: $a_H/b_H > a_L/b_L$. Given that state H is higher cost, the optimal levels of ratification under unconditional reciprocity satisfy $s_H' < s_L'$. That is, the high-cost state's choice with unconditional reciprocity is always lower than the low-cost state's choice.

If a state's optimal level of ratification under unconditional reciprocity exceeds the level of obligation under the original treaty, the state has no opportunity to introduce an over-provision and becomes a nonreserving state. On the other hand, if the state's optimal level of ratification under unconditional reciprocity is less than the treaty level of obligation, the state is reluctant to ratify the treaty in full, choosing to introduce a reservation and become a reserving state. With unconditional reciprocity, the high-cost state H always selects a lower ratification level than the low-cost state and thus is more likely to be the reserving state for any treaty obligation. More generally, given any treaty obligation s_T, if $s_H' < s_T \leq s_L'$, state H is a reserving state and state L is a nonreserving state. If $s_H' < s_L' < s_T$, then both states are reserving states. Finally, if $s_T \leq s_H' < s_L'$, then H and L are both nonreserving states.

2.2. Treaty Ratifications in a Bilateral Equilibrium

Under the reciprocity regime dictated by Article 21 of the Vienna Convention, within the range of mutually agreeable levels of treaty ratification, each state realizes that higher levels of mutual obligation are better than lower levels and chooses accordingly. Thus, if there are multiple mutually acceptable equilibria under reciprocity, the highest level of mutual ratification will be chosen.[15] Depending on the relative magnitudes of s'_H, s'_L, and the content of the original treaty obligation s_T, each state might make reservations or ratify the treaty in full. Consider the alternative cases in turn.

2.2.1. Case 1: Bilateral Reservations

This case happens when the two states prefer lower levels of obligation than that specified in the original multilateral treaty ($s'_H < s'_L < s_T$). Figure 16.1 shows the reaction functions of the two states. From the viewpoint of state H, if state L prefers too low a level of ratification, the best it can do is to adopt the same level of ratification: $s_H = s_L$. If the opponent state chooses too high a level of ratification, state H will not be forced to ratify at any level higher than its private optimum: $s_H = s'_H$. The reaction function of state H first follows the 45-degree line, and then becomes horizontal. Likewise, the reaction function of state L first follows the 45-degree line, and then becomes vertical. Both reaction functions stop at the level specified in the treaty s_T. With these reaction functions, the highest level of ratification mutually agreeable to the states s'_H is the equilibrium ratification level for the two states.

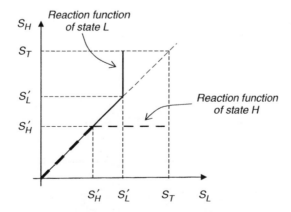

FIGURE 16.1 Bilateral Reservation Strategies Equilibrium ratification: S'_H

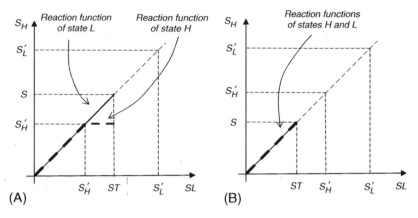

FIGURE 16.2(A) Unilateral Reservation Strategy   FIGURE 16.2(B) No Reservation

2.2.2. Case 2: Unilateral Reservation

This case takes place when one state (state H) prefers a level of obligation lower than the treaty specification, while the other state (state L) is content with the treaty as originally formulated: $s'_H < s_T < s'_L$. Figure 16.2A shows that the reaction function for state H is similar to that in case i, while the reaction function for state L no longer has a kink because state L prefers too high a level of ratification. Given these reaction functions, the equilibrium ratification level for both states is again s'_H.

2.2.3. Case 3: No Reservation

This case occurs when both states prefer high levels of ratification: $s_T < s'_H < s'_L$. Figure 16.2B shows the reaction functions for both states. In this case, both states ratify the treaty in full and the equilibrium level of ratification for both states is consistent with the original treaty obligation s_T.

2.3. Distributive Effects of Bilateral Reciprocity under Article 21

We now examine the distributive effects of the reservation process introduced by Article 21 of the Vienna Convention on the two representative states. We concentrate on the asymmetric impact of reservations subject to the reciprocity regime, comparing the outcome induced by Article 21 to the preexisting regime in which no unwanted reservations could be introduced. Following the same order of presentation, we investigate the effects in each case.

2.3.1. Case A. Bilateral Reservations: H and L Are Both Reserving States

As observed before, whenever the original treaty specifies a high obligation such that $s'_H < s'_L < s_T$, both states introduce reservations to the treaty and reach a level of mutual ratification s'_H. Because s'_H maximizes the payoff function for state H under unconditional reciprocity, state H is better off after the ratification process than under any other level of treaty obligation. It is not clear whether state L is better off or worse off after ratification. Recall that s'_L maximizes the payoff function under unconditional reciprocity for state L. The relationships $s'_H < s'_L < s_T$ imply that s'_H falls on the left hand side of the maximum and s_T falls on the right hand side of the maximum of the payoff function. Thus, the move from the original treaty obligation s_T to the lower ratification level chosen by the other state can either improve or worsen state L's welfare. Thus, when both states introduce reservations, the high-cost state is better off, but the welfare change for the low-cost state is indeterminate.

2.3.2. Case B. Unilateral Reservation: H Is a Reserving State and L Is a Nonreserving State

The original treaty obligation falls between the privately optimal treaty levels for the two states, $s'_H < s_T \leq s'_L$. Here the high-cost state introduces a reservation. The low-cost state has no incentive to introduce a reservation, but can at least invoke the reciprocal effects of the high-cost state's reservation against such state.[16] In this bilateral subtreaty relationship, the equilibrium ratification s'_H is determined by the high-cost state. As in the last case, the high-cost state H is better off after the ratification process, because it achieves its first-best treaty level under reciprocity. Unlike in the previous case, the low-cost state L is worse off because the equilibrium ratification s'_H is further from the optimal level of state L than the level of treaty obligation s_T. Thus, when there is a unilateral reservation, the welfare of the reserving state is always improved while the welfare of the nonreserving state is worsened.

2.3.3. Case C. No Reservation: H and L Are Both Nonreserving States

The treaty obligation is lower than the private optimal levels for the relevant states, $s_T \leq s'_H < s'_L$, so that neither state has an incentive to introduce a reservation even though both have an option to do so. Both states ratify the treaty in full in equilibrium. When no reservations are introduced by either state, welfare does not change after the ratification process.

2.4. The Multilateral Setting

So far the bilateral relationship of representative states H and L which are parties to a multilateral treaty is considered. Now contemplate the multilateral effects of treaty ratification under Article 21 of the Vienna Convention with N participating states. Each state benefits from other states' acceptance and ratification of a treaty obligation, and incurs cost by agreeing to fulfill the treaty obligations by ratifying the treaty. When a uniform treaty obligation crumbles into a network of bilateral treaty obligations, the overall benefit of a participating state is determined by the sum of the benefits derived from each subtreaty relationship in which it participates. The payoff for state i, P_i, is the sum of all P_i^j where P_i^j is the payoff derived by state i from interacting with state j in the bilateral subtreaty relationship, similar to those introduced previously. Let the level of treaty ratification of state j as it affects state i be denoted by s_{ji} and the level of treaty ratification of state i as it affects state j be denoted by s_{ij}. The benefit enjoyed by state i from the level of ratification by state j is $b_i s_{ji}$, and the cost incurred by state i for its level of treaty ratification with state j is $a_i s_{ij}^2$. The net payoff for state i from the treaty relationship with state j, P_i^j, is $b_i s_{ji} - a_i s_{ij}^2$ where $b_i > a_i$. Thus, the total payoff for state i from participating in the multilateral treaty is given by the summation of the bilateral payoffs from the various subtreaty relationships and is given by

$$P_i = \sum_{\substack{j=1 \\ j \neq i}}^{N} P_i^j = \sum_{\substack{j=1 \\ j \neq i}}^{N} (b_i s_{ji} - a_i s_{ij}^2) \qquad 16.5$$

The formulation of the states' payoffs in equation (16.5) assumes that state i's benefit in entering in a treaty interaction with state j is independent from its interaction with other states. This condition implies that the ideal ratification level between two nonreserving states remains at s_T (full compliance with the treaty) irrespective of whether other states introduce reservations. Treaty ratification choices are strategically independent, which is reasonable in many situations. For example, the benefits derived from a treaty abating trade barriers between two states generally do not depend on whether other states ratify the trade treaty. Likewise, benefits derived by one state from an asylum treaty with another state do not depend on the choices of third-party states.[17]

As before, the optimal level of mutual ratification for state i in its relationship with any other state, say state j, could be found by maximizing the payoff assuming unconditional reciprocity $b_i s_{ij} - a_i s_{ij}^2$. To maximize this payoff, state i would choose $s_i' = b_i/2a_i$—the optimal level of ratification under unconditional reciprocity.

The N states participating in the formation and ratification of the treaty are ranked from 1 to N such that state 1 is the highest cost state, and state N is the lowest cost state:[18]

$$\frac{a_1}{b_1} > \frac{a_2}{b_2} > \ldots > \frac{a_N}{b_N}, \text{ or }, s_1' < s_2' < \ldots < s_N' \qquad 16.6$$

In the process of bargaining for a mutually acceptable treaty level, it is likely that the states would agree to an intermediate level of treaty obligation. This is true because states are expected to bargain until the sum of their payoffs under reciprocity is maximized. The aggregate payoff function for all signatory states is maximized when states undertake a level of treaty obligation s_T falling between the privately optimal levels of ratification for the states at both ends of the cost distribution: state 1 and state N.[19] In other words, there exists a state M between 1 and N such that the treaty obligation s_T satisfies:

$$s_M' = \frac{b_M}{2a_M} < s_T < \frac{b_{M+1}}{2a_{M+1}} = s_{M+1}' \qquad 16.7$$

Recall that if the optimal level of ratification under unconditional reciprocity is greater than or equal to the original treaty obligation s_T, the state would be a nonreserving state. Thus, all states from $M+1$ to N are nonreserving states. On the other hand, states 1 through M have incentives to introduce reservations to the treaty. To study the reciprocal reservation mechanism provided in Article 21 of the Vienna Convention in this multilateral context, we consider three separate cases.

2.5. Nonreserving States

The first group of cases includes situations in which state i is a nonreserving state. Here $i \geq M + 1$ and $s_i' = b_i/2a_i > s_T$. The content of the treaty relationship between a nonreserving state i and another state j depends on whether j is itself a reserving or nonreserving state. If j is a nonreserving state $(j \geq M + 1)$, the bilateral subtreaty relationship between the two states is characterized by full ratification (s_T) because neither state has an incentive to introduce a reservation. Thus, the opportunity to introduce unilateral reservations made possible by Article 21 of the Vienna Convention has no impact on the welfare of state i when going through the process of ratification with another nonreserving state.

On the other hand, when i is a nonreserving state and j is a reserving state ($j \leq M$), then state j must be higher cost compared to state i. The unilateral reservation introduced by state j leads to an equilibrium level of treaty ratification s_j'. The welfare of state i, the nonreserving low-cost state, is negatively affected by the possibility offered by Article 21 of the Vienna Convention to introduce unilateral reservations.

Recall that the total payoff for state i from the multilateral treaty is given by the summation of the various bilateral payoffs with all other signatory states, as in (16.5). The equilibrium payoff for state i after the ratification process under Article 21 should naturally be separated into two parts. The first part represents payoffs obtained from interacting with reserving states (1 to M), and the second part is given by payoffs from interacting with other nonreserving states ($M + 1$ to N). Recalling that the nonreserving states are those ranked from $M + 1$ to N, the equilibrium payoff for a nonreserving state i is given by the following:

$$P_i = \sum_{j=1}^{M} (b_i s_j' - a_i s_j'^2) + \sum_{\substack{j=M+1 \\ j \neq i}}^{N} (b_i s_T - a_i s_T^2)$$

16.8

$$[i \text{ a nonreserving state}, i \geq M + 1]$$

The equilibrium payoff in (16.8) shows that state i suffers an insufficient level of ratification in M cases but receives the full treaty payoff in the remaining $N - M - 1$ bilateral subtreaty relationships.

2.6. Reserving States

In the second group of cases, state i is a reserving state: $i \leq M$ and $s_i' = b_i/2a_i < s_T$. The interaction of a reserving state i with another state depends on whether the latter is a reserving or nonreserving state. If the other state j is a nonreserving state, state i is higher cost compared to state j, with $j \in \{M+1, \ldots, N\}$. The mutual level of treaty ratification is determined by the high-cost state i's ratification at level s_i'. The welfare of state i, the reserving state, is improved by the opportunity to introduce unilateral reservations under Article 21 of the Vienna Convention.[20]

When state i interacts with another reserving state j, the resulting equilibrium level of ratification depends on whether state i or state j is higher cost.[21] Because all states are ranked in decreasing order in terms of relative cost, state i is relatively high cost in comparison to state j, when such a state falls in the range $j = i+1, \ldots, M$. The equilibrium level of ratification s_i' in these cases is determined by the high-cost state i. Here, the welfare of state i, the reserving state, is also improved by the opportunity to introduce reservations against other reserving, and yet lower-cost, states.

Different results are obtained when state i is a lower-cost state relative to the other reserving states, 1 through $i - 1$. In spite of the common use of reservations, each bilateral subtreaty relationship is characterized by an equilibrium level of ratification s_j' which is determined by the relatively high-cost state j, where $j \in \{1, \ldots, i-1\}$. In each of these interactions with relatively high-cost states, the changes in welfare for the low-cost state i are indeterminate under the process of reservation and ratification set forth by Article 21. This result reflects the indeterminacy already observed in case A above.

The equilibrium payoff for state i following various reservations under Article 21 should again be separated into two parts. The first part is given by payoffs from interacting with other reserving and relatively high-cost states (1 to $i - 1$). The second part is given by payoffs from interacting with other reserving and relatively low-cost states ($i+1$ to M) or nonreserving states ($M+1$ to N). Recalling that the reserving states are those ranked from 1 to M, the equilibrium payoff for a reserving state i is given by the following:

$$P_i = \sum_{j=1}^{i-1}(b_i s_j' - a_i s_j'^2) + \sum_{j=i+1}^{N}(b_i s_i' - a_i s_i'^2)$$

16.9

$$[i \text{ a reserving state}, i \leq M]$$

The equilibrium payoff in (16.9) shows that state i suffers an insufficient level of ratification in $i - 1$ cases but obtains its optimal payoff in the remaining $N - i$ bilateral subtreaty relationships.

Comparing the payoff for a nonreserving state in (16.8) with the payoff for a reserving state in (16.9), we see that the reserving state is faced with undesired reservations from fewer states than the nonreserving state because there are fewer terms in the first summation in (16.9) than in the first summation in (16.8). Meanwhile in the remaining bilateral relations, the reserving state controls the level of treaty obligations in a larger number of cases, while the nonreserving state is constrained by the level of the treaty s_T and obtains the full treaty payoff in fewer cases. This means that the process of treaty reservations set forth by Article 21 gives an advantage to reserving states over nonreserving states.

2.7. The Highest-Cost State

Given our criterion for ranking states, state 1 is the highest-cost state. Given a treaty obligation s_T, the highest-cost state would be a reserving state. The possibility for state 1 to introduce unilateral reservations under Article 21 of the Vienna Convention implies that this state's reservation would affect the levels of treaty ratification in its relationship with all other states. Thus the highest cost state's welfare is improved by the opportunity to introduce reservations in every bilateral subtreaty interaction. As a special case of the equilibrium payoff formulated for the general case of a reserving state, the first term in equation (16.9) disappears because no other reserving state has a higher cost than state 1. Consequently, the equilibrium payoff for state 1 with reciprocal effects of reservations is the following.

$$P_1 = \sum_{j=2}^{N} (b_1 s_1' - a_1 s_1'^2) \qquad \text{16.10}$$

The equilibrium payoff in (16.10) shows that state i obtains its optimal payoff in all $N - 1$ subtreaty relationships and never suffers excessive treaty reservations by other states.

Comparing the payoff for the highest-cost state in (16.10) with the payoff for the representative reserving state in (16.9), we see that the highest-cost state never faces undesired reservations from other states. This can be seen from the fact that the first summation in (16.9) disappears in (16.10).

The highest-cost state effectively controls the level of ratification so that its optimal treaty level prevails in all bilateral treaty relations with other states. This shows that treaty reservations set forth by Article 21 not only give an advantage to reserving states over nonreserving states, but they also give an increasing advantage to states that prefer lower levels of international treaty obligations.

2.8. Other Considerations

As a first step toward understanding the impact of Article 21 on the states' obtainable payoffs, our model treated the content and membership of the underlying treaty as exogenous. The prospect of unilateral reservations affects terms of the underlying treaty and often affects states' incentives to negotiate treaties. When states can anticipate ratification strategies of other states, they may take such effects into account in determining the content and participation to the treaty. Given the highlighted workings of Article 21, there are different ways in which heterogeneous states could react to the reservations regime in a multilateral treaty.

First, states may anticipate the bias effect of unilateral reservations under Article 21 and choose not to enter into multilateral treaty arrangements with high-cost states. High-cost states could corrode the benefits of low-cost states by lowering commitment levels at the ratification stage. This helps explain why treaty membership is confined in many situations to relatively homogeneous states that share a common goal with similar cost-benefit ratios. Thus, different groups of states form different multilateral treaties with limited participation, rather than attempting to coalesce in a multilateral treaty with universal participation. Examples include regional treaties for economic development, trade treaties among industrialized countries, and outer space exploration agreements. By entering into treaties with fewer participants with similar interests, states ensure a higher level of homogeneity and reduce the risk of treaty corrosion via unilateral reservations.

Second, states may realize that benefits can be obtained from international cooperation extended to heterogeneous states. The heterogeneity of states often implies, however, that different states have different ideal treaty ratification levels. The reservation mechanism set forth by Article 21 gives high-cost states a greater opportunity to reach their ideal points relative to low-cost states. The joint-payoff maximizing arrangement frequently lies between the ideal levels of high-cost and low-cost states. In these situations, treaty arrangements are not the fruit of consensus, but of compromise. Often, high-cost states can be enticed to undertake higher levels of treaty participation with side payments or lateral concessions. In these cases, an implicit price can be found in the side concessions made by one state to one or more other states in the process of treaty negotiations. For example, states whose privately optimal levels of treaty obligations below the aggregate optimum may be induced to accept higher levels of obligation in exchange for side benefits of some sort. Sufficient side payments could reduce the degree of heterogeneity between states by turning a high-cost state into a relatively low-cost state, or vice versa. Once the joint-payoff optimum is achieved, the content of the treaty could still be undermined by subsequent reservations of states that prefer lower levels of obligation. It is thus in the interest of all states to exclude ex post unilateral reservations. Our analysis illustrates why in practice, when treaties involve side payments or lateral concessions, parties often opt out of the regime of Article 21, with an explicit preclusion of ex post unilateral reservation under Article 19(a) of the Vienna Convention.

Third, heterogeneous states may anticipate the effect of Article 21 and yet wish to extend participation to as large a group of states as feasible. This may be the case for treaties for which the objectives can be better achieved with widespread participation, such as environmental, economic integration, and human rights treaties. Here compromise leads participating states to undertake asymmetric obligations such as different timing for implementing new emission standards, partial waivers for developing countries, and accommodating different cultural traditions in the interpretation of human rights principles.

A specific example is the WTO regime, where many heterogeneous states have contracted on a number of issues ranging from trade in goods to intellectual property rights. The WTO contains several provisions on special and differential (s'n'd) treatment in favor of developing countries. This amounts to a situation where the treaty imposes asymmetric obligations on the negotiating states. The WTO avoids reservations by anticipating the potential effect of ex post reservations and agreeing to reach an equilibrium that lowers the burden on high-cost states. Thus, the treaty outcome can be seen as anticipating the bias of Article 21, adjusting the initial treaty arrangement to the likely outcome of a uniform treaty corroded by subsequent reservations. The s'n'd-type provisions have the dual advantage of allowing parties to maximize the joint advantage ex ante and to increase the transparency and predictability of the final result through explicit negotiations. In situations such as environmental and human rights protection treaties, widespread treaty participation is more important than uniformity of international obligations and it may be appropriate to allow occasional nonstrategic reservations necessitated by internal political or constitutional constraints of the participating states.

Finally, even if it is possible for states to foresee the likely ratification choices of other states, it may be difficult to adjust the substantive terms of the treaty to anticipate such results. Treaty provisions are drafted for general and uniform application, even though the generality and uniformity of the effects may be undermined by subsequent reservations. It would be difficult to draft treaty provisions that anticipate the complex bilateral and multilateral effects of unilateral reservations. In the practice of international law where treaty reservations are observed, not every reservation can be attributed to a lack of rational foresight by the signatory states.

3. Asymmetric Effects of Reservations under the Vienna Convention

Under the reservations regime in force prior to the Vienna Convention, unanimity principles governed the effects of unilateral reservations at the time of treaty accession and ratification. Under such a regime, reservations become effective only if all other states give their consent. This prevents nonreserving states from being made worse off by unilateral reservations introduced by another signatory state at the time of ratification.

The strength of the reservations regime introduced by the Vienna Convention lies in complex multilateral treaties, where significant negotiating (and renegotiating) cost savings can be achieved when minor deviations from the agreement are allowed through reservations. Our investigation unveils an interesting effect of the process of treaty ratification introduced by the Vienna Convention on the Law of Treaties. Behind the apparent neutrality of the reciprocity principle, reservations under Article 21 create a bias where states with a comparative disadvantage in treaty implementation have a systematic advantage. Given the opportunity to introduce reservations, Article 21 tilts the balance in favor of high-cost and low-benefit states who can take advantage of the mechanism of reciprocity. The bias brought about by the introduction of the reciprocity principle in treaty reservations thus had potential distributive effects between different groups of states.[22]

These effects of Article 21 never became a matter of open contention during several years of preparatory work that preceded development of rules on treaty reservations. The main argument for changing the existing reservation rules was based on the need for greater flexibility brought about by the increasing diffusion of multilateral treaties in world politics. Giving states greater flexibility in accepting terms of a treaty avoids undesirable holdups in the ratification process and ultimately fosters greater state participation. On the other hand, states that opposed changes in the law of treaty reservations feared that any departure from the unanimity principle would contradict past practice and run the risk of casting a shadow of ambiguity over treaty language.[23] In wrestling with this problem, the U.N. General Assembly asked the International Court of Justice to offer its guidance on the question of reservations, and also turned to the International Law Commission for its expertise.[24] Neither of these official opinions indicates an explicit awareness of the bias effects of the reciprocity principle.

In spite of the lack of open discussion of this matter, it is interesting to look back at the peculiar split between supporters and opponents of Article 21. Reciprocity under Article 21 was strongly advocated by less developed countries, such as India and other non-European countries, and was opposed by more established European nations and the United States.[25] In light of our findings, note that poorer or developing states often face higher treaty implementation and compliance costs or enjoy lower benefits from the fulfillment of international obligations, while richer nations generally advocate for and are willing to undertake higher levels of international obligations. Several treaties, for example, explicitly impose more stringent obligations on wealthier or industrialized states. The Montreal Protocol on Ozone-Depleting Substances takes this to an extreme by having wealthier nations subsidize 100 percent of the poorer nations' compliance costs. This treaty outcome is a good illustration of our "hidden bias" hypothesis, because poorer states bear no costs and receive some benefits.

This chapter has identified the source of the bias in the unequal opportunity to introduce reservations. A high-cost state, one who gains less relative to the costs it bears than other states, wishing to avoid application or to reduce the content of a given treaty provision, has the opportunity to do so via unilateral reservations. No symmetric opportunity is given to other states who desire to add provisions to a treaty or to raise the content of a treaty obligation under an existing provision. High-cost nations thus have an intrinsic advantage over low-cost states in shaping the content of multilateral treaty relations. The actual allocation of this advantage across different categories of states depends a great deal on context. Although this bias may often favor poorer and developing nations that face higher cost-benefit ratios in treaty implementation, it may in other situations favor larger and powerful nations, whose well-being depends less critically on international cooperation. For example, since NAFTA the United States is much more reserved in sharing its intellectual property rights with other countries.Further research should examine the applicability of these results to other situations where reciprocity constrains the strategic behavior of different parties, for example, most favored nation clauses. Different alternative mechanisms that may help avoid or minimize the identified limitations of Article 21 of the Vienna Convention should also be considered.

Conclusions

ACCORDING TO A FUNDAMENTAL PRINCIPLE of constitutional design, powers should be allocated to the branch and level of society or government that can best exercise them. This principle can be applied to the question of lawmaking in order to select sources of law that will exploit the comparative advantage of different legal and social institutions in the production of laws. In this book we have considered four different methods of lawmaking, which we described as (1) lawmaking through legislation; (2) lawmaking through adjudication; (3) lawmaking through practice; and (4) lawmaking through agreement.

We have considered various distinguishing features of these alternative sources of law, evaluating their relative advantages in the production of law. Previous work on the economics of lawmaking focused on the public choice dimension of alternative lawmaking processes, considering, among other things, issues of minimization of lawmaking costs, agency problems in representation, as well as issues of stability of collective decision-making outcomes. In this book we have utilized a combination of neoclassical and public choice instruments, in the hope of bridging the gap between the law and economics and the public choice literature. Besides its methodological efforts, this research project has been intellectually most rewarding and has shed light on some interesting features of sources of law that had remained unclear in the previous literature.

⁂ 1. Lawmaking Costs

A traditional criterion for evaluating alternative sources of law is that of minimization of rulemaking costs. According to this criterion, the mechanisms for law creation should be chosen in order to minimize the transaction costs of collective decision making and political bargaining. This cost minimization problem involves the evaluation of two different costs: (1) direct costs of decision making, such as the costs of reaching a majority consensus in a political context, and/or the cost of litigation or adjudication in a judicial context; (2) indirect or external costs, such as the cost imposed on a minority group by the rules chosen by a majority coalition. The objective of cost minimization is, once again, related to public choice considerations of collective decision making the imperfect process of collective decision making through political representation. In this book we have identified additional factors that may affect the costs of lawmaking under the various categories that we considered.

In Part I we considered the case of lawmaking through legislation applying the systematic framework of investment theory. Lawmakers can be viewed as making investment decisions that create present lawmaking costs and which generate future benefits. Within this framework, we studied the optimal degree of specificity of laws and the functionality of rules or standards in conditions of uncertainty (Chapter 2). Specific rules may require larger up-front investments, inasmuch as they require a large outlay in the initial acquisition of information, but the choice of well-specified rules may reduce operating costs later. A broader standard requires smaller initial investments but may require larger outlays in its interpretation and enforcement. In our analysis we discussed a cost factor which has often been overlooked. Lawmaking costs are at least partially sunk and lawmaking investments can dissipate when exogenous changes affect the regulated environment over time. Rules and standards, however, are characterized by different sunk investments. Legal rules can become obsolete as a result of exogenous changes, and the optimal design of legislation should account for the costs of legal obsolescence.

We further applied the instruments of modern investment theory to consider the issue of optimal timing of legal intervention (Chapter 3), identifying some misleading applications of net present value calculations. Legal systems can be regarded as making investment decisions for which timing is an important determination. Also in that chapter we proceeded setting aside the usual issues considered in public choice theory, such as the unavoidable effect of political discount rates in cost-benefit calculations under uncertainty. Building upon the insights of option pricing theory, we considered how the choice of optimal timing in lawmaking can be derived considering the option-like characteristics of lawmaking decisions.

If we analogize the lawmaking process to a production process in the marketplace, the sources of lawmaking through adjudication dis-cussed in Part II may appear as quite an inefficient production process.

The common law process, by shifting some of the law making functions to the judiciary, entrusts courts with the task of conceiving and refining laws while adjudicating specific cases. From a production point of view, such a process forgoes the economies of scale and scope that might be exploited by specialized legislative bodies. The common law process, however, by relying on the adversarial efforts of the parties, utilizes information available to the parties in litigation. Parties have direct information on the costs and benefits of alternative rules and courts may be regarded as having an informational advantage over central legislative bodies, given the opportunity of judges to infer the litigants' preferences from the choices they make during a case. Courts have a further informational advantage in observing the revealed preference of the parties with respect to applicable law. Modern legal systems generally provide a set of default rules that govern their relationships absent parties' decisions to the contrary (e.g., in contract law). When parties opt out of the default rules (through ex ante choices), they reveal their preferences for alternative laws. If courts observe a large number of parties routinely opting out of the default rules, it becomes evident that such rules have failed their cost-minimization task and do not approximate the will of the majority. In these cases, courts have a comparative informational advantage over legislators in designing and revising default legal rules.

In Part III we discussed the case of lawmaking through practice, for which we can distinguish two distinct costs: (1) the cost of decentralized creation of a customary law and (2) the cost of judicial acknowledgement of such an existing custom. The costs of customary law creation are relatively minimal. Most rules of customary law are derived from the observation of widespread practice followed by individuals in society. In this context, customary rules are a costless byproduct of the economic and social interactions of individuals in society. Such practices are not being carried out with the objective of creating binding laws, and the legal recognition of such practices as binding laws adds no cost to the activities involved. The cost for courts to identify a rule of customary law may, however, be considerable. Customs are intangible sources of law and their content does not enjoy any objective articulation in written law. The identification of custom thus requires knowledge of past practice and investigation of the beliefs shared by those who engaged in the practice: a process that can be difficult to carry out and, hence, costly. A point of advantage of customary sources of law is related to the fact that custom is formed through the independent action of individuals in society, without the need for their express agreement to the emerging rule. Because most rules of custom, though requiring a very high level of participation, do not require unanimity, holdup problems and other transaction-associated costs are generally avoided in the formation of customary legal rules. No single individual in society can prevent the emergence and recognition of a general custom.

In Part IV we considered the case of lawmaking through agreement, such as treaties and other agreements between international actors capable of having lawmaking effect. Treaties are a unique source of law, given their strictly consensual nature. Unlike other sources of law, capable of being enforceable against individuals who actively opposed their adoption, treaty law only binds parties that have affirmatively agreed to be bound. Substantial creation costs are generally associated with this source of law. Multilateral treaty negotiations are difficult to administer and may take long periods of time. The rate of successful formation and ratification of multilateral treaties is low, due to the difficulties of reaching a consensus among participants with diverse needs and expectations (Chapter 14).

The various sources of law also have different levels of external costs. As public choice theory has shown in the case of political decision making, direct and external costs of lawmaking are negatively correlated (Buchanan and Tullock 1962). The tradeoff between direct and external costs is easily illustrated by the consideration of the two extreme cases of unanimity and dictatorship in a voting context. If deliberations require a unanimous vote, the risk of external costs disappears (every voter has a veto power against undesired proposals), but transaction costs are at their highest. In the opposite case of dictatorship, the risk of external costs is much higher (a dictator can single-handedly impose costs on all others), but direct lawmaking costs are lowest, given that no consensus or political bargaining is necessary.

In this book we have shown that analogous tradeoffs between direct and external costs exist for the various sources of law that we have considered, although the content and interpretation of such costs differ substantially in each case. As suggested by public choice theory, in evaluating the various sources of law, it is important to give careful consideration to the different performances of alternative lawmaking processes from the vantage point of this criterion of cost minimization. The results of this book provide a contribution to this line of research, shedding some light on these important questions. In the case of lawmaking through adjudication discussed in Part II, we have seen the possibility that present litigants may impose external costs on future litigants through the creation of precedents (Chapter 7), considering the effect of alternative doctrines of precedent on the dynamics of legal evolution (Chapter 8). The sources of lawmaking through practice considered in Part III require a very high level of participation and consensus. This reduces, though does not eliminate, the risk of imposing external costs on unwilling minorities. But, as a result of such high thresholds of required participation, customary laws are relatively slow in their emergence and evolution. The sources of lawmaking through agreement considered in Part IV are different from all other sources of lawmaking, inasmuch as the rules produced through treaty agreements generally affect and bind only the signatory states. Similar to constraints of privity in contract law, third parties cannot be negatively affected (at least, not directly) by a treaty agreement that they did not sign or ratify. External costs of lawmaking are thus excluded with respect to this source of law.

2. Agency Costs and Political Representation

A well-known concern in public choice theory relates to agency problems in representation. Lawmaking mechanisms should be designed to minimize such problems, ensuring that the underlying preferences of the individuals subject to the law are reflected in the lawmaking process. For the case of lawmaking through legislation, this requires the choice of collective decision-making procedures that will promote the alignment of the incentives of political representatives and the incentives of the represented citizens. In the presence of perfect incentive alignment, agency problems in political representation will disappear. Likewise, in the case of lawmaking through adjudication, judge-made law should approximate the rules that private parties would have chosen if engaging in an ex ante choice of applicable law. On the basis of these analyses, the hypothesis of efficiency of the common law was developed. The proponents of this hypothesis suggest that common law rules enjoy a comparative advantage over legislation in the avoidance of agency problems and other public choice failures, facilitating the evolutionary selection of efficient laws.

The discussion in Part II of this book revealed, however, that the creation of laws through adversarial adjudication is not free from biases and shortcomings of its own. These results support the concerns raised by public choice scholars and theorists of the efficiency hypothesis (Rubin, Curran, and Curran 2001; Zywicki 2003). The identified biases in the production of law through adjudication are not the effect of agency problems or lack of political representation of the judicial body. Rather, these are biases and shortcomings that are created despite the existence of an unbiased and politically representative judiciary (Chapter 6), and even in the absence of ideology on the part of judges (Chapter 7).

Likewise, in Part III, we discussed the existence of inertia in the formation of customary law (Chapter 10), as well as some possible distortions in the subsequent evolution of customary law (Chapter 12). Also these effects are generated by factors that do depend on public choice failures. Customary law avoids the interface of third-party decision makers (such as legislators and judges) and is derived directly from the observation of the behavioral choices of individuals in society. In a customary law setting, the group of lawmakers thus coincides with the subjects of the law and agency problems are generally absent. Yet, even setting aside the concerns for representation, our discussion identified a different group of problems that affect the process of customary law formation.

In Part IV we discussed another bias observed in the case of lawmaking through agreement (Chapter 16). The source of bias in the process of treaty formation is due to the lack of equal opportunity for states to introduce reservations. Also in this case, this bias is not attributable to public choice failures and its effects should be added to possible additional distortions created by agency problems in the representation of states in the negotiation of treaties.

3. Legal Stability

A third problem relevant for the institutional design of lawmaking concerns the cost of instability and intransitivity of collective choices (Easterbrook 1983; Rizzo 1987; Cooter 2000). Although stability cannot be used as a proxy for efficiency, lawmaking processes should allow Condorcet alternatives to prevail when they exist. If Condorcet winners do not exist, "democratic politics becomes a contest, not to satisfy the preferences of a unique majority, but to determine which majority's preferences will be satisfied" (Cooter 2000). As observed in the literature, when political cooperation fails and instability arises, several legal institutions and doctrines come to the rescue to minimize instability and select among cyclical alternatives (Stearns 1994). In these situations, lawmaking processes should be designed in order to minimize the welfare costs of legal instability. In particular, Cooter (2000) explains how democratic constitutions pursue these goals of stability by separating powers among the branches of government, by guaranteeing individual rights, and creating a framework of competition for political office. In a world where political bargaining exists, the existence of enforcement mechanisms within politics will promote stability and reduce costly intransitivity of collective outcomes.

In Part I we considered the case of lawmaking through legislation and the optimal rate of innovation in law (Chapter 3). Lawmakers can choose both the timing and the specificity of legal rules. The solution to these interrelated lawmaking problems is likely affected by legal, social, and economic conditions. In Part II we considered lawmaking through adjudication, examining the effect of various doctrines of precedent in promoting stability (Chapter 8). Our results complement the analysis of Stearns (1994), who considers the role of standing doctrines and *stare decisis* as evolved institutions aimed at reducing instability in the absence of a Condorcet majority consensus. In Part III we considered lawmaking through practice. In the case of customary law, we discussed the process of formation and evolution of customary law, unveiling its ability to generate stable rules in different game-theoretic situations. We studied the process through which customary rules can change over time (Chapter 12). We modeled the effects of persistent objector and subsequent objector doctrines in the formation and change of customary law. In Part IV we considered lawmaking through agreement, discussing the process of formation and evolution of treaty law. We modeled international treaty formation and analyzed the different modalities with which the content of treaty law can change over time in response to solicitations of acceding states. We considered the rules governing accession to international treaties, distinguishing between closed, semi-open, and open treaties (Chapter 14).

4. Toward an Institutional Design of Lawmaking

In this book we have revisited the important questions concerning the institutional design of lawmaking through the lens of economic theory. Alternative sources of law have been evaluated considering their respective advantages and disadvantages in the production of laws. Our findings shed new light on the process of law formation, suggesting that the comparative evaluation of alternative sources of law requires an appropriate analysis of the structural processes present in the originating environment. Despite the sophisticated mathematical techniques of economic analysis, previous scholarship still lacked a systematic assessment of the efficiency of alternative sources of law. This book constitutes a first step in that direction, investigating the incentives structures underlying the lawmaking processes under consideration. Prior to formulating normative corollaries, our findings should be evaluated in conjunction with the results reached in the extensive literature of public choice and constitutional political economy, considering the influence of market and nonmarket institutions on legal regimes. Undoubtedly, the field is still far from a point of maturity. Our contribution offers some building blocks for the understanding of the comparative advantages of alternative lawmaking processes in supplying efficient laws, and will hopefully contribute to the development of some useful criteria of institutional design of lawmaking.

Notes

Chapter 2 Optimal Specificity of Laws

1 Although some contributions in the literature model the choice between rules and standards as a binary choice rather than two extremes on a spectrum, others model rules and standards as a binary choice only for ease and the simplification of the model, recognizing that rules and standards are terms of art used to exemplify specificity of law (e.g., Kaplow 1992 and 1995).

2 Ehrlich and Posner (1974) have advanced the notion that total cost should ultimately control a legislature's determination. Kaplow (1992) further clarifies various issues discussed here.

3 In this context, Ehrlich and Posner (1974) predict that rules will be more frequently adopted in areas of the law characterized by homogeneous conduct.

4 In addressing the important question of access to justice by the poor, Calabresi (1979) raised the issue between the degree of specificity of legal rules and the need—or lack of need—for lawyers.

5 We make reference to the degree of specificity of rules adopting the prevailing distinction between *rules* and *standards*. As pointed out by Ellinghaus and Wright (2005), this distinction is qualitatively analogous to the distinction adopted by European scholars between *rules* and *general principles*.

6 This is consistent with Ehrlich and Posner (1974).

7 Here we set aside the other component of the marginal benefit of greater specificity, V_S.

8 $ds^*/dN = (V_S - C_S)/|(N \cdot V_{SS} - F_{SS} - N \cdot C_{SS})| > 0.$

9 $d\omega/ds^* = (N \cdot V_{S\omega})/|(N \cdot V_{SS} - F_{SS} - N \cdot C_{SS})| < 0.$

10 $ds^*/d\lambda = F_{S\lambda}/(NV_{SS} - F_{SS} - NC_{SS}) < 0.$

11 $ds^*/d\sigma = NC_{S\sigma}/(NV_{SS} - F_{SS} - NC_{SS}) > 0.$

12 $ds^*/d\kappa = (F_{S\kappa} + NC_{S\kappa})/(NV_{SS} - F_{SS} - NC_{SS}).$

13 Note that $ds^*/d\kappa < 0$ if $F_{S\kappa} > -NC_{S\kappa}$, and $ds^*/d\kappa > 0$ if $F_{S\kappa} < -NC_{S\kappa}$.

14 Type I and type II errors in this context imply that a rule was applied to cases where it should have been inapplicable, or it was not applied to situations to which it should have been applied. Normatively, this balancing should be carried out from an ex ante perspective, but hindsight bias makes it difficult for courts not to be influenced by the fact that, in the case at bar, the risk has materialized, leading to an over-inclusiveness of the rule (Rachlinski 2000).

15 See, e.g., Immergut (1992) and Tsebelis (2002) on the use of standards in the context of veto points.

16 For example, vague standards may be a way to meet contradictory political demands (Brunsson 1989) or to exploit narrow political windows of opportunity (Heritier 1999).

17 Articles 516 through 710 of the French *Code Civil* of 1804.

18 Articles 1101–1369 and 1582–1701 of the French *Code Civil* of 1804.

19 Articles 1382–86 of the French *Code Civil* of 1804.

20 Articles 1984–2010 of the French *Code Civil* of 1804.

21 Articles 711–1100 of the French *Code Civil* of 1804.

22 Articles 406–684 of the Italian *Codice Civile* of 1865.

23 Articles 1097–1139, 1157–1377, and 1447–1548 of the Italian *Codice Civile* of 1865.

24 Articles 1151–56 of the Italian *Codice Civile* of 1865.

25 Articles 1737–63 of the Italian *Codice Civile* of 1865.

26 Articles 720–1096 of the Italian *Codice Civile* of 1865.

27 Sections 854–1296 of the German Civil Code (*Bürgerliches Gesetzbuch*) of 1900.

28 Sections 241–514 of the German Civil Code (*Bürgerliches Gesetzbuch*) of 1900.

29 Sections 823–53 of the German Civil Code (*Bürgerliches Gesetzbuch*) of 1900.

30 Sections 164–81 of the German Civil Code (*Bürgerliches Gesetzbuch*) of 1900.

31 Sections 516–34 and 1922–2385 of the German Civil Code (*Bürgerliches Gesetzbuch*) of 1900.

32 Articles 3:107–295; 5:1–147 of the Netherlands Civil Code of 1990. See the trilingual translation of the Code (English, French, and Dutch) by P.P.C. Haanappel and E. Mackaay (Kluwer, Deventer, Pays-Bas et Boston, MA 1990).

33 Articles 6:1–161, 213–79; 7:1–50 of the Netherlands Civil Code of 1990.

34 Articles 6:162–83 of the Netherlands Civil Code of 1990 (some articles left empty initially).

35 Articles 3:60–79; 7:400–418 of the Netherlands Civil Code of 1990.

36 Articles 4:1–233, 7.3.1–7.3.12c of the Netherlands Civil Code of 1990 (some provisions in force since 1/1/2003).

37 Articles 576–806 and 840–41 of the Draft Civil Code of Israel of 2004.

38 Articles 114–228, 241–435, 498–520, and 520–75 of the Draft Civil Code of Israel of 2004.

39 Articles 4, 436–486 and 843 of the Draft Civil Code of Israel of 2004.

40 Articles 99–113 of the Draft Civil Code of Israel of 2004.

41 Eleven provisions (Articles 229–40) of the Draft Civil Code of Israel of 2004 concern gifts. The Draft Civil Code of Israel does not cover matters related to succession law, because of the difficulty of finding a politically acceptable solution due to the conflicting religious traditions and rules on the matter. The point was explicitly stated by Israeli Chief Justice Barak, who served as Chair of the Codex Committee.

See the Proceedings of the Conference for the 200th Anniversary of the Code Napoleon, University of Haifa (Israel), May 30–June 1, 2004 (M. Rabello, ed.).

42 The Draft European Civil Code does not cover matters related to property law, the regulation of which remains governed by the national law of the member states.

43 This count was computed from the June 2004 Draft of the European Civil Code, available at http://www.sgecc.net (last visited 6/20/04). These articles are placed in Book II, Chapters 2–8; Book III, Chapters 1–2 and 4–7; and Book IV, Chapters 1–2 of the European Draft Code. An additional 46 provisions under consideration by the Commission are not included in the numbering of the Draft Code as of June 2004.

44 These articles are placed in Book V, Chapters 1–7 of the European Draft Code.

45 These articles are placed in Book III, Chapter 3; and Book IV.C, Chapters 1–2 of the European Draft Code.

46 The Draft European Civil Code does not cover matters related to wills and estates, the regulation of which remains governed by the national law of the member states.

Chapter 3 Optimal Timing of Legal Intervention

1 Gersen and Posner (2007) argue that rules governing the timing of legal intervention (what they call "timing rules") should be established to minimize agency problems and to reduce the risk of deliberative pathologies.

2 See Pindyck (1991) who stresses the equivalence between the decision to invest and the decision to exercise an option, reviewing the literature in the field. As a result of these contributions, the investment literature now generally views the investment decision as a problem of option valuation.

3 In fact undoing bad lawmaking can be a costly process, whether it is repeal of legislation or overturning precedent in common law. In each case, there is considerable cost to learning the new rule (even if it implies going back to an old rule), and adjusting expectations accordingly.

4 The short-run benefits may be conspicuous when legislation is aimed at preventing irreversible losses, as several irreversible benefits may exist that offset, to some degree, the sunk cost of legal intervention. Imagine, for example, the case of legal intervention concerning the protection of endangered species or the preservation of the ozone layer, where timely intervention may generate benefits otherwise unobtainable at a later time. Likewise, the quantification difficulties to solve a specific timing problem may be exacerbated by society's changing valuation of legal, moral, or ethical principles and the dynamic effects of legal intervention on the evolution of individual preferences and values.

5 In the general industrial organization literature, an investment is considered irreversible whenever the capital is firm or industry specific and has a substantially lower value if used in a different firm or industry. In the law and economics literature, see also Baird and Morrison (2001), considering the irreversibility of bankruptcy decisions and optimal timing of liquidation.

6 These principles apply to a much broader range of problems involving legal intervention in situations of uncertainty and sunk costs. Similar issues may

arise in situations where individuals, firms, or institutions face short-term organizational costs when subjected to a legal change. These costs are for the most part sunk, because they cannot be recouped if the legal rule reverts to the preexisting form. In evaluating the optimal timing and frequency of change of legal rules, the lawmaker should account for such private adjustments costs and should measure the opportunity cost of investing now rather than delaying legal intervention.

7 Given some binding budget, time, or political constraint on the part of the legislature, there is an opportunity cost of adopting a new rule, represented by the forgone possibility to enact a new rule in the subsequent time period. Legislators face such constraints in their activity, which renders the ideal models of unconstrained optimization hardly descriptive of real-life legislative problems.

8 Likewise any rate of return $\alpha + \delta$ that exceeds the market return may conversely suggest that there is too little investment in lawmaking.

9 The analysis in this section follows Dixit and Pindyck (1994), Dixit (1992), and the body of work on investment under uncertainty.

10 There is no discretion on the part of the lawmaker on the degree of specificity of the rule. In later extensions, the distinction between rules and standards should be reintroduced to study the trade-off between the optimal timing and specificity of legal rules.

11 These steps form a geometric series. Hence this is called a geometric or a proportional Brownian motion.

12 The model presented in this section utilizes a geometric Brownian motion. In real-life applications, it may not be always clear what the correct stochastic process is and which functional form should be used. For example, in some areas of legal intervention, stationary processes may be appropriately used, whereas in others nonstationary processes may provide a better fit. The choice of a geometric Brownian motion may be sensible for, say, some situations concerning technological innovation and new scientific discoveries, other regulated environments may be better represented by other stochastic functional forms. One could argue, for example, that over the long run, the level of unemployment or the level of criminality may follow a mean-reverting process, where the mean reflects the long-run equilibrium expected value of unemployment or criminality. In this respect, it is important to keep in mind Dixit and Pindyck (1994: 77–78) warning on the need to rely on both theoretical considerations and historical data in order to determine, with any degree of confidence, whether a given variable should be assumed to follow a stationary or nonstationary process. Although the choice of a specific stochastic form is necessary to generate precise results, for the purpose of our analysis, the specification of the stochastic variable is not crucial for the qualitative results. For a review of the various results under different stochastic assumptions in the investment theory literature, see also Pindyck (1991).

13 Note that the solution of (3.5) should be $P(V) = A'V^\chi + AV^\beta$, where $\chi < 0$ and $\beta > 1$. However, because the opportunity cost of waiting should be zero if V is zero, we have $A' = 0$. Hence $P(V) = AV^\beta$ where $\beta > 1$ is the appropriate solution

to (3.5). Direct substitution of P, P', and P'' into (3.5) shows that β must satisfy the quadratic equation (3.7).

14 In fact, the dotted portion of curve VW ceases to have a valid interpretation as the value of waiting in lawmaking. Otherwise, paradoxically, waiting will always be better than lawmaking, with no legal intervention ever being undertaken.

15 Recall that β is defined by equation (3.7). Define the left-hand side of equation (3.7) to be Q. Then equation (3.7), $Q = 0$, implies that $\partial Q/\partial\beta \cdot \partial\beta/\partial\sigma + \partial Q/\partial\sigma = 0$. It can readily be seen that $\partial Q/\partial\beta > 0$ as $\beta > 1$. Also, $\partial Q/\partial\sigma > 0$ from (3.7). Hence we see that $\partial\beta/\partial\sigma < 0$. From (3.8), we see that $\partial V^*/\partial\sigma = \partial V^*/\partial\beta \cdot \partial\beta/\partial\sigma$ and $\partial V^*/\partial\beta < 0$. Therefore, we conclude that $\partial V^*/\partial\sigma > 0$. Likewise, $\partial V^*/\partial\alpha > 0$ and $\partial V^*/\partial\delta < 0$ can be found in a similar fashion.

16 In terms of physical or financial investment, it would be relatively easy to assign a dollar value to this option. The value of the option in the context of investment in an asset is discussed extensively in Dixit and Pindyck (1994). See also Pindyck (1991) for a relatively nontechnical treatment of the subject of irreversibility and investment. It is more difficult to do this in the context of legal change, giving up an option reduces the choices available to the lawmaker in terms of the timing of future changes to the legal rule.

17 In the investment literature, a number of researchers, including Pindyck (1988) and Dixit (1989), have explored the analogy with financial options. In particular, Pindyck (1991) observes that an irreversible investment opportunity is like a call option, which gives the holder the opportunity to pay an exercise price and receive an asset in consideration for such price. Similar to a sunk investment, the exercise of a call option is irreversible. As Pindyck (1991: 1111) points out, "although the asset can be sold to another investor, one cannot retrieve the option or the money that was paid to exercise it."

18 One of the first models of irreversible investment was developed by McDonald and Siegel (1986) who pointed out that the investment opportunity is equivalent to a perpetual call option.

19 Our model could be easily modified to show that there may be value of waiting even in the absence of uncertainty.

20 The conclusions of this chapter are consistent with Heiner's (1986) economic interpretation of the doctrine of *stare decisis*, despite its very different origin.

21 As shown in the economic development literature, a major cost of political and economic instability may be its depressing effect on investment.

22 This is one reason advanced for leaving legislation to the states in the United States, rather than the federal government. The idea is that states will compete to provide legislation, and the most efficient legislation will eventually come to dominate, even though there will be duplication of legislative investment in the path toward the efficient legislation. See, for example, Kobayashi and Ribstein (2001) for an argument in favor of "competition among the states" in the regulation of privacy in cyberspace.

23 In the standard investment literature, Roberts and Weitzman (1981) present a model of sequential investment that allows for learning during a multistage investment process, with results that depart from the standard net present value approach as well as from the basic option pricing result.

24 Interestingly, in the absence of learning, the use of a simple net present value rule can allow legal innovation that is inefficient, given the forgone value of the option to wait. Conversely, in the presence of learning, the net present value rule can reject proposals for legal innovation that are efficient.

25 For a study of optimal investment in the absence of stochastic random walks of costs and benefits, see Roberts and Weitzman (1981), with application to research and development and exploration projects. This is the basis of the competition among states rationale used by Kobayashi and Ribstein (2001) and others.

26 On the other hand, there should be no additional consideration of the learning benefits of the law when such learning can occur independently of legal innovation.

27 In the existing literature, the problem of optimal degree of specificity of legal rules was first discussed by Ehrlich and Posner (1974) and Schwartz and Scott (1995) who structured their seminal papers around the dichotomous distinction of rules versus standards. Ehrlich and Posner (1974) offer a formal optimization model that is static. Schwartz and Scott (1995) model rule making in the context of private legislatures as a single-shot, multistage game. However, as Kaplow (1992) points out, (in the only other study on the topic with a similar degree of rigor, though from a different angle), it is possible to have a complex rule and a simple standard. This, in effect, uses a different definition of what is a rule and what is a standard. Kaplow (1992) takes the choice of legal rule as a given, and considers the problem of whether an individual will choose to acquire information about the existing law.

28 A related question is what choice of technology will be optimal. The lawmaker could choose to specialize in rules, and invest in a lawmaking technology that is best suited for that purpose. Alternatively, the lawmaker could choose to create a legal system that could incorporate both rules and standards; in effect, choose a technology that permits flexible output. In either case, we assume that the investment is irreversible, and the external environment changes in a stochastic manner. See He and Pindyck (1992) for a rigorous discussion of an analogous problem in investment—choice of technology.

29 Much of the investment literature focuses on continuous investment variables allowing for marginalization of cost and revenue. Lawmaking rarely possesses such properties of continuity and differentiability, but this factor does not change the fundamental rule for investing. The lawmaker must account for the opportunity cost of innovating at present time rather than waiting in choosing the optimal timing of lawmaking.

30 This problem has some similarity to the problem addressed by Majd and Pindyck (1987) where a firm invests continuously until the project is completed.

31 For example, the Uruguay Round Agreement provided for ten years for the phase-out of various trade barriers, including the Multi Fiber Agreement. It also provided for long periods of time to implement other laws, such as those required for the protection of intellectual property rights under TRIPS. The long time horizon adds to the uncertainty over the final value. But the political and other costs are sufficiently large that the multistage implementation is usually essential for the agreement to be reached in the first place.

Chapter 4   Optimal Territorial Scope of Laws

1 Alesina, Angeloni, and Schuknecht (2005: 276).

2 Given that we assume economies of scope both at the local and at the central level, the same is true, *mutatis mutandis*, if we decentralize some functions.

3 The literature on rule competition has formulated an "efficiency hypothesis," according to which a market for legal rules characterized by freedom of choice and competition in the supply of law should favor the evolution and spread of efficient rules (see, among others, Ogus 1999 and references therein).

4 The principle of mutual recognition first appeared in 1978, when the European Court of Justice, in the *Cassis de Dijon* case, ruled that a product lawfully sold in one member state has to be admitted in all member states. Since then, mutual recognition has been applied to set standards for many products and services, like banking, insurance and financial services (see Neven 1992).

5 In this simple model we assume that cooperation between the central and the regional government is not feasible. A regulatory function is either efficiently allocated at central or at the regional level. Removing this assumption would imply that the function can take values between 0 and 1, where 0 means that a particular level (say central or regional) does not perform that function whereas 1 means that it performs it fully. An intermediate value would signify cooperation between levels. We leave such extension for future research.

6 See Schäfer (2006). The idea of economies of scale is also included in Art. 5 of the Treaty on European Union (TEU or Maastricht Treaty), stating that the Community must demonstrate the need to interfere at the local level by proving the existence of either "economies of scale or cross-border externalities."

7 In order to simplify notation and without loss of generality, in our model of subsidiarity we will refer to the concept of economies of scale, to include both cost- and coordination-driven economies.

8 In this respect, the negative referendum results in France and the Netherlands, who rejected the EU constitution, are a signal that these countries perceived their switching costs as unbearably high.

9 This assumption reflects the idea that, the more centralized and harmonized is the management of the political and legal functions of a region, the less costly it will be to transfer even more functions at the central level. This assumption is consistent with a definition of switching costs as financial costs of legal and political change. The more centrally managed a given region, the less costly it will be to increase centralization even more. The opposite assumption would also be interesting to explore and would be more consistent with a definition of switching costs as social and political costs. We will discuss it briefly in Section 5.2.

10 Notice that this is an assumption on the dynamic behavior of switching costs and has no implications for the size of such costs when one or more functions are shifted simultaneously. It that case, it would seem plausible to assume that switching costs increase with the number of functions transferred at the same time.

11 See Pelkmans (2006). If cooperation between different layers of government were allowed, the test should comprise a fourth step, and the third step

would be changed. In the new third step, the possibility of cooperation would be verified. Then, in the fourth step, whenever cooperation is feasible, the optimal level of centralization would be established.

12 See Inman and Rubinfeld (1998).

13 The "Early Warning Mechanism" proposed by the European Commission on May 10, 2006, and "welcomed" by the European Council, looks like a move toward a unanimity-based mechanism, if not toward a form of decentralized federalism. The early-warning mechanism would render national parliaments "subsidiarity watchdogs." According to the mechanism, national parliaments would have the power to raise objections to EU legislative proposals that they believe violate the subsidiarity principle (see Cooper 2006).

14 Clearly, an extension of the case of majority voting requires more than two regions.

15 In a two-region setting, it obviously never possible to find a situation where the centralized test is passed and both countries reject centralization at the local level.

16 A similar result, where satisfaction of inequality (4.8) does not imply that the test is passed at the local level, can also be proved in case both regions had to pay equal shares of the general cost $C^{1C}(2f_1, 0)$.

17 Given that the structure of costs evolves over time, according to previous centralization decisions, the final allocation of policy responsibilities will always be efficient in our setting.

18 As we have proved in the previous section, if the subsidiarity test is passed at the local level, then it is passed also at the central level, whereas the opposite is not necessarily true. That is why we have chosen to assume that the test is performed at the local level, because we consider the case where the success in the test implies higher chances of success in subsequent tests and we want the result to be as general as possible.

19 This condition would be always satisfied in the symmetric case, where countries are characterized by the same cost functions.

20 It is always possible that functions that failed the subsidiarity test in the past are proposed again for a new test later on, when more centralization has occurred and the chances of success are therefore enhanced. However, this is likely to raise substantial political switching costs and usually requires also a change in public opinion.

21 Alternatively, if the subsidiarity test is performed at the central level, the test would fail if

$$C^{2C}(0, 2f_2) + C_1^{1R}(f_1, 0) + C_2^{1R}(f_1, 0) + [k_1^R(f_2 \mid 0) + k_2^R(f_2 \mid 0)]$$
$$> \sum_{j=1}^{2} \left[C_1^{jR}(f_1, f_2) + C_2^{jR}(f_1, f_2) \right].$$

22 However, it is not given that rule competition always selects the best rule. See Carbonara and Parisi (2007b).

23 This argument is supported, among others, by Ogus (1999).

24 Centralization is a sufficient condition for harmonization. If a policy function is centralized, then also its regulation is harmonized. The opposite, by definition, is not necessarily true. Using rule competition local levels can harmonize with other regions to incorporate the most efficient rule, lowering the cost of performing a function while still maintaining that role under local control.

25 Notice that it does so also for the expression of the test performed at the central level, where the right-hand side of (4.8) becomes $N \times \min \left\{ \sum_{j=1}^{2} c_i^{jR} (f_1, f_2) \right\}$.

Chapter 5   Lawmaking through Adjudication

1 For a comprehensive presentation of the main formulations of the efficiency hypothesis, in its various theoretical incarnations, see Rubin (2006), who also presents several of the important critiques moved to this hypothesis.

2 The empirical findings presented by Niblett, Posner and Shleifer (2008) reveal that the law did not converge to any stable resting point and evolved differently in different states. The authors examine a 35-year long sample of appellate-court decisions from 465 and conclude that the law did not converge to any stable resting point and evolved differently in different states. The authors explain their findings suggesting that legal evolution is influenced by plaintiffs' claims, the relative economic power of the parties, and nonbinding federal precedent.

Chapter 6   Litigation and the Evolution of Legal Remedies

1 See, however, the opposing claims of some public choice theorists (most notably, Tullock 1980 and 1997) who look at pervasive shortcomings of the common law process in the formation of legal rules. For a review of the seminal papers that contributed to the formulation of the efficiency of the common law hypothesis, and of their critics, see Posner and Parisi (1997).

2 When the assumption that both parties have equal stakes in the dispute is relaxed (e.g., where one party is a repeat player and has a stake in future similar cases), the rate of success in litigation begins to deviate from the hypothesized baseline, and the model predicts that the repeat player prevails more frequently. Priest and Klein present a great deal of data both from their own empirical investigations and from major empirical studies of the legal system since the 1930s. Although they caution against concluding that these data confirm the selection hypothesis, largely due to measurement problems, the data are nonetheless encouraging.

3 In the literature, adverse selection models generally incorporate asymmetric information. In our model, there is no asymmetric information. Adverse selection refers to the fact that the controlling party (the plaintiff) selects cases according to the likelihood of success, much like sellers select used cars to put on the market. Asymmetric information in the used car market refers to the missing knowledge of the noncontrolling party: the buyer has no knowledge of the quality of the used car. In our model, there is no missing knowledge. If anything, the noncontrolling

party (the judge) has better information about his own ideology. Judges, however, have no opportunity to initiate litigation and cannot decide a case that has not been filed.

4 In this chapter we consider the traditional question of how the selection of disputes affects the process of evolution of legal rules. We thus confine our attention to the activity of judges in the decision-making process, because judges alone decide issues of law. A different logic may explain the growth of damage awards by juries and other trends in the assessment of issues of fact.

5 In real life this information may be available before filing (e.g., in the case of a single judge court or a district with a homogeneous ideological bent) or after filing (e.g., parties know which judge has been assigned the case and thus can abandon the suit before a final decision). In both cases, rational estimation of the judges' predisposition influences the decision whether to pursue, or to continue, litigation. Only those cases that pass this initial phase potentially lead to the creation of legal precedents.

6 This leads to a low rate of conservative-driven marginal precedents in our model. The same result could have been achieved by assuming trembling-hand errors, with differential rates of production of marginal precedents by conservative versus liberal judges. With such an assumption, the flow of liberal precedents in our model would constitute the net effect of liberal precedents.

7 As discussed in Chapter 5, law and economics has had difficulty explaining judicial behavior in economic terms in part because the federal judiciary is structured to remove economic incentives from judges. Posner (1994) articulates a positive economic theory of the behavior of federal appellate judges, using a model in which judicial utility is primarily a function of income, leisure, and judicial voting. Posner believes that an appellate judge's utility function additionally contains preferences for a good reputation, popularity, prestige, and avoiding reversal. Posner supports the notion that the conditions of judicial employment enable and induce judges to vote their values, among which Posner believes efficiency to be particularly influential. Posner analogizes judicial decision making to political voting. There is pure utility in voting, as evidenced by participation in popular elections in which individuals incur a net cost in order to participate in the political process. This analogy suggests that voting on cases is one of the most important sources of judicial utility due to the deference judges' opinions receive from lawyers and the public. Judges further derive a utility in deciding whom or what to vote for. Judges balance this utility against the opportunity cost of decision making. Posner further suggests that the pursuit of leisure explains why judges adhere to *stare decisis*, but not rigidly. With rigid adherence, they would lose the utility of discretionary power, but when judges' views are consistent with current law or when they have no opportunity to depart from current law, they strongly prefer to use precedent as a way to minimize their decision-making efforts.

8 The so-called asymmetric revolution theory of legal evolution suggests that conservative judges are more prone to respect precedents, whereas liberal judges feel less constrained by precedential rules. This creates a differential rate of

change in common law, because liberal-type legal innovations are more likely to dominate conservative-type changes in the law. Thus, any correlation between liberal judicial ideology and expansion of liability implies an increase in the scope of legal remedies over time. As mentioned above, this explanation relies on the assumption that conservative judges are more inclined to abide by legal precedents than liberal judges. Although this assumption may beg empirical confirmation, we provide an alternative hypothesis, suggesting that regardless of the political propensity of judges with respect to past precedents, adverse selection mechanisms may be at work in certain areas of the law. Interestingly, these selection mechanisms do not necessarily generate efficient innovation in the legal system.

9 The ideological labels of *conservative* and *liberal* are used for illustrative purposes. Some areas of the law may reverse the matching of conservative/liberal and pro-defendant/pro-plaintiff. But the qualitative dynamics of our model would not be altered.

10 Note that our selection mechanism assumes away the opportunity for forum shopping and thus looks at the most restrictive scenario in which each case has its natural forum, with no option for the litigants to divert litigation to a different forum. The results of our model would be reinforced if plaintiffs were given an opportunity to engage in forum shopping. This would lead to a potential exacerbation of the bias in legal evolution. For a discussion of the effects of adverse selection in forum shopping, see Parisi and Ribstein (1998), Parisi and O'Hara (1998) and Moore and Parisi (2002). For a public choice analysis of the effects of forum shopping in the evolution of judge-made law, see also Rubin, Curran, and Curran (2001).

11 Needless to say, additional forces likely affect the degree of judicial discretion. Judges may face different incentives and constraints in consideration of their appointment and reelection prospects, affecting their freedom to interpret laws liberally.

12 For further analysis of the effect of these procedural asymmetries on the strategic incentives to litigate, see Moore and Parisi (2002).

Chapter 7 Judicial Path-Dependence and Legal Change

1 For an analysis of the precedential systems of *jurisprudence constante* in civil law and mixed jurisdictions, see Dennis (1993), Dainow (1974), and Moreno (1995). For a comparative study of the rule of precedent, including the Spain, Finland, Norway, Sweden, Germany, France, and the UK, see MacCormick and Summers (1997).

2 See, however, the opposing claims of some public choice theorists (most notably, Tullock 1980 and 1997) who look at pervasive shortcomings of the common law process in the formation of legal rules. For a review of the seminal papers that contributed to the formulation of the efficiency of the common law hypothesis, and of their critics, see Posner and Parisi (1997).

3 See, however, the work of Shavell (1982), (1997), and (1999), as well the work of Menell (1983), Kaplow (1986), and Rose-Ackerman and Geistfeld (1987).

These authors examine the divergent private and social incentives of potential litigants, indicating that parties may not always select cases in a way that leads to efficient rules.

4 When the assumption that both parties have equal stakes in the dispute is relaxed (e.g., where one party is a repeat player and has a stake in future similar cases), the rate of success in litigation begins to deviate from the hypothesized baseline, and the model predicts that the repeat player prevails more frequently. Priest and Klein (1984) use data both from their own empirical investigations and from major empirical studies of the legal system since the 1930s. Although they caution against drawing conclusions from the data, largely due to measurement problems, their results nonetheless provide support to the selection hypothesis.

5 The selection hypothesis advanced by Fon and Parisi (2003a) differs from Priest and Klein (1984) and Hadfield (1992). Along the lines of Rubin and Bailey (1994), Fon and Parisi develop an alternative model of legal evolution which takes into account some important public choice components, such as the role of judges and ideology. Whereas Rubin and Bailey focus on the role of lawyers in changing the law, Fon and Parisi consider the role of judges' ideology.

6 For a previous analysis of path-dependence in courts, see Kornhauser (1992), who identifies the critical interaction between the dichotomous nature of adjudication (i.e., courts produce yes or no decisions and cannot express a maybe) and the force of precedents as an important source of path-dependence. Also relevant is the analysis of Kornhauser and Sager (1986) unpacking the notion of "court decision" in multijudge court panels.

7 In real life this information may be available before filing or after filing. In both cases, rational estimation of the probability of success influences the decision whether to pursue, or to continue, litigation. Only those cases that pass this initial phase potentially lead to law-creating legal precedents.

8 The interpretation of loss L as the damages that may be awarded to defendant in the event of a successful counterclaim may benefit from an extension of the model in which the probability of success of the plaintiff's claim is independent from the probability of success of the defendant's counterclaim. Unlike the traditional interpretation of L a-la-Rubin (1977) or the possible interpretation of L as court-imposed sanctions (e.g., fines for frivolous litigation), the probabilities of success of the principal claim and the counterclaim are not complementary.

9 In many real-life situations, plaintiffs face different choices of litigation expenditures, C. In turn, different litigation efforts affect the probability of success p and the expected magnitudes of W and L. In the following, we assume that the parties rationally choose the most effective litigation effort. The parameters in the model refer to such choice of expenditure in litigation, and the resulting probabilities of success and expected judicial award.

10 We would like to thank an anonymous referee for helping us clarify these two dimensions of the litigation problem.

11 Note that our formulation does not include the forgone settlement payment, because we concentrate on the existence of a positive-net-return claim as a

precondition of a viable dispute. In this respect, our formulation differs from Priest and Klein (1984).

12 The dotted curve represents the hyperbola $W/L = 1/p - 1$, showing the trade-off between the win-loss ratio W/L and p when the expected return R/L is zero with $C = 0$.

13 Points to the southwest of the zero-expected-return curve in Figure 7.1b correspond to negative expected returns.

14 The equation for the zero expected returns for positive litigation cost is $\frac{W}{L} = \frac{1}{p}(\frac{C}{L} + 1) - 1$. Note that the zero-expected-return curve for $C = 0$ intersects the P-axis at $P = 1$, whereas the zero-expected-return curve for $C > 0$ stops at $W/L = C/L$ when $p = 1$. Both zero-expected-return curves asymptotically approach the vertical axis.

15 For the purpose of the present analysis, we assume that the threshold π is exogenously determined by the legal system. Obviously, the findings in this chapter should have normative implications and illuminate the institutional choice of the optimal threshold π.

16 This no-filing region is given by $\left\{(p, W/L)/p < \frac{C/L+1}{W/L+1}\right\}$.

17 The region of contraction in the scope of remedies and the region of gradual consolidation of positive judicial precedents are respectively given by $\left\{(p, W/L)/\frac{C/L+1}{W/L+1} \leq p < \pi = \frac{1}{2}\right\}$ and $\left\{(p, W/L)/\frac{C/L+1}{W/L+1} \leq p\right.$ and $\left.\pi = \frac{1}{2} < p \leq 1\right\}$.

18 In Chapter 8, we develop a dynamic model of evolution of precedents where judges are influenced by recent jurisprudential trends and fads in case law. The higher the level of uniformity in past precedents, the greater the persuasive force of case law. The evolution of case law is modeled, considering the possibility for consolidation, corrosion, and stability of legal rules. For a previous contribution on judge-made law in a dynamic setting, see von Wangenheim (1993).

Chapter 8 Theories of Legal Precedent

1 As discussed in Chapter 5, the legal doctrine of *stare decisis* (literally to stand by things that have been settled) implies that courts should adhere to past legal precedent on issues of law when deciding pending cases.

2 As more extensively discussed in Chapter 5, the doctrine of *jurisprudence constante* doctrines hold that judges should only consider themselves bound to follow a consolidated trend of decisions. Judicial decisions do not become a source of law until they mature into a prevailing line of precedents (Lambert and Wasserman 1929; Dainow 1974; Dennis 1993). For further analysis of the precedential systems of *jurisprudence constante* in civil law and mixed jurisdictions, see Moreno (1995). For a comparative study of the rule of precedent, including Spain, Finland, Norway, Sweden, Germany, France, and the UK, see MacCormick and Summers (1997).

3 For example, causes of action in torts have historically increased in number and scope of application under both common law and civil law systems (Lawson 1955; Lawson and Markesinis 1982; Parisi 1992). Yet in other areas of the law such as

contracts and property, the domain of legal remedies has not experienced similar expansion.

4 Landes and Posner (1976) adopt a similar approach for the analysis of legal precedent, treating the body of legal precedents created by judicial decisions in prior periods as a "capital stock" that yields a "flow" of information which depreciates over time as new unforeseen events change the scenario governed by existing precedents. In this setting, new capital investments take the form of production of new precedents.

5 Daughety and Reinganum (1999) pay special attention to the interjurisdictional aspect of precedents, studying the "persuasive influence" of other appeals courts' decisions on an appeals court's behavior.

6 As noted in Priest and Klein (1984), the set of disputes selected for litigation constitutes neither a random nor a representative sample of the set of all disputes: judges can only rule on cases they see.

7 Among the earliest contributors to this literature, see also Landes (1971).

8 In Chapter 6, building upon existing literature on the evolution of judicially created law, we consider a model of legal evolution in which judges have varying ideologies and propensities to extend the domain of legal remedies and causes of action. The selection hypothesis advanced there differs from Priest and Klein (1984) and Hadfield (1992). Along the lines of Rubin and Bailey (1994), and Fon and Parisi (2003a), in Chapter 6 we presented an alternative model of legal evolution which takes into account some important public choice components. However, while Rubin and Bailey focus on the role of lawyers in changing the law, we consider the role of judges' ideology.

9 For example, this is generally so in Louisiana state case law. Under the Supremacy Clause, however, Louisiana judges are sometimes bound by a single decision issued by the U.S. Supreme Court or Court of Appeals for the 5th Circuit.

10 For example, a threshold $B = 1/2$ implies that a simple majority of precedents on a given legal issue is regarded as persuasive authority, increasing the chances of success for future similar cases.

11 In most civil law judicial traditions, the outcome of the case is drafted and is presented as simply inevitable. The opinion does not reveal doubts that the court may have had in reaching its decision and leaves no room for dissent (Merryman 1969; Parisi 1992).

12 The influence of past cases on current court decisions may vary from system to system and may be influenced both by institutional constraints and judges' incentives. Daughety and Reinganum (1999) derive consistent decision making through a Bayesian updating; Levy (2005) considers the specific incentives of careerist judges. Posner (1994) also explicitly analyzes judges' incentives in decision making. Factors such as reputation, appointment to higher courts, and promotion all play a role in shaping judges' preferences for consistency and/or departure from past decisions.

13 We thank an anonymous referee for pointing out this interesting paradox.

14 In the limiting case where B equals 1/2 the model will have three equilibria, two stable ones (with consolidation or corrosion of remedies) and one unstable (with 50% split case law).

Chapter 9 Lawmaking through Practice

1 The law and economics literature has previously considered other forms of private custom, applicable in commercial settings within specialized trades. Most notably, Bernstein (1995 and 2001) considers the use of custom in the diamond and cotton industries.

2 The practical significance of this requirement is that it narrows the range of enforceable customs: only those practices recognized as socially desirable or necessary will eventually ripen into enforceable customary law. Once there is a general consensus that members of a group ought to conform to a given rule of conduct, a legal custom can emerge when some level of spontaneous compliance with the rule obtains. As a result, observable equilibria that are regarded by society as either undesirable (e.g., a prisoner's dilemma or an uncooperative outcome) or unnecessary (e.g., a common practice of greeting neighbors cordially) will lack the qualitative element of legal obligation, and therefore will not generate enforceable legal rules.

3 Article 38(1) of the Statute of the International Court of Justice provides that "[t]he Court, whose function is to decide in accordance with international law such disputes as are submitted to it, shall apply . . . international customs, as evidence of a general practice of law." Similarly, § 102(1) of the Restatement of the Foreign Relations Law of the United States (3d) provides that "[a] rule of international law is one that has been accepted as such by the international community of states (a) in the form of customary law."

Chapter 10 Fostering the Emergence of Customary Law

1 Rawls (1971) employs Harsanyi's model of stochastic ignorance in his theory of justice. However, the Rawlsian "veil of ignorance" introduces an element of risk aversion into the choice between alternative states of the world, thus altering the outcome achievable under Harsanyi's original model, with a bias toward equal distribution (i.e., with results that approximate the Nash criterion of social welfare). For an extensive treatment, see Roemer (1996 and 1998). Further analysis of the spontaneous formation of norms and principles of morality can be found in Sen (1977); Ullmann-Margalit (1977); and Gauthier (1986).

2 Other important contributions in the literature focus on the relationship between law and social norms—a relationship that is germane but different to the one under consideration, inasmuch as customary rules are recognized as proper sources of law, whereas social norms and other private customs are not. Most importantly on this topic, see Posner (1999 and 2000) and Bernstein (1993 and 1996). For a comprehensive collection of reference articles, see Posner (2007).

3 In the existing literature, compliance with customary norms is occasionally modeled as an aspect of individual preferences or as a constraint on individual behavior (Rabin 1995; Young 1993, 1998). In our specific context, we can assume that first-, second-, and third-party enforcement mechanisms are at work, such that ex post opportunistic departures from a previously accepted rule are excluded.

4 Fon and Parisi (2003b and 2006) show that the presence of homogeneous players is a necessary condition for the emergence of optimal customary rules. An important insight derived from their model is that even when heterogeneous players face ex ante uncertainty over their future roles, their actions will approximate those obtained in the ideal case of identical players.

5 In the absence of perfect incentive alignment, the discount factor plays an important role. In the existing literature, in situations with a probability of future interaction, the discount factor's role is critical. The discount factor captures two analytically distinct elements. First, it acts as a function of the players' time preference. Second, the discount factor is a proxy for the probability of future interactions. Environments promoting a high probability of future interaction and a low time preference are more likely to induce socially optimal equilibria (Axelrod, 1981 and 1984).

6 A related area of research in the social norms literature considers the role of morality and internalized obligations as a means for inducing cooperation in conflict games (see, e.g., Gauthier 1986 and Ullmann-Margalit 1977). Internalization of the norm is a source of spontaneous compliance. For example, individuals internalize obligations when they disapprove of and punish other individuals' deviations from the rule, or when they directly lose utility when the norm is violated.

7 As a historical illustration of an environment that reflected these conditions, we can think of the formative period of the medieval law merchant (*lex mercatoria*), when traveling merchants acted in the dual capacity of buyer and seller. When they articulated a rule of law that was favorable to them as sellers, it could have had the opposite effect when they acted as buyers, and vice-versa. This role-reversibility changed an otherwise conflicting set of incentives (buyer versus seller) into one that converged toward symmetrical and mutually desirable rules (see also Benson 1989 and 1990; and Greif 1989).

8 Certainly, the emergence of consensus for a given rule does not exclude the possibility of subsequent opportunistic deviation by some individuals when roles are later reversed. This is a typical enforcement problem. Where rules are breached following role reversal, norms play a collateral yet crucial role in sanctioning case-by-case opportunism.

9 The group's ability to impose a sanction obviously depends on an individual's accountability for his past behavior. In this setting, Benson (1992: 5–7) explores the role of reputation in situations of repeated market interaction, observing that reputation serves as a source of collective knowledge regarding past actions.

10 We will relax this assumption later, considering the difficulties arising from potential coordination problems when rescuers cannot systematically rely on participation by all others in the rescue.

11 The envelope theorem implies that $\partial P^R/\partial a < 0$, $\partial P^R/\partial b > 0$, and $\partial P^R/\partial r < 0$.

12 In the Appendix, it is proved that $\partial P^R/\partial N < 0$.

13 This assumption will be relaxed later to consider cases of imperfect coordination and incomplete sharing of the initial rescuing costs.

14 Olson's (1971) seminal contribution to the theory of collective action provides an important basis for the thesis that cooperation is less likely in large group environments. More recent contributions have generated results that are partially at odds with the conventional wisdom. De Cremer and Leonardelli (2003) examine the idea that cooperation is driven by the need to belong, reaching the conclusion that customs of cooperation are more likely in large-group environments. Likewise, Haag and Lagunoff (2003), considering the size and structure of group cooperation, also suggest that cooperation is greater in larger groups. The experimental literature supports the traditional theory of group size, revealing that under most environments cooperation more likely results when the group is quite small, or when some factor such as reputation or coercion is present. The relevance of group size to cooperation has also been studied by psychologists. Sherif and Hovland (1961) study the effect of group size on communication and cooperative attitude. Sherif and Sherif (1969) attempt to quantify theories about effects on custom development from changing group size, etc.

15 This is shown by the result $\partial P^R / \partial N < 0$ in the Appendix.

16 The comparative statics of the respective participation and effort levels shows that $\partial P^R / \partial N < 0$, $\partial e^R / \partial N > 0$, $\partial P^I / \partial N < 0$, and $\partial e^I / \partial N = 0$.

Chapter 11 Customary Law and Articulation Theories

1 According to these theories, in the process of ascertaining the existence and content of customary rules, the states' statements and expressions of belief are relevant. D'Amato (1971 and forthcoming) considers articulation as a formative element of international customary law. In D'Amato this element operates in conjunction with state practice and abstention. In this chapter we utilize D'Amato's concept of articulation, but push this notion beyond its intended scope. Our model of articulation processes allows states to express their consensus over potential rules prior or concurrent to the time of their action through practice. When articulation occurs before any customary practice, articulation can replace actual action and by itself generate a rule of customary law. In both cases, custom emerges when states undertake an action that is consistent with their expression of normative views contained in their prior or concurrent articulations.

2 Goldsmith and Posner (2005) more extensively challenge conventional theories of international law that base custom on some sense of exogenous obligation by the states.

3 See, however, the Goldsmith and Posner (2000) discussion of the use of coercion by a powerful state to impose rules of international law.

4 We make no claims with respect to the long-term stability of the rule that emerges. In fact, our analysis is perfectly consistent with that of Goldsmith and Posner (1999 and 2000), who argue that the behavioral regularity will disappear if the normative interests of the nations change. In this chapter we allow, however, for the rule to have some short-term binding effects, constraining states from departing from an accepted rule, in pursuit of their circumstantial short-term interests.

5 In some instances, following a given practice would satisfy both the circumstantial and the normative interests of the states. Put differently, participation may be Pareto superior at each time period. All states would benefit from the compliance with the custom during each time period. Following the emerging custom would always be a dominant strategy for all states. Consequently, such practices would become self-enforcing because no state would ever face a temptation to depart from them. Thus, at the limit, the recognition and enforcement of such practices as rules of customary law would be unnecessary. These practices fall outside the scope of the present analysis, because they would not pose strategic compliance problems.

6 In the more general case of customary practice, this implies assuming away situations in which the initiators of the customary practice can create a benefit for themselves, regardless of the other states' participation and reciprocal compliance.

7 For a more general model of reciprocity in cooperation problems, see Fon and Parisi (2003b).

8 Note that $\sum_{t=0}^{\infty} 1/(1+r)^t = (1+r)/r$.

9 Specifically, $\partial P^C/\partial a = (-\pi^2 b^2)/[4a^2 r(r+1-\pi)] < 0$, $\partial P^C/\partial b = \pi^2 b/[2ar(r+1-\pi)] > 0$, $\partial P^C/\partial r = [-\pi^2 b^2(2r+1-\pi)]/[4ar^2(r+1-\pi)^2] < 0$, $\partial P^C/\partial \pi = [b^2[2\pi(r+1-\pi)+\pi^2]]/[4ar(r+1-\pi)^2] > 0$.

10 If the state faces a discount rate of 100%, *all* future benefits count as much as this period's cost. Setting the present marginal cost and the future marginal benefit equal gives $e^C = b/2a$. This is exactly $e^C = b/2ar$ when $r = 1$. On the other extreme, assume that the state cares about the future greatly and hence the discount rate r becomes very small. Then the sum of *all* future benefits far exceeds this period's cost, and the state prefers to provide a large amount of effort, given the promise of future reciprocation. The fact that $e^C = b/2ar$ increases without bound as r approaches 0 is consistent with this intuition.

11 Specifically, the comparative statics are: $\partial e^C/\partial a = -\pi b/[2a^2(r+1-\pi)] < 0$, $\partial e^C/\partial b = \pi/[2a(r+1-\pi)] > 0$, $\partial e^C/\partial r = -\pi b/[2a(r+1-\pi)^2] < 0$, $\partial e^C/\partial \pi = b(r+1)/[2a(r+1-\pi)^2] > 0$.

12 In particular, $\partial^2 e^C/\partial \pi^2 = b(r+1)/[a(r+1-\pi)^3] > 0$.

13 Note that opposite results would hold if the states engaged in the initial practice in the pursuit of their circumstantial interest, rather than their normative interest. In that case, a lower probability that the practice consolidates in a custom would facilitate the initial participation, because the states could capture the full benefit from participation without fearing the perpetual effect of such a custom in the future.

14 D'Amato (1971) allows for the alternative sequence of articulation occurring prior to or concurrently with the state act (practice). In D'Amato, however, not much emphasis was placed on the timing of practice and articulation, for the understandable reason that international law treats the two elements as qualitatively different from each other (one is a physical act, the other is a human characterization), rendering any discussion of the temporal order between the two items mostly irrelevant under positive international law.

15 In this setting, Harsanyi (1955) suggests that optimal social norms are those that would emerge through the interaction of individual actors in a social setting with impersonal preferences. The impersonality requirement for individual preferences is satisfied if the decision makers have an equal chance of finding themselves in any one of the initial social positions and they rationally choose a set of rules to maximize their expected welfare. Rawls (1971) employs Harsanyi's model of stochastic ignorance in his theory of justice. However, the Rawlsian "veil of ignorance" introduces an element of risk aversion in the choice between alternative states of the world, thus altering the outcome achievable under Harsanyi's original model, with a bias toward equal distribution (i.e., with results that approximate the Nash criterion of social welfare). Further analysis of the spontaneous formation of norms and principles of morality can be found in Sen (1977); Ullmann-Margalit (1977); and Gauthier (1986).

16 Unlike social norms that rely on private and social enforcement mechanisms, customary rules are recognized as proper sources of law and enjoy enforcement mechanism comparable to those of proper law. Most comprehensively on the economics of social norms, see Posner (2000), who interestingly shows that the relationship between legal and social norms is nonadditive: sometimes law can add a legal sanction, but this legal intervention does not necessarily enhance the effect of preexisting forms of extralegal regulation, but actually undermine them. See also the interesting evidence presented by Gneezy and Rustichini (2000 and 2003). The availability of legal enforcement mechanisms for customary law, does not necessarily exclude the presence of ex post compliance problems with court decisions. This is particularly evident in the system of public international law—a system that relies heavily on sources of customary law. For a well-documented analysis of ex post compliance problems in international law, see Ginsburg and McAdams (2004) and Posner (2004).

17 In attempting to solve one of the problems associated with the notion of *opinio iuris*, namely the troublesome problem of circularity, legal scholars (notably, D'Amato 1971) have considered the crucial issue of timing of belief and action in the formation of customary rules. The traditional approach emphasizes the awkward notion that individuals must believe that a practice is already law before it can become law. This approach basically requires the existence of a mistake for the emergence of a custom: the belief that an undertaken practice was required by law, when instead, it was not. Obviously, this approach has its flaws. Placing such reliance on systematic mistakes, the theory fails to explain how customary rules can emerge and evolve over time in cases where individuals have full knowledge of the state of the law.

18 This formulation of the notion of articulation obviously encompasses different possible factual scenarios, not all of which would find a readily applicable treatment under positive international law. Under current law the element of articulation is not sufficient in itself to constitute custom. If separated from practice, articulation processes would render custom formation similar to an informal legislative process, given the possibility for new rules of international

law to be generated via meeting of the minds of state actors. This informal legislative process would be difficult to implement in a multilateral setting, because it would potentially impose excessive costs on third-party states in the monitoring and objection to states' articulations. See, however, the ICJ pronouncement in the case of *Military and Paramilitary Activities in and against Nicaragua* (*Nicaragua v. U.S.*), Merits, 1986 ICJ REP. 14 (Judgment of June 27), readily criticized by D'Amato (1987: 101).

19 Here, it is interesting to point out a strong similarity between the legal and the economic models. Articulations that are made prior to the unveiling of conflicting contingencies can be analogized to rules chosen under a Harsanyian veil of uncertainty.

20 Specifically, the comparative statics are: $\partial e^A/\partial a = -\pi b/[2a^2(1-\pi)] < 0$, $\partial e^A/\partial b = \pi/[2a(1-\pi)] > 0$, $\partial e^A/\partial r = 0$, and $\partial e^A/\partial \pi = b/[2a(1-\pi)^2] > 0$.

21 This can be easily seen comparing the result $\partial e^A/\partial T = 0$ with those obtained for the case of traditional customary processes where $\partial e^C/\partial T < 0$.

Chapter 12 Stability and Change in Customary Law

1 See Viller (1985: 24). Stability of the practice over time is interpreted with some flexibility according to the circumstances. There is no universal minimum duration for the emergence of customary rules. Customary rules have evolved from both immemorial practice and single acts. Still, French scholars have traditionally advocated the passage of forty years for the emergence of an international custom, while German doctrine has generally required thirty years (Tunkin 1961; Mateesco 1947). Naturally, the longer the time required to form a valid practice, the less likely it is for custom to be an effective substitute for treaty law (or formal legislation, in the domestic setting), and to adapt to changing circumstances over time.

2 Regarding the interpretation of the condition of consistency or universality, international legal theory is ambivalent. Charney (1986) suggests that the system of international relations is analogous to a world of individuals in the state of nature, and dismisses the idea that unanimous consent by all participants is required before binding customary law is formed.

3 This element is also often described as necessary and obligatory convention (Kelsen 1939 and 1945; D'Amato 1971; Walden 1977).

4 Asylum and diplomatic immunity rules are among the oldest examples of customs that emerged in line with these requirements. Already in ancient Greece the practices of granting asylum for political reasons and giving immunity to diplomatic missionaries were accompanied by the belief that those practices fulfilled a fundamental necessity of international relations, given the fact that their violation would have seriously undermined the stability of peaceful relations of states. See Kelley (1992).

5 For further discussion of the persistent objector doctrines in international customary law, see also Akehurst (1974–75) and Charney (1985). For a dissenting

view on the legality and desirability of the persistent objector's exemption from customary law, see D'Amato (forthcoming).

6 *Asylum case (Columbia v. Peru)*, 1950 I.C.J. 266, 272–78.

7 *Fisheries Case (United Kingdom v. Norway)*, 1951 I.C.J. 116, 124–31.

8 According to Stein (1985: 458), in order for the doctrine to apply, it is sufficient that a state makes its objection "manifest during the process of the rule's emergence." See also the *Fisheries Case (United Kingdom v. Norway)*, 1951 I.C.J. 116 (Judgment of December 18); *Asylum Case (Columbia v. Peru)*, 1950 I.C.J. 266 (Judgment of June 13).

9 *Jus cogens* encompasses peremptory rules that serve the most fundamental interests of the international community and that should be obeyed by all states without exception (Loschin 1996: 158–63). *Jus cogens* principles cannot be overridden by the persistent objector doctrine because *jus cogens* stands for fundamental and essential norms of justice which no state can be allowed to disobey (McClane 1989: 25).

10 The reason that newly independent states are given time to gain the status of a persistent objector is the necessity to support a newly independent state's sovereignty and equality (Viller 1985: 16–17).

11 Before practices mature into a custom, states face a voluntary participation problem similar to that studied by Fon and Parisi (2006). They investigated bilateral custom under reciprocity and discussed the ability of custom formation to generate Kaldor-Hicks efficient customs. This paper extends those findings to persistent objector and subsequent objector doctrines.

12 The interpretation of probabilities α_i and β_i can be illustrated by the following example. Imagine that a customary rule imposes an affirmative duty on coastal states to rescue foreign vessels within a range of 200 miles from the state's coastline. Then α_i represents the probability that state i's vessels may need rescue and benefit from the customary rescue rule. This probability depends on the number of vessels that fly state i's flag when navigating the high seas. β_i represents the probability that state i may be called upon to rescue other states' vessels. This probability depends on the extent of state i's coastline and navigation routes in its proximity.

13 In our rescue example, the effort level e represents the standard of care or investment of resources that states undertake when rescuing other states' vessels under the customary practice.

14 A discount rate reflects the state's time preference on the uncertainty concerning the effective emergence of a custom. See Fon and Parisi (2006) for more discussion.

15 Persistent objector states may opt out in full or in part from excessive customary obligations. There is no symmetric opportunity for persistent objector states to force a level of customary obligation higher than the emerging custom. Obviously, differences among states based on asymmetric preferences can be settled by means of bilateral or multilateral treaties specifying specific treaty obligations for the states. Such tailoring of international obligations to the needs of states is not possible under general customary law, given the initial need for uniform customary practices.

16 For example, with respect to our hypothetical rescue rule, rejection of the custom implies that the state prefers a self-help approach in which each state faces the burden of rescuing its own ships, even when far from the state's own coastline, without the assistance of other states in closer proximity to the accident. Under the self-help regime, states must assist their own vessels each time they are in trouble.

17 This can be easily understood in the rescue example. The cost of rescuing a ship far from the state's coastline is different from the cost to the state of rescuing a foreign vessel in the proximity of its coast.

18 As a second-best solution, in the face of a persistent objection, other states take advantage of the reciprocal effects of a unilateral objection, allowing them to adopt the same customary level against the objecting state. In this context, the persistent objector doctrine constitutes an example of weak reciprocity studied in Fon and Parisi (2003b).

19 If the probability ratio of receiving benefit and performing under custom α_i/β_i is small, state i is less likely to receive a benefit than to face the burden of future implementation of the custom. State i can be considered a low-benefit or high-cost state. Thus, in this case it is more likely for state i to fully oppose the custom.

20 See Wolfke (1993: 66): "A state may certainly not unilaterally at will refuse the legal consequences of its previous consent to accept a practice as law."

21 The *rebus sic stantibus* principle is often referred to as the law of changed circumstances. It allows a state to terminate an existing obligation on the grounds of fundamental and unforeseen changes in circumstances, as long as the changes were not caused by the state invoking the excuse (Brownlie 1990).

22 A fundamental change in circumstances may be the basis of an exemption from international law only if it increases "the burden of the obligations to be executed to the extent of rendering the performance something essentially different from that originally undertaken." *Fisheries Jurisdiction Case* (1973).

23 Villiger (1985: 17) discusses the difficulties in recognizing subsequent objectors' unilateral departures and the need to obtain acquiescence from other states: "Their position is untenable, in part, because other states have come to rely on the subsequent objector originally conforming to the rule. Also, general customary law is binding on all states and cannot, in the words of the Court, be subject of 'any right of unilateral exclusion exercisable at will by any one of [the international community members] in its own favor'" (quoting *North Sea Cases* ICJ Reports 1969). See also Stein (1985: 458).

24 This process bears some similarity with the rules governing the amendment of international treaty law. Under § 334 (3) of the *Restatement of the Law, Third Foreign Relations Law of the United States:* § 334. Amendment or Modification of International Agreement. (1) An international agreement may be amended by agreement between the parties. [. . .] (3) Two or more of the parties to a multilateral agreement may agree to modify the agreement as between themselves alone if such modification [. . .] would not be incompatible with the rights of the other parties to the agreement or with its object and purpose." Under this provision, an amendment is permissible and takes effect for the states that

agree to it even if other states do not agree to the amendment. See also 1969 *Vienna Convention on the Law of Treaties*, Article 41(2).

25 The change in customary law takes effect for the departing states and the states that provide implicit consent via acquiescence unless the rule of customary law is one of *jus cogens* or the change to the two states' practice adversely affects the interests of third party states.

26 Note, however, that while a subset of states can modify the effects of a customary rule by subsequent practice or modify a treaty obligation by subsequent treaty amendment, international law is still ambivalent on the issue of modification of treaties via subsequent practice. The International Law Commission proposed an article providing that a treaty could be modified by subsequent practice indicating agreement to such modification. As explained in the Reporter's Notes to the *Restatement of the Law, Third Foreign Relations Law of the United States*, that proposal was deleted after the delegation of the United States, among others, objected that an agreement might be deemed amended as a result of unauthorized actions by state officials. Kearney and Dalton (1970: 525). The question of modification by subsequent practice tends to merge into that of interpretation by subsequent practice under § 325, Comment c. See also *Decision of Arbitration Tribunal concerning International Air Transport Services Agreement between France and the United States*, 16 R. Int'l Arb. Awards 5 (1964).

27 Unlike persistent objectors who raise objections prior to facing a compliance problem when the custom is not yet binding, subsequent objectors manifest their objections by departing from an already binding rule of customary law.

28 This can be seen from (12.7).

29 Other first-party states that become subsequent objectors also react to the original subsequent objector state. The content of the custom between two first-party states who both want to depart from the existing custom, perhaps to different levels, is governed by the subsequent objector doctrine in ways similar to those explicitly considered in this section.

30 Unlike persistent objectors who can gain an exemption from an emerging custom by unilaterally objecting, subsequent objectors can only gain an exemption from a rule of customary law if their departure from an existing custom is not opposed by other states.

31 In the presence of uniform exogenous changes to the states, optimal effort levels are denoted with a prime.

32 Naturally, a uniform change for all states can have a mitigating effect on the subsequent objector's departure. For example, if the cost of performing has decreased, the first-party state is induced to undertake a higher level of effort. This counteracts the need for the first-party state to minimize the effort level to reduce the immediate burden of compliance. Likewise, the decrease in cost also has different impacts on second- and third-party states. We concentrate on the case where it is more likely for the existing custom to erode.

33 In the presence of asymmetric exogenous changes to the parameters, the states' optimal effort levels are denoted with a double prime.

34 The corresponding acquiescence constraint for the second-party state is

$$b'e + \frac{1}{r'}(\alpha'b'e - \beta'a'e^2) \geq b'e^* + \frac{1}{r'}(\alpha'b'e^* - \beta'a'e^{*2}).$$

35 As suggested by Goldsmith and Posner (1999), a more complex formulation of the customary relationship should account for the possibility that the customary practice results from coercion or is affected by the states' relative power, shedding light on how a custom could be transformed by a change in the states' interest and relative power. This idea is further developed in their more recent book (Goldsmith and Posner 2005), where the authors argue that while customary law may play an important role in creating state reliance, the reasons for state compliance with custom should be searched elsewhere. States seek to maximize their interest at any given time, and their compliance with norms of custom may due to a variety of factors, ranging from coercion, to forms of sustainable cooperation and coordination of the states' interest-oriented behavior, to states' coincidence of interests.

36 Most recently, Kontorovich (2006) expressed skepticism with respect to the effective reach of customary international law in situations involving several heterogeneous states.

Chapter 13 Lawmaking through Agreement

1 Vienna Convention on the Laws of Treaties, May 23, 1969, Art. 15, *available at* http://www.un.org/law/ilc/texts/treatfra.htm.

Chapter 14 Formation and Accession to Treaties

1 Vienna Convention on the Laws of Treaties, May 23, 1969, Art. 15, *available at* http://www.un.org/law/ilc/texts/treatfra.htm.

2 Int'l L. Comm'n, *Draft Articles on the Law of Treaties*, Arts. 8–9, 1962, Vol. II. U.N.Y.B of the Int'l L. Comm'n 167–68, U.N. Doc. A/CN.4/144. For further analysis of the International Law Commission's proposal, see Kelsen (1966: 479–80).

3 See, Association of Southeast Asian Nations (ASEAN) Web site, at http://www.aseansec.org/64.htm.

4 Treaty on the Non-Proliferation of Nuclear Weapons, July 1, 1968, art. IX(3), 21 U.S.T. 483, 492–93, 729 U.N.T.S. 161, 174.

5 *Id.*

6 General Act of Arbitration for the Pacific Settlement of International Disputes (Geneva, September 26, 1928).

7 Case Concerning the Aerial Incident of 10 August 1999 (*Pakistan v. India*), 2000 ICJ 12 (2000).

8 *Id.* at 19.

9 Pakistan argued that the Schedule to Indian Independence transferred unto India and Pakistan all international rights and obligation upon India and Pakistan, excluding those regarding territorial issues and international organizations. *Id.* at 19–20.

10 *Id.* at 25. The Court rejected each of the jurisdictional claims put forth by Pakistan and found that it lacked jurisdiction over the matter.

11 Agreement on an International Energy Program, TIAS 8278, 27 U.S.T. 1685; 1974 U.S.T. LEXIS 278.

12 *Id.* at *45.

13 Center for International Forestry Research (CIFOR), TIAS 11960, 1993 U.S.T. LEXIS 16 at *1 (March 5, 1993).

14 *Id.*

15 The EEC example is a hybrid case—with some features of a semi-open treaty and other features of a closed treaty. Although the organs of the community approve accession with a majority vote, an intergovernmental conference is necessary (with proper state ratification) in order for a new accession to become effective. At this stage, incumbent member states have the power to impose conditions for accession of new states. These conditions are often imposed with reference to (1) the modes for extending membership and the composition or representation within EC institutions; and (2) the acceptance of all past regulations and implementation of all past directives within a given period (generally rather long). Some bargaining takes place and modifications are made at this stage.

16 *Id.* at Art. XII, 33 I.L.M. at 1150.

17 *Id.*

18 See Bishop (1971: 119) and Kelsen (1966: 478–79). Hedlund (1994: 295) observes that one feature of a treaty to enhance competition in the global airline market would be an open accession clause.

19 Argentina-Brazil-Bulgaria-Chile-Slovak Republic-Organization for Economic Cooperation and Development: Convention on Combating Bribery of Foreign Public Officials in International Business Transactions, December 18, 1997, 37 I.L.M. 1, 6 (1998).

20 The variable N appears twice in the benefit function, B. It has both a direct effect on the benefit from participating in a treaty (i.e., widespread membership may affect benefits) and an indirect effect through the treaty content (i.e., changes in membership may affect treaty content).

21 Using the same payoff and benefit-from-treaty functions as in case (A), the effort level $(b_i + \alpha)/2a_i$ is the treaty content desired by both states.

22 Treaties signed by one country to cede a city or a port to another country may fit this scenario. In the Treaty of Nanking (1842) which ended the first opium war, China opened additional ports of trade, eliminated trade barriers, ceded the offshore island of Hong Kong to Britain, and allowed Britain's drug trade to continue despite the Chinese ban. Signing the treaty helped the Chinese to avoid further war with the British.

23 This is the basic Nash bargaining problem that Nash (1950) discussed. In our notation, this is the case when $2 = 1/2$.

24 See the related issues on Bilateral Investment Treaties discussed in Section 3.

25 Figure 14.1 makes an implicit assumption that the cost of negotiation for an additional entrant equals the original negotiation cost to create the treaty. If the negotiation cost for the incumbent state is lower in the case of accession by a

third state than in the case of forming the treaty, for example, then the vertical intercept of V_1^3 should be higher than the vertical intercept of V_1^2.

26 From the first-order condition, $ds_T^*/dN = -\pi_{SN}/(\partial^2 V_1^1/\partial s_T^2 + \pi_{SS})$. Because $\partial^2 V_1^1/\partial s_T^2 < 0$ and $\pi_{SS} \leq 0, ds_T^*/dN > 0$ when $\pi_{SN} > 0$ (the case of complements) and $ds_T^*/dN < 0$ when $\pi_{SN} < 0$ (the case of substitutes).

27 The assumptions of the Median Voter theorem include single-picked preferences and nonalienation. In this context, single-picked preferences with respect to simply that states prefer treaty obligations closer to their ideal first-best point than treaty obligations that are further away. Nonalienation implies that all states have an interest in participating in the deliberation through voting and that even states holding extreme preferences will not withdraw from the collective deliberation or be alienated from the decision process.

28 Treaties left open for accession usually limit admissibility of reservations at the time of accession. This precommitment strategy limits strategic behavior and holdup problems by third states at the time of accession. States wishing to accede to an existing open treaty have little opportunity to renegotiate treaty terms or to request unilateral exemptions or concessions.

Chapter 15 Ratification and Reservations

1 Vienna Convention on the Law of Treaties, concluded May 23, 1969, entered into force Jan. 27, 1980, 1155 U.N.T.S. 331 [hereinafter Vienna Convention]. The United States is not a party to the Vienna Convention; however, the international community generally accepts the Convention as an authoritative codification of treaty law.

2 For a recent analysis and explanation of the weakness of multilateral treaties, see Posner (2006).

3 The precise language of the treaty is as follows:
1. A reservation established with regard to another party in accordance with articles 19, 20, and 23: (a) modifies for the reserving State in its relations with that other party the provisions of the treaty to which the reservation relates to the extent of the reservation; and (b) modifies these provisions to the same extent for that other party in its relations with the reserving State.

4 For a more extensive discussion of Article 21 of the Vienna Convention on treaty reservations, see Parisi and Sevcenko (2003) from which the following synopsis is drawn.

5 On the role played by reciprocity in international law and international relations, see Keohane (1986), Greig (1994), and Parisi and Ghei (2002).

6 For a brief history of the contested definition of reservation, see Pellet (1998).

7 The compatibility of a reservation "with the object and purpose of the treaty" constitutes the benchmark test for its admissibility. Signatory states decide for themselves whether the reservation can be considered compatible with the object and purpose of the treaty. If a state believes that the reservation of another state is incompatible with the purpose and object of the treaty, it can oppose such reservation with an objection. As a result of a state's objection, the relevant treaty

provisions will become inapplicable between the reserving state and the objecting state. Ultimately, disagreements concerning the admissibility of reservations may necessitate a dispute settlement mechanism, and many treaties indeed contemplate such dispute resolution procedures.

8   Article 20 outlines the circumstances under which reservations must be accepted by other parties; otherwise, if a state does not object to a reservation from another state within a set amount of time, its silence is construed as tacit acceptance.

9   Although the percentage of treaties with reservations rose after World War II, the high point remained at only 6% of treaties in force, as of 1980. This means that a state makes, on average, one reservation to a multilateral treaty every ten years. The impressive finding is that in 85 percent of all multilateral treaties that allowed reservations, no state introduced any reservations and only 61 treaties had more than three. Gamble (1980: 378–79).

10   Ratification levels greater than 1 can be interpreted as a state's hypothetical willingness to ratify a treaty that creates even higher obligations than the current treaty, if faced with an opportunity to do so.

11   Thus, the reaction function of state 1 is given by $s_1 = s_2$ if $s_2 < b/2a$ and $s_1 = b/2a$ if $s_2 \geq b/2a$.

12   The reaction function of state 2 is given by $s_2 = s_1$ if $s_1 < d/2c$ and $s_2 = d/2c$ if $s_1 \geq d/2c$.

13   The desired level of cooperation for the two states is not equal except in the special case in which the states have identical marginal benefit-cost ratios in spite of their asymmetric payoff functions.

14   The payoffs are $\pi_1^*(b/2a, b/2a) = b^2/4a$ and $\pi_2^*(b/2a, b/2a) = [b(2ad - bc)]/4a^2$.

15   Note that the subscript 1 for marginal cost MC and marginal benefits MB does not refer to state 1. Instead, it refers to the level of treaty ratification provided by state 1. Clearly, private marginal cost and social marginal cost coincide in as much as the cost of treaty ratification is borne by the ratifying state. On the other hand, the private marginal benefit enjoyed by state 1 is provided by the ratification choice of state 2, and vice versa.

Chapter 16   The Hidden Bias of Treaty Law

1   The precise language of Article 21(1) of the Vienna Convention on the Law of Treaties follows: "1. A reservation established with regard to another party in accordance with articles 19, 20 and 23: (a) modifies for the reserving State in its relations with that other party the provisions of the treaty to which the reservation relates to the extent of the reservation; and (b) modifies these provisions to the same extent for that other party in its relations with the reserving State."

2   Parisi (1998), Parisi and Ghei (2002), and Parisi and Sevcenko (2002) suggest that the reciprocal effects of unilateral reservations introduced by Article 21 (1) of the Vienna Convention create a valuable constraint against strategic reservations.

3 The Vienna Convention combines codification of customary international law and creation of new legal norms through progressive development, although the line between the two is not necessarily clear.

4 Malkin (1926: 141–62) provides numerous examples of how the unanimity principle developed through the practice of states in the formation and ratification of international treaties, with reference to the International Sanitary Conventions held in Venice in 1892, Dresden in 1893, and Paris in 1894. Sinclair (1984: 55) provides an additional example of strict application of the unanimity principle in various pre–World War I treaties, as shown by the opposition to unilateral reservations in The Hague Peace Conference of 1899.

5 Documentation is available at GAOR, 14th session, annexes, a.i. 65 (1959). The position of India is described in A/4188 and that of the Secretary General in A/4235. The debate revealing the different positions of states on the issue of reservations is available at A/4311 paras 5–24.

6 According to Rosenne (1989), "the 1959 debate in the General Assembly is important for its strong reaffirmation that there was to be no return to the absolute unanimity practice in any guise," although no further movement forward occurred until the Waldock Commission of 1962.

7 For a more extensive description of the development of the regime of treaty reservations from the nineteenth century to the adoption of the Vienna Convention on Treaties, see Sinclair (1984) and Rosenne (1989).

8 Reciprocity is the foundation of diplomatic immunity, the laws of war, and a mechanism for dealing with breaches of treaty provisions. For a general analysis of reciprocity in international law, see Parisi and Ghei (2002).

9 The difficulty of finding a viable solution to this issue is evidenced by the debate and work that preceded the Vienna Convention. For further historical analysis, see Parisi and Sevcenko (2002).

10 The proposition that reserving states are bound to the treaty as modified by the greater of the reservations follows from the reciprocal effects of reservations under Article 21 (1)(b) whenever the level of treaty ratification is single-dimensional (e.g., level of abatement, expenditures in enforcement).

11 Reservations have no reason to exist in a simple two-country setting with a single dimension of treaty commitment. States negotiating in this environment know that reservations are possible and therefore negotiate substantive terms of the treaty, excluding the opportunity for later unilateral reservations. This makes the final terms more transparent, ensuring that neither side is surprised by the other's reservations. For this reason, Vienna Convention Article 20(4)(c) implies that unilateral reservations are not allowed in a bilateral treaty.

12 The multilateral problem facing an individual state can be viewed as the aggregation of multiple bilateral problems faced by the state. Thus, the bilateral problem is the typical problem confronting a representative state in a multilateral treaty relationship.

13 This model is adopted from the asymmetric nonlinear model developed in Fon and Parisi (2003b). The functional forms of benefits and costs ensure that marginal cost eventually exceeds marginal benefit. It is assumed that marginal benefit is constant and that marginal cost is increasing.

14 The subscript refers to the state. The superscript L is redundant here but this notation makes it easier to generalize when each state interacts with more than one state.

15 We appeal to the intuitive criterion as formulated by Cho and Kreps (1987) and Rasmusen (1989) to assume that among multiple equilibria, the parties always coordinate toward the equilibrium that is mutually preferred by the players.

16 In this context, the nonreserving state obtains a lower treaty level than its ideal level, but avoids the costs of full treaty compliance in the face of the other state's partial ratification.

17 Extensions of this model could contemplate strategic substitutes and strategic complements. The decision of one state to depart from full treaty compliance could alter the cost-benefit calculations of those who remain. If compliance levels are strategic substitutes, nonreserving states may increase their obligations beyond the level specified in the treaty. Examples include some environmental treaties, where failure of some states to ratify the treaty may need to be counterbalanced by higher preservation efforts by participating states. If compliance levels are strategic complements, nonreserving states may reduce their obligations below the specified treaty level. This may be the case when the nonparticipation of some states reduces the benefits of participation for the other states. Examples include coordination treaties creating network externalities (e.g., technological standards), the value of which depends on the level of participation and resulting diffusion.

18 For convenience we assume strict inequality for ranking the cost-benefit ratios. The results can be modified if weak inequalities are involved.

19 As an extremely simplified example, take the payoff functions for state H and L discussed earlier. The aggregate payoff function under reciprocity is $b_H s - a_H s^2 + b_L s - a_L s^2$. The level of treaty obligation that maximizes this payoff is $s_T = (b_H + b_L)/2(a_H + a_L)$. It can be proved that s_T is greater than $b_H/2a_H$ and less than $b_L/2a_L$. For other details, see the discussion on reciprocal social optimum in Fon and Parisi (2007).

20 This is discussed in case B above. In this specific case where i is the reserving state, state i plays the role of H and j plays the role of L.

21 This is discussed in case A above.

22 From an economic point of view, states are expected to take into account these distributive effects when "pricing" the treaty agreement. However, in spite of many similarities between treaties and contracts, multilateral treaty obligations are generally undertaken by states without any side payment. In these situations no price system is capable of capturing the distributive effects of the reservation rule.

23 The General Assembly asked the International Law Commission to "study the question of reservations to multilateral conventions both from the point of view of codification and from that of progressive development" (Resolution 478 (V) of November 16, 1950). See also *Report of the International Law Commission on the work of its forty-ninth session 12 May_18 July* U.N. GAOR, 52nd Sess., Supp. No. 10, U.N. Doc. A/52/10 (1997) discussed in Parisi and Sevcenko (2002).

24 Even after the Court rendered its opinion, the ILC input still was relevant because the Court, relying on the abstract nature of an advisory opinion, left many questions unanswered about how a regime would work that did not require unanimous acceptance of reservations.

25 The debate that followed India's request for accession to the Inter-Governmental Maritime Organization is informative of the positions taken by the various nations on the general issue of reservations. As discussed above, this documentation is available at GAOR, 14th session, annexes, a.i. 65 (1959). Position of India is described in A/4188 and that of the Secretary General in A/4235. Rosenne (1989) suggests that the fall of the unanimity rule and allowance of reservations is a product of the demise of European dominance in international relations. The United States ultimately failed to ratify the Vienna Convention on the law of treaties. In practice the United States closely scrutinizes reservation provisions prior to signing a multilateral treaty, to avoid applicability of other default mechanisms of reservation.

References

Abbott, Kenneth W. 1989. "Modern International Relations Theory: A Prospective for International Lawyers." *Yale Journal of International Law* 14: 335–411.

Akehurst, Michael. 1974–75. "Custom as a Source of International Law." *British Yearbook of International Law* 47: 1–54.

Alesina, Alberto F., Ignazio Angeloni, and Federico Etro. 2005. "International Unions." *American Economic Review* 95: 602–15.

Alesina, Alberto, Ignazio Angeloni, and Ludger Schuknecht. 2005. "What Does the European Union Do?" *Public Choice* 123: 275–319.

Arce, Daniel G. 2001. "Leadership and the Aggregation of International Collective Action." *Oxford Economic Papers, Oxford University* 53: 114–37.

Aristotle [350 B.C.] 2000. *Nicomachean Ethics*. Edited and translated by Roger Crisp. New York: Cambridge University Press.

Axelrod, Robert M. 1981. "The Emergence of Cooperation among Egoists." *American Political Science Review* 75: 306–18.

———. 1984. *The Evolution of Cooperation*. New York: Basic Books.

Baird, Douglas G., and Edward R. Morrison. 2001. "Bankruptcy Decision Making." *Journal of Law, Economics and Organization* 17: 356–72.

Barro, Robert J. 1991. "Economic Growth in a Cross Section of Countries." *Quarterly Journal of Economics* 106: 407–43.

Beemelmans, Hubert. 1997. "State Succession in International Law: Remarks on Recent Theory and State Praxis." *Boston University International Law Journal* 15: 71–123.

Benson, Bruce L. 1989. "The Spontaneous Evolution of Commercial Law." *Southern Economic Journal* 55: 644–61.

———. 1990. *The Enterprise of Law: Justice without the State*. San Francisco: Pacific Research Institute.

———. 1992a. "Customary Law as a Social Contract: International Commercial Law." *Constitutional Political Economy* 3: 1–27.

———. 1992b. "The Evolution of Values and Institutions in a Free Society: The Under-Pinnings of a Market Economy." *International Journal on the Unity of Sciences* 5: 411–42. Reprinted in *Values and the Social Order*, Vol. I, ed. G. Radnitzky and H. Bouillon, 87–125. Aldershot: Avebury, 1995.

Bentham, Jeremy. [1776] 1977. "A Fragment on Government." In *A Comment on the Commentaries and a Fragment on Government.* Edited by J. H. Burns and H. L. A. Hart, 393–501. London: University of London Althone Press.

Berman, Harold J., and Charles J. Reid, Jr. 1996. "The Transformation of English Legal Science: From Hale to Blackstone." *Emory Law Journal* 45: 437–522.

Berman, Harold J., and Felix J. Dasser. 1990. "The 'New' Law Merchant and the 'Old': Sources, Content, and Legitimacy." In *Lex Mercatoria and Arbitration: A Discussion of the New Law Merchant,* 21–36. Dobbs Ferry: Transnational Juris Publications.

Bermann, George A. 1994. "Taking Subsidiarity Seriously: Federalism in the European Community and the United States." *Columbia Law Review* 94: 331–456.

Bernstein, Lisa. 1993. "Social Norms and Default Rules Analysis." *Southern California Interdisciplinary Law Journal* 3: 59–90.

———. 1995. "Opting Out of the Legal System: Extralegal Contractual Relations in the Diamond Industry." *Journal of Legal Studies* 21: 115–57.

———. 1996. "Merchant Law in a Merchant Court: Rethinking the Code's Search for Immanent Business Norms." *University of Pennsylvania Law Review* 144: 1765–1821.

———. 2001. "Private Commercial Law in the Cotton Industry: Creating Cooperation through Rules, Norms, and Institutions." *Michigan Law Review* 99: 1724–90.

Binmore, Ken, and Larry Samuelson. 1994. "An Economist's Perspective on the Evolution of Norms." *Journal of Institutional and Theoretical Economics* 150: 45–63.

Bishop, William W., Jr. 1971. *International Law: Cases and Materials.* 3rd ed. Boston: Little & Brown.

Black, Duncan. 1958. *The Theory of Committee and Elections.* Cambridge, UK: Cambridge University Press.

Blackstone, William. [1764] 1979. *Commentaries on the Laws of England.* Chicago: University of Chicago Press.

Bowles, Samuel, and Herbert Gintis. 2001. "The Evolution of Strong Reciprocity." *Journal of Theoretical Biology* 213: 103–19.

Brownlie, Ian. 1990. *Principles of Public International Law.* 4th ed. Oxford: Clarendon Press.

Brunsson, Nils. 1989. *The Organization of Hypocrisy. Talk, Decisions, and Actions in Organizations.* Chichester, UK: Wiley.

Buchanan, James M., and Gordon Tullock. 1962. *The Calculus of Consent. Logical Foundations of Constitutional Democracy.* Ann Arbor, MI: University of Michigan Press.

Buergenthal, Thomas, and Harold G. Maier. 1990. *Public International Law.* St. Paul, MN: West Group.

Calabresi, Guido. 1979. "Access to Justice and Substantive Law Reform: Legal Aid for the Lower Middle Class." In *Access to Justice, Vol. III: Emerging Issues and Perspectives.* Edited by Mauro Cappelletti and Bryant Garth, 169–256. Varese: Sijthoff and Noordhoff.

Calamandrei, Piero. 1965. *Opere Giuridiche,* (Edited by Mauro Cappelletti). Naples, Italy: Morano.

Carbonara, Emanuela, and Francesco Parisi. 2007a. "The Economics of Legal Harmonization." *Public Choice* 132: 367–400.

———. 2007b. "Choice of Law and Legal Evolution: Rethinking the Market for Legal Rules." *Minnesota Legal Studies Research Paper* No. 07–38.

Carbonnier, Jean. 1974. "Authorities in Civil Law: France." In *The Role of Judicial Decisions and Doctrine in Civil Law and in Mixed Jurisdictions*. Edited by J. Dainow, 91–118. Baton Rouge, LA: Louisiana State University Press.

Carozza, Paolo G. 2003. "Subsidiarity as a Structural Principle of International Human Rights Law." *American Journal of International Law* 97: 38–79.

Charney, Jonathan I. 1985. "The Persistent Objector Rule and the Development of Customary International Law." *British Yearbook of International Law* 56: 1–24.

Chinkin, Christine. 1993. *Third Parties in International Law*. Oxford: Clarendon Press.

Cho, In-Koo, and David M. Kreps. 1987. "Signaling Games and Stable Equilibria." *Quarterly Journal of Economics* 102: 179–221.

Coase, Ronald H. 1960. "The Problem of Social Cost." *Journal of Law and Economics* 3: 1–44.

Cooper, Ian. 2006. "The Subsidiarity Early Warning Mechanism: Making It Work." *Intereconomics* 41: 254–57.

Cooter, Robert D. 1992. "Against Legal Centrism." *California Law Review* 81: 417–29.

———. 1994a. "Decentralized Law for a Complex Economy. Hayek Symposium." *Southwestern Law Review* 23: 443–51.

———. 1994b. "Structural Adjudication and the New Law Merchant: A Model of Decentralized Law." *International Review of Law & Economics* 14: 215–27.

———. 1996. "Decentralized Law for a Complex Economy: The Structural Approach to Adjudicating the New Law Merchant." *University of Pennsylvania Law Review* 144: 1645–96.

———. 2000. *The Strategic Constitution*. Princeton, NJ: Princeton University Press.

Cooter, Robert D., and Lewis Kornhauser. 1980. "Can Litigation Improve the Law without the Help of Judges?" *Journal of Legal Studies* 9: 139–63.

Cooter, Robert D., and Daniel L. Rubinfeld. 1989. "Economic Analysis of Legal Disputes and Their Resolution." *Journal of Economic Literature* 27: 1067–97.

D'Amato, Anthony A. 1971. *The Concept of Custom in International Law*. Ithaca: Cornell University Press.

———. 1987. "Trashing International Customary Law." *American Journal of International Law* 81: 101–5.

———. Forthcoming. *A Groundwork for International Law*. Unpublished manuscript (on file with author).

Dainow, Joseph, ed. 1974. *The Role of Judicial Decisions and Doctrine in Civil Law and Mixed Jurisdictions*. Baton Rouge, LA: Louisiana State University Press.

Dari-Mattiacci, Giuseppe, and Bruno Deffains. 2005. "Uncertainty of Law and the Legal Process." Working Paper No. 2005-10, Amsterdam Center for Law & Economics. SSRN. http://ssrn.com/abstract=869368.

Daughety, Andrew F., and Jennifer F. Reinganum. 1999. "Stampede to Judgment: Persuasive Influence and Herding Behavior By Courts." *American Law and Economics Review* 1: 158–89.

David, Renè. 1972. *French Law: Its Structure, Sources, and Methodology*. Baton Rouge, LA: Louisiana State University Press.

De Cremer, David, and Geoffrey Leonardelli. 2003. "Cooperation in Social Dilemmas and the Need to Belong: The Moderating Effect of Group Size." *Group Dynamics: Theory, Research, and Practice* 7: 168–74.

Dennis, James L. 1993. "The John Tucker, Jr. Lecture in Civil Law: Interpretation and Application of the Civil Code and the Evaluation of Judicial Precedent." *Louisiana Law Review* 54: 1–17.

Depoorter, Ben, and Francesco Parisi. 2003. "Legal Precedents and Judicial Discretion." In *Encyclopedia of Public Choice*. Edited by C. K. Rowley and F. Schneider, 343–47. Boston: Kluwer Academic Publishers.

Dixit, Avinash. 1989. "Entry and Exit Decisions under Uncertainty." *Journal of Political Economy* 97: 620–38.

———. 1992. "Investment and Hysteresis." *Journal of Economic Perspectives* 6: 107–32.

Dixit, Avinash K., and Robert S. Pindyck. 1994. *Investment under Uncertainty*. Princeton: Princeton University Press.

Downs, Anthony. 1957. *An Economic Theory of Democracy*. New York: Harper and Row.

Easterbrook, Frank. 1983. "Statutes' Domains." *University of Chicago Law Review* 50: 533–52.

Ehrlich, Isaac, and Richard A. Posner. 1974. "An Economic Analysis of Legal Rulemaking." *Journal of Legal Studies* 3: 257–86.

Eisenberg, Melvin A. 1988. *The Nature of the Common Law*. Cambridge, MA: Harvard University Press.

Ellickson, Robert C. 1991. *Order without Law: How Neighbors Settle Disputes*. Cambridge, MA: Harvard University Press.

———. 1994. "The Aim of Order without Law." *Journal of Institutional and Theoretical Economics* 150: 97–100.

———. 2001. "The Market for Social Norms." *American Law and Economics Review* 3: 1–49.

Ellinghaus, Manfred P., and Edmund W. Wright. 2005. "The Common Law of Contracts: Are Broad Principles Better Than Detailed Rules? An Empirical Investigation." *Texas Wesleyan Law Review* 11: 399–420.

Evans, Jim 1987. "Change in the Doctrine of Precedent during the Nineteenth Century." In *Precedent in Law*. Edited by L. Goldstein, 35–72. Oxford: Clarendon Press.

Farzin, Y. Hossein., Kuno J. M. Huisman, and Peter M. Kort. 1998. "Optimal Timing of Technology Adoption." *Journal of Economic Dynamics and Control* 22: 779–99.

Feess, Eberhard, and Erich Schanze. 2003. "Reciprocity-Induced Cooperation: A Comment." *Journal of Institutional and Theoretical Economics* 159: 93–96.

Fon, Vincy, and Francesco Parisi. 2003a. "Litigation and the Evolution of Legal Remedies: A Dynamic Model." *Public Choice* 116: 419–33.

———. 2003b. "Reciprocity-Induced Cooperation." *Journal of Institutional and Theoretical Economics* 159: 1–17.

———. 2003c. "The Hidden Bias of the Vienna Convention on the Law of Treaties." Law and Economics Working Paper Series No. 03–08, George Mason University.

———. 2004. "Judicial Precedents in Civil Law Systems: A Dynamic Analysis." Law & Economics Research Paper No. 04–15, George Mason University. http://ssrn.com/abstract=534504.

———. 2006. "Customary Law and Articulation Theories: An Economic Analysis." *International Law and Management Review* 2: 201–232.

———. 2007. "Matching Rules." *Managerial and Decision Economics* 28: 1–14.

Fon, Vincy, Francesco Parisi, and Ben Depoorter. 2005. "Litigation, Judicial Path-Dependence, and Legal Change." *European Journal of Law and Economics* 20: 43–56.

Fuller, Lon L. 1969. *The Morality of Law*. Revised edition. New Haven: Yale University Press.

Gamble, John K. 1980. "Reservations to Multilateral Treaties: A Macroscopic View of State Practice." *American Journal of International Law* 74: 372–94.

Gauthier, David. 1986. *Morals by Agreement*. Oxford: Clarendon Press.

Gersen, Jacob, and Eric A. Posner. 2007. "Timing Rules and Legal Institutions." *Harvard Law Review* 121: 543–90.

Ginsburg, Thomas, and Richard McAdams. 2004. "Adjudicating in Anarchy: An Expressive Theory of International Dispute Resolution." *William and Mary Law Review* 45: 1229–1339.

Gintis, Herbert M. 2000. *Game Theory Evolving: A Problem-Centered Introduction to Modeling Strategic Behavior*. Princeton, NJ: Princeton University Press.

Gneezy, Uri, and Aldo Rustichini. 2000. "A Fine Is a Price." *Journal of Legal Studies* 29: 1–17.

———. 2003. "Incentives, Punishment and Behavior." In *Behavioral Economics*. Edited by Colin Camerer, George Loewenstein, and Matthew Rabin. Princeton, NJ: Princeton University Press.

Goldsmith, Jack L., and Eric A. Posner. 1999. "A Theory of Customary International Law." *University of Chicago Law Review* 66: 1113–77.

———. 2000. "Understanding the Resemblance between Modern and Traditional Customary International Law." *Virginia Journal of International Law* 40: 639–72.

———. 2005. *The Limits of International Law*. New York: Oxford University Press.

Goodman, John C. 1979. "An Economic Theory of the Evolution of the Common Law." *Journal of Legal Studies* 7: 393–406.

Grady, Mark F. 1995. "Legal Evolution and Precedent." *Annual Review of Law & Ethics* 3: 147–82.

Greif, Avner. 1989. "Reputation and Coalitions in Medieval Trade: Evidence on the Maghribi Traders." *Journal of Economic History* 49: 857–82.

Greig, Donald W. 1994. "Reciprocity, Proportionality, and the Law of Treaties." *Virginia Journal of International Law* 34: 295–403.

Grossman, Gene M., and Elhanan Helpman. 1996. "Electoral Competition and Special Interest Politics." *Review of Economic Studies* 63: 265–86.

Haag, Matthew, and Roger Lagunoff. 2003. "On the Size and Structure of Group Cooperation." Working Paper No. 03-02, Georgetown University. http://papers.ssrn.com/sol3/papers.cfm?abstract_id=335160.

Hadfield, Gillian K. 1992. "Biases in the Evolution of Legal Rules." *Georgetown Law Journal* 80: 583–616.

Hale, Matthew. [1713] 1971. *The History of the Common Law of England.* Chicago: University of Chicago Press.

Harsanyi, John C. 1955. "Cardinal Welfare, Individualistic Ethics, and Interpersonal Comparisons of Utility." *Journal of Political Economy* 63: 309–21.

Hatzis, Aristides N. 2003. "Having the Cake and Eating It Too: Efficient Penalty Clauses in Common and Civil Contract Law." *International Review of Law and Economics* 22: 381–406.

Hayek, Friedrich A. 1967. "The Results of Human Action but Not of Human Design." In *Studies in Philosophy, Politics and Economics*, 96–105. Chicago: University of Chicago Press.

———. 1973. "Nomos: The Law of Liberty." *Law, Legislation and Liberty* 1: 94–123.

He, Hua, and Robert S. Pindyck. 1992. "Investment in Flexible Production Capacity." *Journal of Economic Dynamics and Control* 16: 575–99.

Heckathorn, Douglas D. 1993. "Collective Action and Group Heterogeneity: Voluntary Provision versus Selective Incentives." *American Sociological Review* 58: 329–50.

Hedlund, Daniel C. 1994. "Toward Open Skies: Liberalizing Trade in International Airline Services." *Minnesota Journal of Global Trade* 3: 259–99.

Heiner, Ronald A. 1986. "Imperfect Decisions and the Law: On the Evolution of Legal Precedent and Rules." *Journal of Legal Studies* 15: 227–61.

Héritier, Adrienne 1999. *Policy-making and Diversity in Europe: Escaping Deadlock.* Cambridge, UK: Cambridge University Press.

Hirshleifer, Jack. 1983. "From Weakest Link to Best Shot: The Voluntary Provision of Public Goods." *Public Choice* 43: 371–86.

Hylton, Daniel N. 1994. "Default Breakdown: The Vienna Convention on the Law of Treaties: Inadequate Framework on Reservations." *Vanderbilt Journal of Transnational Law* 27: 419–51.

Immergut, Ellen M. 1992. *Health Politics: Interests and Institutions in Western Europe.* Cambridge, UK: Cambridge University Press.

Inman, Robert P., and Daniel L. Rubinfeld. 1998. "Subsidiarity and the European Union." *NBER Working Paper* No. 6556.

Johnston, Jason S. 1995. "Bargaining under Rules versus Standards." *Journal of Law, Economics, and Organization* 11: 256–81.

Kaplow, Louis. 1986. "Private versus Social Costs in Bringing Suits." *Journal of Legal Studies* 15: 371–85.

———.1992. "Rules versus Standards: An Economic Analysis." *Duke Law Journal* 42: 557–629.

———. 1994. "The Value of Accuracy in Adjudication: An Economic Analysis." *Journal of Legal Studies* 23: 307–401.

———. 1995. "A Model of the Optimal Complexity of Legal Rules." *Journal of Law, Economics, and Organization* 11: 150–63.

———. 2000. "General Characteristics of Rules." *Encyclopedia of Law and Economics*. Edited by Boudewijn Bouckaert and Gerrit De Geest. Cheltenham, UK: Edward Elgar.

Karasik, David R. 1997. "Securing the Peace Dividend in the Middle East: Amending GATT Article XXIV to Allow Sectoral Preferences in Free Trade Areas." *Michigan Journal of International Law* 18: 527–64.

Kearney, Richard D., and Robert E. Dalton. 1970. "The Treaty on Treaties." *American Journal of International Law* 64: 495–561.

Kelly, John M. 1992. *A Short History of Western Legal Theory.* Oxford: Clarendon Press.

Kelsen, Hans. 1939. "Théorie du Droit International Coutumier." *Revue Internationale de la Théorie du Droit*, New Series 1: 253–74.

———. 1945. *General Theory of Law and the State.* Cambridge, MA: Harvard University Press.

———. 1966. *Principles of International Law.* Edited by Robert W. Tucker. New York: Holt, Reinhart, & Winston.

Keohane, Robert O. 1986. "Reciprocity in International Relations." *International Organizations* 40: 1–27.

King, Gary, Robert O. Keohane, et al. 1994. *Designing Social Inquiry: Scientific Inference in Qualitative Research.* Princeton, NJ: Princeton University Press.

Klein, Benjamin. 1996. "Why Hold-Ups Occur: The Self-Enforcing Range of Contractual Relationships." *Economic Enquiry* 34: 444–63.

Klick, Jonathan, and Francesco Parisi. 2003. "The Disunity of Unanimity." *Constitutional Political Economy* 14: 83–94.

Kobayashi, Bruce H. 1996. "Case Selection, External Effects, and the Trial/Settlement Decision." In *Dispute Resolution: Bridging the Settlement Gap.* Edited by D. A. Anderson, 17–49. Greenwich, CT: JAI Press.

Kobayashi, Bruce H., and Larry E. Ribstein. 1997. "Federalism, Efficiency and Competition." Presented at the Center for the Study of Public Choice, George Mason University (November 1997). http://papers.ssrn.com/sol3/papers.cfm?abstract_id=110071.

———. 2001. "A Recipe for Cookies: State Regulation of Consumer Marketing Information." Working Paper No. 01–04, George Mason University. http://www.law.gmu.edu/faculty/papers/docs/01-04.pdf.

Kontorovich, Eugene. 2006. "Inefficient Customs in International Law." *William and Mary Law Review* 48: 859–922.

Kontou, Nancy. 1994. *The Termination and Revision of Treaties in the Light of New Customary International Law.* Oxford: Clarendon Press.

Kornhauser, Lewis. 1989. "An Economic Perspective of Stare Decisis." *Chicago-Kent Law Review* 65: 63–92.

———. 1996. "Conceptions of Social Rule." In *Social Rules: Origin, Character, Logic, Change.* Edited by David Braybrooke, 203–16. Boulder, CO: Westview Press.

———. 1992. "Modeling Collegial Courts I: Path Dependence." *International Review of Law and Economics* 12: 169–85.

Kornhauser, Lewis, and Lawrence G. Sager. 1986. "Unpacking the Court." *Yale Law Journal* 96: 82–117.

Lambert, Edouard, and Max J. Wasserman. 1929. "The Case Method in Canada and the Possibilities of Its Adaptation to the Civil Law." *Yale Law Journal* 39: 1–21.

Landes, William M. 1971. "An Economic Analysis of the Courts." *Journal of Law and Economics* 14: 61–107.

Landes, William M., and Richard A. Posner. 1975. "The Independent Judiciary in an Interest-Group Perspective." *Journal of Law and Economics* 18: 875–901.

———. 1976. "Legal Precedent: A Theoretical and Empirical Analysis." *Journal of Law & Economics* 19: 249–307.

Lawson, F. Harry. 1955. *Negligence in the Civil Law*. Oxford: Clarendon Press.

Lawson, F. Harry, and Basil S. Markesinis. 1982. *Tortious Liability for Unintentional Harm in the Common Law and the Civil Law*. Cambridge, UK: Cambridge University Press.

Levy, Gilat. 2005. "Careerist Judges." *Rand Journal of Economics* 36: 275–97.

Loschin, Lynn. 1996. "The Persistent Objector and Customary Human Rights Law: A Proposed Analytical Framework." *U.C. Davis Journal of International Law & Policy* 2: 147–72.

MacCormick, Neil D., Robert S. Summers, and Arthur L. Goodhart, eds. 1997. *Interpreting Precedent: A Comparative Study*. Aldershot: Ashgate Publishing.

Mahoney, Paul, and Chris William Sanchirico. 2005. "General and Specific Legal Rules." *Journal of Institutional and Theoretical Economics* 161: 329–46.

Majd, Saman, and Robert S. Pindyck. 1987. "Time to Build, Option Value and Investment Decisions." *Journal of Financial Economics* 18: 7–27.

Majone, Giandomenico. 2001. "Nonmajoritarian Institutions and the Limits of Democratic Governance: A Political Transaction-Cost Approach." *Journal of Institutional and Theoretical Economics* 157: 57–78.

Malkin, William H. 1926. "Reservations to Multilateral Conventions." *British Yearbook of International Law* 7: 141–62.

Mateesco, Nicholas M. 1947. *La Coutume dans les Cycles Juridiques Internationaux*. Paris: A. Pedone.

Mattei, Ugo. 1988. *Stare Decisis*. Milano, IT: Guiffre.

———. 1997. *Comparative Law and Economics*. Ann Arbor: University of Michigan Press.

McClane, J. Brock. 1989. "How Late in the Emergence of a Norm of Customary International Law May a Persistent Objector Object?" *ILSA Journal of International Law* 13: 1–26.

McDonald, Robert, and Daniel R. Siegel. 1985. "Investment and Valuation of Firms When There Is an Option to Shut Down." *International Economic Review* 26, no. 2: 331–49.

———. 1986. "The Value of Waiting to Invest." *Quarterly Journal of Economics* 101: 707–28.

McGinnis, John O., and Ilya Somin. 2007. "Should International Law Be Part of Our Law?" *Stanford Law Review* 54: 1175–1247.

Menell, Peter S. 1983. "A Note on Private versus Social Incentives to Sue in a Costly Legal System." *Journal of Legal Studies* 12: 41–52.

Merryman, John. 1969. *The Civil Law Tradition: An Introduction to the Legal Systems of Western Europe and Latin America.* Palo Alto: Stanford University Press.

Moore, Kimberly A., and Francesco Parisi. 2002. "Forum Shopping in Cyberspace." *Chicago-Kent Law Review* 77: 1325–58.

Moreno, Richard D. 1995. "*Scott v. Cokern*: Of Precedent, Jurisprudence Constante, and the Relationship between Louisiana Commercial Laws and Louisiana Pledge Jurisprudence." *Tulane European & Civil Law Forum* 10: 31–60.

Mueller, Dennis C. 1989. *Public Choice II.* Cambridge, UK: Cambridge University Press.

Nash, John F. 1950. "The Bargaining Problem." *Econometrica* 18:155–62.

Neven, Damien J. 1992. "Regulatory Reform in the European Community." *American Economic Review* 82, no. 2: 98–103.

Niblett, Anthony, Richard Posner, and Andrei Shleifer. 2008. "The Evolution of a Legal Rule." *NBER Working Papers* No. 13856, National Bureau of Economic Research.

Nicholson, Michael. 1989. *Formal Theories in International Relations.* Cambridge, UK: Cambridge University Press.

Ogus, Anthony. 1999. "Competition between National Legal Systems: A Contribution of Economic Analysis to Comparative Law." *International and Comparative Law Quarterly* 48: 405–18.

Olson, Mancur. 1965. *The Logic of Collective Action.* Cambridge, MA: Harvard University Press.

———. 1971. *On the Logic of Collective Action: Public Goods and the Theory of Groups.* Cambridge, MA: Harvard University Press.

Parisi, Francesco. 1992. *Liability for Negligence and Judicial Discretion.* 2nd ed. Berkeley: University of California Press.

———. 1995. "Toward a Theory of Spontaneous Law." *Constitutional Political Economy* 6: 211–31.

———. 1998. "Customary Law." In *The New Palgrave Dictionary of Economics and the Law*, 572–78. London: Macmillan Reference.

———. 2000a. "The Cost of the Game: A Taxonomy of Social Interactions." *European Journal of Law and Economics* 9: 99–114.

———. 2000b. "Spontaneous Emergence of Law: Customary Law." In *Encyclopedia of Law & Economics.* Vol. 5, 603–630. Northampton: Edward Elgar Publishing.

Parisi, Francesco, Vincy Fon, and Nita Ghei. 2004. "The Value of Waiting in Lawmaking." *European Journal of Law and Economics* 18: 131–48.

Parisi, Francesco, and Nita Ghei. 2003. "The Role of Reciprocity in International Law." *Cornell International Law Journal* 36: 93–123.

———. 2005. "Legislate Today or Wait Until Tomorrow? An Investment Approach to Lawmaking." *Journal of Public Finance and Public Choice* 23: 19–42.

Parisi, Francesco, and Erin O'Hara. 1998. "Conflict of Laws." *New Palgrave Dictionary of Economics and the Law.* Vol. 1, 386–95. London: MacMillan Publishing.

Parisi, Francesco, and Larry Ribstein. 1998. "Choice of Law." *New Palgrave Dictionary of Economics and the Law.* Vol. 1, 236–41. London: MacMillan Publishing.

Parisi, Francesco, and Catherine Sevcenko. 2003. "Treaty Reservations and the Economics of Article 21 of the Vienna Convention." *Berkeley Journal of International Law* 21: 1–26.

Pelkmans, Jacques. 2006. "An EU Subsidiarity Test Is Indispensable." *Intereconomics* 41: 249–54.

Pellet, Alain. 1998. "Special Rapporteur, Third Report on Reservations to Treaties." UN Doc. A/CN.4/491/Add. 1, 1998.

Perry, Clive, et al. 1996. *Perry and Grant Encyclopaedic Dictionary of International Law.* New York: Oceana Publications.

Pindyck, Robert. S. 1988. "Irreversibility Investment, Capacity Choice, and the Value of the Firm." *American Economic Review* 78: 969–85.

———. 1991. "Irreversibility, Uncertainty and Investment." *Journal of Economic Literature* 29: 1110–48.

Posner, Eric A. 1996. "Law, Economics, and Inefficient Norms." *University of Pennsylvania Law Review* 144: 1697–1744.

———. 2000. *Law and Social Norms.* Cambridge, MA: Harvard University Press.

———. 2004. "The Decline of the International Court of Justice." *University of Chicago Law & Economics, Olin Working Paper* No. 233.

———. 2006. "International Law: A Welfarist Approach." *University of Chicago Law Review* 73: 487–544.

———. 2007. *Social Norms, Nonlegal Sanctions, and the Law.* Cheltenham Glos, UK: Edward Elgar.

Posner, Richard A. 1973. "An Economic Approach to Legal Procedure and Judicial Administration." *Journal of Legal Studies* 2: 399–458.

———. 1981. "A Reply to Some Recent Criticisms of the Efficiency Theory of the Common Law." *Hofstra Law Review* 9: 775–94.

———. 1989. "Legislation and Its Interpretation: A Primer." *Nebraska Law Review* 68: 431–53.

———. 1994. "What Do Judges and Justices Maximize? (The Same Thing Everybody Else Does)." *Supreme Court Economic Review* 3: 1–41.

———. 2006. "The Role of the Judge in the Twenty-First Century." *Boston University Law Review* 86: 1049–68.

Posner, Richard A., and Francesco Parisi. 1997. "Law and Economics: An Introduction." In *Law and Economics.* Edited by R. A. Posner and F. Parisi. International Library of Critical Writings in Economics Series. Lyme, NH: Edward Elgar Publishing.

Priest, George L. 1977. "The Common Law Process and the Selection of Efficient Rules." *Journal of Legal Studies* 6: 65–82.

Priest, George L., and Benjamin Klein. 1984. "The Selection of Disputes for Litigation." *Journal of Legal Studies* 13: 1–55.

Rabin, Matthew. 1995. "Moral Preference, Moral Constraints, and Self-Serving Biases." Economics Working Papers, University of California at Berkeley.

Rachlinski, Jeffrey J. 2000. "A Positive Psychological Theory of Judging in Hindsight." In *Behavioral Law and Economics.* Edited by Cass R. Sunstein, 95–115. Cambridge, UK: Cambridge University Press.

Rasmusen, Eric. 1989. *Games and Information: An Introduction to Game Theory*. 2nd ed. Cambridge, MA: Blackwell Publishers.

Rawls, John. 1971. *A Theory of Justice*. Cambridge, MA: Harvard University Press.

Ribstein, Larry E. 1993. "Choosing Law by Contract." *Journal of Corporation Law* 18: 245–300.

Rizzo, Mario J. 1987. "Rules versus Cost Benefit Analysis in the Common Law." In *Economic Liberties and the Judiciary*. Edited by J. A. Dorn and H. G. Manne, 865–84. Fairfax, VA: George Mason University Press.

Roberts, Kevin, and Martin L. Weitzman. 1981. "Funding Criteria for Research, Development, and Exploration Projects." *Econometrica* 49: 1261–88.

Roemer, John E. 1996. *Theories of Distributive Justice*. Cambridge, MA: Harvard University Press.

———. 1998. *Equality of Opportunity*. Cambridge, MA: Harvard University Press.

Romano, Roberta. 1985. "Law as a Product: Some Pieces of the Incorporation Puzzle." *Journal of Law, Economics & Organization* 1: 225–83.

Rose-Ackerman, Susan, and Mark Geistfeld. 1987. "The Divergence between Social and Private Incentives to Sue: A Comment on Shavell, Menell, and Kaplow." *Journal of Legal Studies* 16: 483–91.

Rose-Ackerman, Susan, and Jennifer Tobin. 2005. "Foreign Direct Investment and the Business Environment in Developing Countries: The Impact of Bilateral Investment Treaties." Law & Economics Research Paper No. 293, Yale University.

Rosenne, Shabtai. 1989. *Developments in the Law of Treaties 1945–1986*. Cambridge, UK: Cambridge University Press.

Rowley, Charles K. 1989. "The Common Law in Public Choice Perspective: A Theoretical and Institutional Critique." *Hamline Law Review* 12: 355–83.

Rubin, Paul H. 1977. "Why Is the Common Law Efficient?" *Journal of Legal Studies* 6: 51–63.

———. 1982. "Common Law and Statute Law." *Journal of Legal Studies* 11: 205–23.

———. 2006. *Evolution of Efficient Common Law*. Cheltenham Glos, UK Edward Elgar.

Rubin, Paul H., and Martin J. Bailey. 1994. "The Role of Lawyers in Changing the Law." *Journal of Legal Studies* 23: 807–31.

Rubin, Paul H., Christopher Curran, and John Curran. 2001. "Litigation versus Lobbying: Forum Shopping by Rent-Seekers." *Public Choice* 107: 295–310.

Sandler, Todd. 1998. "Global and Regional Public Goods: A Prognosis for Collective Action." *Fiscal Studies* 19: 221–47.

Schäfer, Hans-Bernd. 2006. "Rules versus Standards in Rich and Poor Countries: Precise Legal Norms as Substitutes for Human Capital in Low-Income Countries." *Supreme Court Economic Review* 14: 113–34.

Schäfer, Wolf. 2006. "Harmonization and Centralization versus Subsidiarity: Which Should Apply Where?" *Intereconomics* 41: 246–49.

Schelling, Thomas C. 1980. *The Strategy of Conflict*. Cambridge, MA: Harvard University Press.

Schwartz, Alan, and Robert E. Scott. 1995. "The Political Economy of Private Legislatures." *University of Pennsylvania Law Review* 143: 595–654.

Sen, Amartya K. 1977. "Rational Fools: A Critique of the Behavioral Foundations of Economic Theory." *Philosophy and Public Affairs* 6: 317–44.

Shavell, Steven. 1982. "The Social versus the Private Incentive to Bring Suit in a Costly Legal System." *Journal of Legal Studies* 11: 333–39.

———. 1993. "Suit versus Settlement When Parties Seek Nonmonetary Judgments." *Journal of Legal Studies* 22: 1–13.

———. 1997. "The Fundamental Divergence between the Private and the Social Motive to Use the Legal System." *Journal of Legal Studies* 26: 575–612.

———. 1999. "The Level of Litigation: Private versus Social Optimality of Suit and of Settlement." *International Review of Law and Economics* 19: 99–115.

Sherif, Muzafer, and Carl I. Hovland. 1961. *Social Judgment, Assimilation and Contrast Effects in Communication and Attitude Change.* New Haven: Yale University Press.

Sherif, Muzafer, and Carolyn W. Sherif. 1969. *Social Psychology.* New York: Harper and Row.

Sinclair, Ian. 1984. *The Vienna Convention on the Law of Treaties.* 2nd ed. Manchester: Manchester University Press.

Spier, Kathryn E., and Michael D. Whinston. 1995. "On the Efficiency of Privately Stipulated Damages for Breach of Contract: Entry Barriers, Reliance, and Renegotiation." *Rand Journal of Economics* 26: 180–202.

Starke, Joseph G. 1989. *Introduction to International Law.* 10th ed. London: Butterworth's.

Stearns, Maxwell L. 1994. "The Misguided Renaissance of Social Choice." *Yale Law Journal* 103: 121.

Stein, Ted L. 1985. "The Approach of the Different Drummer: The Principle of the Persistent Objector in International Law." *Harvard International Law Journal* 26: 457–82.

Sturgis, Robert. 1995. *Tort Cost Trends: An International Perspective.* Weatogue, CT: Tellinghast, Towers and Perrin.

Sugden, Robert. 1984. "Reciprocity: The Supply of Public Goods through Voluntary Contributions." *Economic Journal* 94: 772–87.

Sullivan, Kathleen M. 1992. "The Justices of Rules and Standards." *Harvard Law Review* 106: 22–123.

Swaine, Edward T. 2001. "Subsidiary and Self-Interest: Federalism at the European Court of Justice." *Harvard International Law Journal* 41: 1–128.

Troper, Michel, and Christophe Grzegorczyk. 1997. "Precedent in France." In *Interpreting Precedents: A Comparative Study.* Edited by D. MacCormick and R. Summers, 103–40. Dartmouth: Dartmouth Publishing Co.

Tsebelis, George. 2002. *Veto Players: How Political Institutions Work.* Princeton, NJ: Princeton University Press.

Tullock, Gordon. 1980. *Trials on Trial: The Pure Theory of Legal Procedure.* New York: Columbia University Press.

———. 1997. *The Case against the Common Law.* Blackstone Commentaries Series, Vol. 1. Cheltenham, UK: Edward Elgar Publishing.

Tunkin, Gregory I. 1961. "Remarks on the Juridical Nature of Customary Norms in International Law." *California Law Review* 49: 419–30.

Ullmann-Margalit, E. 1977. *The Emergence of Norms*. Oxford: Clarendon Press.

Villiger, Mark E. 1985. *Customary International Law and Treaties*. The Netherlands: Martinus Nijhoff Publishers.
Von Wangenheim, Georg. 1993. "The Evolution of Judge Made Law." *International Review of Law and Economics* 13: 381–411.

Wagner, Richard E. 1998. "Common Law, Statute Law, and Economic Efficiency." *New Palgrave Dictionary of Economics and the Law*. Vol. 1, 313–17. London: MacMillan Publishing.
Walden, Raphael M. 1977. "The Subjective Element in the Formation of Customary International Law." *Israel Law Review* 12: 344–64.
Wegner, Gerhard. 1997. "Economic Policy from an Evolutionary Perspective: A New Approach." *Journal of Institutional and Theoretical Economics* 153: 485–509.
Wolfke, Karol. 1993. *Custom in Present International Law*. 2nd ed. Netherlands: Kluwer Academic Publishers.

Young, H. Peyton. 1993. "The Evolution of Conventions." *Econometrica* 61: 57–84.
———. 1998. *Individual Strategy and Social Structure*. Princeton: Princeton University Press.

Zywicki, Todd. 2003. "The Rise and Fall of Efficiency in the Common Law: A Supply-Side Analysis." *Northwestern Law Review* 97: 1551–1634.

Index

economies of scale in adjudication,
    relevance of, 16
efficiency hypothesis, 7–8, 285*n*3
efficiency of common law hypothesis,
    73–74, 86, 98–99
    demand-side explanations, 74–77.
        See also demand-side theories
    supply-side explanations, 77–78.
        See also supply-side models
Ehrlich, Isaac, 4, 284*n*27
equilibrium level of ratification, 258, 259,
    262, 263
equilibrium payoff, 262–64
Etro, Federico, 52
European Commission, 52, 55
European Economic Community (EEC),
    218–19, 303*n*15
European national codes, 25–27
European Union (EU), 8, 52–54, 57, 69.
    See also Treaty on European Union
ex ante legal rules, 6, 9, 11, 106
ex post interpretation of laws, 6, 11
ex post regulation by courts, 22

federalism, centralized *vs.*
    decentralized, 60
French *Code Civil*, 25–27

General Act of Arbitration of 1928, 217–18
General Agreement on Tariffs and Trade
    (GATT), 219
German national code, 25–27
Goldsmith, Jack L., 134–35, 202

harmonization, 7, 52, 64–66. *See also*
    centralization
    subsidiarity principle and, 59–63
Harsanyi, John C., 297*n*15
human rights and subsidiarity, 56

ideological decision making (judicial
    discretion), 88–94
incentives. *See also under* customary law
    (custom) formation
    alignment of private and social
        cooperation, 140
incremental legal intervention, 34–35,
    47–48
India, 218

institutional design of lawmaking, toward
    an, 277–78
International Law Commission, 216–17
interpretive standards, 91. *See also*
    judicial discretion
investment
    lawmaking as, 33–37
    lawmaking compared with, 31
Italian *Codice Civile*, 26

judge-made law, 73, 288*n*7
    economics, 81–83
judicial discretion, 88–94
judicial path dependence, 107, 290*n*6
    defined, 78
    under different doctrines of precedent,
        78–81, 101
    dynamic subsidiarity and, 63–68
    and legal evolution, 101–9
jurisprudence constante (doctrine), 78–81,
    100–101, 106, 291*n*2
    dynamics, 119*f*
    legal evolution under, 113–24
jus cogens, 299*n*9

Kaplow, Louis, 76–77, 284*n*27
Klein, Benjamin, 86
Kornhauser, Lewis, 290*n*6

law
    value of, 34–35
law-as-a-product metaphor, 7
lawmaking. *See also specific topics*
    cost components, 13–16
    cost of waiting in, 36–37
    methods of, 271
    with obsolescence and economies in
        adjudication, 12–13, 17–18. *See also*
        optimal specificity of laws/legislation
    sunk costs in, 35–36
    through agreement, 209–13
lawmaking costs, 271–75
    direct *vs.* indirect/external, 271–72,
        274–75
laws. *See also specific topics*
    frequency of application, and optimal
        specificity, 16
    obsolete, 12–13, 17–18
League of Nations, 217